Verlag der Buchhandlung Walther König

Susan Philipsz

You — Are — Not — Alone

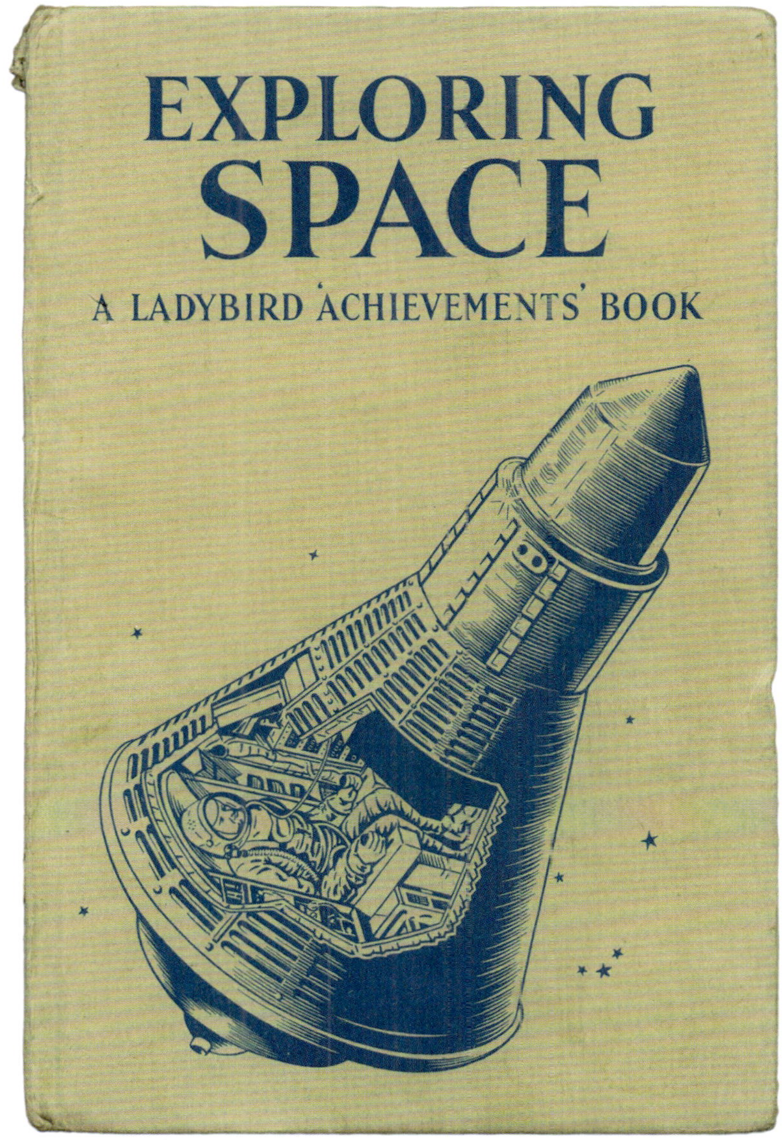

Dedicated to Michael Starley, 1975–2012

Co-Published by
Artangel, London
Tanya Bonakdar Gallery, New York
Bonniers Konsthall, Stockholm
Isabella Bortolozzi Galerie, Berlin
Edinburgh Art Festival, Edinburgh
Ludwig Forum für Internationale Kunst, Aachen
Modern Art Oxford, Oxford
Museum of Contemporary Art, Chicago
Pro Arte Foundation, Helsinki

Edited by
James Lingwood
and Brigitte Franzen

Introduction

There is a marked economy to Susan Philipsz's work. For the most part, it comprises a sound and a place—or more precisely a recording of a voice or of instruments replayed in a public place. When you encounter one of Philipsz's works, it feels as if the sound is coming from the fabric of the place itself, emanating from stone or concrete, emerging from water or just hanging in the air. At the same time, there is an intimate quality to the voice. It feels as if the woman is singing to herself, to a friend, or to you.

This economy of means shouldn't belie the precision with which Philipsz conceives each specific work. She draws on a vast repertoire of music and song, from madrigals and lullabies to anthems and laments, and a deep understanding of music's place within both vernacular culture and the grand narratives of history; its integral role as a carrier of the memories, hopes and longings of peoples. For each new work, she reflects on the specific cultural matter embedded in a given, or chosen, place. The weft of history entangles with the warp of memory; the material and the immaterial commingle. An interior world meets another world, much larger. The sound is within you, and around you.

You Are Not Alone comprises ten works realised in ten different places over the past six years; in Münster, Stockholm, Helsinki, Oxford, Berlin, Chicago, Glasgow, London, Edinburgh and Kassel. Nothing, of course, can really replicate the experience of being there, of hearing the voices or the strings resonate in situ. The sound arrests you, slows you, makes you pay attention to the place you're in, and the state you're in.

The places range from parks and rivers to quiet streets, public squares and railway stations. It's no coincidence that several of these places — from the Central Hall of the Railway Station in Helsinki to a platform in the Hauptbahnof in Kassel, the River Clyde in Glasgow or the River Thames in London—are places of constant movement, of people arriving or departing, of water flowing away, for there is an elegiac quality to Philipsz's work, a sense of time passing, the importance of holding on to experience for as long as possible. Each of Philipsz's work is inextricably of a time and place. Recognising its elusive nature, the publication gathers a range of material which informed the conception and shaping of each work in turn, together with the lyrics of the songs, photographs of each place and a critical reflection or testimony about each project in turn. The publication extends to a web-based audio guide, which features excerpts of each work, interviews with the artist and links to further audio-visual material.

This publication is a collective effort, enabled by some of the museums, galleries and organisations around the world who have worked with Susan Philipsz over recent years. For their generous collaboration, we would like to thank Tanya Bonakdar, Tanya Bonakdar Gallery, New York; Sara Aarhenius, Director, Bonniers Konsthall, Stockholm; Isabella Bortolozzi, Isabella Bortolozzi Galerie, Berlin; Sorcha Carey, Director Edinburgh Art Festival; Madeleine Grynsztein, Director, Museum of Contemporary Art, Chicago; David Thorp, Acting Director, Modern Art Oxford, and Paula Toppila, Executive Director, Pro Arte Foundation, Helsinki.

We join them in thanking the authors Sara Aarhenius, Katrina Brown, Carolyn Christov-Bakargiev, Maeve Connolly, Steven Connor, Barbara London, Dieter Roelstraate, Anna Sophia Schultz and Ross Sinclair, Florian Ludwig for his exceptional work on the design of the book, Eoghan McTigue for his tireless efforts in keeping everything moving forward, and Susan Philipsz, with whom each of us in turn enjoyed such a memorable collaboration.

Brigitte Franzen,
Director, Ludwig Forum

James Lingwood,
Michael Morris,
Co-Directors, Artangel

www.susanphilipszyouarenotalone.com

Contents

The Lost Reflection — Münster — 9
Immaterial Sculpture — 20
Brigitte Franzen

Lowlands — Berlin — 25
Glasgow — 34
Lowlands — 44
Katrina M. Brown

I See a Darkness — Stockholm — 47
New York — 50
Night Walks Grand, Yet Silent — 58
Sara Arrhenius

You Are Not Alone — Oxford — 61
Berlin — 72
Reverberations in Time and Space — 82
Maeve Connolly

When Day Closes — Helsinki — 87
To Watch, to Listen, to Sing a Lullaby — 96
Carolyn Christov-Bakargiev

Surround Me — London — 101
Surround Me — 140
Steven Connor

Seven Tears — Aachen — 145
An Echo of Melancholy — 156
Anna Sophia Schultz

We Shall Be All — Chicago — 163
Who By Song — 172
Dieter Roelstraete

Timeline — Edinburgh — 177
Socialism in her Heart: A Melodic Reverie in the Key of G. The Seven Harmonies of the Timeline — 186
Ross Sinclair

Study for Strings — Kassel — 191
Study for Strings — 204
Barbara London

The Lost Reflection

Münster, 2007

Torminbrücke Münster, 2007. Two-channel sound installation. 2 minutes, 5 seconds. Skulptur Projekte Münster '07.

I recorded myself singing the soprano and mezzo soprano parts of Jacques Offenbach's barcarolle from *The Tales of Hoffmann*. My voice was split across two separate channels and the recordings call out to each other from across the two sides of the lake. The barcarolle begins as a call and response duet. Both voices come together in harmony only to separate again. I noticed that the pathways underneath the Torminbrücke have two platforms facing each other on either side. From the pathway the bridge is reflected in the water. The water also reflects dappled light onto the underside of the concrete structure giving it a dream-like atmosphere. The way that sound travels across water and the acoustics under the bridge create a kind of enchanted space that also heralds an unknown danger.

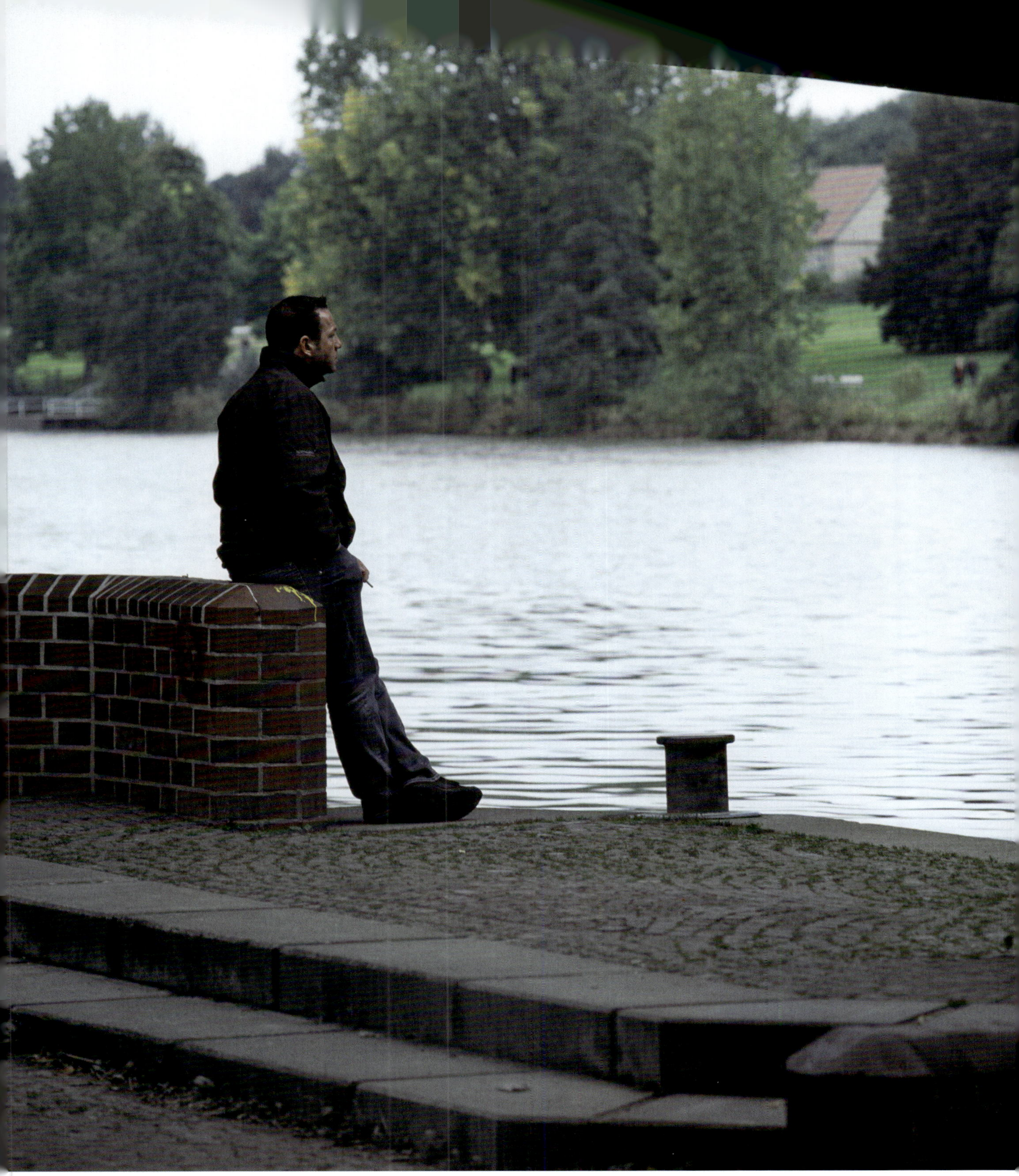

Joy – ous night, ———— O night ___ of love, ———— Your mys – tic shad – ows

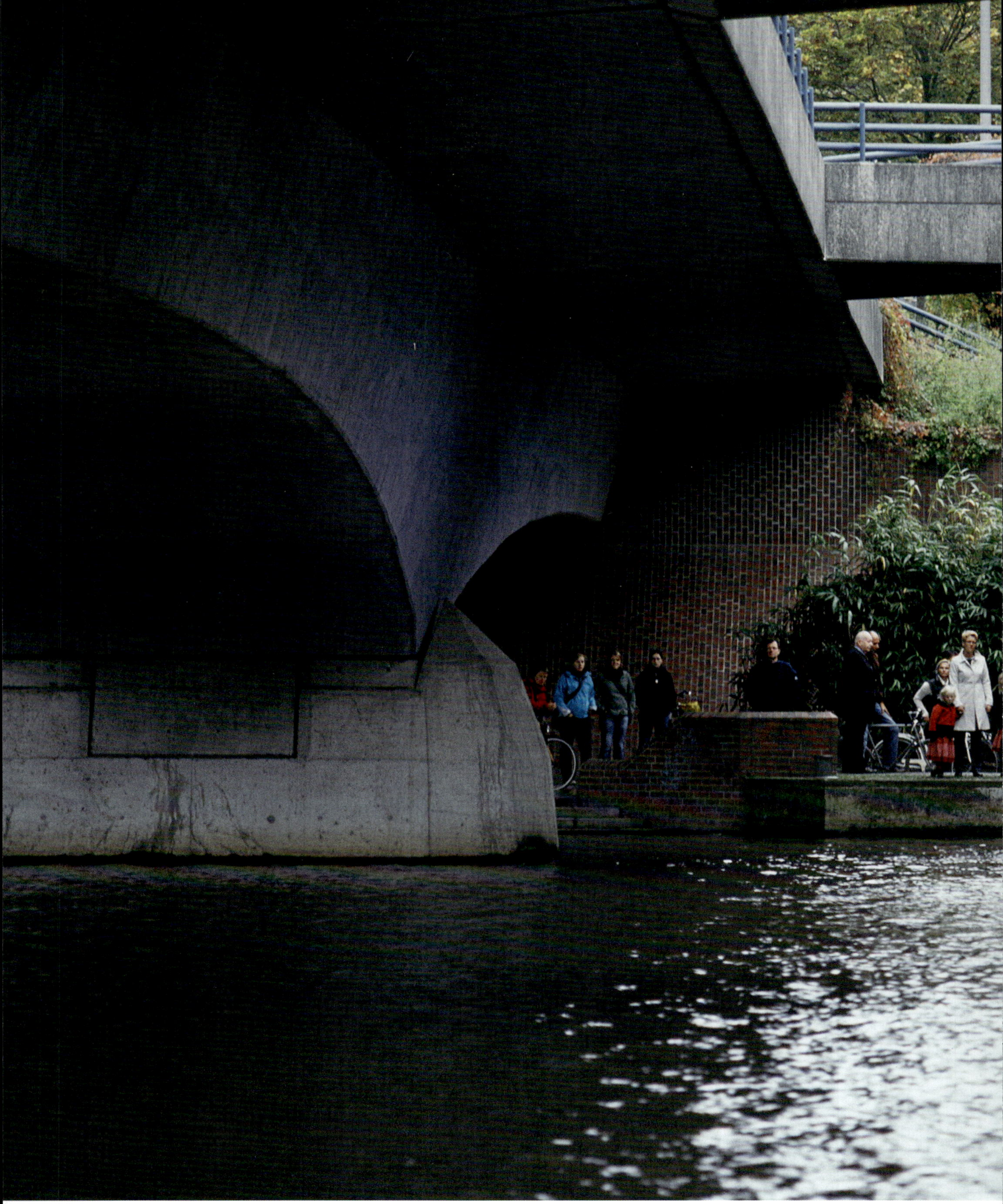

bless us! Star – ry heav – ens high a – bove, Oh, Joy – ous night, O night of love!

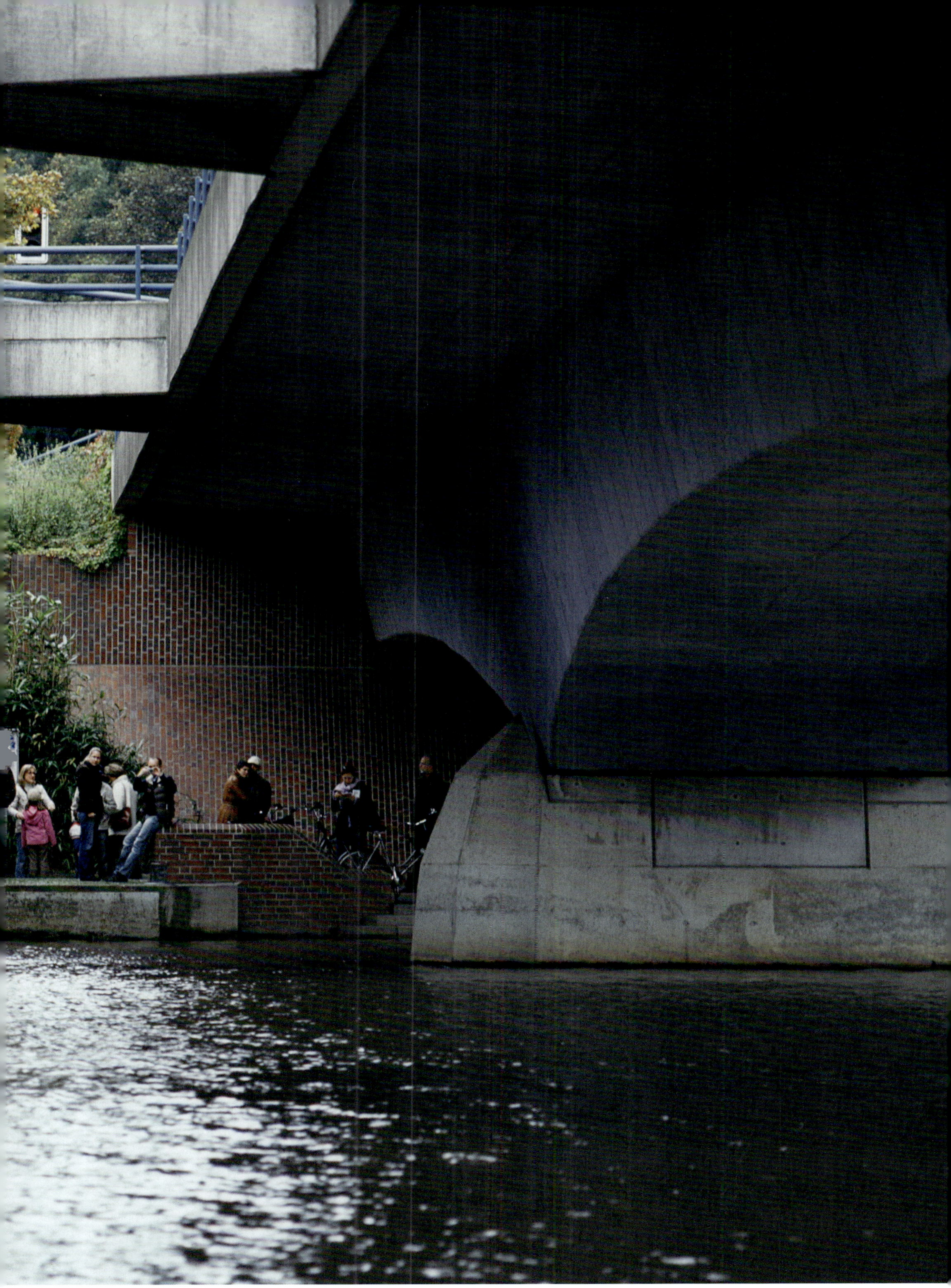

Time is fleet and bears a – way, The pas-sions that pos-ses us,

Time is fleet and bears a – way, The pas-sions that pos-ses us,

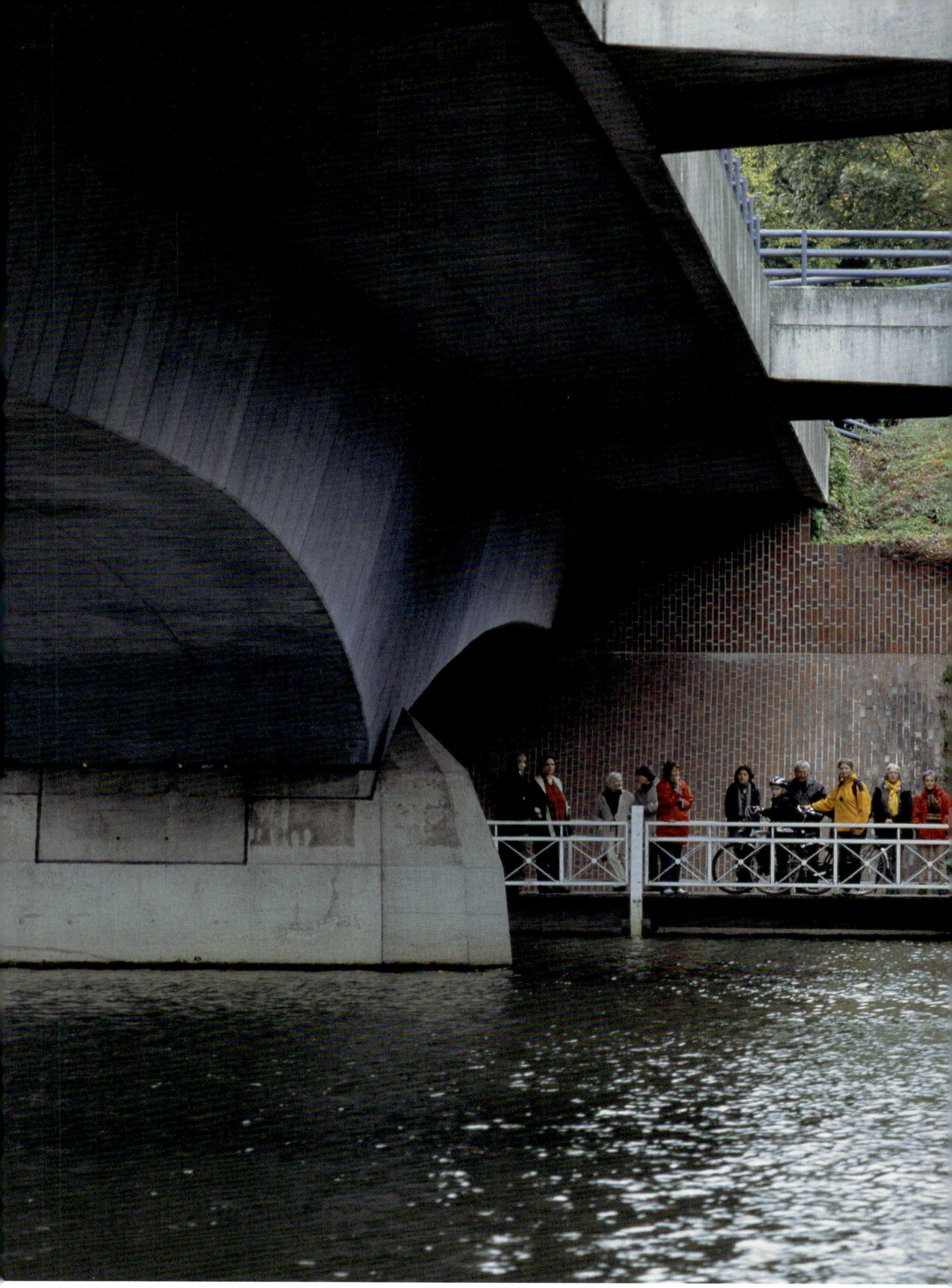

Far from this en – chant – ed shore——Re–tur–ning nev – er more

Far from this en – chant – ed shore——Re–tur–ning nev – er more——En – joy——

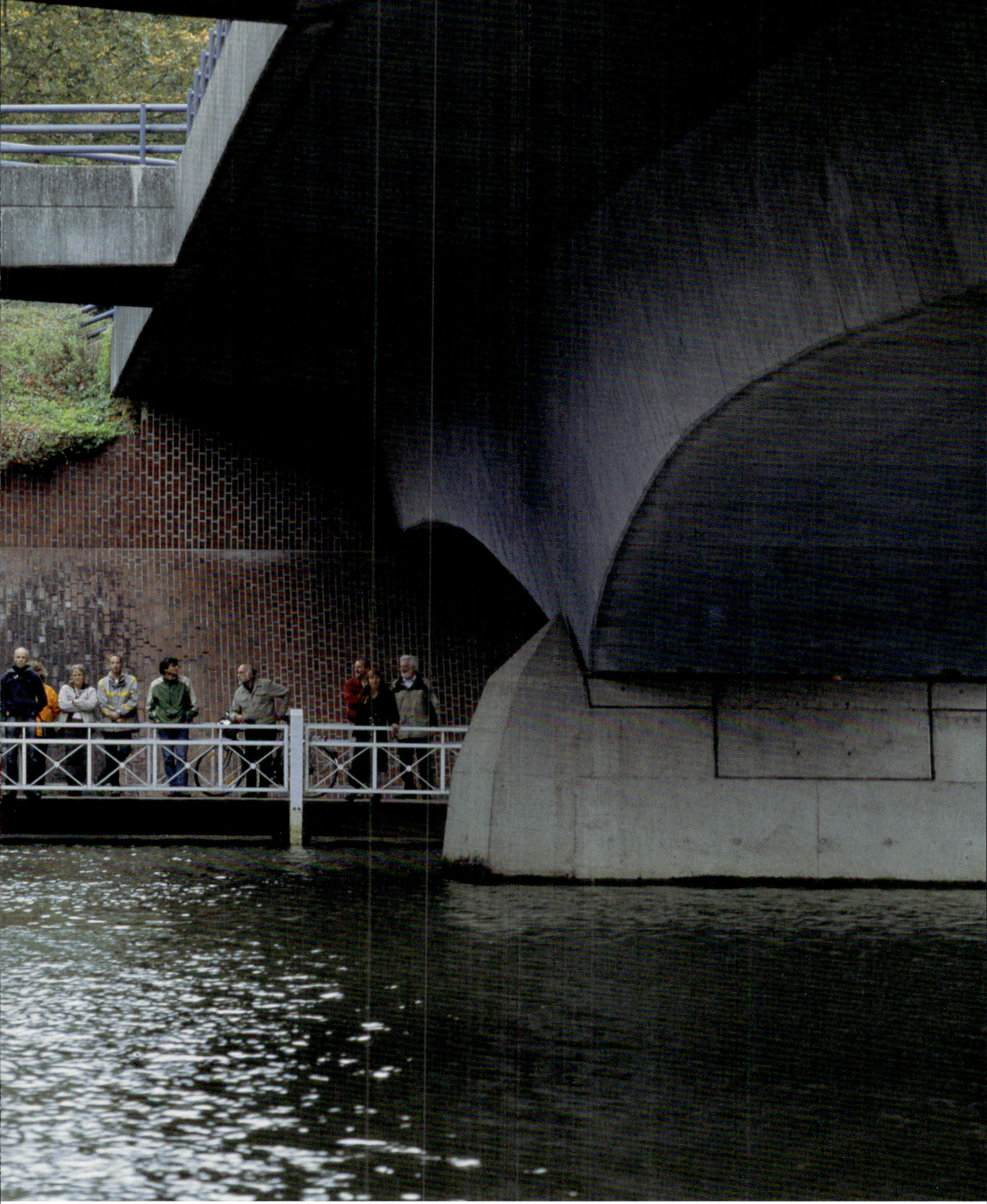

Before the dawn of day______

——while we may———Your be – lov – ed ca – res—————ses

Correspondence between Kasper König and Susan Philipsz, 2005–7.

Aerial image of Münster and environs. Photograph: Roman Mensing / artdoc.de. Courtesy: Vermessungs- und Katasteramt, Stadt Münster.

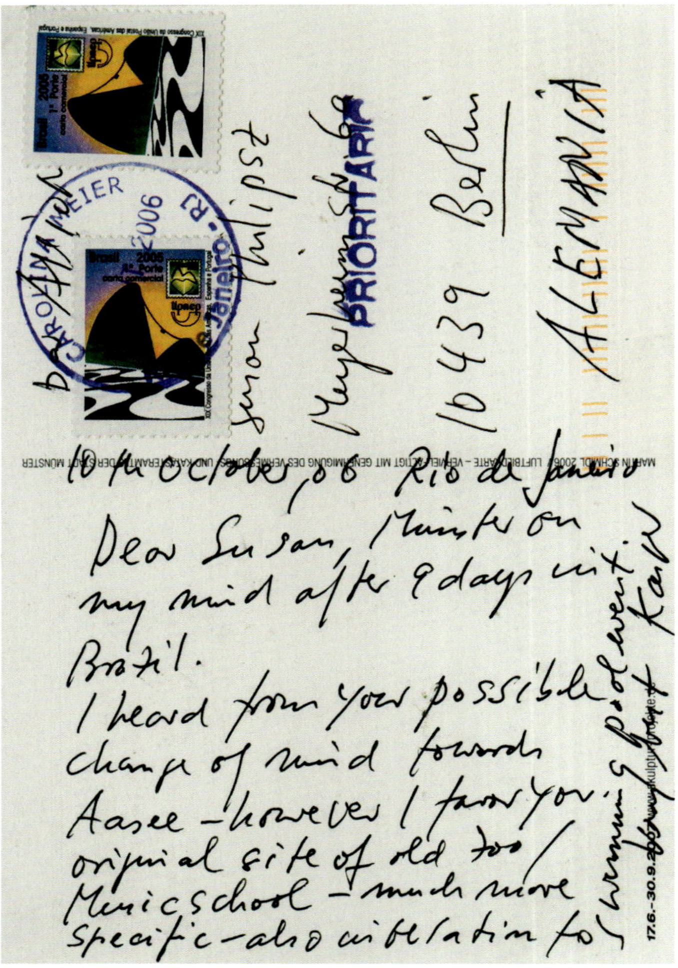

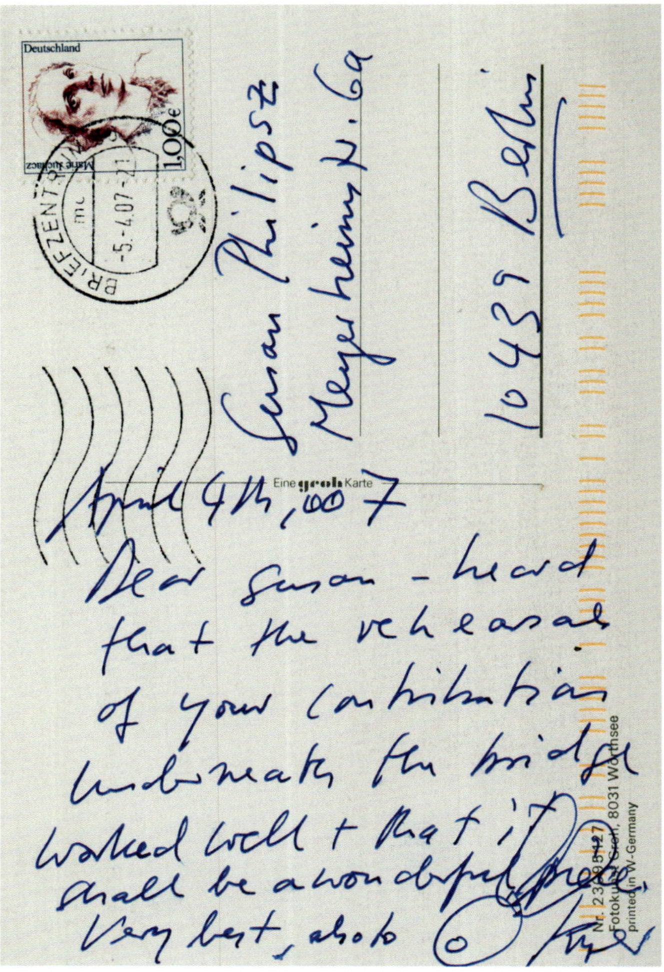

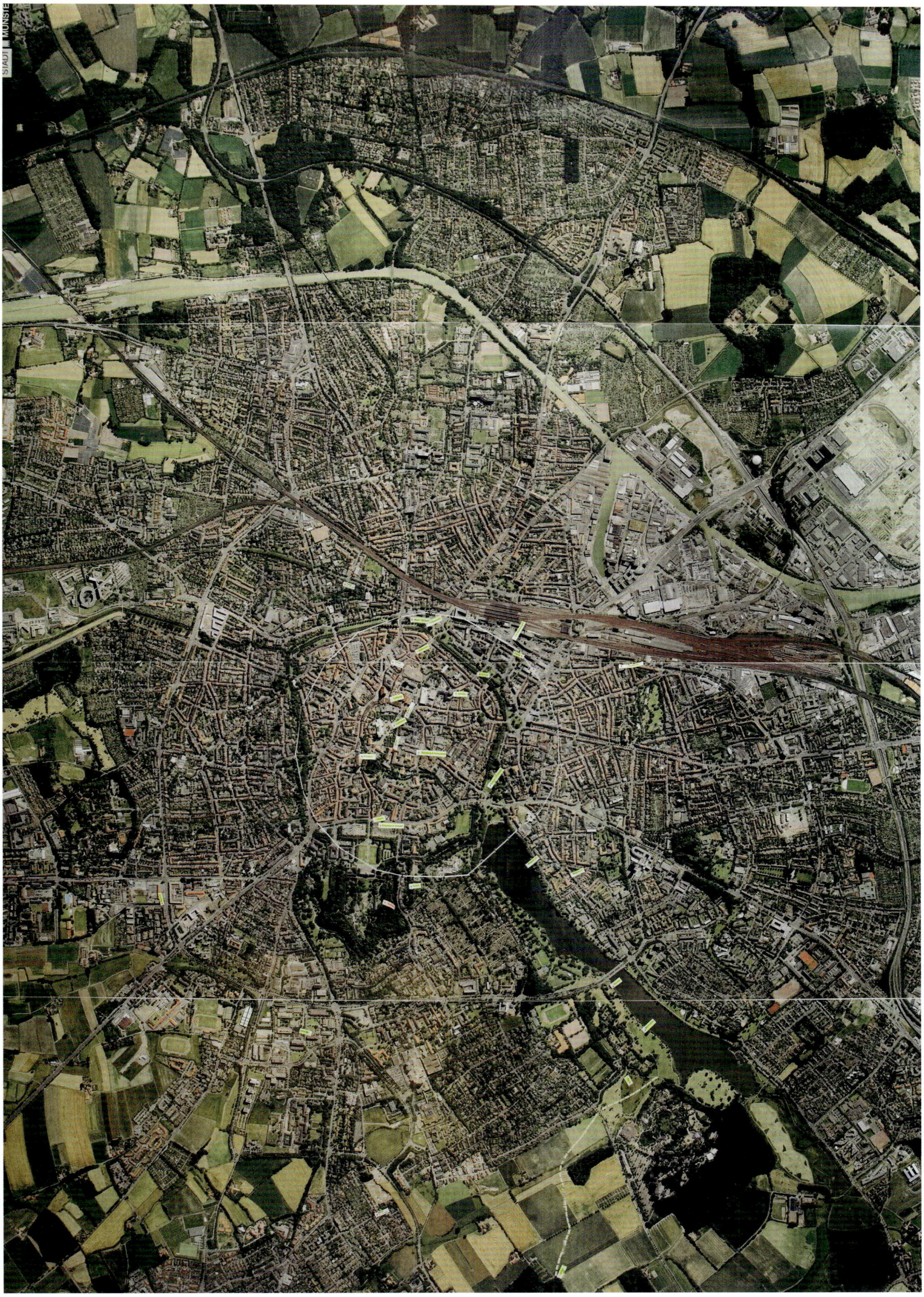

Torminbrücke

When I first arrived in Münster, I was given a map, a bike and was left to my own devices. After cycling round the promenade a few times I started to become interested in the Aasee, an artificial lake in the centre of the city. The opening stretch of water is quite wide and despite the artificial nature of the Aasee, I was still able to see it as a space for projection. It was only when I went cycling under the Tormin Bridge that spans the Aasee that everything seemed to fall into place. Passing under the bridge I liked the way it instantly got darker, the way the sounds echoed and then, within a few seconds, you emerged back into the daylight again. I'd read that *The Tales of Hoffmann* was based on stories by the author E.T.A. Hoffmann. Siting my work in the dark underside of the bridge seemed to fit.

The Tales of Hoffmann, Michael Powell & Emeric Pressburger, 1951. Source: BFI, Courtesy: Studiocanal.

Sir Thomas Beecham conducting the Royal Philharmonic Orchestra in Shepperton Studios. Source: BFI, Courtesy: Studiocanal.

Michael Powell directing Robert Rounseville and Ludmilla Tcherina in *The Tale of Giulietta*. Source: BFI, Courtesy: Studiocanal.

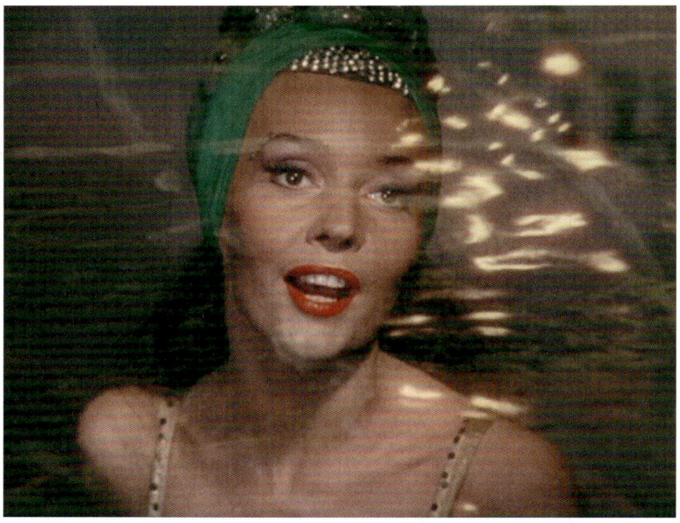

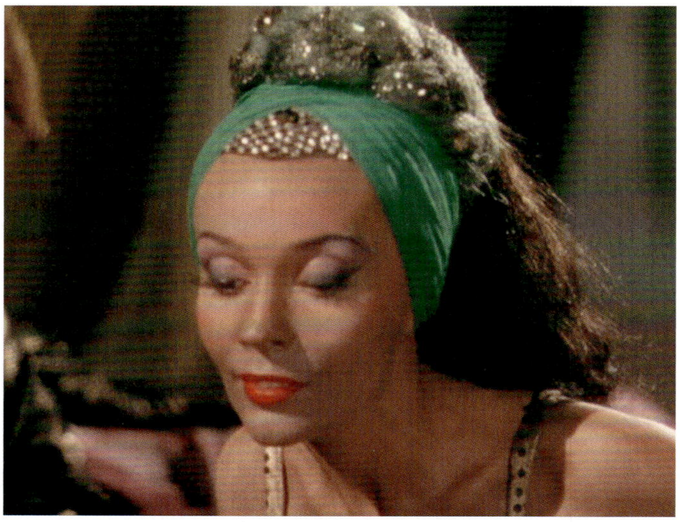

The Tale of Giulietta

There is a famous barcarolle in *The Tales of Hoffmann*, an opera written by the German composer Jacques Offenbach, that I learned at school. All I knew about it then was that it was a duet where each person seemed to call to the other across the water. The barcarolle features in the opening scene of *The Tale of Guilietta*, a story about how the courtesan Guilietta steals Hoffmann's reflection from the enchanted mirror and therefore captures his soul. There's a great film adaptation by Michael Powell and Emeric Pressburger, where Guilietta's reflection takes on a life of its own and begins to sing the barcarolle to her embodied form.

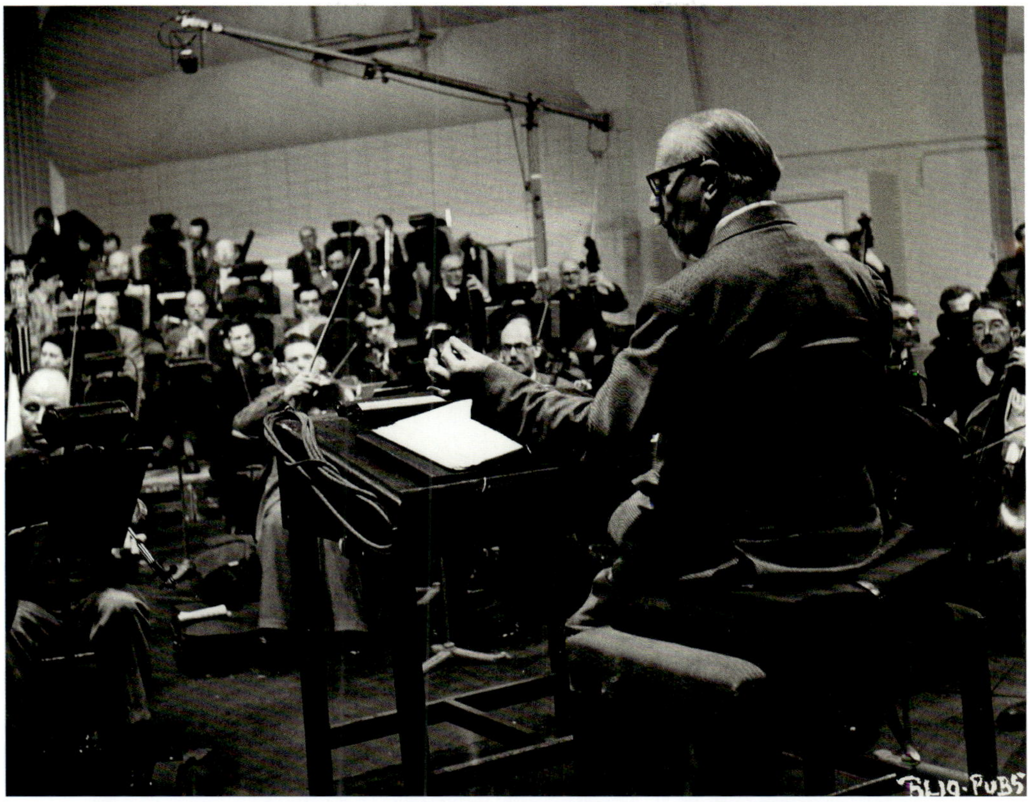

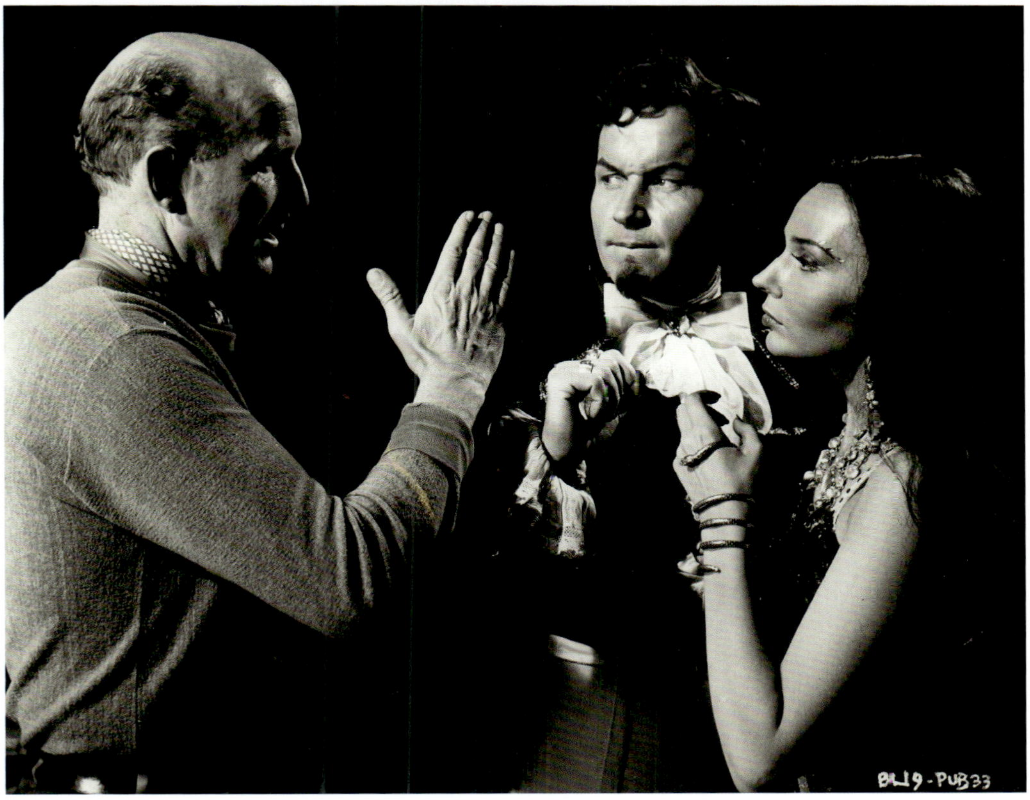

A Pre-recorded Soundtrack

Powell and Pressburger began the project after hearing Sir Thomas Beecham playing the score on piano and singing all of the parts one afternoon at Powell's hotel, La Voile d'Or. Sir Thomas Beecham gave the first UK performance of *The Tales of Hoffmann* in 1910, and, as its leading authority, not only gave the idea to Powell & Pressburger but also became the film's musical director. Working to a pre-recorded soundtrack opened up numerous possibilities for the filmmakers. For Powell, whose formative years in film production were during the silent era, this meant *The Tales of Hoffmann* could be shot like a silent film, with the camera free to roam around the enormous sets that had been constructed on the giant sound stage at Shepperton studios.

Immaterial Sculpture

Brigitte Franzen

The Aasee in Münster is a lake fed by the Aa River. This is man-made nature, a reservoir in the guise of a lake designed to protect the city from flooding and to help improve civic hygiene. Construction began as early as 1914 and continued through the 1920s as a state job-creation scheme. Back then the lake stretched to the Tormin Bridge, the location of Susan Philipsz's installation *The Lost Reflection*. In the 1970s the expanse of the lake was doubled to its current size. In contrast to many other inner-city parks, the Aasee Park is not an island of nature surrounded by the city on all sides. Rather, it guides visitors from the centre of the city to the edge, out to more natural surroundings. It is a singular location and it comes as no surprise that several artists have been drawn to the Aasee over the course of the Münster Sculpture Projects (held every ten years from 1977 onwards) and have identified particular sites around the lake. In a very specific way the lake and its surrounding park have always been one of the fixed points in the urban space of the Münster Sculpture Projects, offering a resonant intersection of political, cultural and social histories within a seemingly natural setting.

Viewed from a distance, the park brings together several artificial landscapes into one, and is almost like a modern variant of the landscape garden so prominent during the Enlightenment. The old and new zoos mark the beginning and end of the grounds. An open-air museum devoted to rural building culture extends the grounds in one direction, along with the Natural History Museum, a popular indoor swimming pool and the distinctive architecture of the former headquarters of the Westdeutsche Landesbank. As a result of the successive sculpture projects, twelve significant sculptures have been sited permanently around the Aasee since 1977.

Susan Philipsz brought a long-held fascination for water to her initial visits to Münster. We considered different approaches, amongst them aquatic ballet with its perfect displays of bodies in water and the technical challenges of transmitting messages over long distances across the sea. Eventually, Philipsz was drawn to a specific location under the Tormin Bridge. She imagined a composition for this unusually tough, even brutal, setting: 145 metres long and 30 metres wide with four lanes of traffic—these are the dimensions of the bridge, as it cuts through the park and inserts a contradictory concrete reality into otherwise relaxing surroundings.

Standing under the bridge, it seems incongruous to hear the famous barcarolle from Jacques Offenbach's opera *The Tales of Hoffmann* echoing across the water: 'Joyous night o night of love, / your mystic shadows bless us / Starry heavens high above, / o joyous night of love. / ... Far, far away ...'

Philipsz recorded the song a capella with two voices. Standing opposite one another on opposite banks of the lake, the visitors hear the barcarolle from across the water, as if the two were mirroring one another. During the Münster Sculpture Projects of 2007 *The Lost Reflection* was played every day from ten in the morning until ten at night. Since 2008 it can be heard at the top of every hour on Sundays between 11am and 5pm.

In Offenbach's opera the barcarolle revolves around the figure of Giulietta. This part draws on the tale *Die Geschichte vom verlorenen Spiegelbilde* (The Story of the Lost Reflection) from *Die Abentheuer der Sylvester-Nacht* (The Adventures of New Year's Eve) which E.T.A. Hoffmann wrote in 1815. In the story, Giulietta, who has made a pact with the devil, steals the reflection of her lover Erasmus Spikher in a desperate bid to carry him away from his family and finally have him all to herself. Generally considered a horror and ghost story, the tale not only confronts (from today's perspective not only grotesque but also ironic) Italian way of life with German earnestness but also presents two diverging images of women. Florence as the place associated with Giulietta represents a contrast to the 'Welschland' of the family, while the courtesan op-

The Tales of Hoffmann, Michael Powell & Emeric Pressburger, 1951. Source: BFI, Courtesy: Studiocanal.

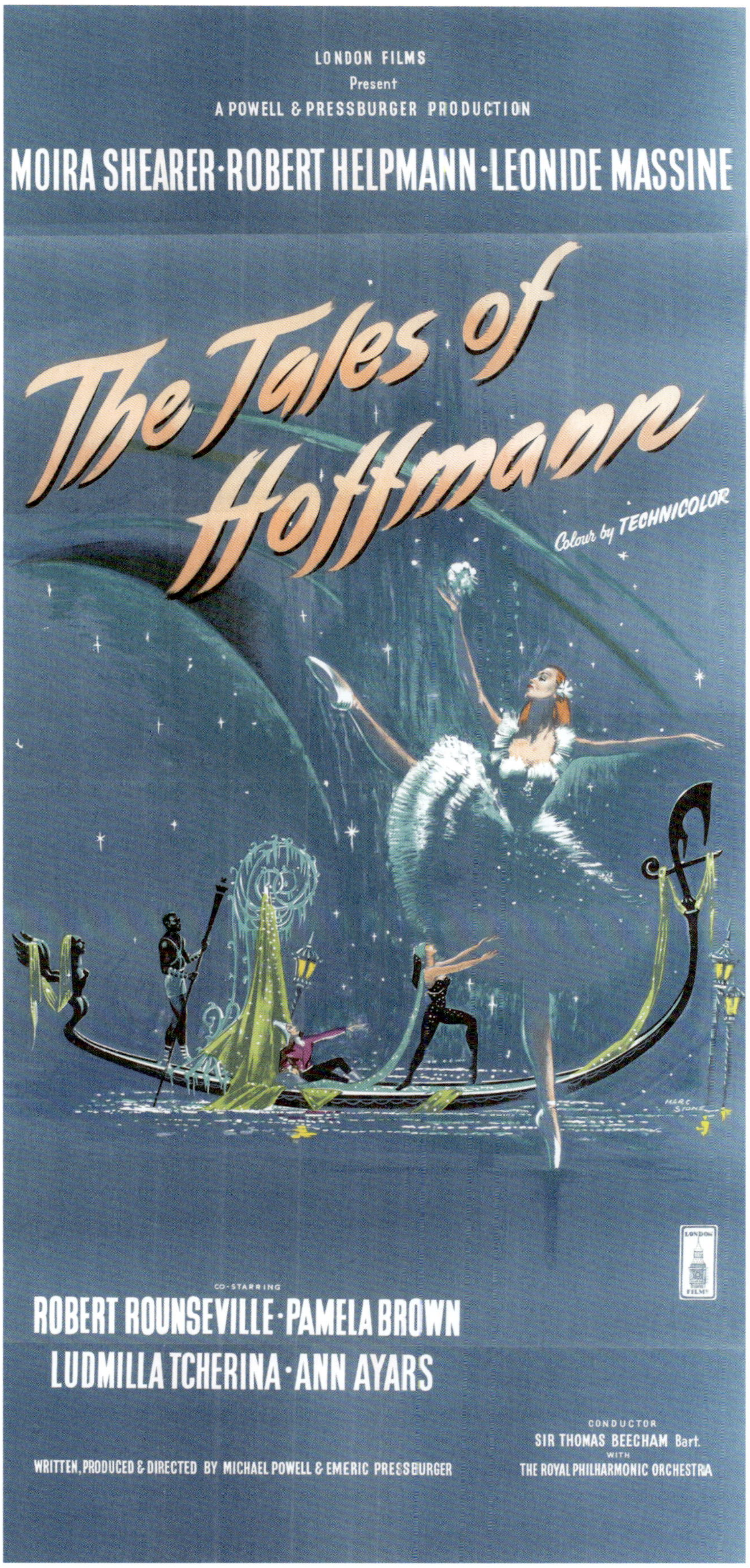

poses the 'devout housewife'. There are also numerous allusions to painting. Rubens, Rembrandt and Callot are called on as references to male fantasies of femininity, including its function for projections and reflections. In some respects the tale seems to anticipate the plot of a road movie, with the travels of the male protagonist triggering a transformation of his character. In the opera however, Offenbach largely dissolves these dichotomies, emphasizing the situation arising when someone loses their reflection and setting the action — bucolic and at the same time violent — in a fictive Venice. The barcarolle, the song of the Venetian gondoliers, celebrates Giulietta's joyous night of love. In contrast to the literary tale, Offenbach casts the author Hoffmann in a rôle and sets him, the focal point of extravagant and bewildering goings-on, as the counterpart to Giulietta. The only figure profiting from this intrigue is the collector of souls Dapertutto, the devil. Offenbach took the composition of the barcarolle from his opera *The Rhine Nixies* (1864).[1]

Even more than the opera, it was the film *The Tales of Hoffmann* directed by Michael Powell and Emeric Pressburger that helped shape Philipsz's project in Münster. Shot in 1951 in London, the film, like the opera, tells the stories of three women. Already at the start of the film, during the opening credits, we can make out the tuning of the instruments and in the background of the barcarolle, the first musical motif can be heard. The plot is set in Nuremberg. As the opening credits roll we see the spires and ornaments of a medieval city at night, closely and ironically interwoven with the music. Weathercocks turn in sync with the music and seem to dance.

The shortened story focuses on Giulietta stealing Hoffmann's reflection as a way to capture his soul. One peculiarity of the film is that Giulietta, played by Ludmilla Tchérina, sings the duet with herself. Her likeness reflected in the water takes up the song. Both Giuliettas — the real and the immaterial, the mirrored one — sing to and with one another. Pressburger and Powell's *Tales of Hoffman* is not merely an opera performance captured on film but, with its beguiling and delicate imagery, is one of the most sophisticated achievements in the genre of opera film. In a way, Münster's particular double bind resonates here: it is a city with visibly medieval and mercantile roots which blossomed again in the post-war years as an administrative stronghold, and it is from this dual image that it draws its present-day atmosphere and identity. The repertoire of images associated with Münster present a cliché of a city of churches and burgher houses (like Nuremberg) and also a prime example of West Germany's redevelopment in the 1950s, as the decision was made to forgo catering for a 'car-friendly' city and to launch a reconstruction programme based on building structures and architectural styles from the past. Today the replicated past is taken to be authentic. Only those willing to plunge deeper into the past become aware of the veneer, the artificiality of these structures. Their atmosphere pervades the texture of the city and can intuitively be sensed as you walk its streets.

Despite the massiveness of the bridge above, the listener experiences an exceptionally empathetic situation underneath. One can hear Philipsz's singing of Offenbach's barcarolle as if reflected across the water from the other side. At times the noise of traffic muddies the sound. Cyclists approach, stop, and sometimes ring their bell to clear the pathway. The bridge is mirrored in the water, the sky is reflected, and before one gazes into the shadowy dim spaces under the bridge, even on drab days one experiences a 'bright', even illuminated, Münster, a city whose Westphalian sky is otherwise so often draped with clouds.

Philipsz carries the artificiality of the situation to the extreme by alluding to Powell and Pressburger's film. She was fascinated by the cinematic staging of the tale, where Giulietta's reflection takes on a life of its own and begins to sing the barcarolle to her embodied form.[2] Similar to the atmosphere of Münster, the film is a pastiche of epochs and fashions; today one would perhaps speak of a post-modern approach. Clearly rooted in the 1950s and drawing on contemporary cinematic devices, the film quotes from diverse times, a specific characteristic of musical performances in general and opera in particular, which are often based on quoting, reciting, reviving, and reinterpreting already existing material. There is a fundamental distinction here to the visual arts, where appropriation and quotation are used, albeit not as part of a repertoire but rather with historical, political and artistic distance. Philipsz does not therefore quote the barcarolle itself, but draws on and employs the opera film of *The Tales of Hoffmann* and the well-known melody of the barcarolle as a product of the mass media, as found footage. She takes the material in all its ambiguity, and assimilates and elaborates it. This specific mode of restaging quotes the musical motif and uses it not simply in isolation, but rather embedded in a spatial and social context. Now referring to the present and a specific context, Philipsz shapes the material and assigns it new meaning. It is possible that many a visitor to the Aasee will become acquainted with the melody for the first time there and perhaps in future deduce its origin the other way around. For such a visitor, the origin of the melody and their memories of it will always be tied to Philipsz's installation. Here the work also deals with loss. The 'lost reflection' characterises a crack marking a rupture between reality and the ideal, between the real conditions of a society responding to the imperative of continuous dynamism and the utopia of the 'good life'.

The Lost Reflection centres around the motif of the mirror. Besides the aspect of reflective doubling, of confronting oneself literally face to face, in a way similar to other metaphors like the labyrinth and the spiral, a host of other connotations are attached to the mirror. Historically, the mirror was seen as an attribute of sagacity.[3] In both literature, for example Lewis Carroll[4], and film, in the work of Jean Cocteau[5], the mirrored surface has been seen as a membrane we can pass through or a water surface that releases us into other psychic states or lives. Again and again the mirror has served as a metaphor for change, both real and surreal. The magical meaning has the same weight as the physical. This juxtaposition of magic and physics, of 'natural nature' (natürliche Natur) and 'art-nature' (Kunstnatur) plays a pivotal role in *The Tales of Hoffmann*. Not least, in *The Lost Reflection* the enormous water surface forms a giant mirror, while the 'reflecting' of the sounds and the doubling of both shores, the two carriageways, people on both sides of the water, the two massive bridge pillars, the twin-channel sound, the two singing voices, the duration of just two minutes, the dual sources of material, namely text and film, the two Giuliettas, and so on, all merge in a play of mirrors, doubles and reflections. For a brief moment we glimpse ourselves in a reflection, lifted out of the world surrounding us.

1 — http://de.wikipedia.org/wiki/Hoffmanns_Erzählungen#Vierter_Akt_.28Giulietta.29/ Retrieved 15.10.2012

2 — Susan Philipsz: *The Lost Reflection*, in: *Skulptur Projekte Münster 07*, hrsg. von Brigitte Franzen, Kasper König, Carina Plath, Köln: König, 2007, s. 197

3 — For more on the mirror, see Jurgis Baltrusaitis, *Le miroir: essai sur la légende scientifique: révélations, science-fiction et fallacies*, (Paris: Elmayan, 1978)

4 — Lewis Carroll, *Alice's Adventures in Wonderland*, first published in London in 1865.

5 — Jean Cocteau, *Le Sang d'un poète*, 1930

Lowlands

Berlin, 2008

Isabella Bortolozzi Galerie, Berlin, 2008. Three-channel sound installation. 8 minutes, 35 seconds.

I loved the song *Lowlands* when I first heard it. It evoked a dark and murky land beneath the sea while at the same time it made me think of the lowlands of Scotland where I'm from. The song began as a Scottish lament but the sailors adopted it as a sea shanty and it changed and developed as it moved from port to port. There are three versions and each version tells the story of a drowned woman returning as a ghost to mourn the fact that she will never be with her lover again. I recorded myself singing each of the three versions and the three recordings were layered over each other, they all begin the same but then gradually change so the lyrics intertwine and overlap, coming together and then parting again. Each version varies in length so that at the end only one lone voice can be heard.

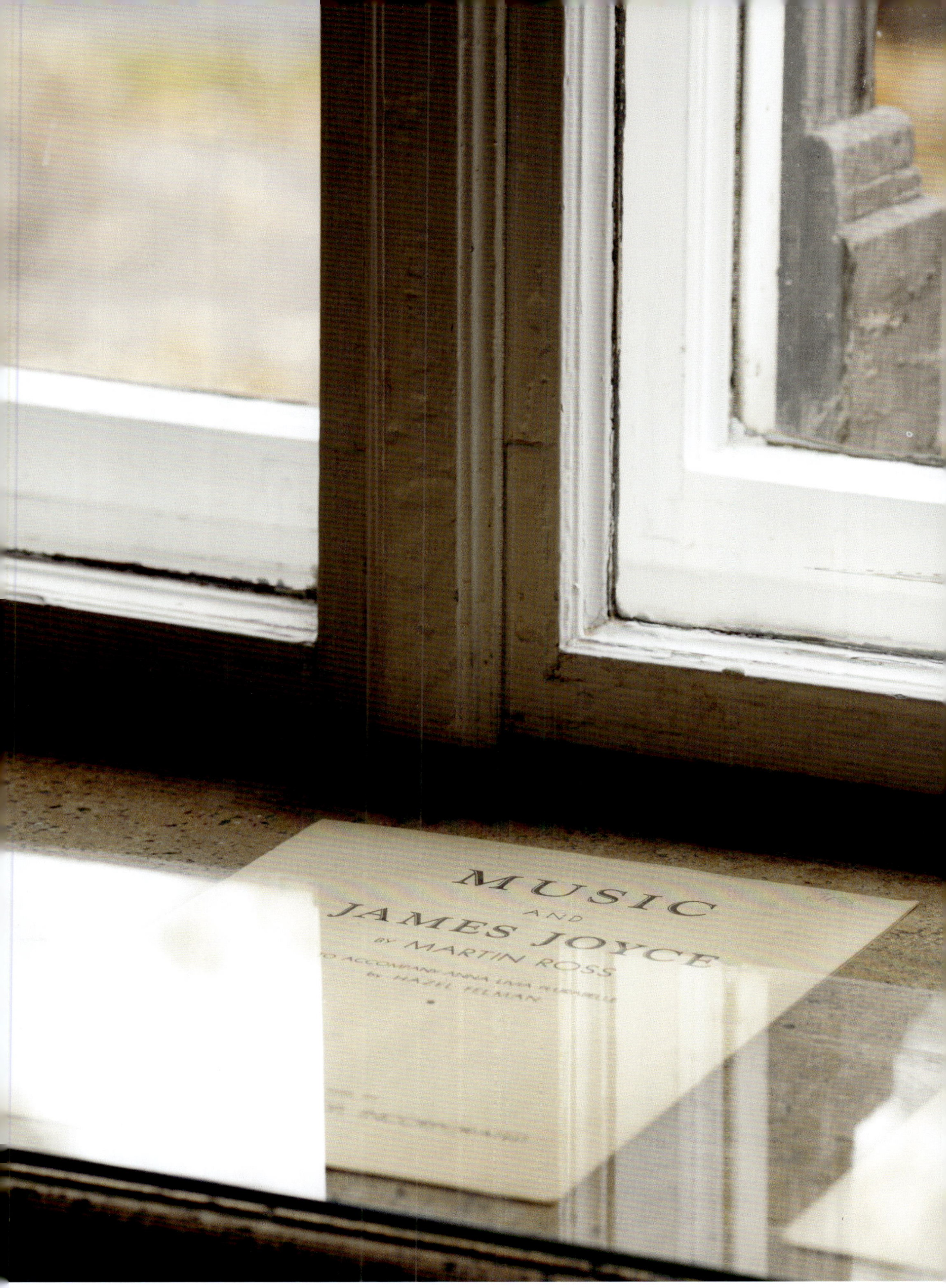

Low — lands, ___ low — lands, awa — y my John———————————Low —lands awa — y I heard them say,

Low — lands, ___ low — lands, awa — y my John———————————Low —lands awa — y I heard them say,

Low — lands, ___ low — lands, awa — y my John———————————Low —lands awa — y I heard them say,

My low — lands awa — y——————I dreamt a dream the__o — ther — night——————————Low — lands, ____low—

My low — lands awa — y——————I dreamt a dream the__o — ther — night——————————Low — lands, ____low—

My low — lands awa — y——————I dreamt a dream the__o — ther — night——————————Low — lands, ____low—

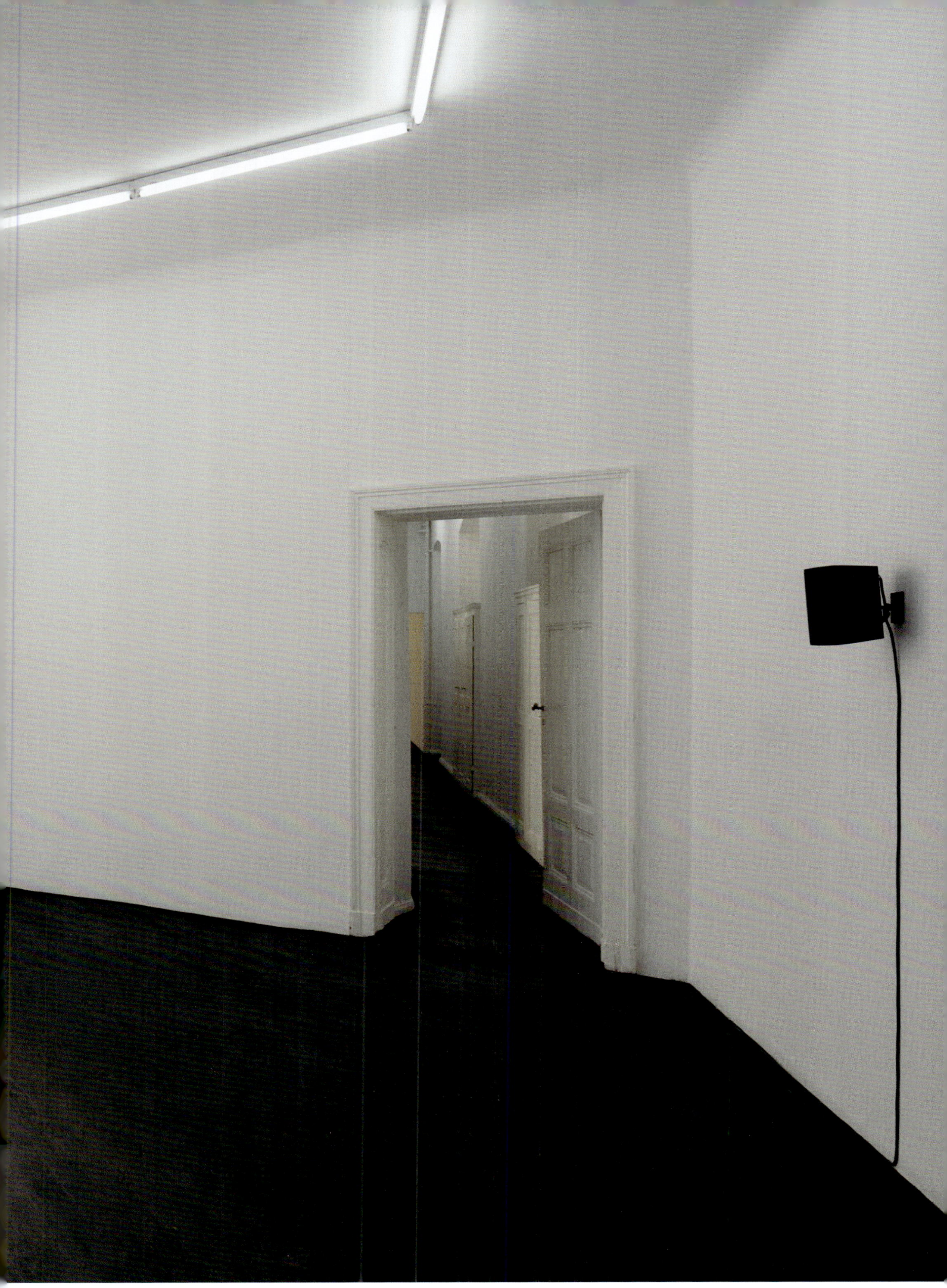

—lands, awa — y my John,——————I dreamt a dream the other night,————————————————My low — lands

—lands, awa — y my John,——————My love she came all__dressed in__white,——————————My low — lands

—lands, awa — y my John,——————I dreamt a dream the other night————————————————My low — lands

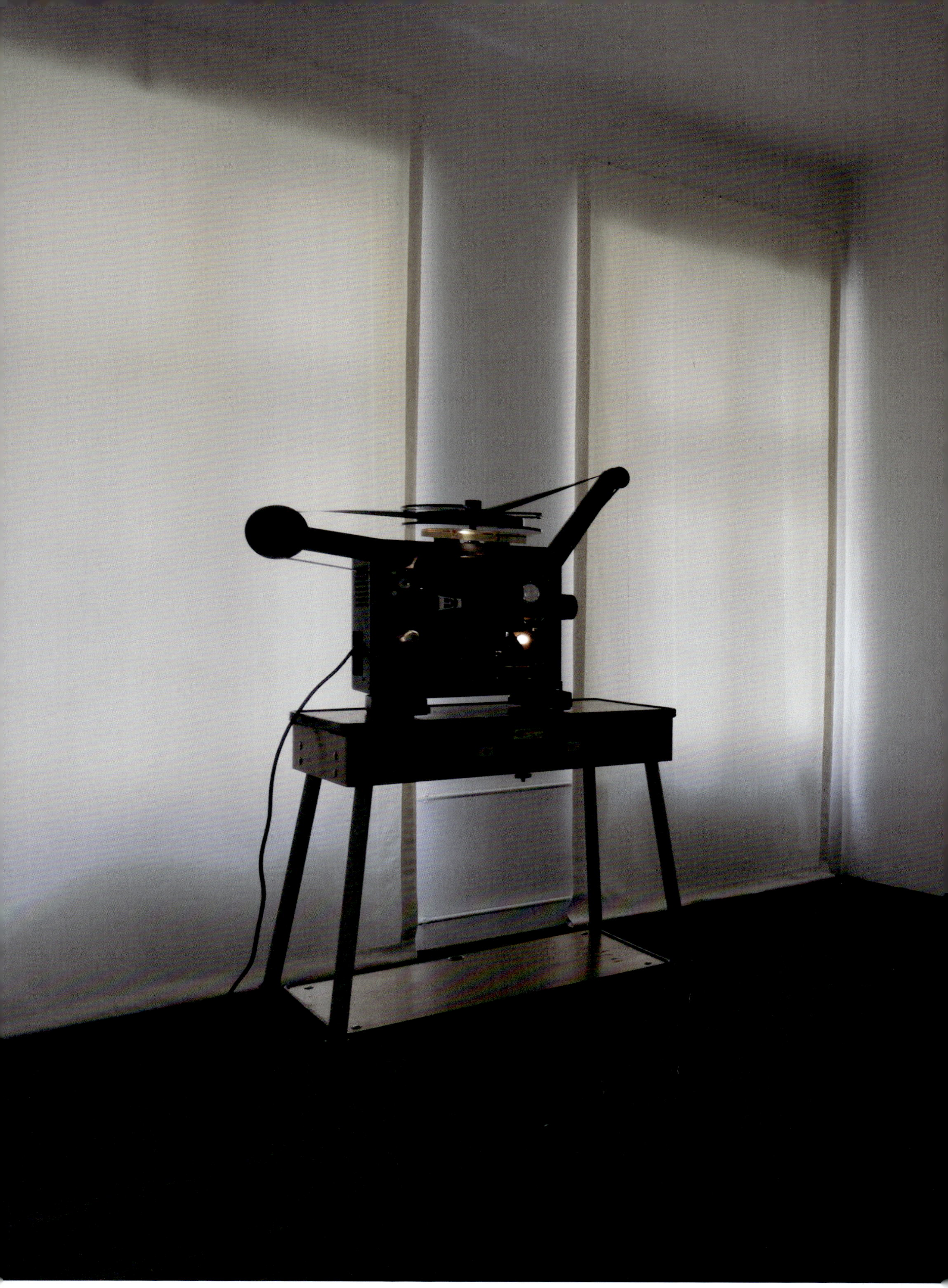

awa — y——————————I dreamt I saw my own true love,——————————Low — lands, ——low—

awa — y——————————I dreamed my love came in my sleep,——————————Low — lands, ——low—

awa — y——————————I dreamed I saw my own true love,——————————Low — lands, ——low—

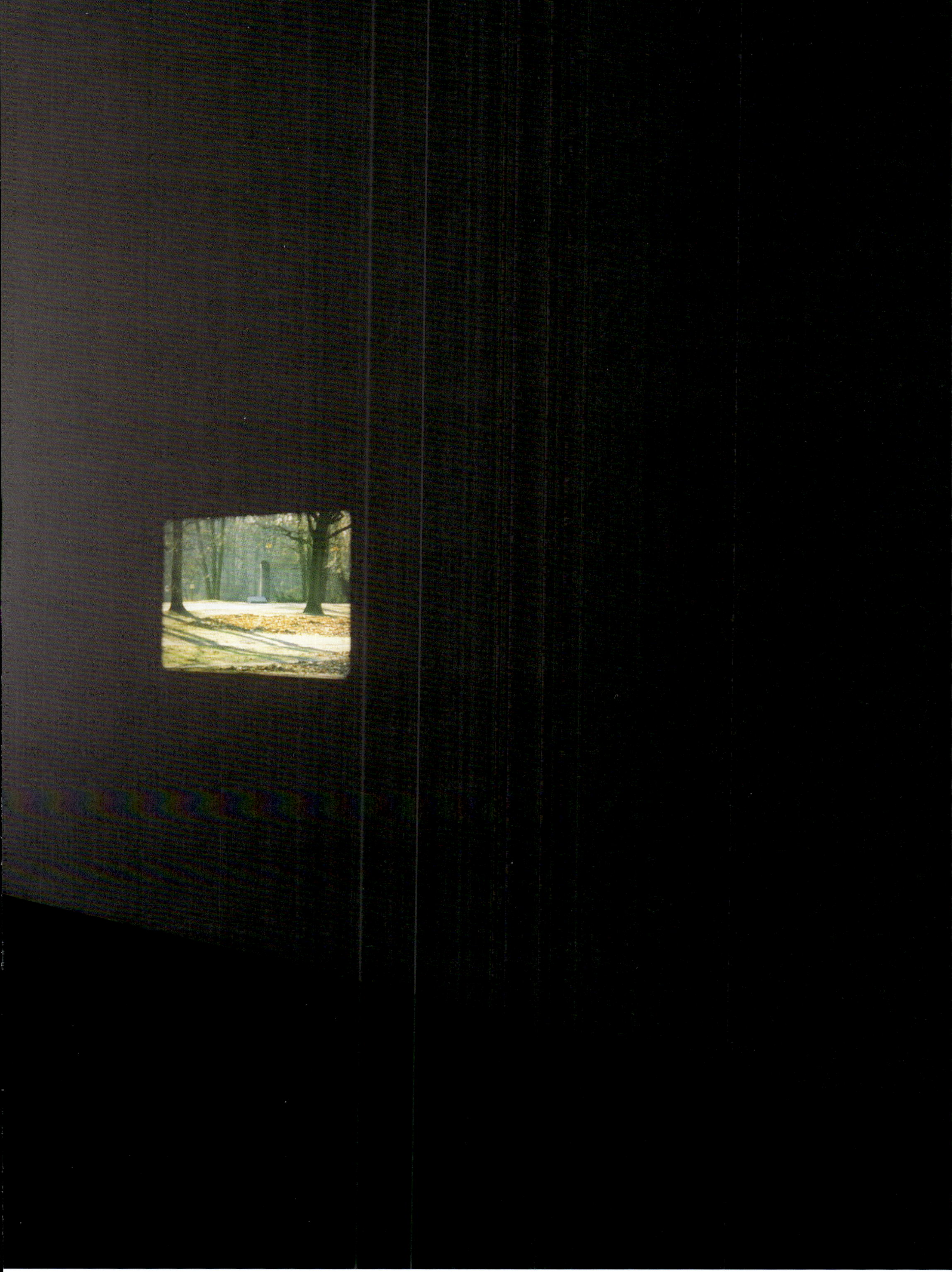

—lands, awa — y my John——————His hair was wet, his eyes above——————My low —lands awa — y

—lands, awa — y my John——————Her cheeks were wet her eyes did weep,——————My low —lands awa — y

—lands, awa — y my John——————She flew to me like some young dove,——————My low —lands awa — y

Proposal for elements of the monuments to Rosa Luxemburg and Karl Liebknecht by Ralf Schüler and Ursulina Schüler-Witte, 1987. Photograph: Christian Tagger. Courtesy: Berlinische Galerie.

Film stills, *Returning* (2004).

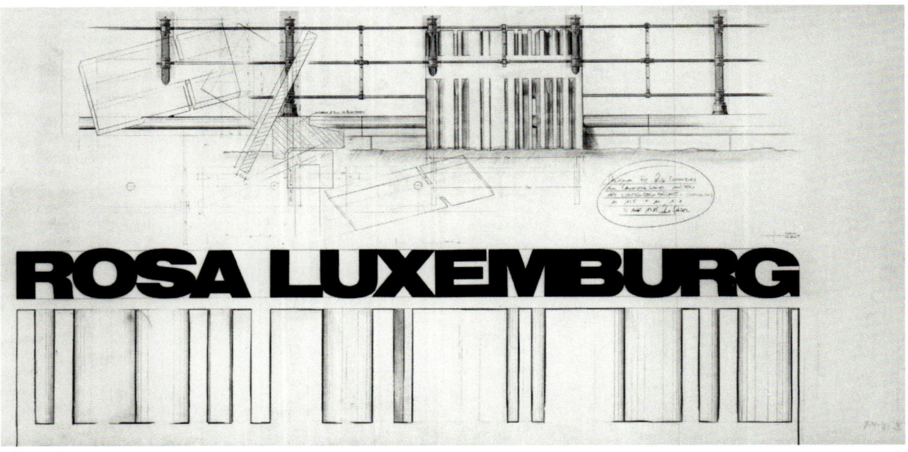

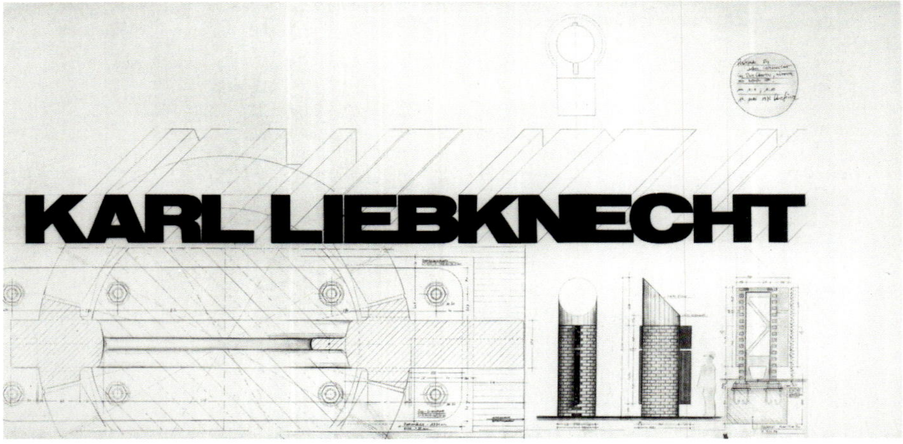

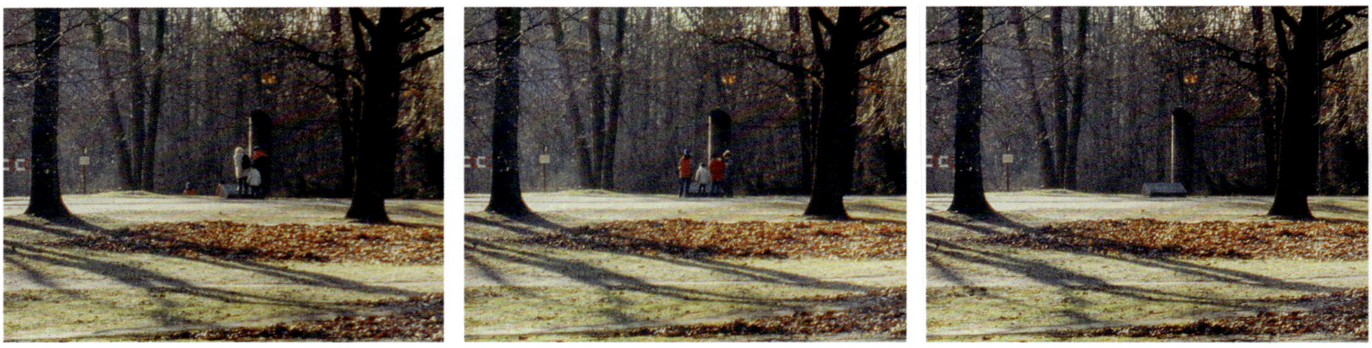

Karl Liebknecht and Rosa Luxemburg

The Spartikus leaders Karl Liebknecht and Rosa Luxemburg were both murdered on the night of the 15 January 1919. Luxemburg's body was thrown into the Landwehrkanal in Berlin. The underwater currents carried her body into the weeds and the corpse was retrieved from the water months later. That sad image came to me as I stood in the room in Isabella Bortolozzi Galerie that looks out over the canal.

The film *Returning* (2004) was shot in a single take, on a Sunday afternoon in January in the Tiergarten in Berlin. It shows a monument sited on the spot Karl Liebknecht was murdered. The static camera records the flow of people passing by the monument: cyclists, dog-walkers, playing kids joggers. Some interrupt their journey to read the inscription and for a few moments contemplate their surroundings.

Anna Livia Plurabelle score. Hazel Felman, 1936. Argus Book Shop Chicago. Collection of the artist.

Edward Smyth's carving of Anna Liffey, part of a series of ornamental sculptures representing Ireland's rivers on the façade of the Customs House, Dublin.

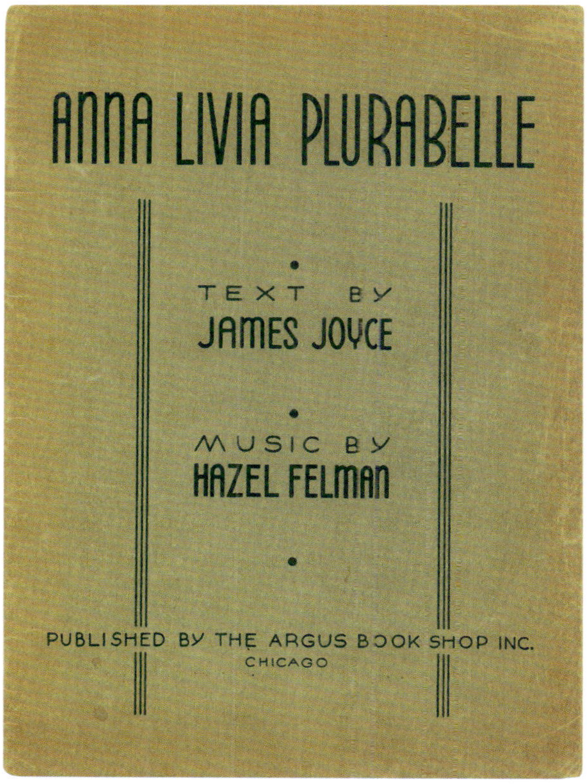

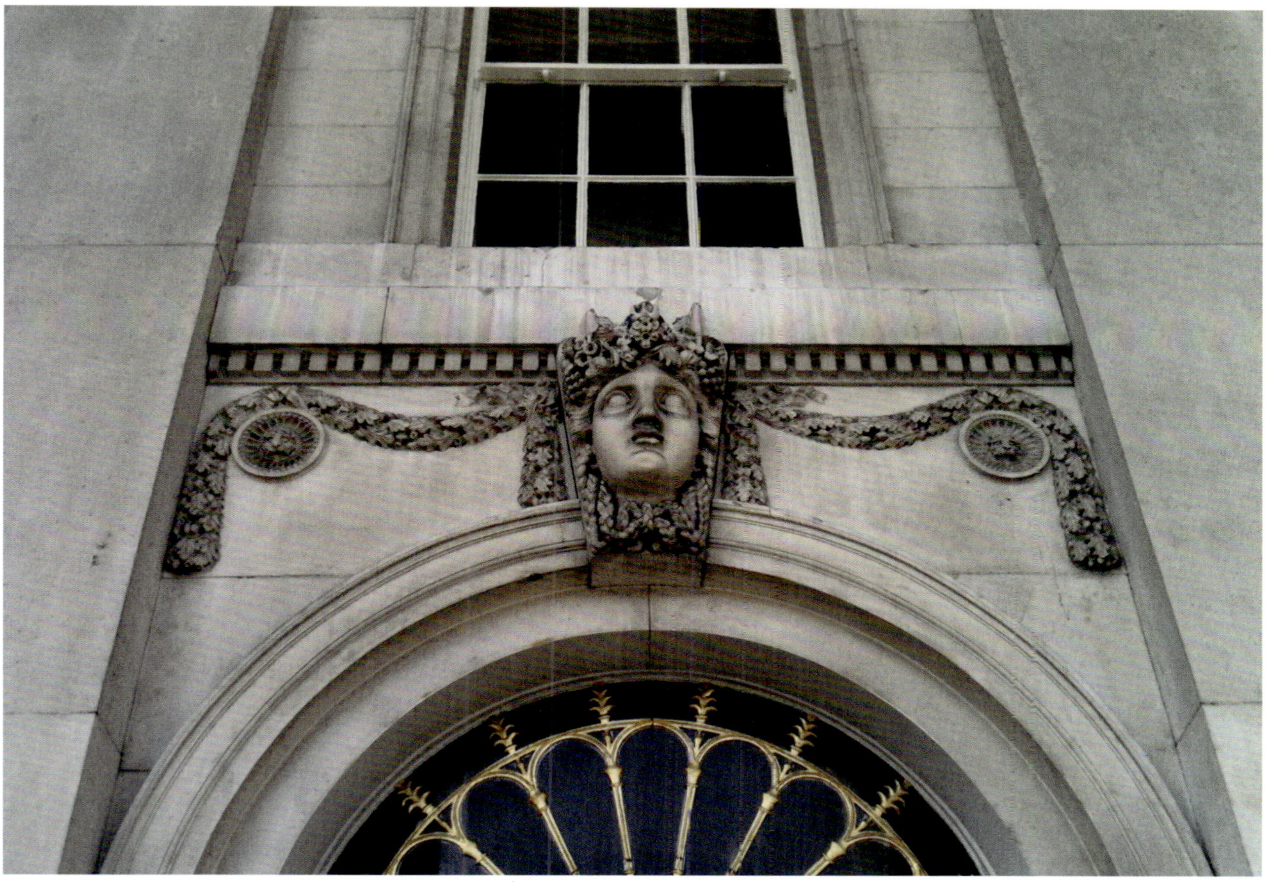

It is said that in his conception of the fictional character Anna Livia Plurabelle, James Joyce merged the characters of the Irish river Goddess Anna Liffey with Livia Schmitz, the wife of Ettore Schmitz (alias the writer Italo Svevo) his patron in Trieste. 'They say I have immortalized Svevo, but I've also immortalized the tresses of Signora Svevo. These were long and reddish-blonde. My sister who used to see them let down told me about them. The river at Dublin passes dye-houses and so has reddish water. So I have playfully compared these two things in the book I'm writing. A lady in it will have tresses, which are really Signora Svevo's.' Richard Ellmann, *James Joyce* (Oxford University Press, Oxford, 1959).

Glasgow, 2010

Clydeside walkway, Glasgow, 2010. Three-channel sound installation. 8 minutes, 35 seconds. Glasgow International Festival of Visual Art.

The Glasgow Bridge, the Caledonian Railway Bridge and the George V Bridge say so much about the history of Glasgow and the undersides of the bridges are like the dark underbelly of the city. Addicts and homeless people take shelter under these bridges and when I was there for my site visit for the Glasgow International Festival of Visual Art I saw flowers taped to the railings to mark a suicide. I was incredibly moved and I immediately knew that this would be the perfect place for a larger-scale outdoor installation of *Lowlands*. We installed the speakers so as to have the three versions of the ballad playing from under each of the three bridges. The underside of the bridges have powerful acoustics and although the speakers were in plain sight it was difficult to locate the source of the sound.

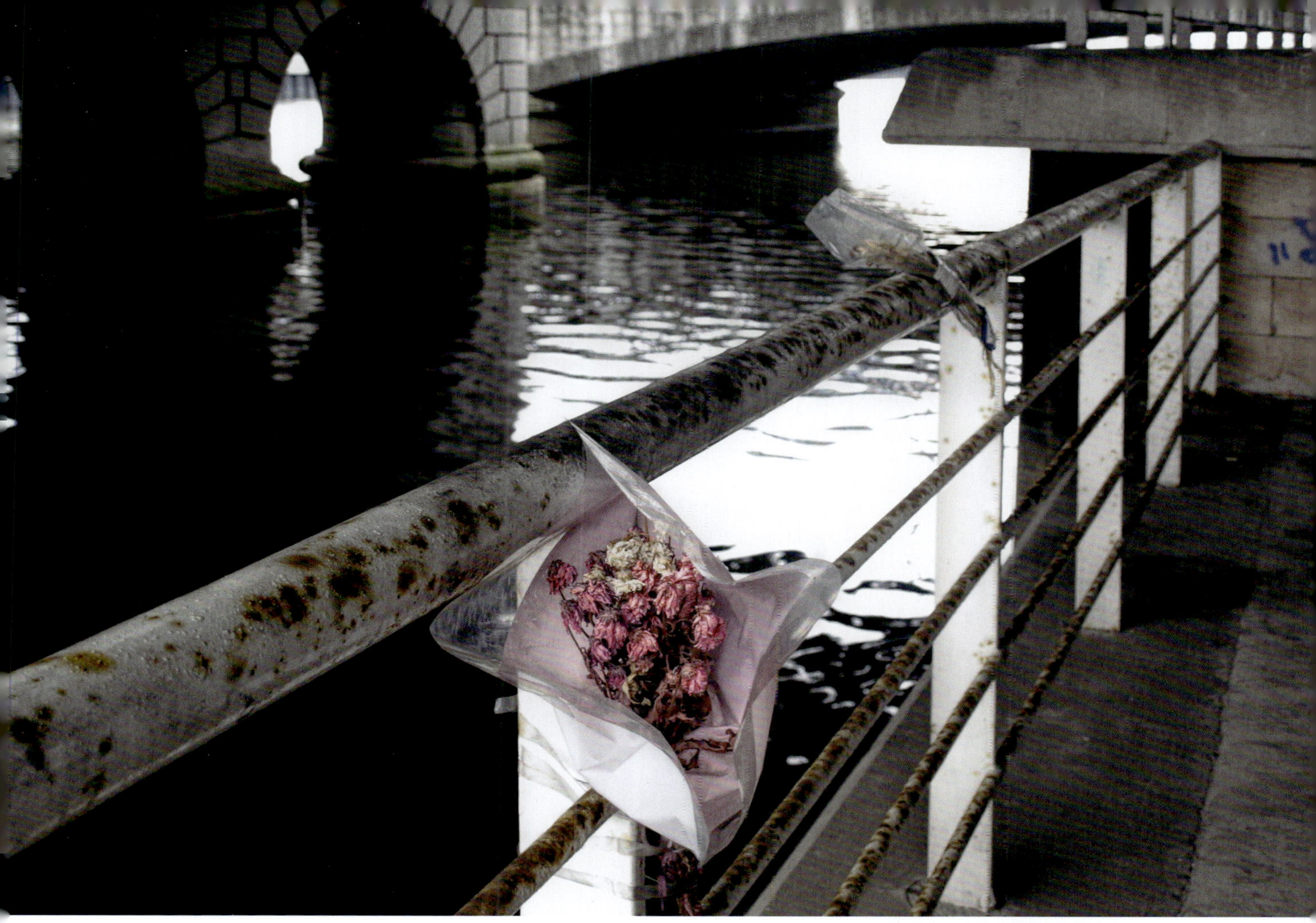

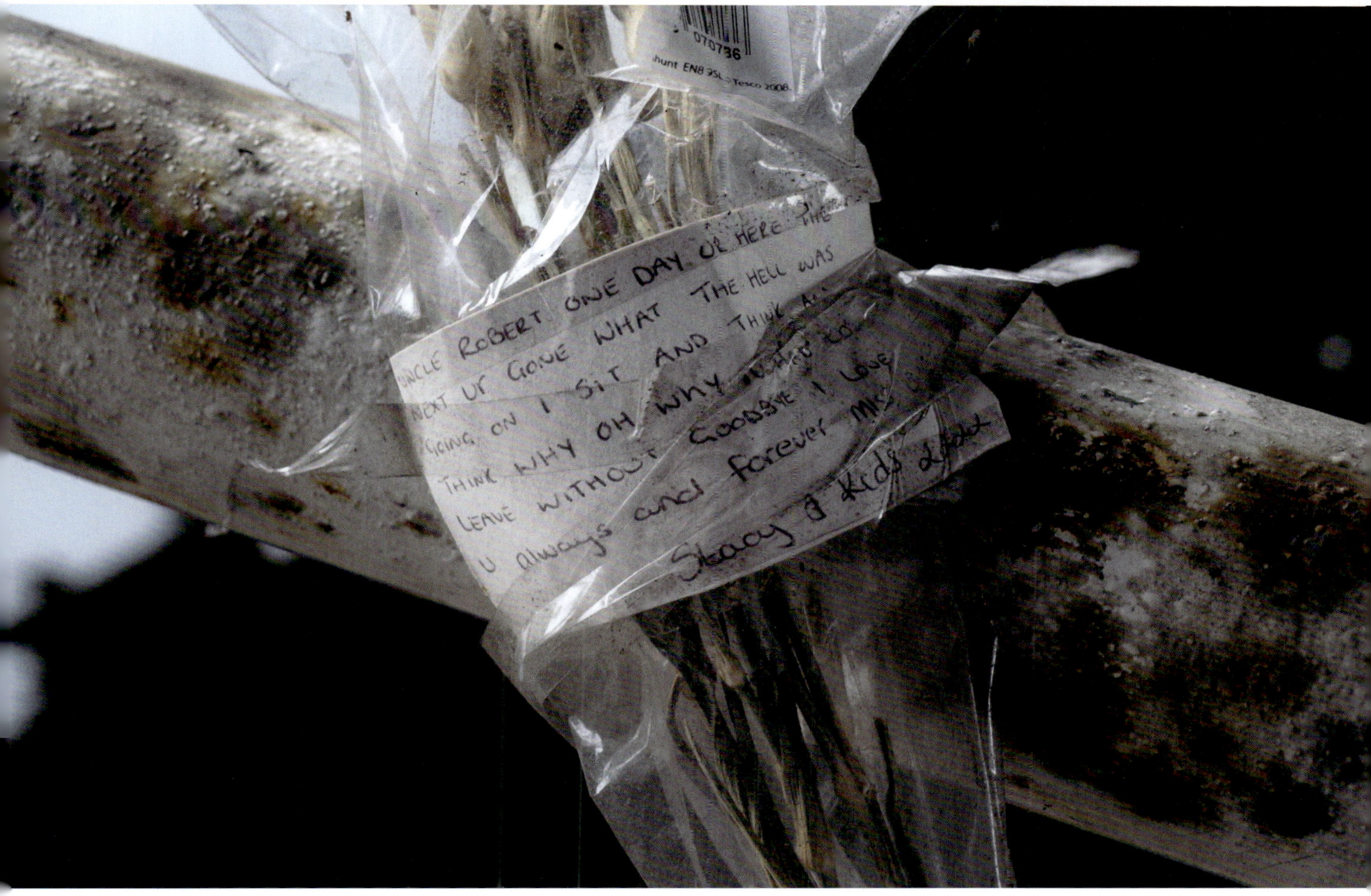

I knew my love was drowned and dead, ———————————— Low — lands, ___ low — lands, awa — y

She came to me as my best bride, ———————————— Low — lands, ___ low — lands, awa — y

This maid she stood close by my side, ———————————— Low — lands, ___ low — lands, awa — y

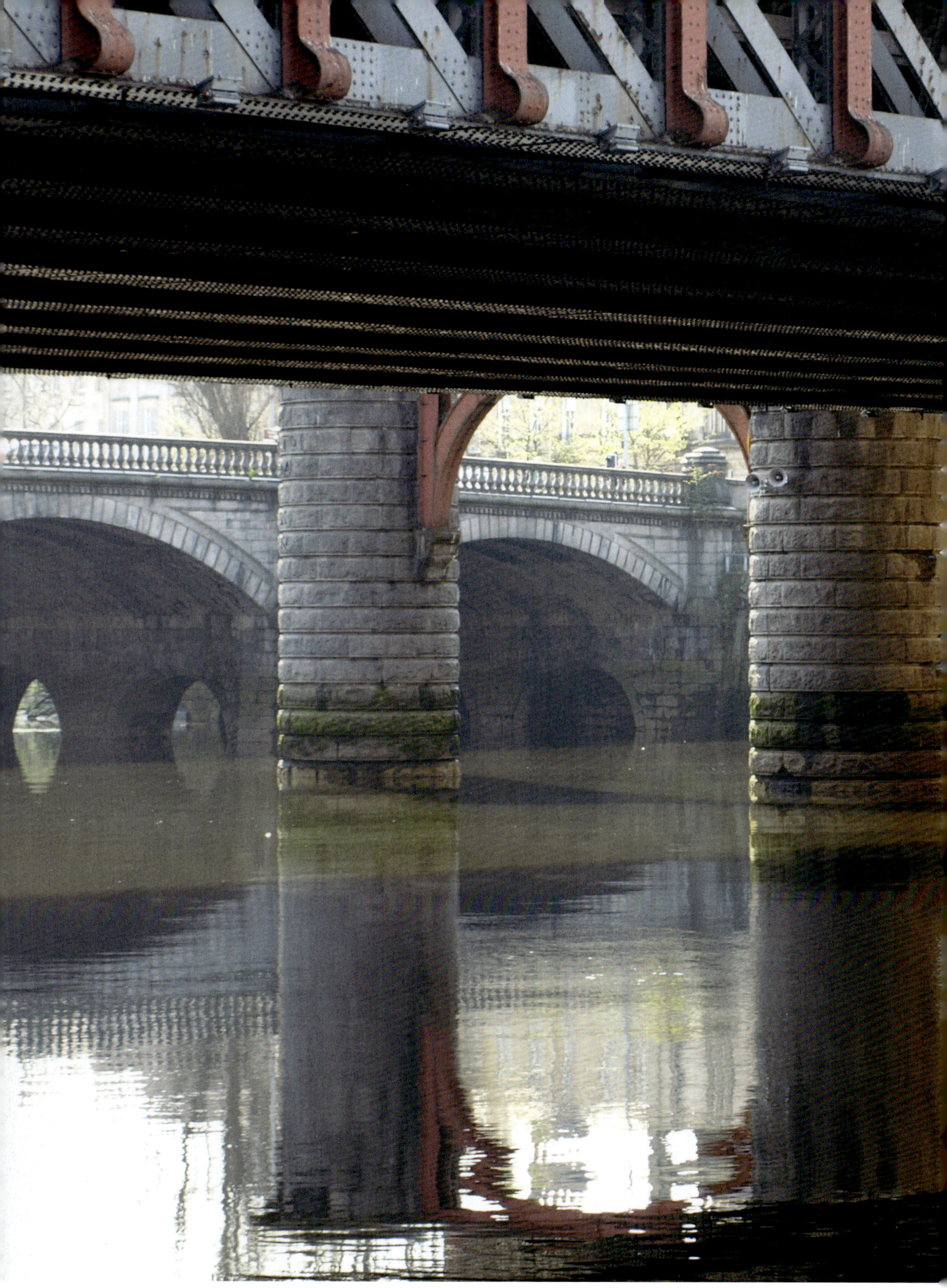

my John—————He stood so still, no word he said——————————————My lowlands awa — y————

my John,—————All dressed in white like — some fair — bride————————————My lowlands awa — y————

my John,—————All dressed in white like — some fair — bride————————————My lowlands awa — y————

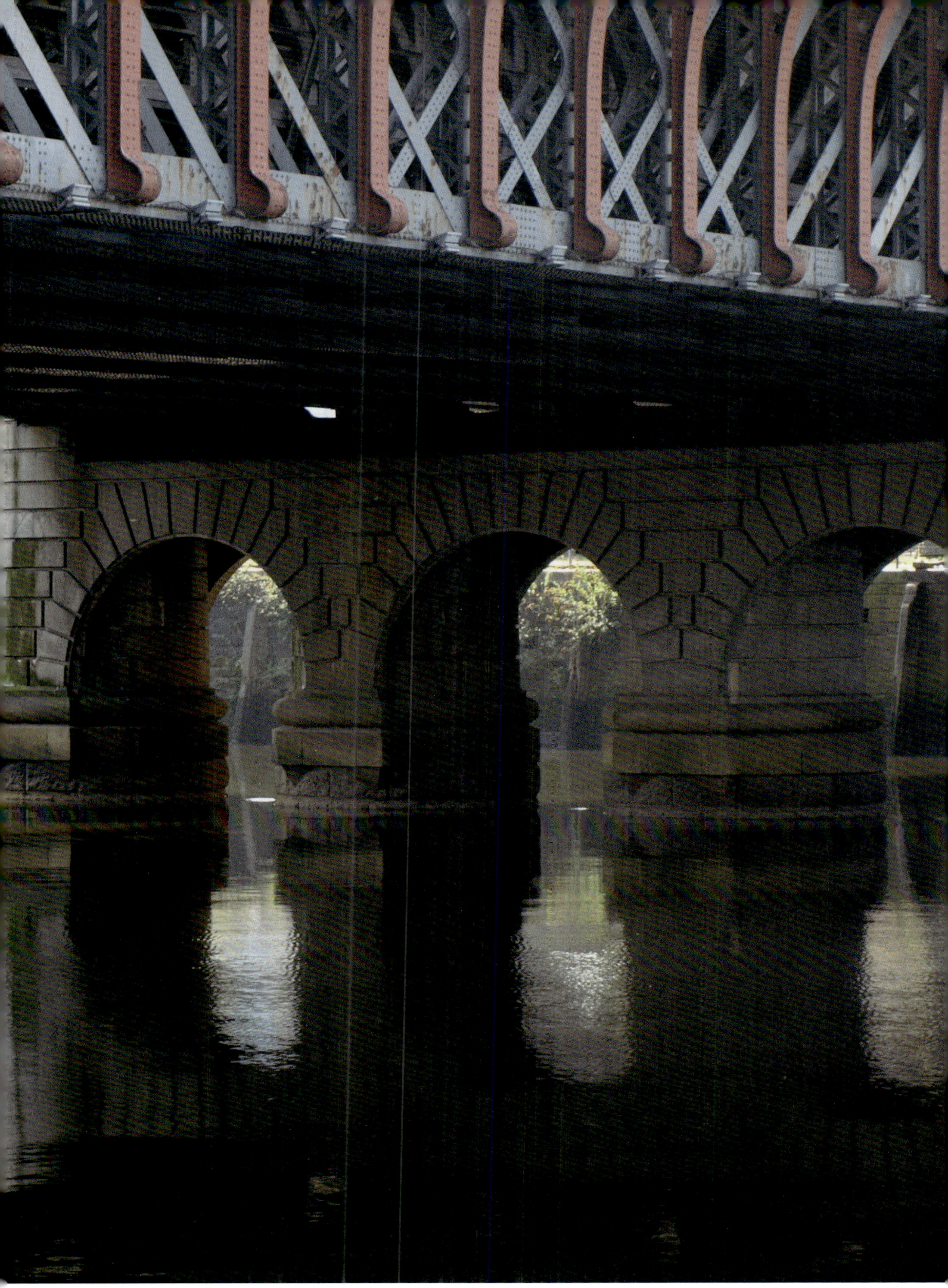

—All dank his hair, all dim his eye——————Low — lands,____ low————————————lands, awa — y

—And bravely in her bosom fair———————Low — lands,____ low————————————lands, awa — y

—She spoke in accents sweet an' low—————Low — lands,____ low————————————lands, awa — y

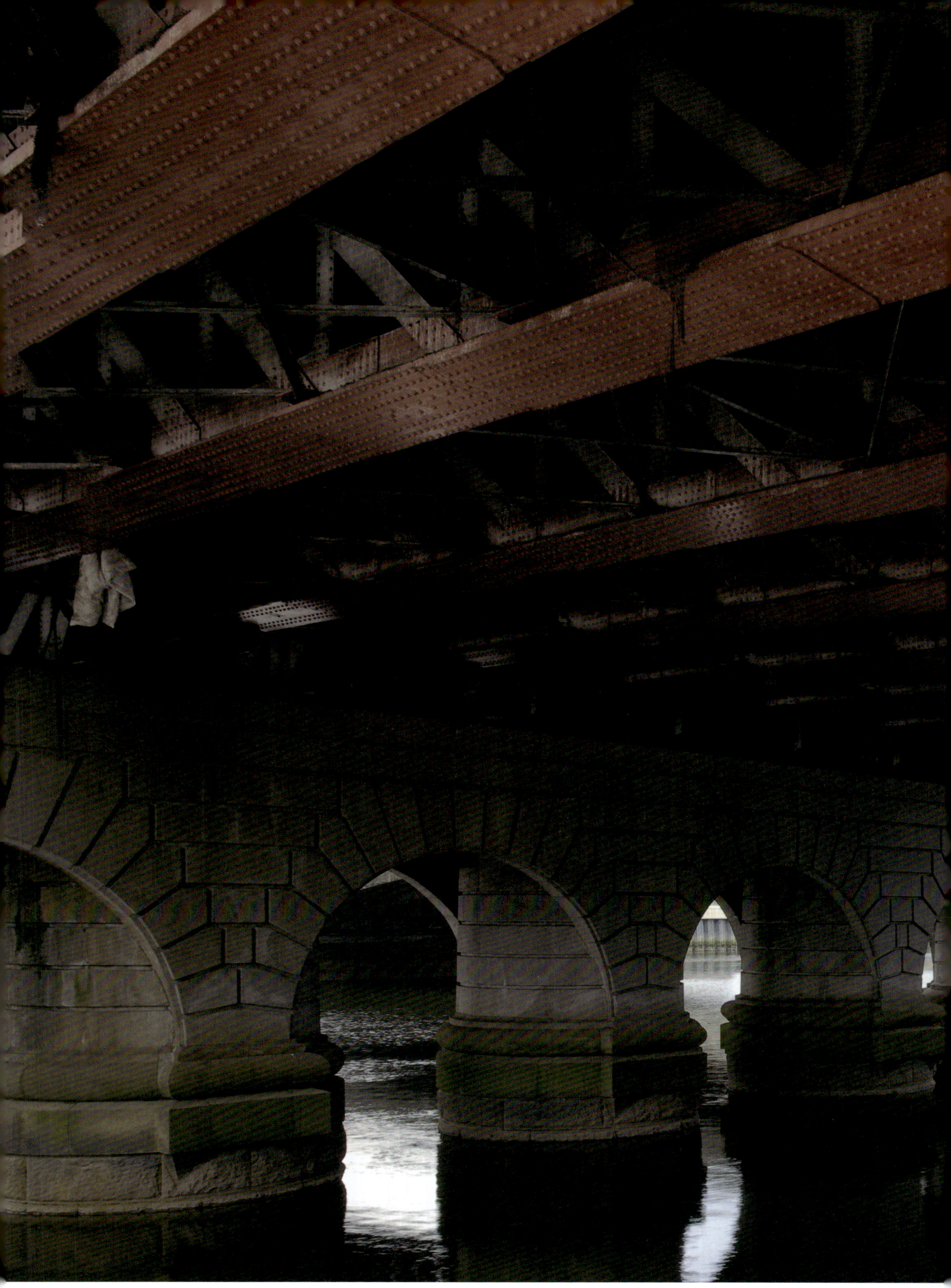

my John,————I knew that he had said goodbye————My low — lands awa — y——

my John,————A red, red rose did my love wear————My low — lands awa — y——

my John,————'I love you dear, this well you know'————My low — lands awa — y——

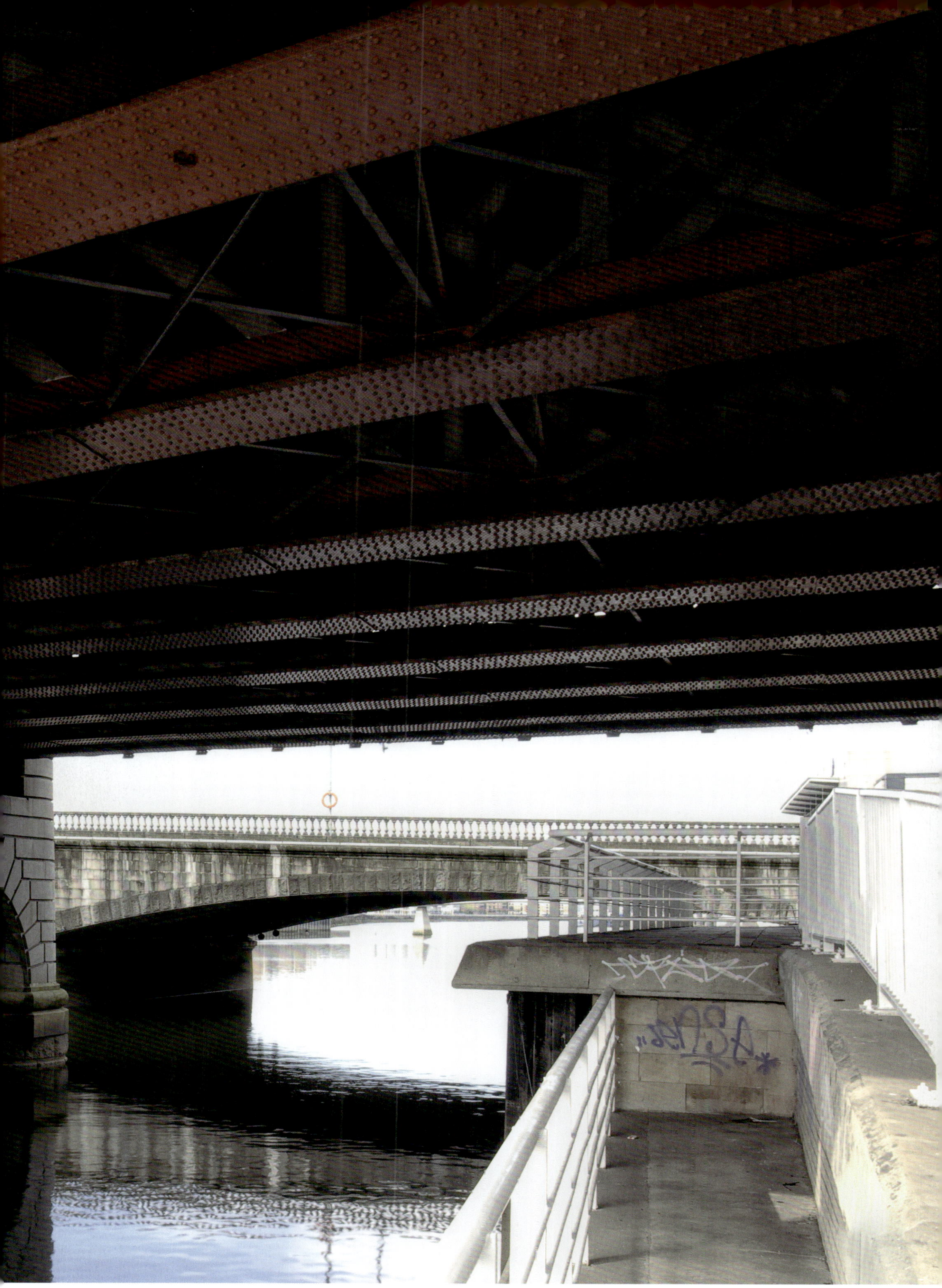

—All green and wet with weeds so cold——— Low — lands, ___ low——————— lands, awa — y my John

—She made no sound no word she said——— Low — lands, ___ low——————— lands, awa — y my John

—And then she sang in sweetest voice——— Low — lands, ___ low——————— lands, awa — y my John

View towards Caledonian Railway Bridge with King George V Bridge under construction, 1926. Courtesy: The Glasgow City Archives and Special Collections.

Installation sketches by Colin Lindsay, Glasgow International Festival of Visual Art, 2010.

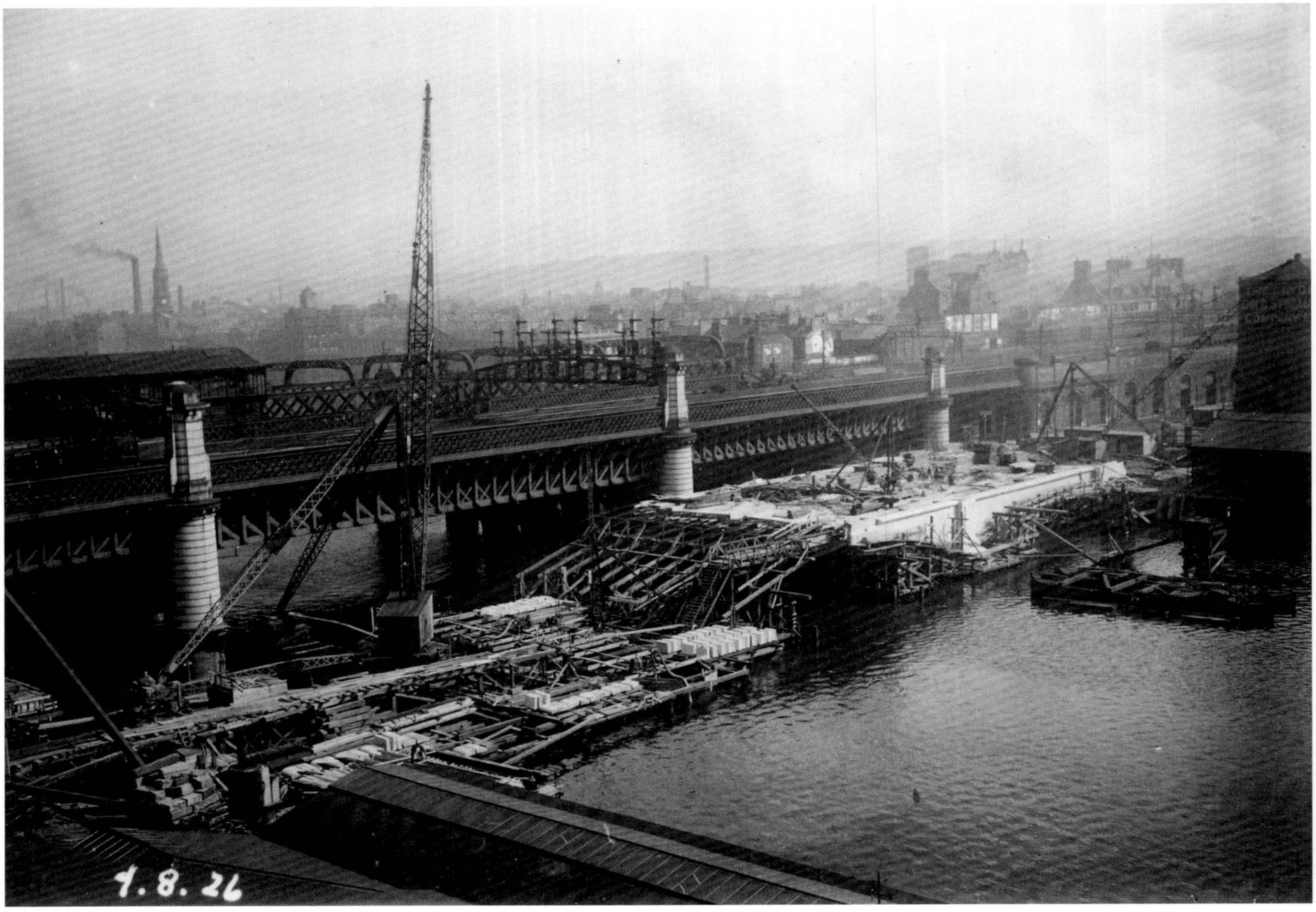

The Sacred Bridge

Throughout the ages bridges and rivers have been associated with the sacred. The Celts regarded rivers as bestowers of life, health, and plenty, and offered them gifts and sacrifices. The most important religious position in ancient Rome was given the title *pontifex maximus* (greatest bridge builder). The word is formed from *pons* and *facere*, which in Greek means 'to perform a sacrifice' and it may refer to the priests who offered sacrifices upon the bridge. Evidence of these rites has been found in the very foundations of the bridges themselves. During excavations there have often been discoveries of offerings and valuable goods thought to appease the spirits of the river. There have even been discoveries of immurement. It was believed that this form of human sacrifice gave the bridge strength.

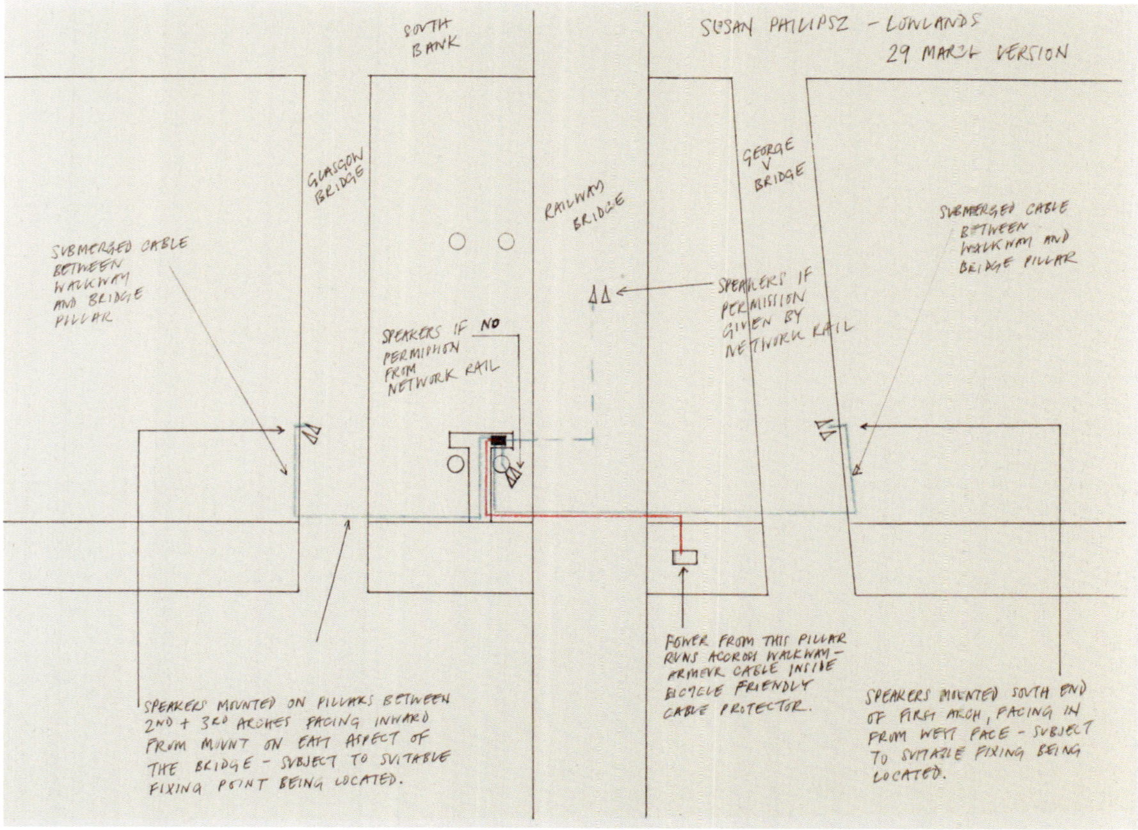

Caledonian Railway Bridge

I anticipated lots of echo and reflections from the barrel-vaulted archways and I thought this would amplify the disembodied voices reverberating around the space. After I had installed my work under the bridge I was waiting on the walkway when a bunch of people suddenly appeared behind me. One of them, who had clearly been drinking, staggered up to me with a bottle in his hand and asked if I could hear those voices too. They told me they were living rough inside the structure of the Railway Bridge. They pointed to some wooden beams above us that spanned the length of the bridge and told me this is where they slept. Sometimes you can see their sleeping bags and blankets hanging down along the underside of the bridge, high above the water.

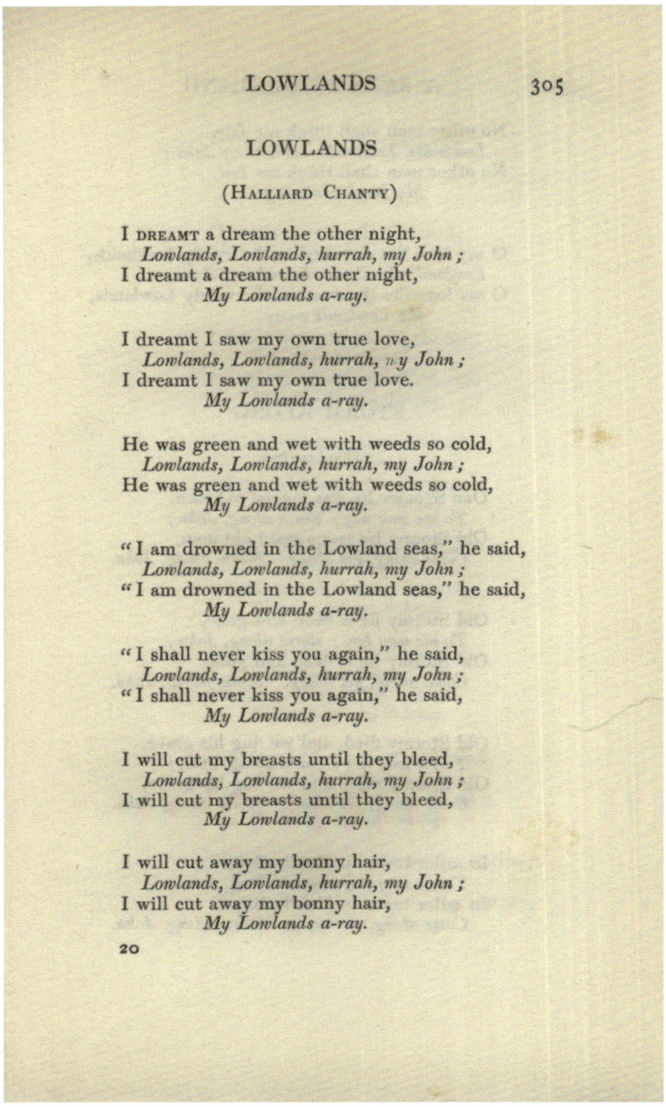
LOWLANDS 305

LOWLANDS

(Halliard Chanty)

I dreamt a dream the other night,
Lowlands, Lowlands, hurrah, my John;
I dreamt a dream the other night,
My Lowlands a-ray.

I dreamt I saw my own true love,
Lowlands, Lowlands, hurrah, my John;
I dreamt I saw my own true love.
My Lowlands a-ray.

He was green and wet with weeds so cold,
Lowlands, Lowlands, hurrah, my John;
He was green and wet with weeds so cold,
My Lowlands a-ray.

"I am drowned in the Lowland seas," he said,
Lowlands, Lowlands, hurrah, my John;
"I am drowned in the Lowland seas," he said,
My Lowlands a-ray.

"I shall never kiss you again," he said,
Lowlands, Lowlands, hurrah, my John;
"I shall never kiss you again," he said,
My Lowlands a-ray.

I will cut my breasts until they bleed,
Lowlands, Lowlands, hurrah, my John;
I will cut my breasts until they bleed,
My Lowlands a-ray.

I will cut away my bonny hair,
Lowlands, Lowlands, hurrah, my John;
I will cut away my bonny hair,
My Lowlands a-ray.

20

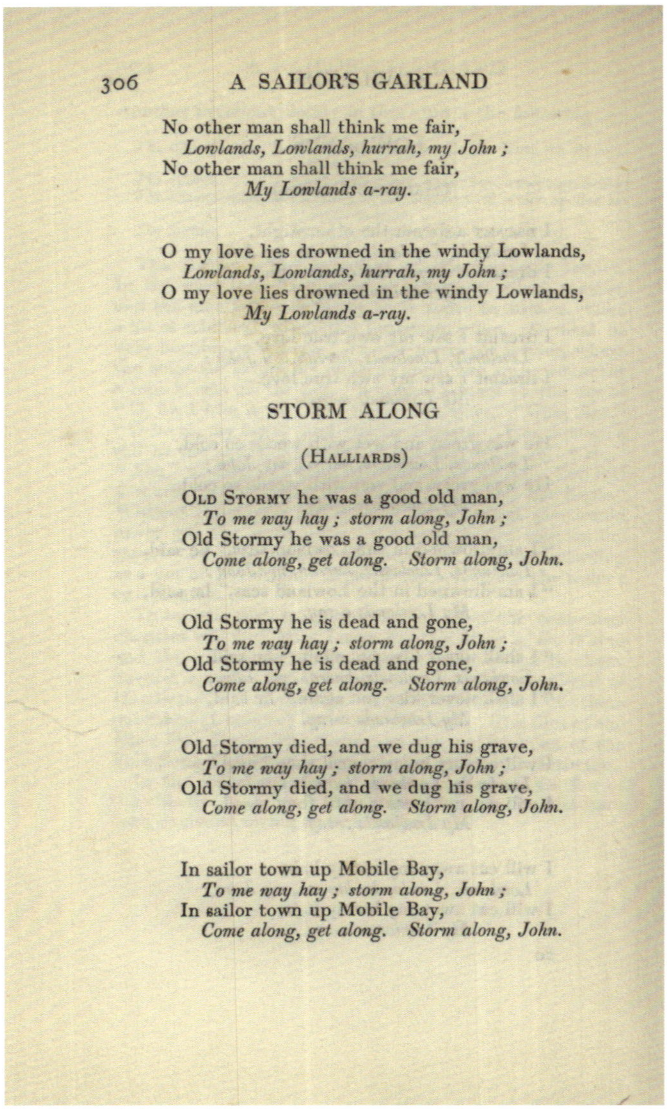
306 A SAILOR'S GARLAND

No other man shall think me fair,
Lowlands, Lowlands, hurrah, my John;
No other man shall think me fair,
My Lowlands a-ray.

O my love lies drowned in the windy Lowlands,
Lowlands, Lowlands, hurrah, my John;
O my love lies drowned in the windy Lowlands,
My Lowlands a-ray.

STORM ALONG

(Halliards)

Old Stormy he was a good old man,
To me way hay; storm along, John;
Old Stormy he was a good old man,
Come along, get along. Storm along, John.

Old Stormy he is dead and gone,
To me way hay; storm along, John;
Old Stormy he is dead and gone,
Come along, get along. Storm along, John.

Old Stormy died, and we dug his grave,
To me way hay; storm along, John;
Old Stormy died, and we dug his grave,
Come along, get along. Storm along, John.

In sailor town up Mobile Bay,
To me way hay; storm along, John;
In sailor town up Mobile Bay,
Come along, get along. Storm along, John.

A Sailors Garland

'There are three varieties of chanty, each kind adapted to its special labour. There is the capstan chanty, sung at the capstan when warping, or weighing anchor, or hoisting topsails with the watch. There is the halliard chanty, sung at the topsail and top-gallant halliards, when the topsails and top-gallant sails are being mast-headed. And there is the sheet, tack, and bowline chanty, used when the fore, main and crossjack sheets are hauled aft, and when the tacks are boarded and the bowlines tautened... The true chanty of the kinds I have mentioned, is a song with a solo part and one or two choruses. The solo part consists of a line of rhyme which is repeated by the solo man after the first chorus has been shouted.' *A Sailor's Garland*, John Masefield (Methuen, London, 1906).

A Sailor's Garland, selected and edited by John Masefield (Methuen, London, 1906). Courtesy: Irvin Department of Rare Books and Special Collections, Ernest F. Hollings Special Collections Library, University of South Carolina Libraries.

Anne w *The Hazards of Love* (EP), Topic Records Ltd, 1964. Courtesy: Topic Records.

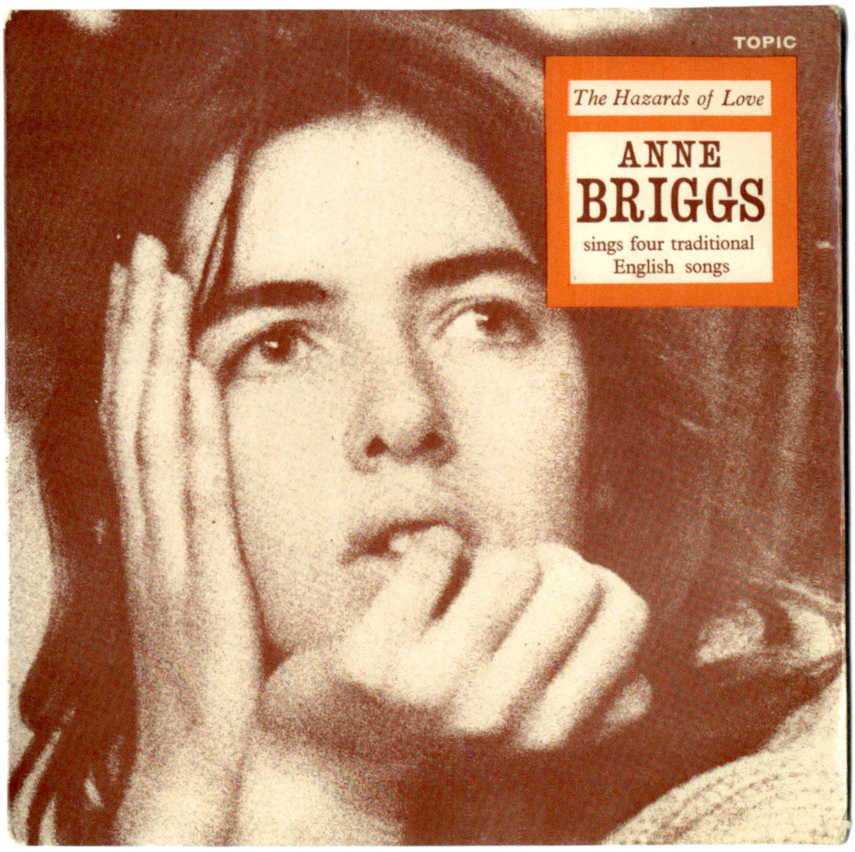

Lowlands Away

The song is a bit of a mystery. It has often been found in tradition in Britain and America but always as a sailor shanty, usually sung while working at the pumps. Two distinct sets of words accompany the tune: one text tells the present story of the dead lover who returns; the other text concerns the work and pay of cotton-lumpers in the port of Mobile, Alabama. More likely, it's a fragment of an Anglo-Scots ballad that lived on among British seamen who passed it on to longshoremen in the Gulf ports. Captain Whall says that in Liverpool in the old days a crew of merchant seamen was often spoken of as "the Johns", so the term "my John" in the ballad is no more personal than "my lad". Anne Briggs sings *Lowlands* not as a shanty but as a ballad, in what is probably something like its original form.

Lowlands

Katrina M. Brown

The bridges that span the River Clyde where it runs through the centre of Glasgow are as grandly named as they are built, and full of the aura of Empire from the city's heyday. There are three major bridges in close proximity, with lesser foot and road bridges either side of them. The Jamaica Street Bridge, first opened in 1836, was originally designed by Scottish civil engineer Thomas Telford, whose prowess with road and bridge building was to earn him the moniker 'The Colossus of Roads'. The Second Caledonian Railway Bridge came into being in 1901, replacing a smaller earlier bridge; and then the George V Bridge completed in 1928. Their substantial mass, evident weight and heft, their impressive engineering, extensive steelworks, solid granite and stone, all stand in contrast to the light, white footbridge of recent years that now stands nearby. They are an enduring image of Glasgow's erstwhile industrial might and are such an integral part of daily city life that I doubt anyone ever has cause to refer to them, and certainly not by their given names. They have melted into the fabric of the city; almost, like the river that flows below them, invisible to the passing traffic.

These bridges stand as much as a symbol of the height of Victorian Glasgow's wealth as 'the second city of Empire' as the buildings that lined the river, many of which are now replaced or redeveloped, some lying derelict. The river is the sole constant — once the very base of Glasgow's international position, the route out to the rest of the world taken by its ships and steel. The only vessels to be seen on this stretch of the river today are occasional dredgers and police boats.

Running along the north bank of the river and beneath these grand structures is a section of the 'Clydeside Walkway', a footpath that is considerably less grand. Despite 'regeneration' and intermittent clean-ups it remains, as Philipsz herself put it 'a little seedy'. The intersection with the railway bridge is a fairly abject place: dark, dank and gloomy, populated mainly by street drinkers and malingerers. There are signs of people sleeping rough on the underside of the railway bridge. By day, there will be the occasional runner or cyclist passing through, quickly.

It was this particular place, in the city in which she grew up, that Philipsz chose as the site for her work for *Glasgow International Festival of Visual Art* in 2010. The site was in many respects a characteristic choice for the artist: off-centre in some respect, somehow transitional or marginal. It was not the first time Philipsz had chosen a waterway: her work for the Münster Sculpture Projects in 2007, *The Lost Reflection*, straddled the Aasee with a duet from Offenbach's *The Tales of Hoffman*, and was sited under a bridge. In Dundee in 2005, another outdoor installation entitled *Atlantis* was made for the banks of the River Tay. Although the chosen site in Glasgow in many ways offered a kind of separation from the urban swarm above and around it, it differs from these other watery locations in that it was full of sound: of traffic passing either side, trains trundling overhead, station announcements echoing from the platforms above. No sound though from the silent, murky river. But resonant with echoes and reflections.

Walking around Glasgow on an early visit to develop her work for the Festival, Philipsz came across the spot immediately beneath the railway bridge. It was at the time marked by a modest bunch of flowers tied to the railing at the water's edge commemorating a recent suicide, sadly not an irregular occurrence. The site called to mind a song, in this instance an old Scottish lament or sea shanty, entitled *Lowlands*. It is one of over 400 sea shanties that were collected by Stan Hugill and published as *Shanties from the Seven Seas* in 1961. Hugill writes of *Lowlands*: 'Originally a pumping song, it was later used at windlass and capstan. It was never too popular, as it was difficult to sing properly — Whall describes it as a "recitative type" of song. It savours of a shore-ballad, with words unusually sentimental for seamen... More than likely it is one of the songs that passed through the shanty mart of the Gulf Ports'. Passed from one crew to another, amended and adapted through time, these songs were sung by sailors 'when engaged in the severest of their many labours'.[1] It is a working song with a repetitive, haunting melody. As recalled by Philipsz, it exists in a number of versions, variations on what Hugill describes as 'the dead lover theme', said to originate in Scotland or the North of England, a pattern that includes two types: those in which the dead lover is male and those in which the dead lover is female.

With a place and a song in mind, Philipsz configured a work of characteristic simplicity. It involved the installation of three speakers, attached to the three bridges, each relaying a recording of Philipsz singing one of the three versions of *Lowlands*. All three were directed back at the spot on the riverside pathway beneath the railway bridge. Starting simultaneously, the songs diverge over the course of the piece, with the longest of the three running for seven minutes, the last few of which are played out in acute isolation. At certain points the three versions converge and overlap — not unlike the railway tracks above. Each starts with the same refrain: 'Lowlands, lowlands, away my John, / Lowlands away I heard them say, / My lowlands away / I dreamed a dream the other night, / Lowlands, lowlands, away my John, (...)'

From here they continue to describe a dream, that of a lost lover returning from a watery grave. In one version, it is a young woman's dream of her lost lover, full of poignant imagery of love lost: 'I knew my love was drowned and dead / He stood so still, no word he said (...)'

And later, in the same version: 'All green and wet with weeds so cold / Around his form green weeds had hold / "I shall never kiss you more", he said, / "Never kiss you more — for I am dead"'.

The woman's pain and torment at the sight of her love culminates in the dramatic: '"I will cut my breasts until they bleed." / His form had gone — in the green weed'. Another version is sung from a male perspective, a sailor seeing a vision of his sweetheart, as if as a harbinger of doom: 'She came to me at my bedside / Dressed all in white like some fair bride'. It is a familiar type of traditional song, if not a familiar song itself, a haunting melody with a melancholic air.

The song is sung in Philipsz's distinctive, gentle lilt. As has been remarked elsewhere, she sings not in the manner of a public performer but more as if she were singing to herself, oblivious to the presence of an audience. It is affectless and feels intensely intimate. Fragile but never actually faltering or failing. She holds the tune. It is though soft, light, direct and all the more potent for it, especially when encountered in this unlikely, dehumanized public space.

Abruptly and through the most minimal, near invisible of means, this somewhat bleak urban no man's land was cast into an ethereal and other-worldly domain. One of dark, watery depths and sinister female figures, in which the waterway becomes the conduit to an underworld. It is a highly evocative combination that brings to mind many a fictional creation, from the Sirens of Greek mythology, whose enchanting voices would lure sailors to their death; to the character of Anna Livia Plurabelle in James Joyce's *Finnegans Wake* (1939), a personification of the River Liffey, who disappears at dawn into the ocean at the close of the book.

In this particular location, the soft, gentle voice resonated around the hard stone surfaces of the bridges and the river-bank, the unhurried pace at odds with the swirling life above. As ever with Philipsz's work, the place inflected the song and the song changed the place. The work caused passers-by to pause, listen, and look out over the river. The combined voices (albeit the same voice in fact) that together suggest a choir, gradually trail off to leave the one remaining voice all the more intensely fragile, recalling multiple losses, long forgotten — lives lost or discarded.

1 — *A Sailor's Garland*, Selected and Edited by John Masefield. (Methuen, London, 1906).

I See a Darkness

Stockholm, 2008 New York, 2010

Jarla Partilager,
Stockholm, 2008.
Tanya Bonakdar Gallery,
New York, 2010.
Five-channel sound
installation. 8 minutes,
30 seconds.

I See a Darkness is always presented in the dark. The speakers are set on plinths and arranged throughout the space like sculptures. The work begins with a call and response duet of the song *I See a Darkness* written by Will Oldham. This is followed by a recording of me picking out the tune of Ravel's *Pavane pour une infante defunte* (Pavane for a Dead Princess) on a piano. Lucia Joyce danced to this tune as a teenager with *Les Six de rythme et couleur*. The final piece is a four-speaker installation of me singing the Neapolitan barcarolle *Santa Lucia*. The lyrics 'My home is far away / For you I'm yearning / Longing to greet the day / Of my returning' allude to feelings of separation and longing and echo Lucia Joyce's later years when she longed to return to her father.

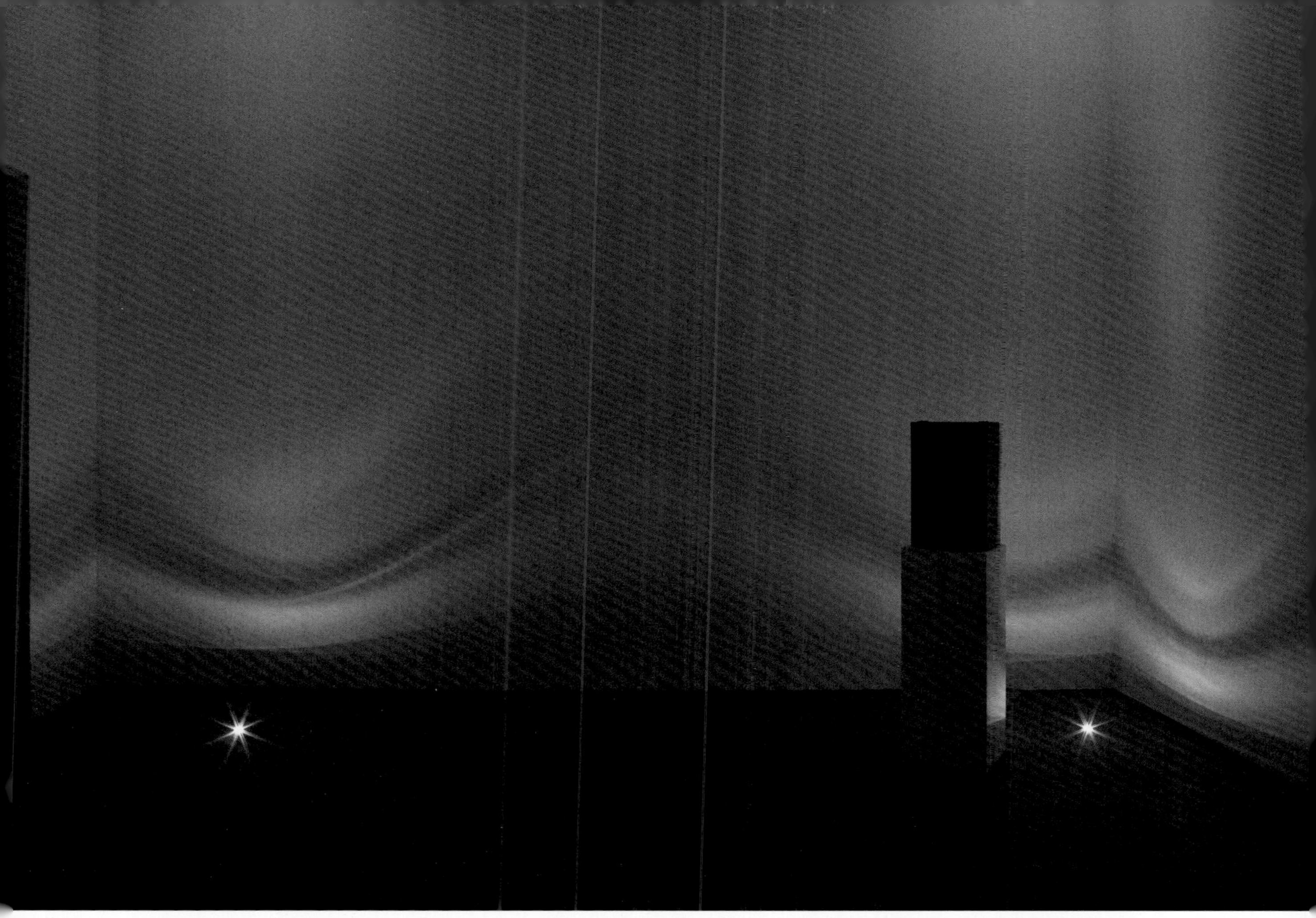

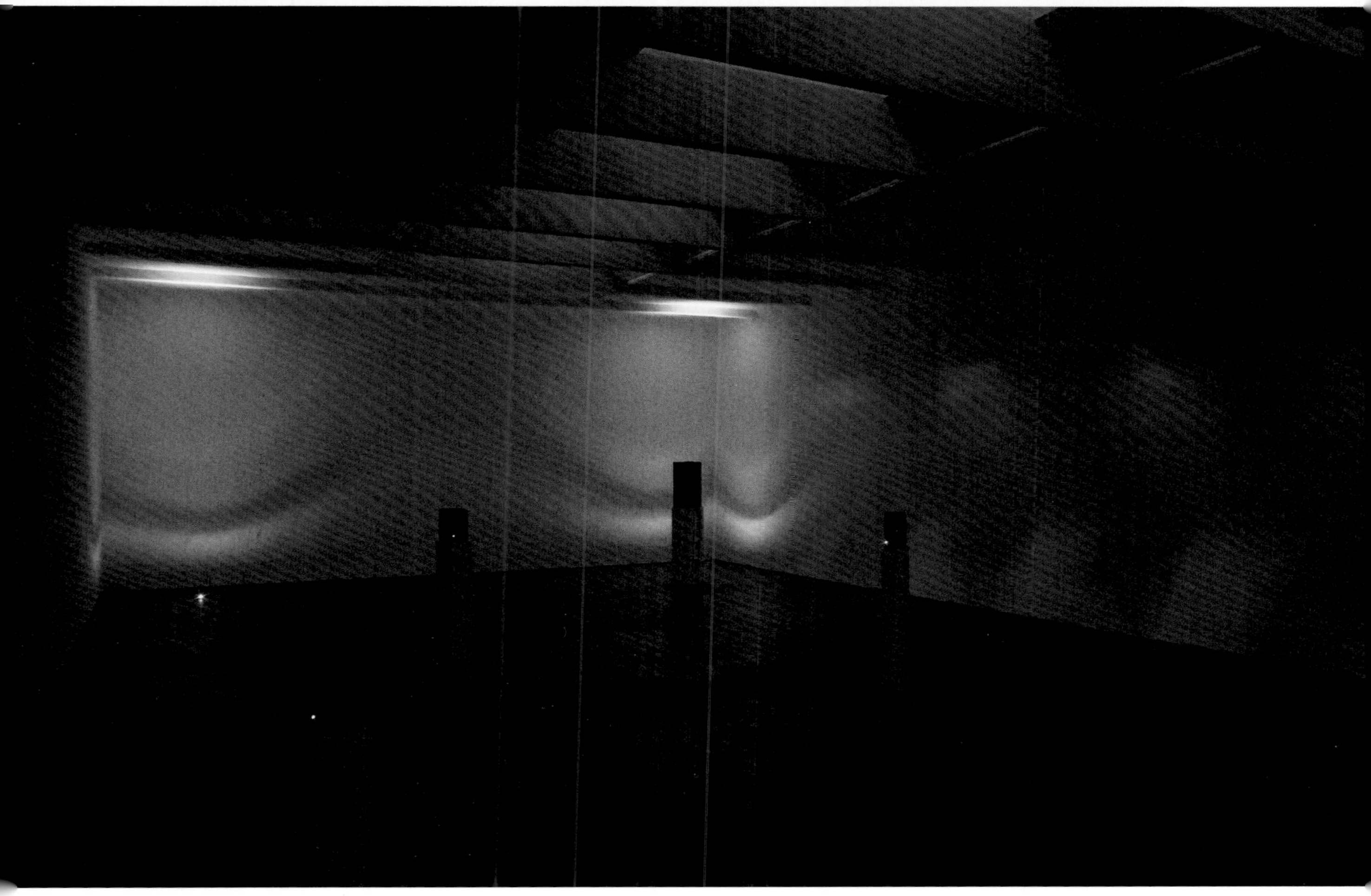

Well, you’re my friend————And can you see————

that’s what you told me————what’s inside of me

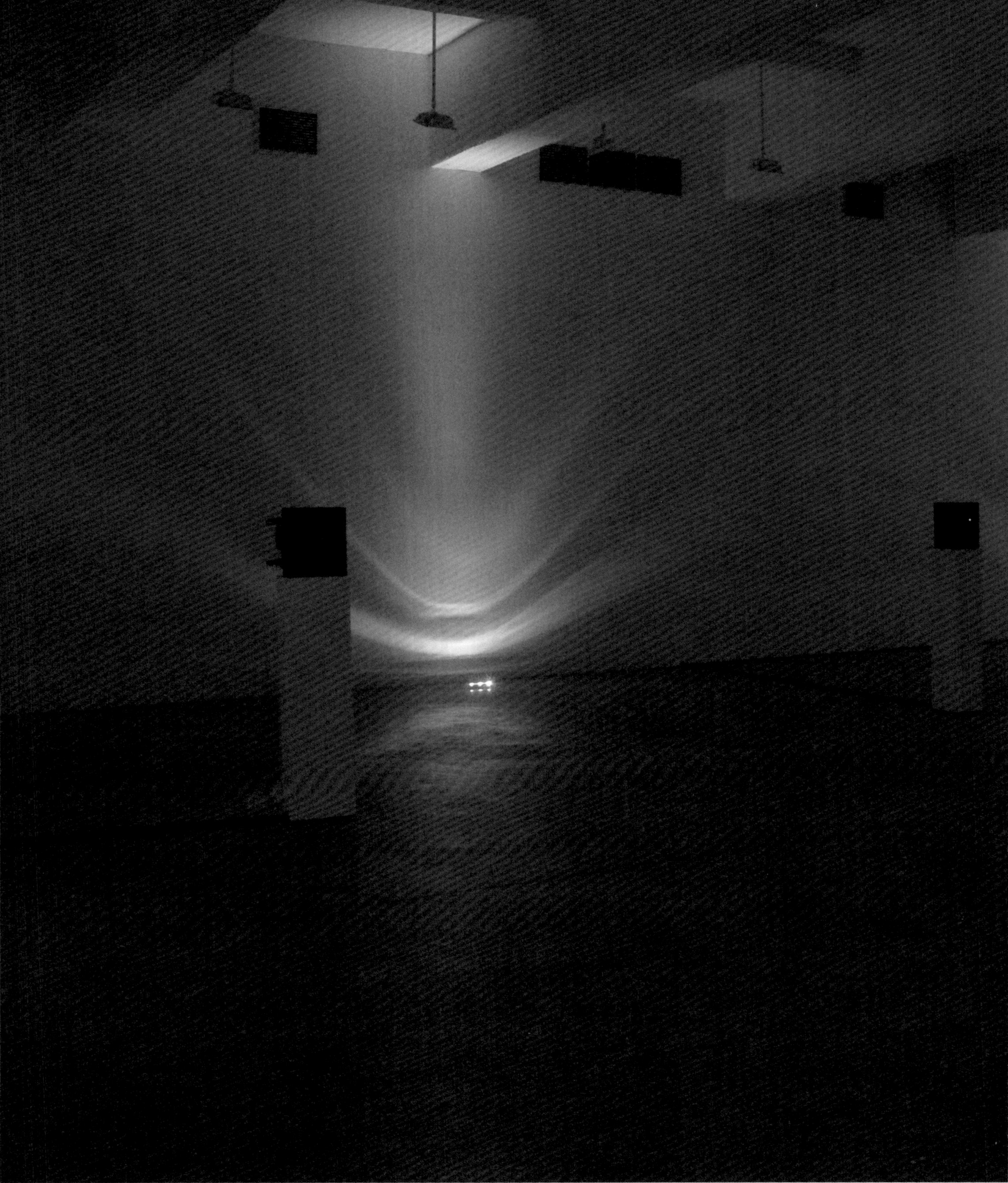

Brightl – y the silver stars——Shine on the water——Softl – y the gentle breeze——Carries our laughter—

Brightl – y the silver stars——Shine on the water——Softl – y the gentle breeze——Carries our laughter—

Brightl – y the silver stars——Shine on the water——Softl – y the gentle breeze——Carries our laughter—

Brightl – y the silver stars——Shine on the water——Softl – y the gentle breeze——Carries our laughter—

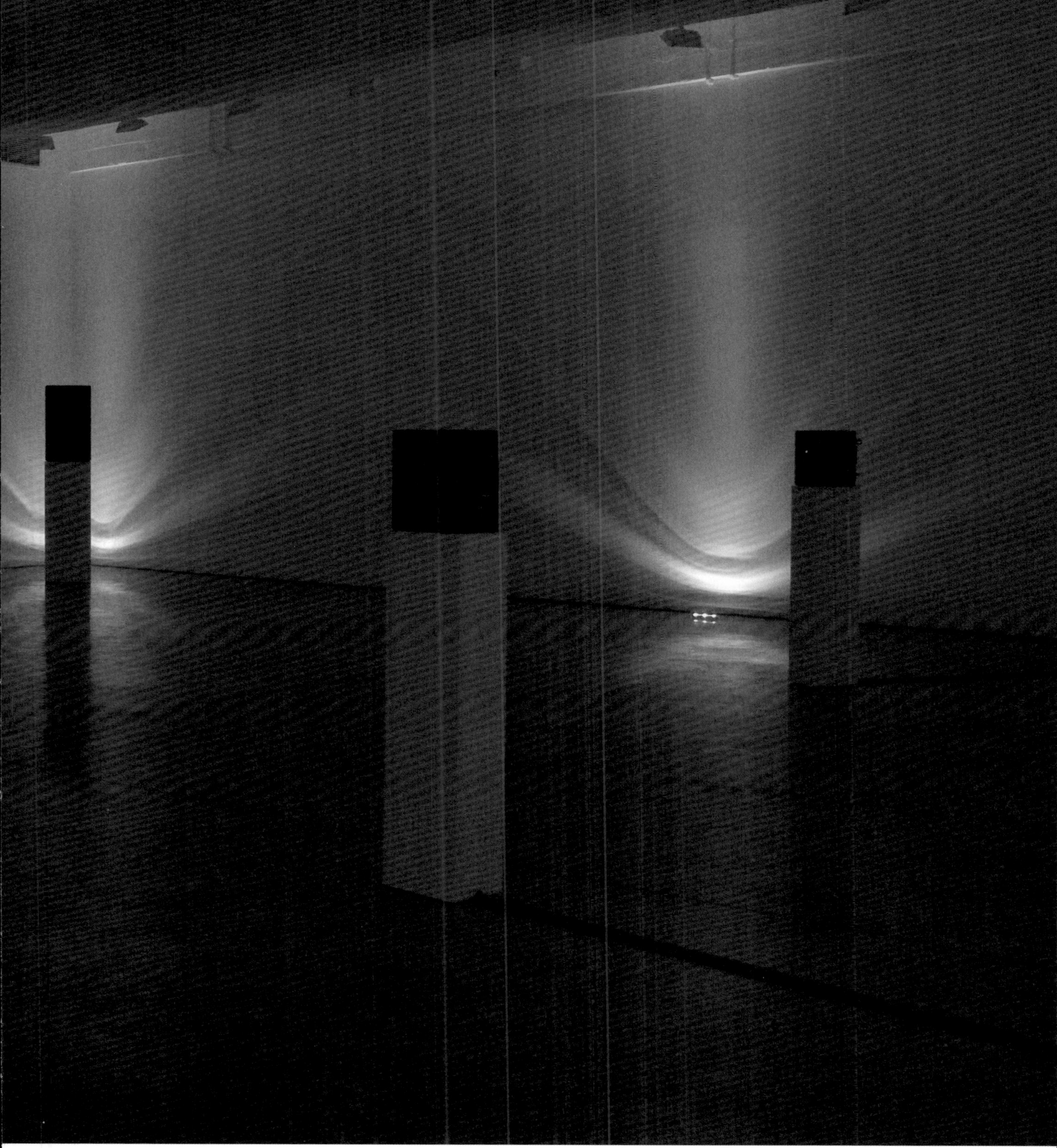

—My home is far_ away——For you I'm yearning———Long–ing to greet the day————Of my return–ing

—My home is far_ away——For you I'm yearning———Long–ing to greet the day————Of my return–ing

—My home is far_ away——For you I'm yearning———Long–ing to greet the day————Of my return–ing

—My home is far_ away——For you I'm yearning———Long–ing to greet the day————Of my return–ing

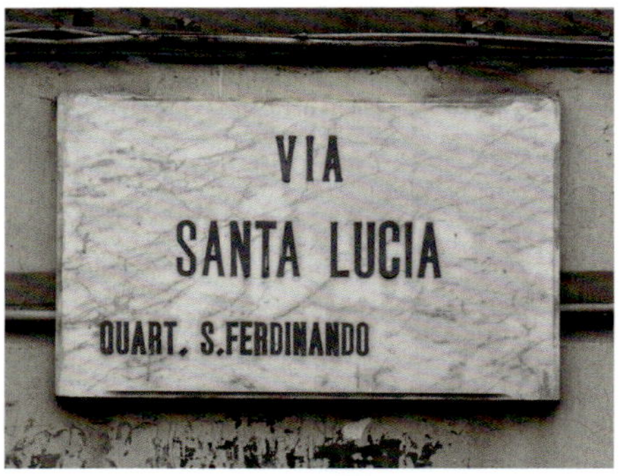

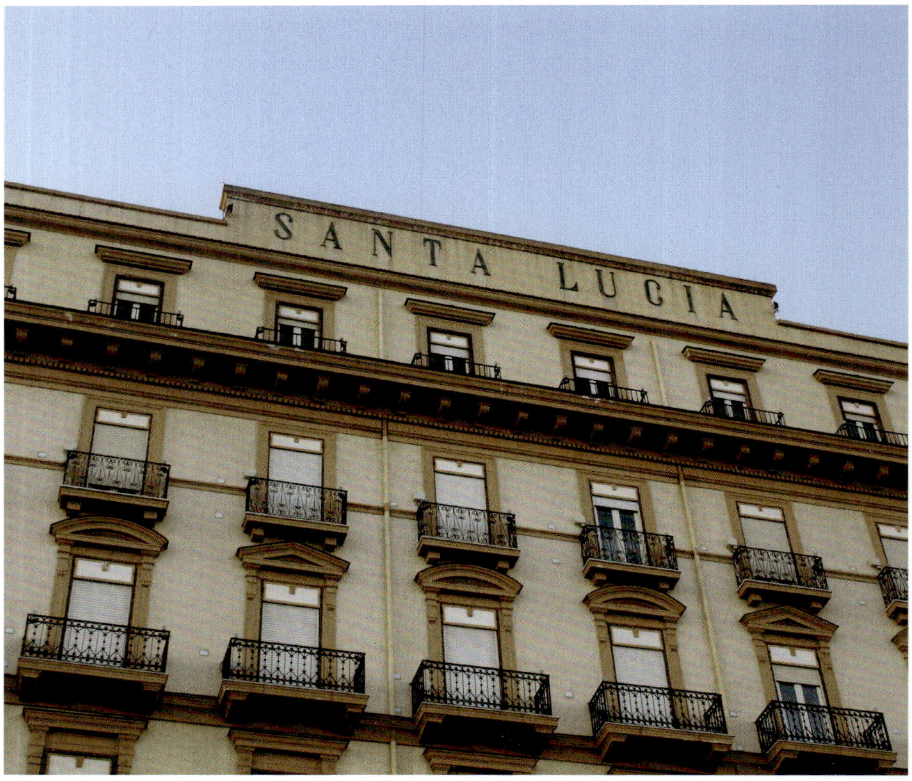

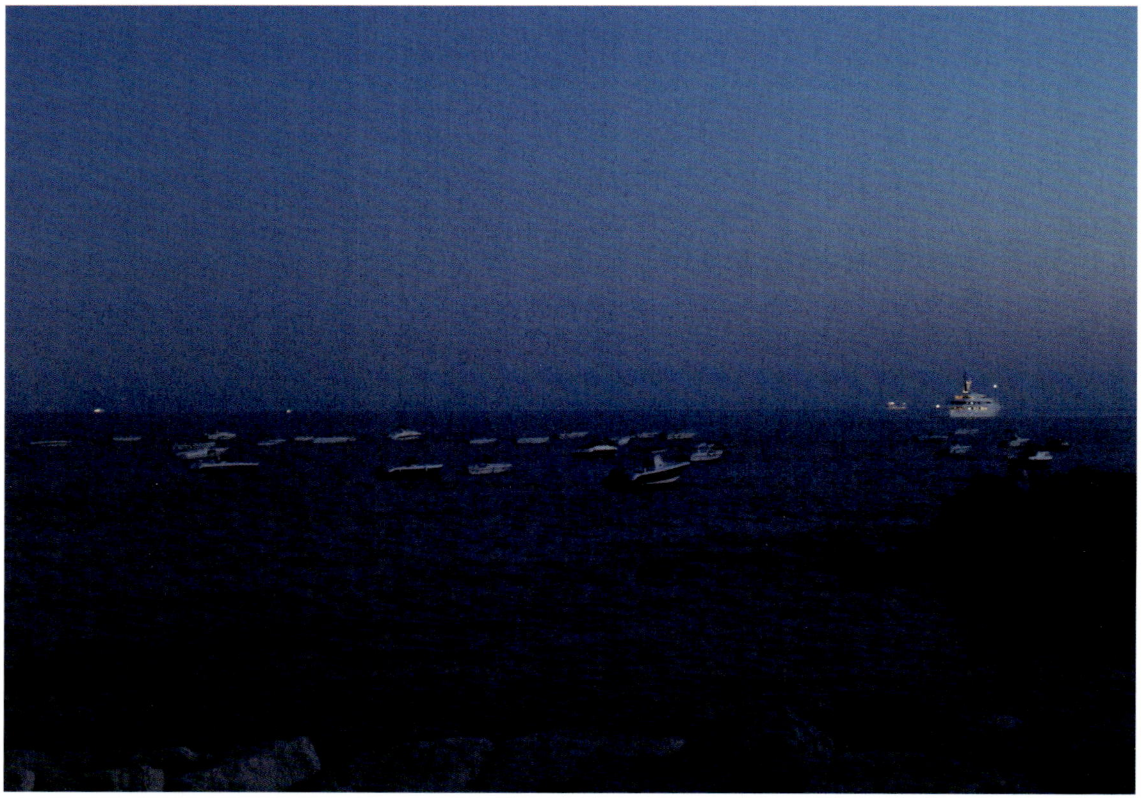

Borgo Santa Lucia

We scheduled the exhibition in Stockholm in December, to coincide with the Santa Lucia festival that is celebrated all over Sweden. The festival takes place on one of the darkest days in the calendar and celebrates the coming of the light. I'd heard about this famous festival and I knew that the Swedes in effect had adopted the Neapolitan song *Santa Lucia* as their own. I was interested in this as it was a song I knew from childhood, a song about a sailor who longs to return home. This song somehow always stayed with me. On a visit to Italy earlier in the year I visited Naples and looking out onto the Bay of Naples I remembered that the song refers to the district in Naples called the Borgo Santa Lucia and I began to realise the potential of the song again.

Correspondence between
Susan Philipsz and
Gerard De Geer, 2008.

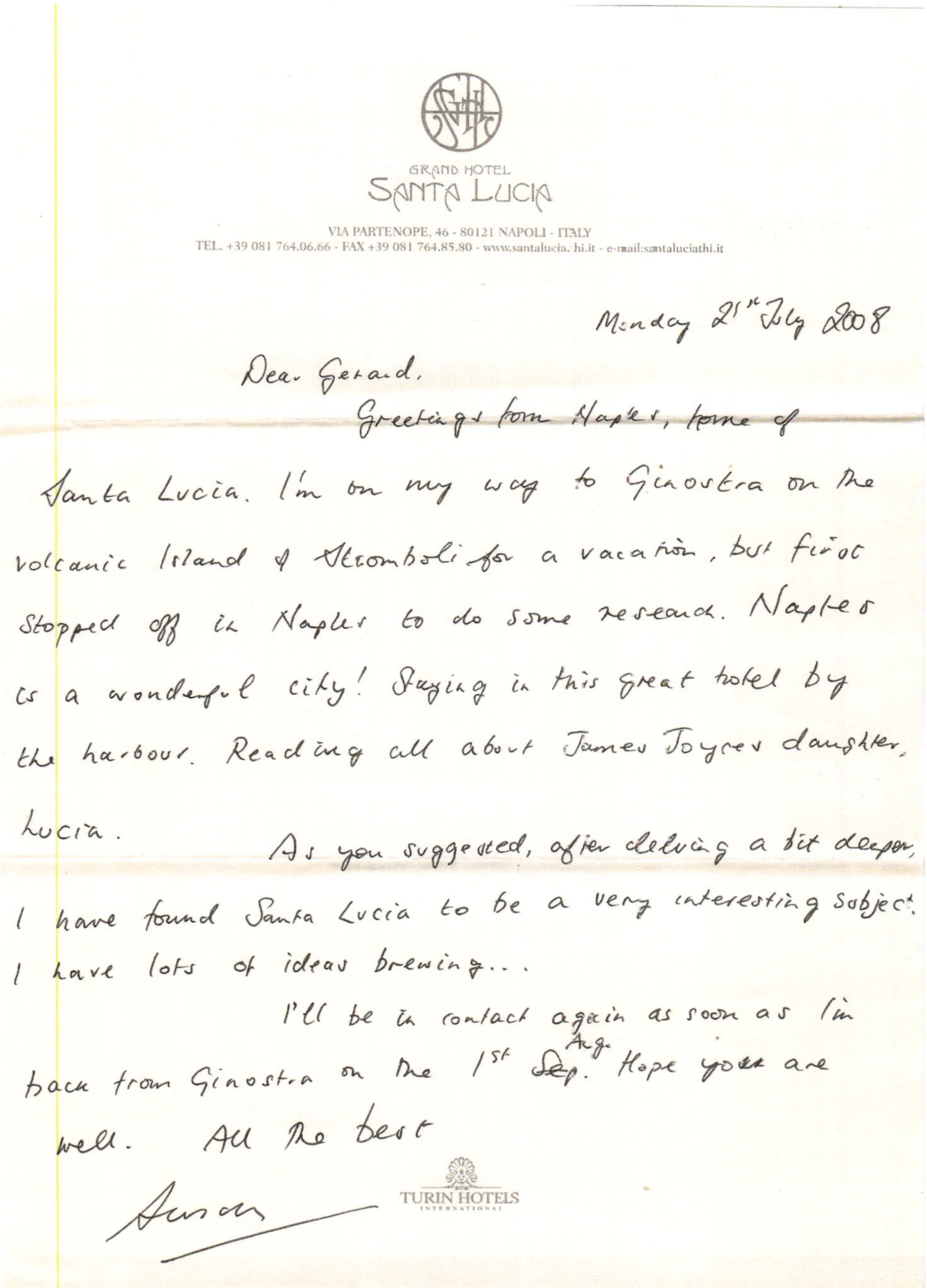

GRAND HOTEL
SANTA LUCIA
VIA PARTENOPE, 46 - 80121 NAPOLI - ITALY
TEL. +39 081 764.06.66 - FAX +39 081 764.85.80 - www.santalucia.thi.it - e-mail:santaluciathi.it

Monday 21st July 2008

Dear Gerard,

Greetings from Naples, home of Santa Lucia. I'm on my way to Ginostra on the volcanic Island of Stromboli for a vacation, but first stopped off in Naples to do some research. Naples is a wonderful city! Staying in this great hotel by the harbour. Reading all about James Joyces daughter, Lucia.

As you suggested, after delving a bit deeper, I have found Santa Lucia to be a very interesting subject. I have lots of ideas brewing...

I'll be in contact again as soon as I'm back from Ginostra on the 1st ~~Sep.~~ Aug. Hope you are well. All the best

Susan

TURIN HOTELS INTERNATIONAL

Lucia Joyce

On my way to Naples I came across a book about James Joyce's daughter Lucia Joyce. This was to become my book for the journey. I was surprised to discover that she was very important in Joyce's development as a writer and that he frequently refers to her in his work. She was to become his muse and was always under his watchful eye. Lucia took after her father; she loved to dance as much as Joyce loved to sing and it seemed that she was destined for great things. However, the more I read about Lucia Joyce the more I began to realise what a tragedy her life was. The family moved continually and in doing so uprooted Lucia's sense of herself. Lucia Joyce slipped into madness and obscurity and lived the remainder of her years isolated in an institution in Northampton, England.

Lucia Joyce, Paris, 1924. Photograph: Bernice Abbot. Courtesy: Howard Greenberg Gallery.

Santa Lucia, 1521. Domenico di Pace Beccafumi. Courtesy: Banca Monte dei Paschi di Siena.

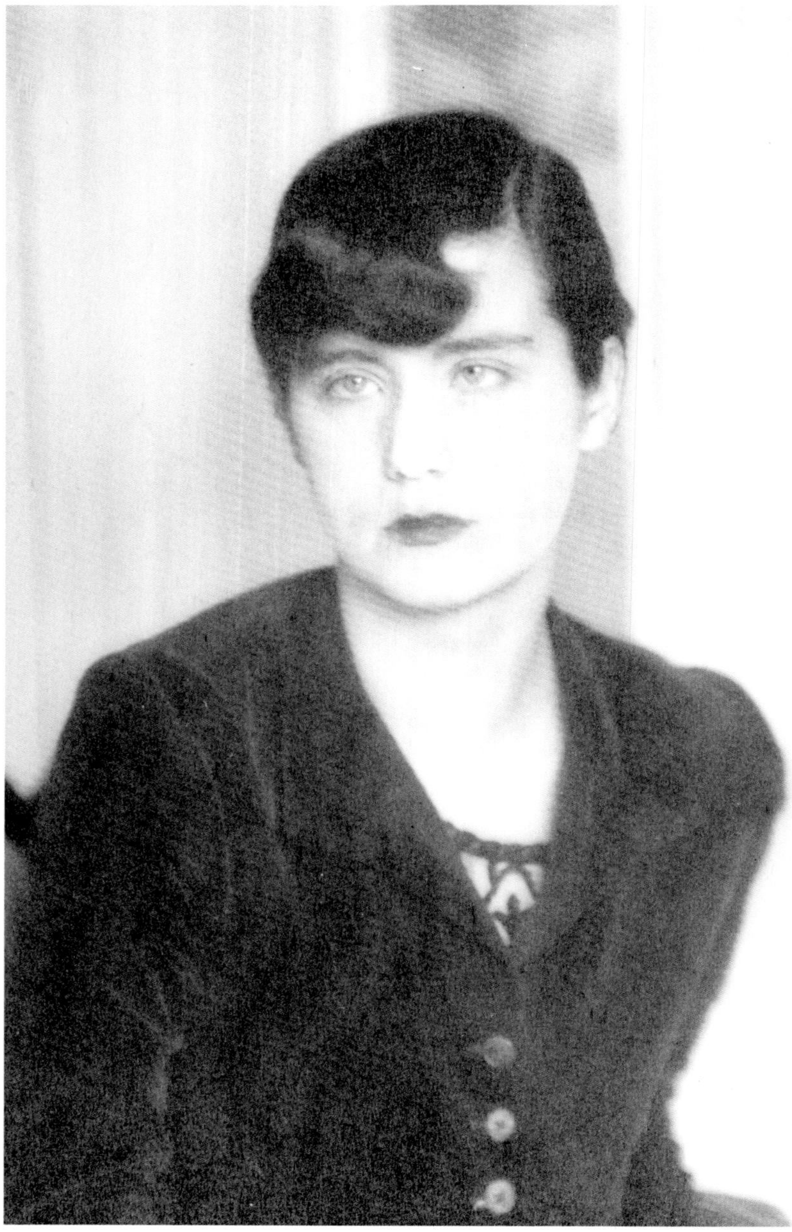

The Syra-Cusa

Lucia Joyce inherited her eyes from her mother's side of the family. Nora Barnacle's sister Peg had a strong cast in one eye. This strabismus was something of which Lucia Joyce was always conscious. Samuel Beckett reputedly based his character 'the Syra-Cusa' upon Lucia after their failed love affair. 'Her eyes were wanton, they rolled and stravagued, they were laskivious and lickerish, the brokers of her zeal, basilisk eyes, the fowlers and hooks of Amourr, burning glasses. Strong piercing black eyes... Eyes – less good, to be frank, than we make out, our pen carried us away. Samuel Beckett, *Dream of Fair to Middling Women* (Black Cat Press, Dublin, 1992).

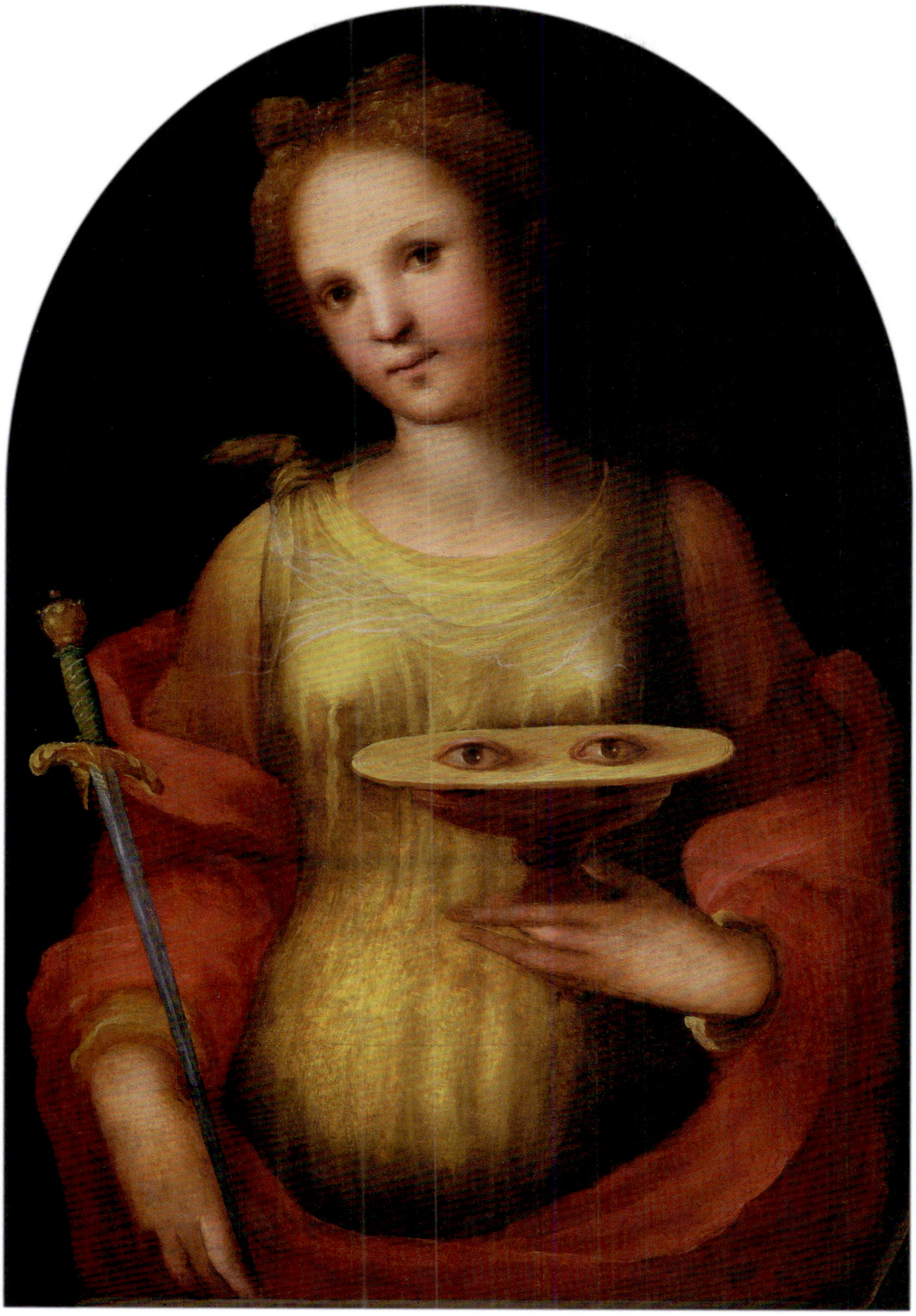

The Light Giver

Santa Lucia came from Syracuse in Sicily. She was the patron saint of light and she has always been described as having beautiful eyes. Legend has it after one admirer complimented her eyes she cut them out and sent them to him. 'If thine eye offend thee, pluck it out and cast it from thee'. The legend concludes with her eyes being restored but she is frequently depicted holding her eyes on a platter.

Santa Lucia's name shares a root (luc-) with the Latin word for light, lux. This has led to her being named as the patron saint of the blind and those with eye-trouble. Santa Lucia will always represent light, while Lucia Joyce's story is one of a bright light slipping into obscurity and darkness.

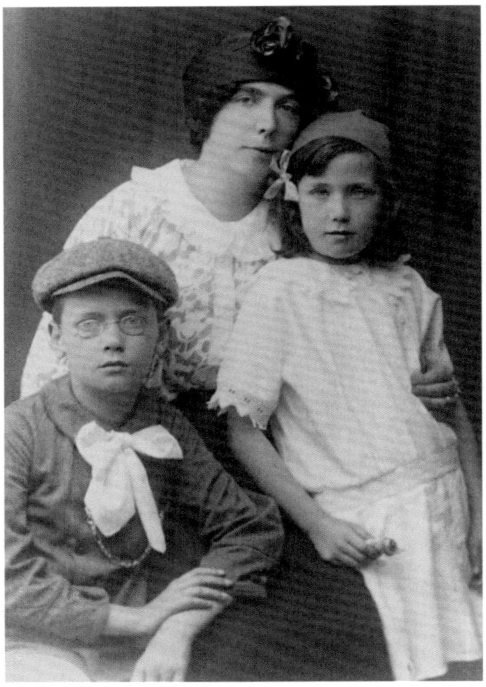

Lucia with Nora and Giorgio Joyce, Zurich, circa 1916. Courtesy: The Poetry Collection of the University Libraries, University at Buffalo, The State University of New York.

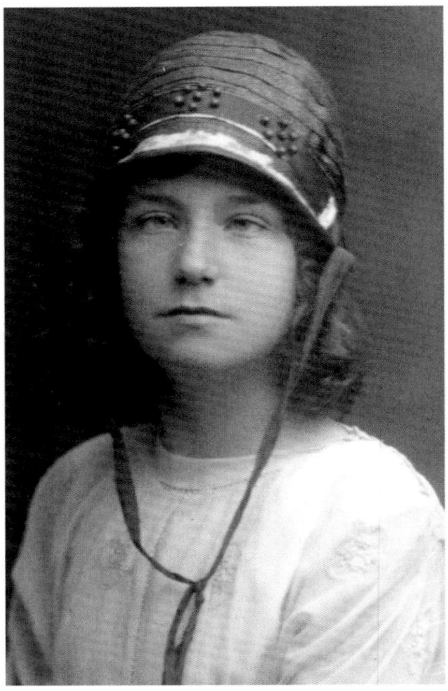

Lucia Joyce as a young girl, wearing hat with streamers, Zurich, circa 1914. Courtesy: The Poetry Collection of the University Libraries, University at Buffalo, The State University of New York.

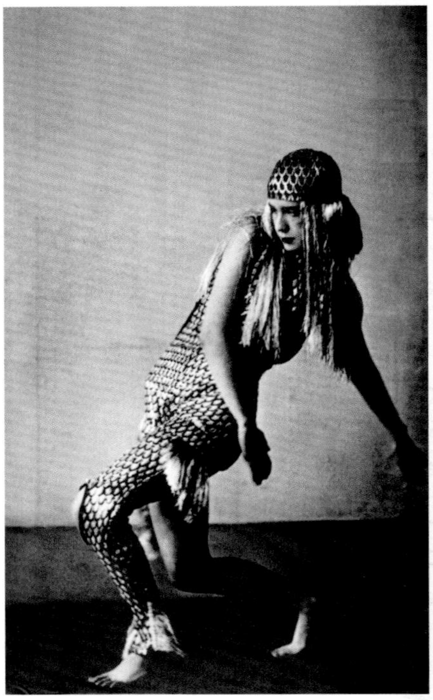

Lucia Joyce dancing in a costume she made hersef for a competition at the Bal Bullier in Paris, May 1929. Photographer unknown. Courtesy: The Stuart Gilbert Collection, Harry Ransom Center, University of Texas at Austin.

The Silver Fish

'She had created a remarkable costume with a moiréd cloth sequined as if in scales. It was sleeveless, to emphasize the creature's slender evanescence, and from the hips protruded delicate gills. Her head was covered with a rounded cap of the same material, from which she had suspended long silver tresses dangling to her waist. The wit of the costume was in its "leggings", for Lucia had swathed only one leg in sequined cloth, leaving the other free to appear and disappear nakedly behind the first. As everyone knows, the allure of a mermaid arises from the frustration of sexual longing that the single tail ensures.'
Carol Loeb Shloss, *Lucia Joyce: To Dance in the Wake*, (Picador, New York, 2003).

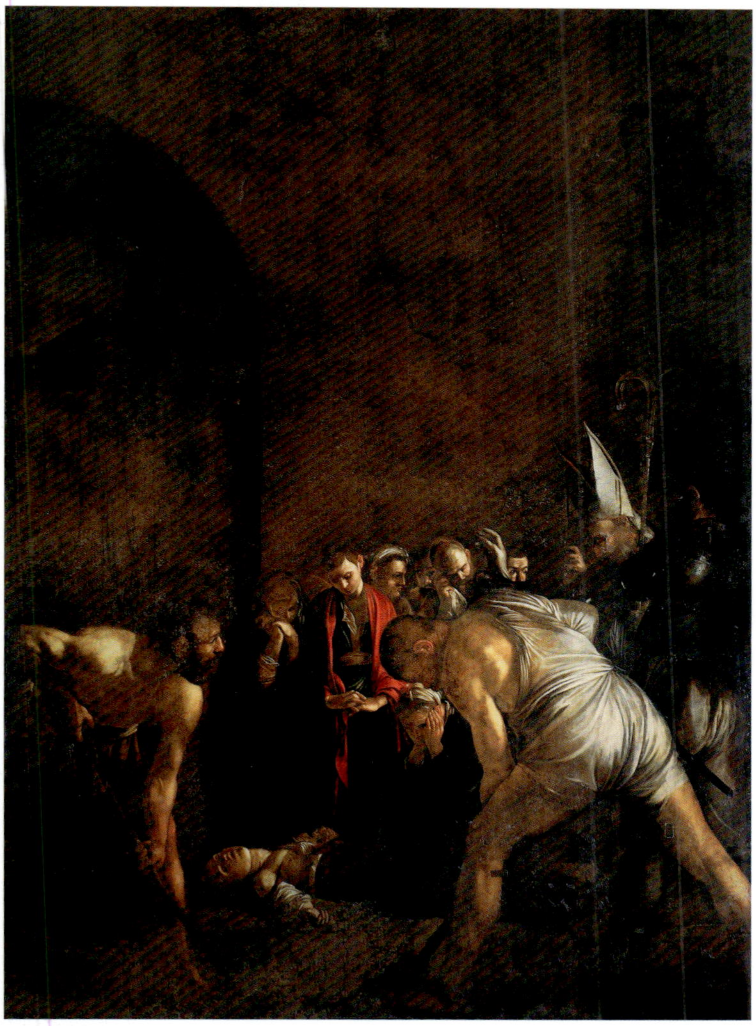

Burial of Santa Lucia, 1608–1609, Caravaggio Courtesy: The church of Santa Lucia al sepolcro, Syracuse, Italy.

Santa Agata appears to Santa Lucia tormented, circa 1625–1640, Peter Paul Rubens. Courtesy: Accademia Carrara, Bergamo.

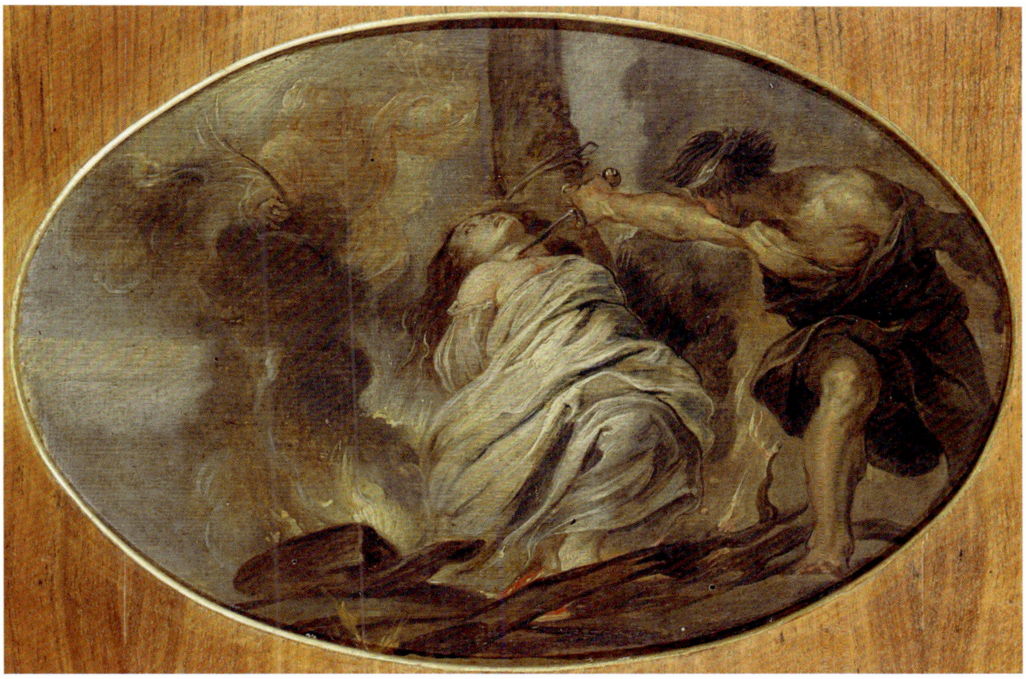

The Martyrdom of Santa Lucia

Santa Lucia vowed to remain celibate in the tradition of St. Agatha. She forsake all male attention during her life in order to devote herself to God. After attempting to distribute her family's wealth among the poor, an angry suitor denounced her to the local Roman authorities, who sentenced her to be removed to a brothel and forced into prostitution. The Christian tradition states that when the guards came to take her away, they could not move her even when they hitched her to a team of oxen. Bundles of wood were then heaped about her and set on fire, but would not burn. Finally, she met her death by the sword.

Night Walks Grand, Yet Silent

Sara Arrhenius

It has been snowing ceaselessly for almost two days and the falling snow muffles the sounds of the city. The houses, the empty streets, the parked cars and the faint streetlights are covered with a thick layer of snow and all that remains to be seen outside my window is the whiteness of snow and the darkness of night. It is early December in Stockholm and it is already fifteen degrees below zero.

This text has been waiting to be written since the beginning of June. Maybe it needed the darkness of winter. Somehow the light of summer nights could never take me back to the sombre, shadowy atmosphere of my first encounter with Susan Philipsz's sound installation *I See a Darkness*. This was four years ago, on another icy evening in Stockholm, at precisely this time of year. Quite a small crowd gathered in the now-closed Stockholm space of Jarla Partilager, moving hesitantly through the darkened rooms, speaking in hushed voices, somehow intimidated by the gloom. Suddenly the sound of Philipsz's distinctive voice comes from loudspeakers in various parts of the space, singing Will Oldham's melancholy *I See a Darkness* in a call-and-response duet, which silences us, enticing us to stand still and listen. A piano piece by Ravel follows, and then the room is filled by the 19th-Century barcarolle *Santa Lucia* sounding out from four separate speakers.

This suite of vocal and musical scores threads together a necklace of different musical traditions and genres. When hearing them juxtaposed, one after another, you become aware of their diverse natures and of how each disparate soundscape creates its own narrative within the space. At the same time, they converse with each other, and with the specific ambience of the rooms. They are both of the moment and from some other time. A sensitivity to the history and spirit of a place often serves as the point of departure for Philipsz's work, and her attentiveness extends to the specificity of rituals in a given culture. The choice of Santa Lucia as one of the songs in this piece made to be experienced in Stockholm in December has a special significance which was powerfully felt by those present that evening. The Swedish celebration of Santa Lucia on the 13th December is in itself a dense collage of religious rituals and cultural traditions. This female bearer of light traditionally wears a crown of lit candles, and carries pagan and Christian beliefs, black magic, childhood chants and adolescent rites of passage in the folds of her long, white cloak. Hearing *Santa Lucia*, I cannot help but recall those dark early mornings of childhood, when the faint, distant sound of the song slowly filled the room with the light and smell of burning paraffin candles. I also remember the vital rite of passage for Swedish adolescents of drinking and partying all through the previous night. In Sweden the ritual of Lucia is an emblem of innocence, as well as of entry into adult experience.

The Catholic Christian setting of the Lucia tradition is a remodeling of an originally pagan celebration. In Sweden's ancient calendar, the 13th December was the carnival of the winter solstice, the longest night of the year. This night was associated with witchcraft and evil powers, and according to tradition one had to wait and watch through the night. This connection with dark deeds continued into Christian times; 'Lusse', the popular name for the night is linked both to Lucifer and to Santa Lucia. Light and darkness walk together through the winter night. It was in the late 19th Century that the Neapolitan song was given Swedish lyrics celebrating the Nordic winter night and Lucia as the bearer of light, instead of the glittering, sunny seas off the coast of Naples.

In this interplay between light and darkness, love and loss, Philipsz introduces a third actor, Lucia Joyce, the daughter of James Joyce and, for a time, the lover of Samuel Beckett. She was a talented child, so much loved by her father that his love and his life as a celebrated writer slowly suffocated her. Her affair with Beckett ended sadly; he admitted that he was more interested in her father than in her. She disappeared into mental illness and out of the official history of the Joyce family. She spent most of her life in mental hospitals, where she died in 1982. In Philipsz's installation she is commemorated as a young girl in Ravel's *Pavane for a Dead Princess*, a slow musical miniature that Lucia Joyce danced to as a promising young student of Isadora Duncan in Paris.

'Oh no, I see a darkness', sings Will Oldham. So, as the patron saint of the blind, did Santa Lucia. Often represented holding out her eyes on a tray in front of her, she offers her blindness to the beholder. Her name means light and her hagiology tells several horrifying stories of how she lost her eyes during her martyrdom. James Joyce's daughter, who bore her name, also had a cast in her eyes, which shows clearly in the photographs of this beautiful young woman who was to die alone in an asylum. Experienced in this darkened room, Philipsz's *I See a Darkness* is replete with references to blindness and to the loss of sight.

The history of western art is also a history of the eye. Sight has been the privileged sense, with painting and now film and photography as its most favoured and most highly valued modes of representation. The prerequisite for these art forms is, of course, light—both in the production of the work, and in its perception. When Philipsz chooses sound, voice and music as her materials, she turns away from the master narrative of the visual, away from the main roads of art history and takes us on a journey which leads us beyond what is visible. She emphasizes the perception of sound and of the body in space. Her way of using music and voices to create architectures of sound in space is maximized in *I See a Darkness* by the dimming of the light in the rooms. The difficulty of fully perceiving the room with your eyes sharpens your hearing and weighs on your movement through the room. Her voice becomes even more present in the space and your awareness of your own body is similarly heightened.

I See a Darkness draws attention to the ways in which the significance and the experience of music are transformed over time and place, and become part of a larger cultural heritage by being shared and reinterpreted. The conversion of the Neapolitan gondoliers' song into a Swedish celebration of winter is, of course, one telling example of this. In a similar way Ravel's *Pavane*, inspired by the slow processional dance that was very popular at the Spanish court in the 17th Century, has also diffused into a wider popular sphere. It can, for example, be heard in its orchestrated version in the film *The Dark Knight Rises* (2012). In Philipsz's art, cultural history and personal memories overlay and influence one another. She uses our associations and memories of certain sounds and songs to construct new narratives and images that transcend their original meanings. Will Oldham's sombre song, with its whiff of late-night drinking and the sharing of sorrows between male friends, becomes something very different when sung *a capella* by a woman's voice in a darkened museum space. The effect of these transpositions in Philipsz's installations is to make us acutely aware of the complexity of every experience of music, of how our understanding of music is never direct and unfiltered, but always built up out of layers of collective and individual, official and intimate histories, traditions and deeply personal memories.

You Are Not Alone

Oxford, 2009

Radcliffe Observatory,
Oxford, 2009.
Four-channel radio
transmission.
31 minutes.
Commissioned by
Modern Art Oxford.

Guglielmo Marconi suggested that sounds once generated never die, they fade but they continue to reverberate as sound waves across the universe. I thought this was a very evocative idea and I began to think about radio as a medium to tune into the immense range of sounds echoing across the universe. *You Are Not Alone* is an instrumental sound installation that is broadcast on HF radio frequencies.

The work was initially installed as a four-channel broadcast at the Radcliffe Observatory in Oxford in 2009 and later as a stereo broadcast at the Haus des Rundfunks in Berlin in 2011. For this work I recorded a number of radio interval signals on a vibraphone. These brief instrumental sequences were transmitted from Modern Art Oxford to a receiver installed at the Radcliffe Observatory.

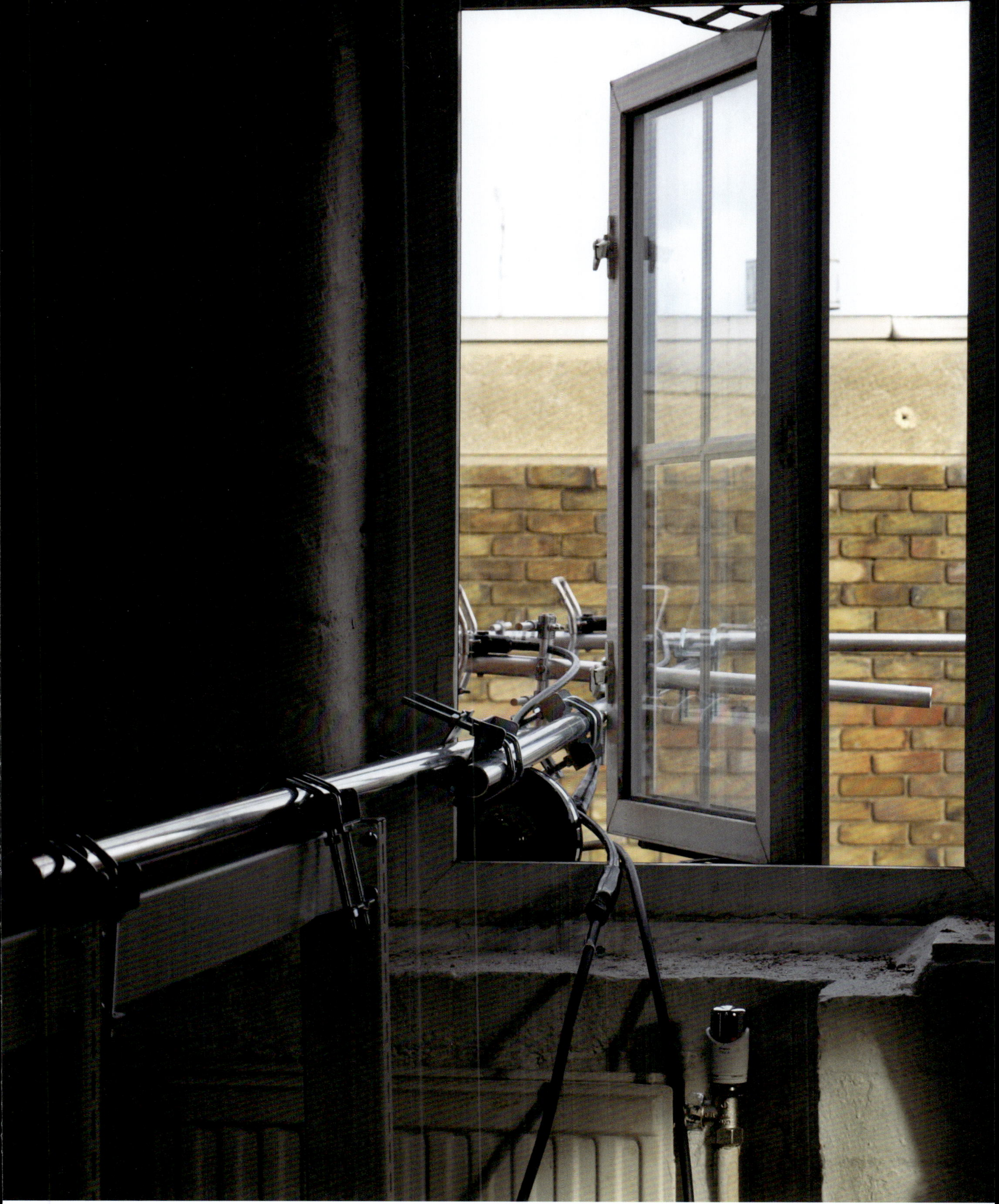

01 —— *Serb Republic Radio, External Service* —— Serbia —— 1993
02 —— *GTRK Chuvashia, Cheboksary* —— Russia —— ongoing
03 —— *Radio South Africa* —— South Africa —— 1965
04 —— *Radio Peking* —— China —— 1980

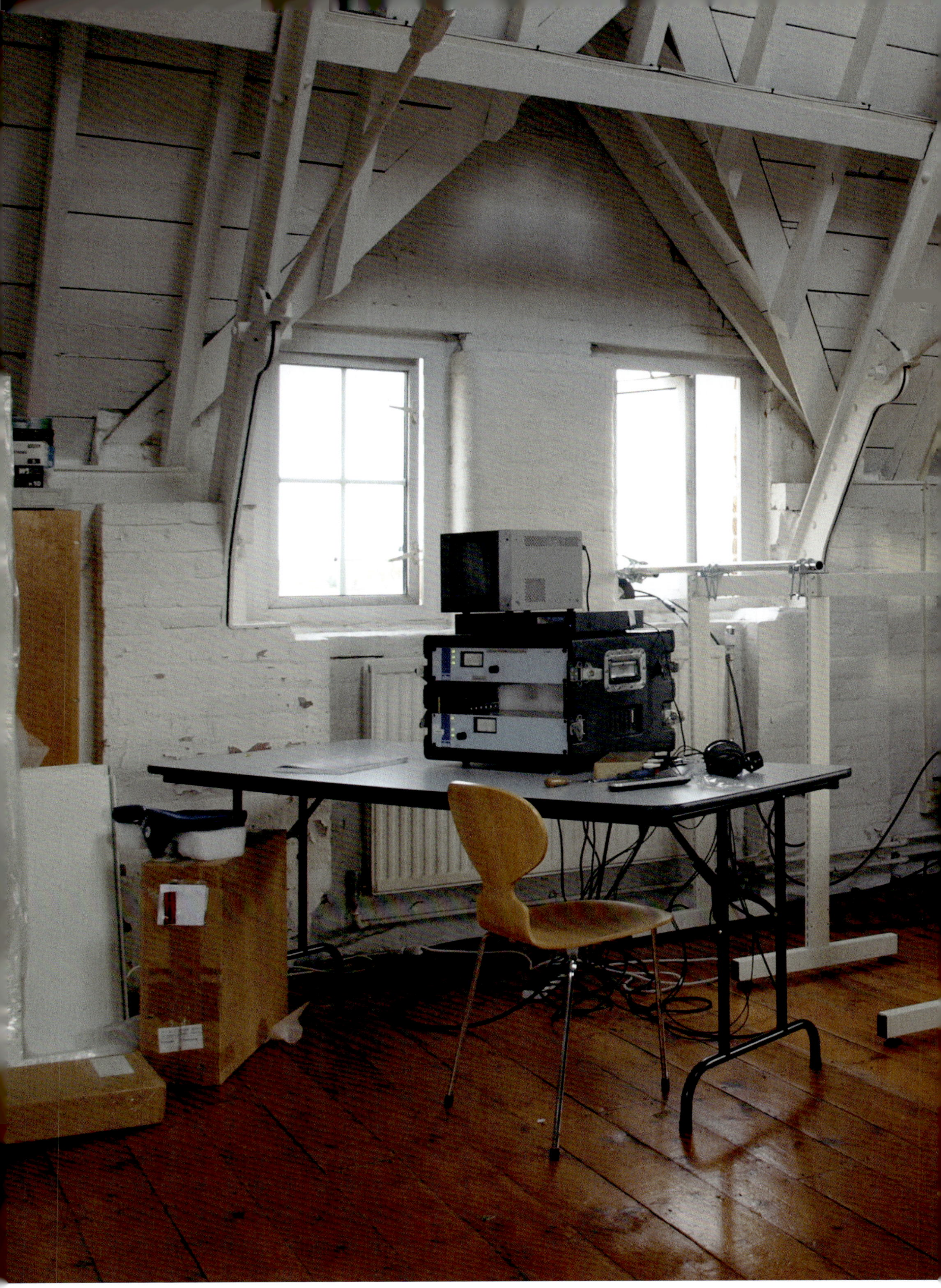

05 ——— *GTRK Saratov* ——— Russia ——— ongoing
06 ——— *Radio Argentina al Exterior* ——— Argentina ——— 1995
07 ——— *Radio Mayak* ——— Russia ——— 1972
08 ——— *Swedish Radio P1* ——— Sweden ——— 1975

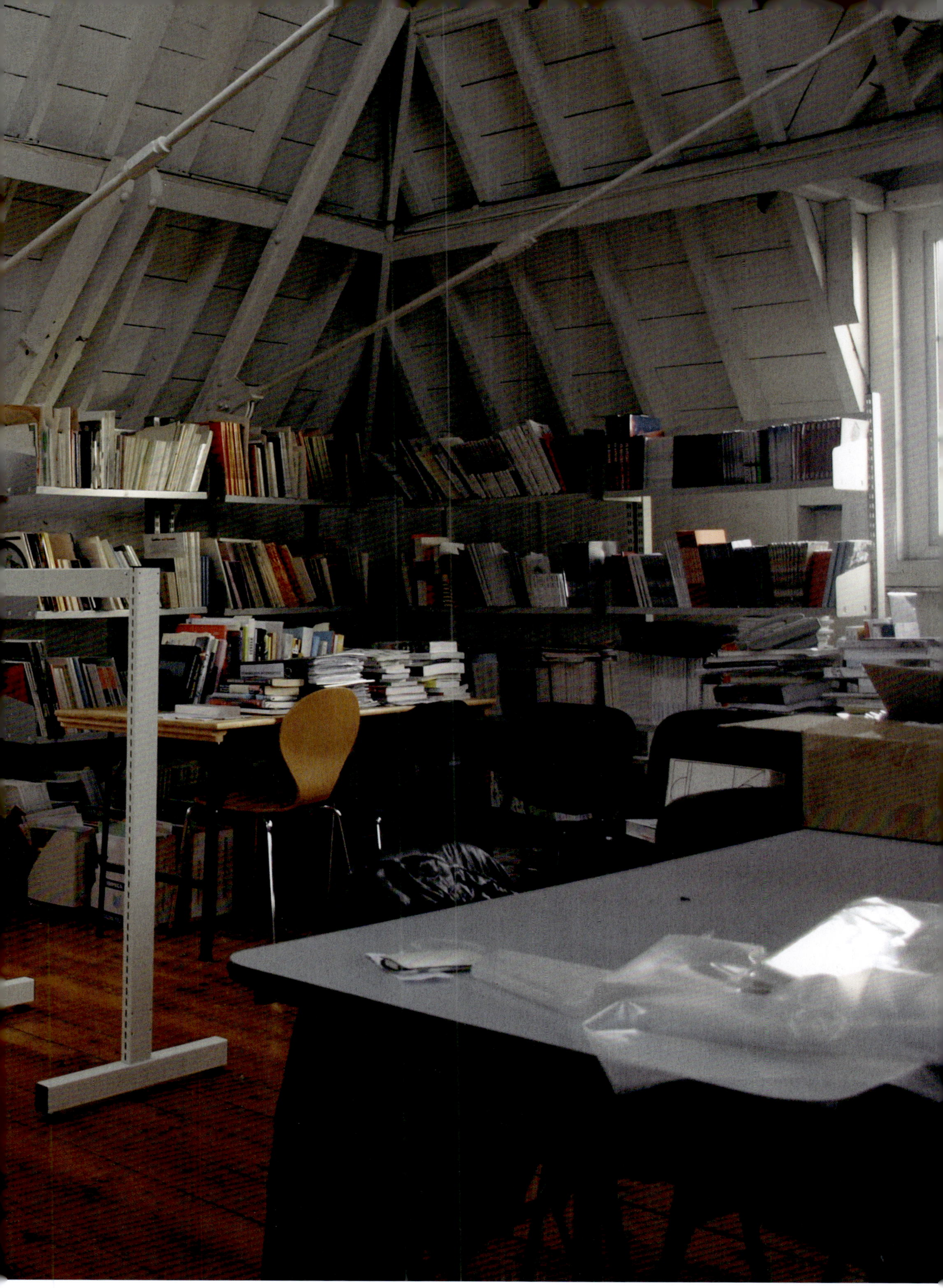

09 — *ELWA* — Liberia — 1975
10 — *Radio Habana* — Cuba — 1982
11 — *Radio Ullan Bator* — Mongolia — 1979
12 — *FEBC, Overseas Service* — Philippines — 1964

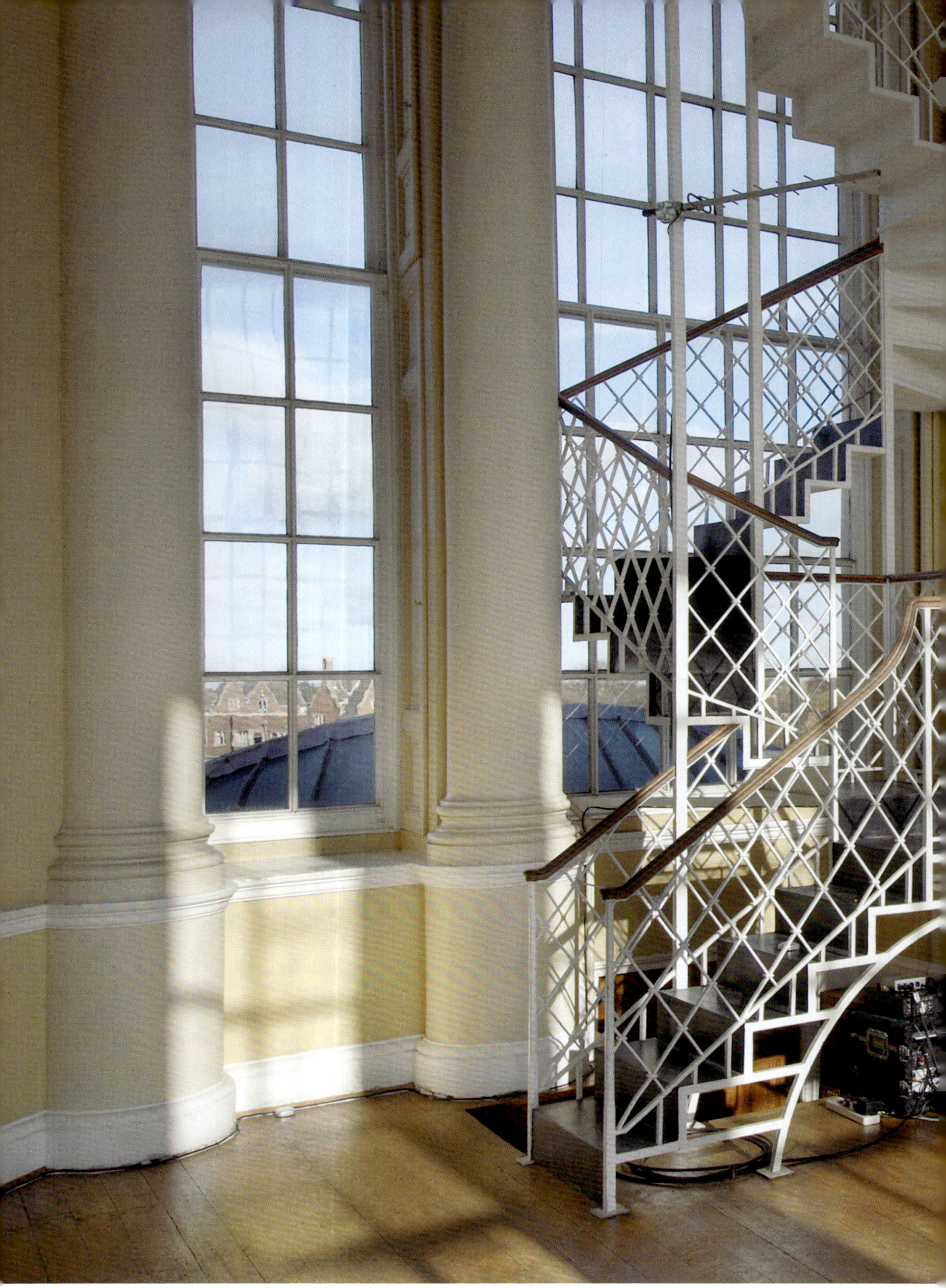

13 — *Azerbaijan Radio* — Azerbaijan — 1983
14 — *Voice of the People of Ho Chi Minh City* — Vietnam — ongoing
15 — *Deutschlandfunk* — Germany — 1974
16 — *Radio Normandie* — France — 1939

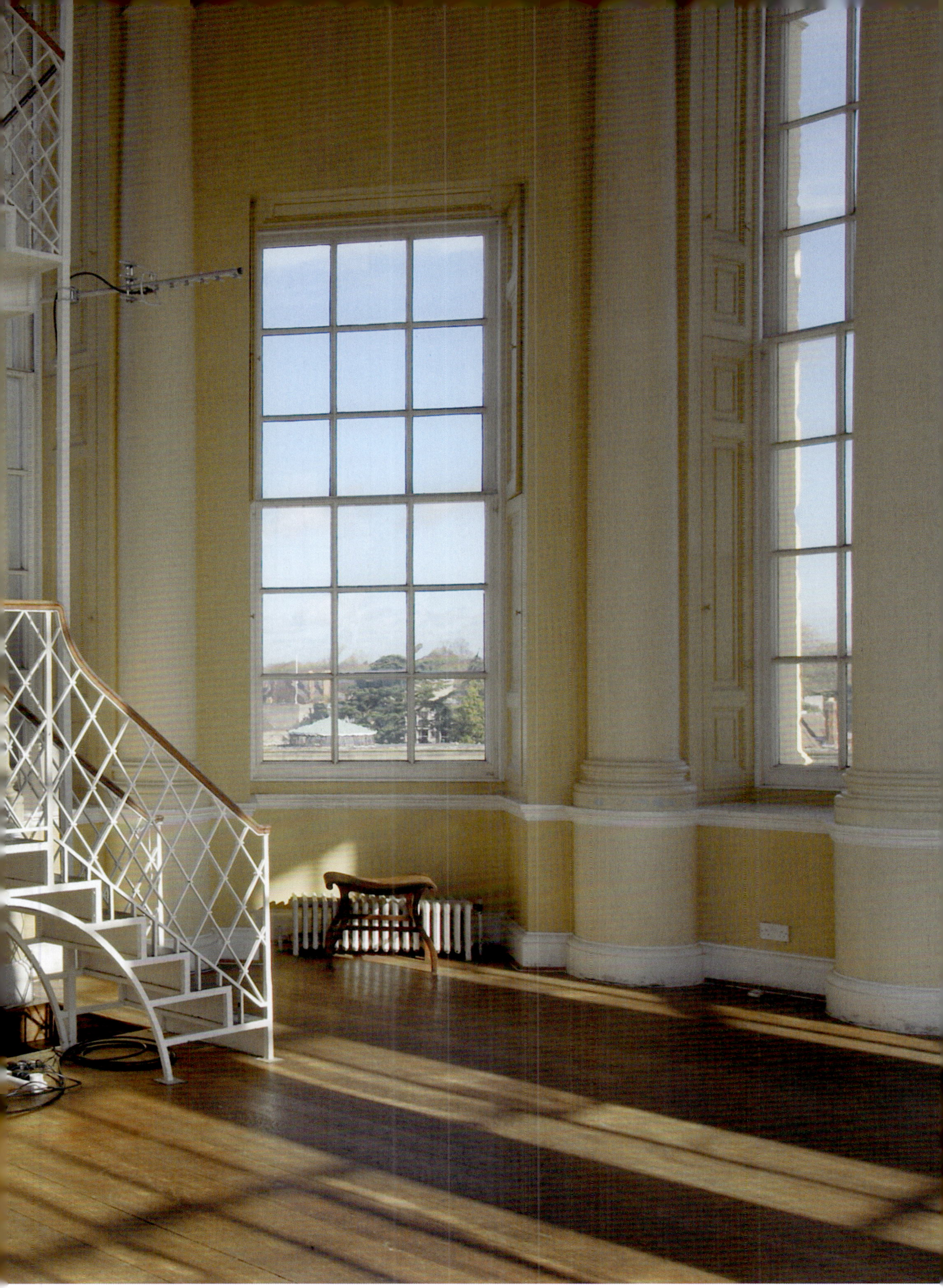

17 — *Utvarp Föroya* — Faroe Islands — 2000
18 — *Radio Pridnestrovye* — Moldova — ongoing
19 — *Rikisutvarpid* — Iceland — 1965
20 — *Radio Ceylon* — Sri Lanka — 1965

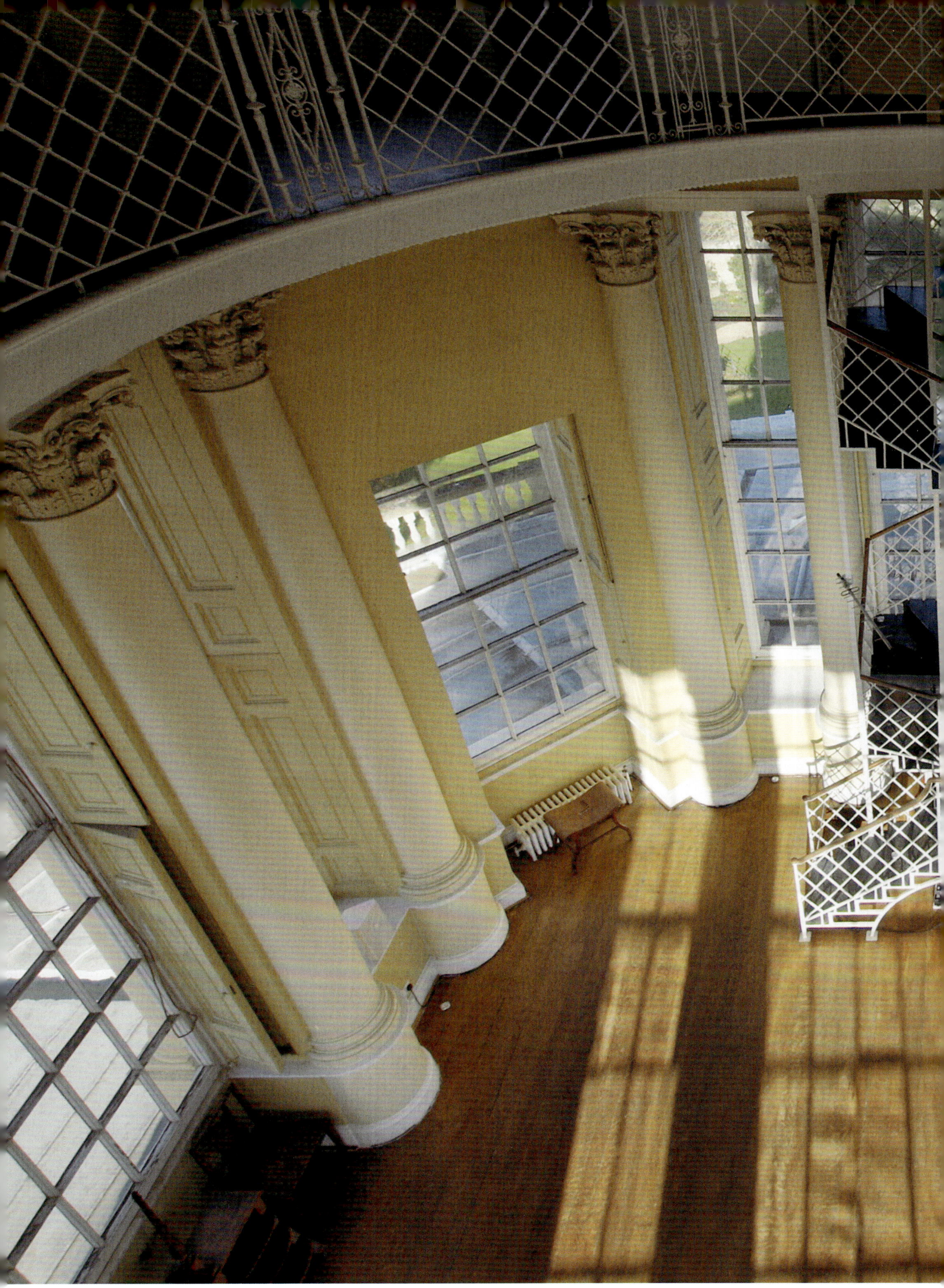

21 — *Murmansk Radio* — Russia — 1975
22 — *Korean Central Broadcasting Station* — North Korea — 1980
23 — *Mother Vietnam (clandestine)* — Vietnam — 1971
24 — *Hessischer Rundfunk* — Germany — 1975

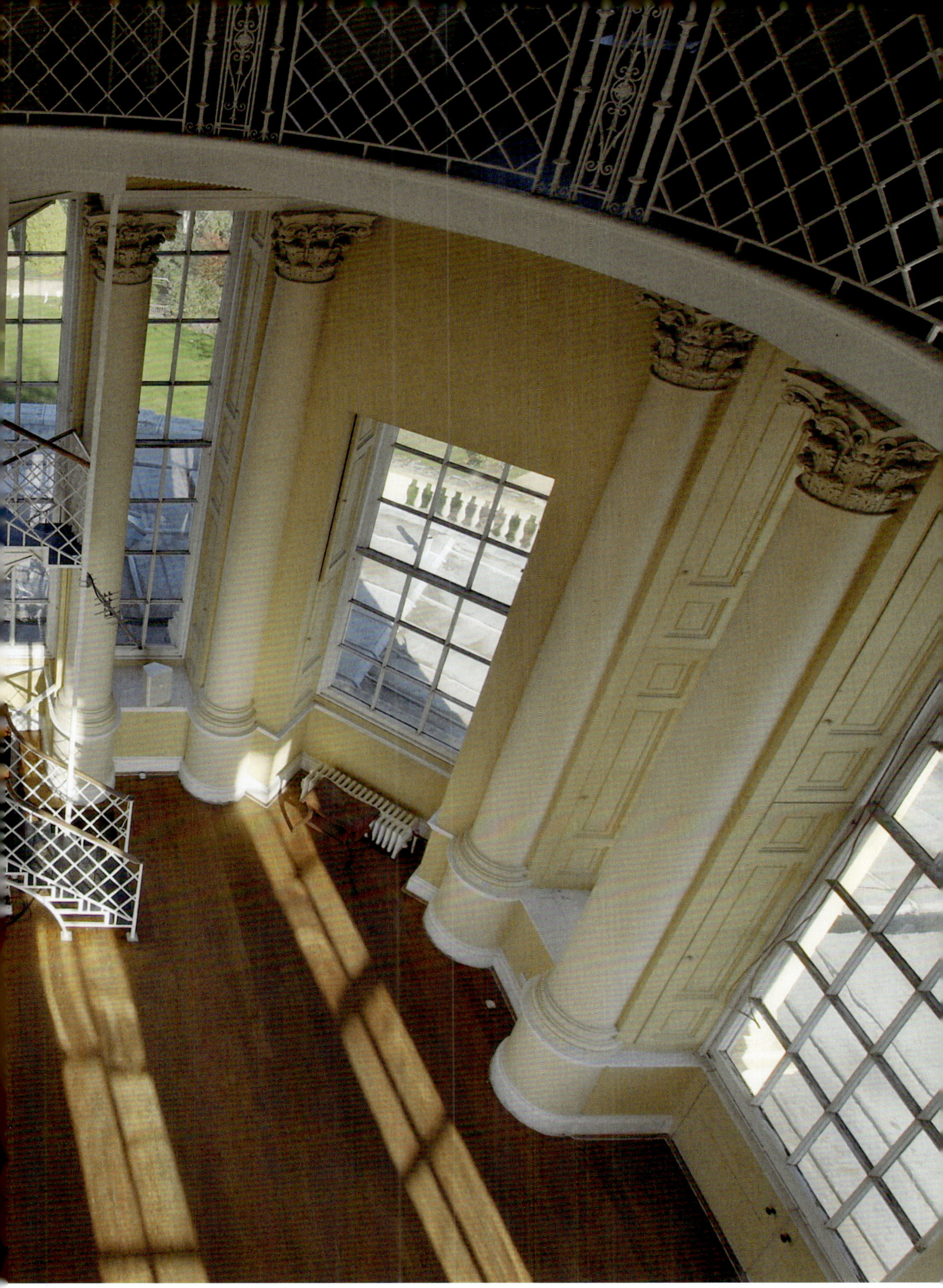

25 — *Radio Greenland* — Greenland — 1961
26 — *Bizim Radio (clandestine)* — Turkey — 1989
27 — *Kasakh Radio* — Kazakhstan — 1978
28 — *Radio Malaysia Sabah* — Malaysia — ongoing

Site of the former Radcliffe Infirmary, 2009. Photograph: Mick Scott.

Aerial View of Oxford indicating Modern Art Oxford and the Radcliffe Observatory. We set up the transmitters in the upper offices of Modern Art Oxford and broadcast to the receivers in the Radcliffe Observatory. Courtesy: Infoterra Ltd & Bluesky.

Elevation and details of the Tower of the Winds, Antiquities of Athens, James Stuart & Nicholas Revett, 1762. Courtesy: Princeton Architectural Press.

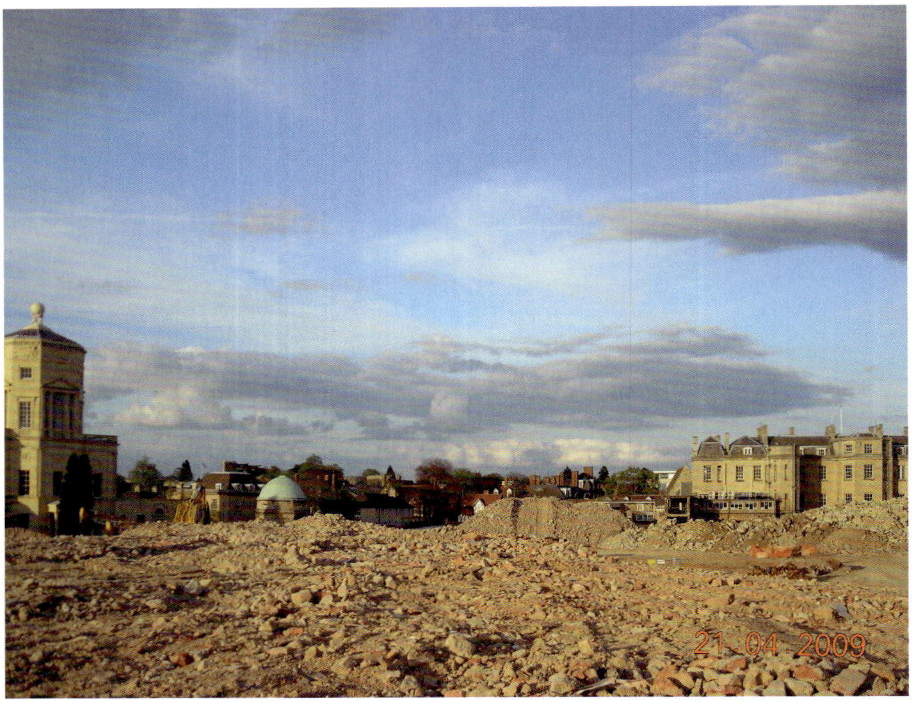

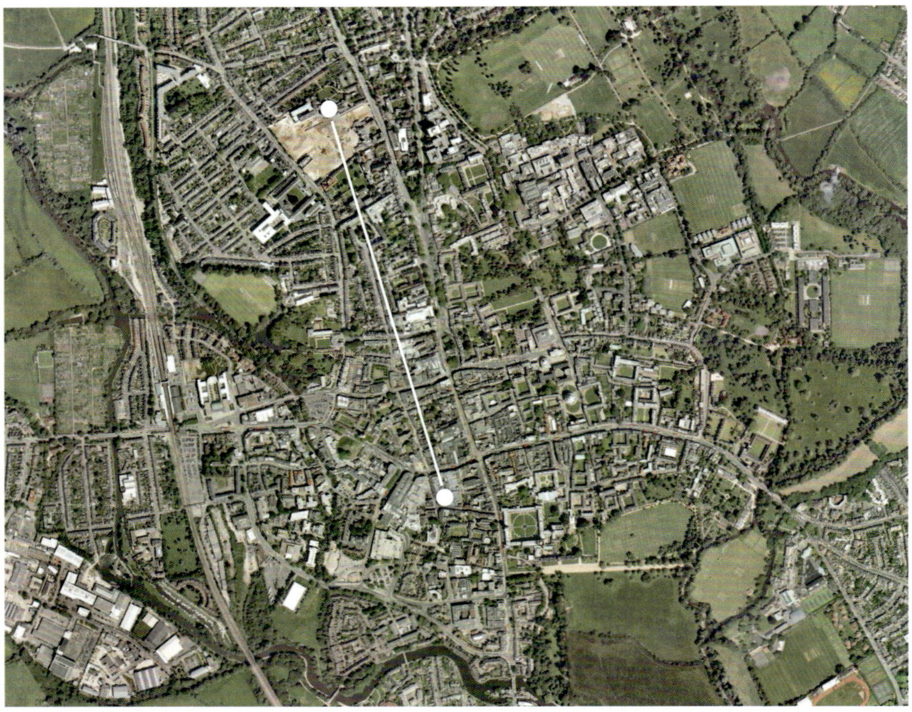

Radcliffe Observatory

Built in the late 18th Century, the Radcliffe Observatory was modelled on a small Tower of the Winds built in the 1st Century BC in Athens. However, due to poor visibility, the observatory was never used and they shipped all the equipment to another location in South Africa. It became a bit of a white elephant and it was only when the neighboring Radcliffe Infirmary was pulled down that the observatory was visible again from a distance. On visiting the building for the first time, I could imagine the ancient winds as they passed through the towers' portals, as well as the telescopes looking out on the night sky. Contemporary cosmologists say that telescopes are like time machines, the deeper they can see into the night sky the further back in time they allow us to travel.

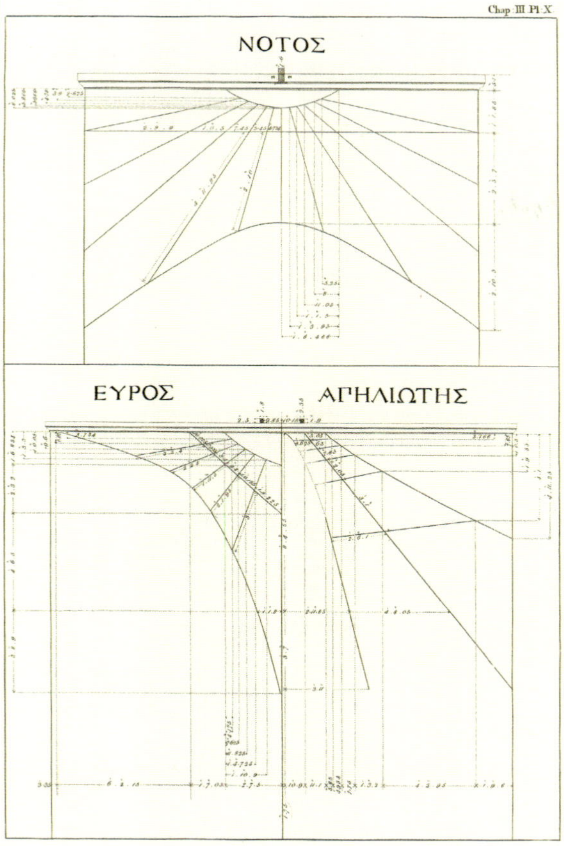

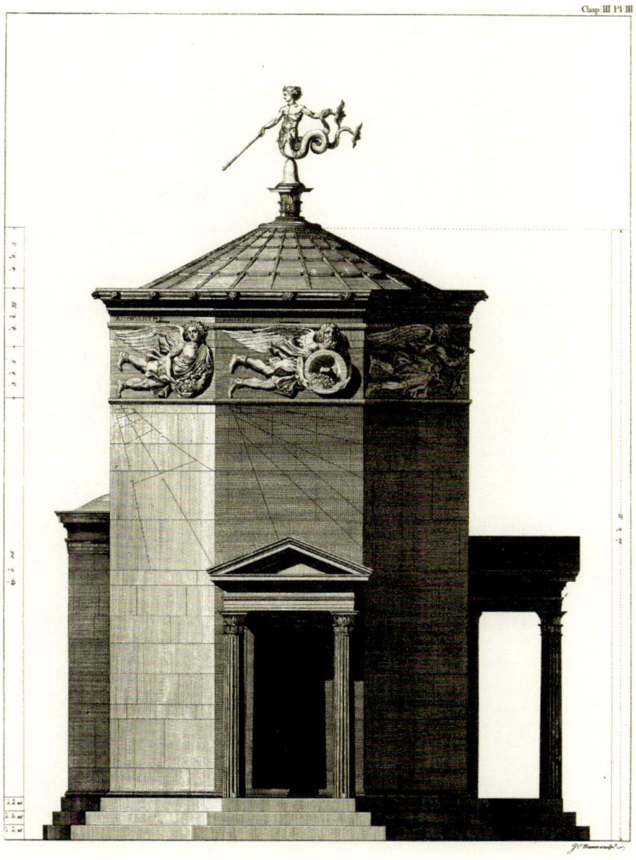

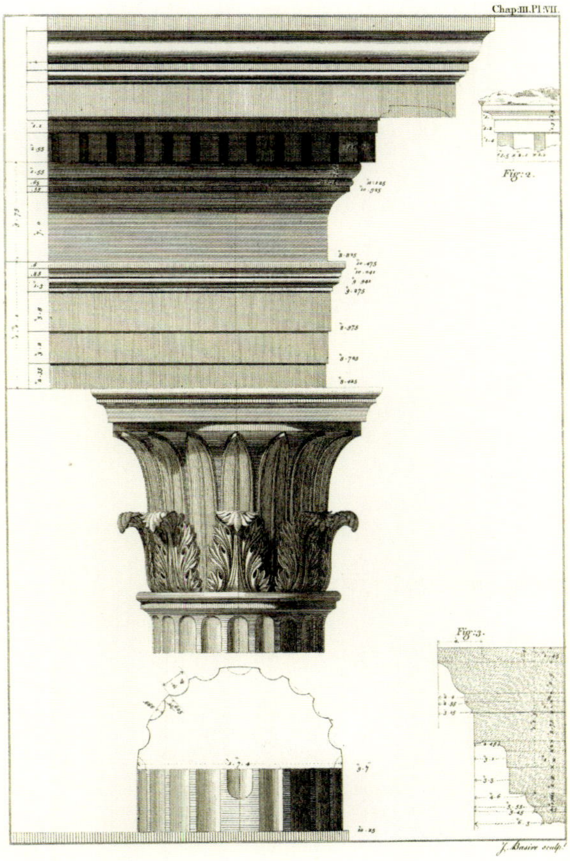

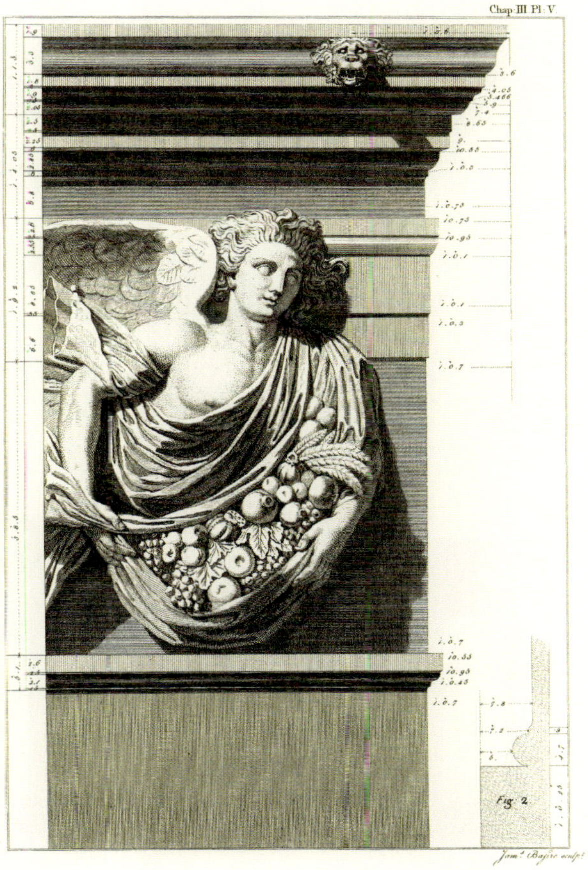

Tower of the Winds

Some have chosen to reckon only four Winds, the East blowing from the equinoctial Sun-rise, the South from the Noon-day Sun, the West from the equinoctial Sun-setting, and the North from the Polar Stars. But those who are more exact, have reckoned eight Winds, particularly Andronicus Cyrrhestes, who on this System erected an Octogon Marble Tower at Athens, and on every Side of the Octogon, he wrought a Figure in Relievo, representing the Wind which blows against that side; the Top of this Tower he finished with a conical Marble, on which he placed a brazen Triton, holding a Wand in his right Hand; this Triton is so contrived that he turns round with the Wind, and always stops when he directly faces it: Pointing with his Wand, over the Figure of the Wind at that Time blowing.

Berlin, 2011

Haus des Rundfunks,
Berlin, 2011.
Two-channel radio
transmission.
31 minutes.

The Haus des Rundfunks on Masurenallee in Berlin has an extraordinary atrium and the acoustics are very special. Although the building remains in use as a broadcasting house the atmosphere is still and calm. A version of *You Are Not Alone*, adapated for this specific location, was presented during the Berlin gallery weekend in 2011. Broadcast in stereo, across the atrium, the transmission began with a version of the final signal from Radio Berlin International, the radio station in former East Berlin, and ended with the signal from Sender Freies Berlin, the station that originally broadcast from the building in the 1950s and which had an important influence on the development of stereophonic broadcasting.

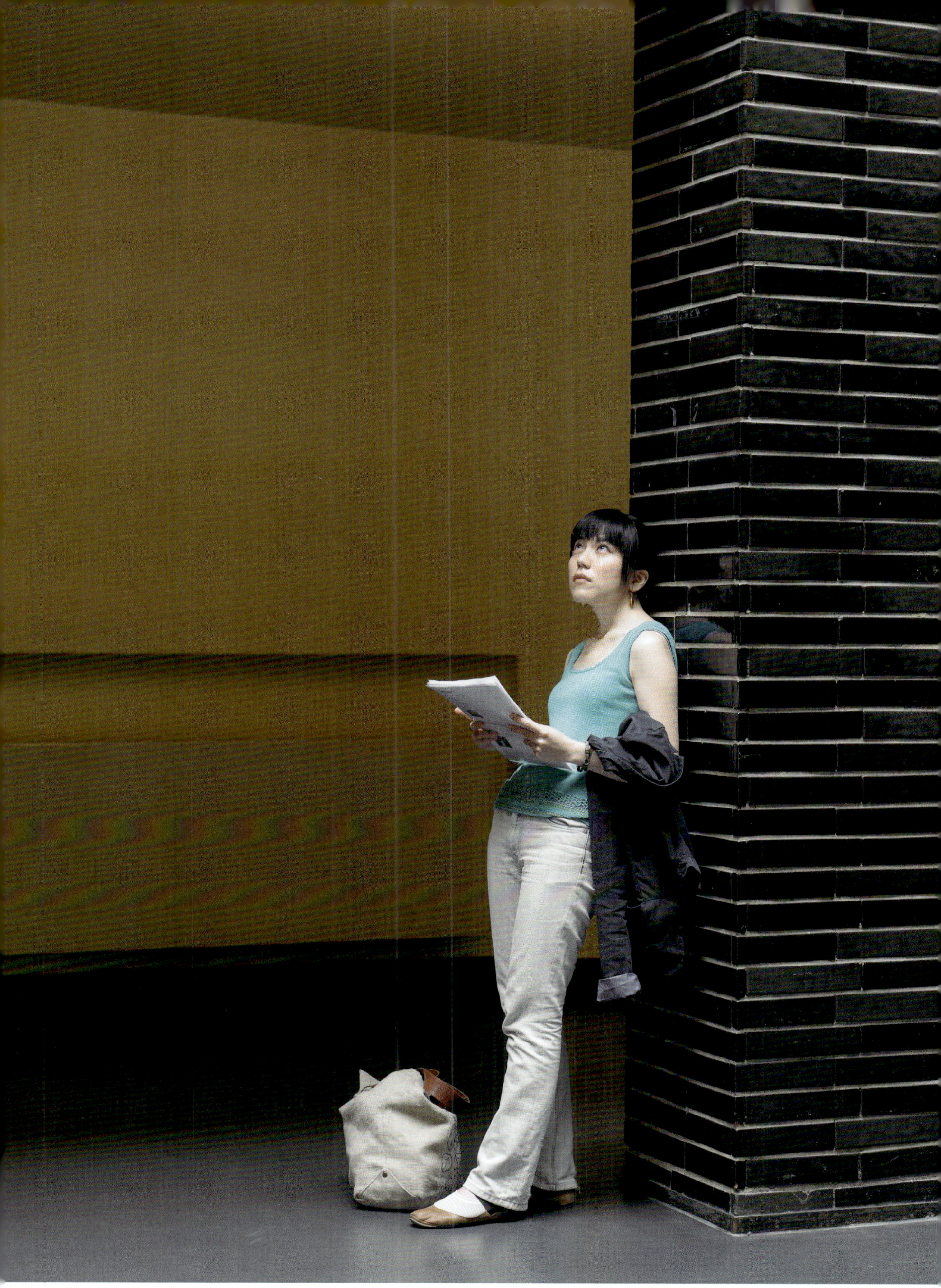

01 —— *Radio Berlin International* —— Germany —— 1990
02 —— *Utvarp Föroya* —— Faroe Is ands —— 2000

03 —— *Radio Pridnestrovye* —— Moldova —— ongoing
04 —— *Rikisutvarpid* —— Iceland —— 1965

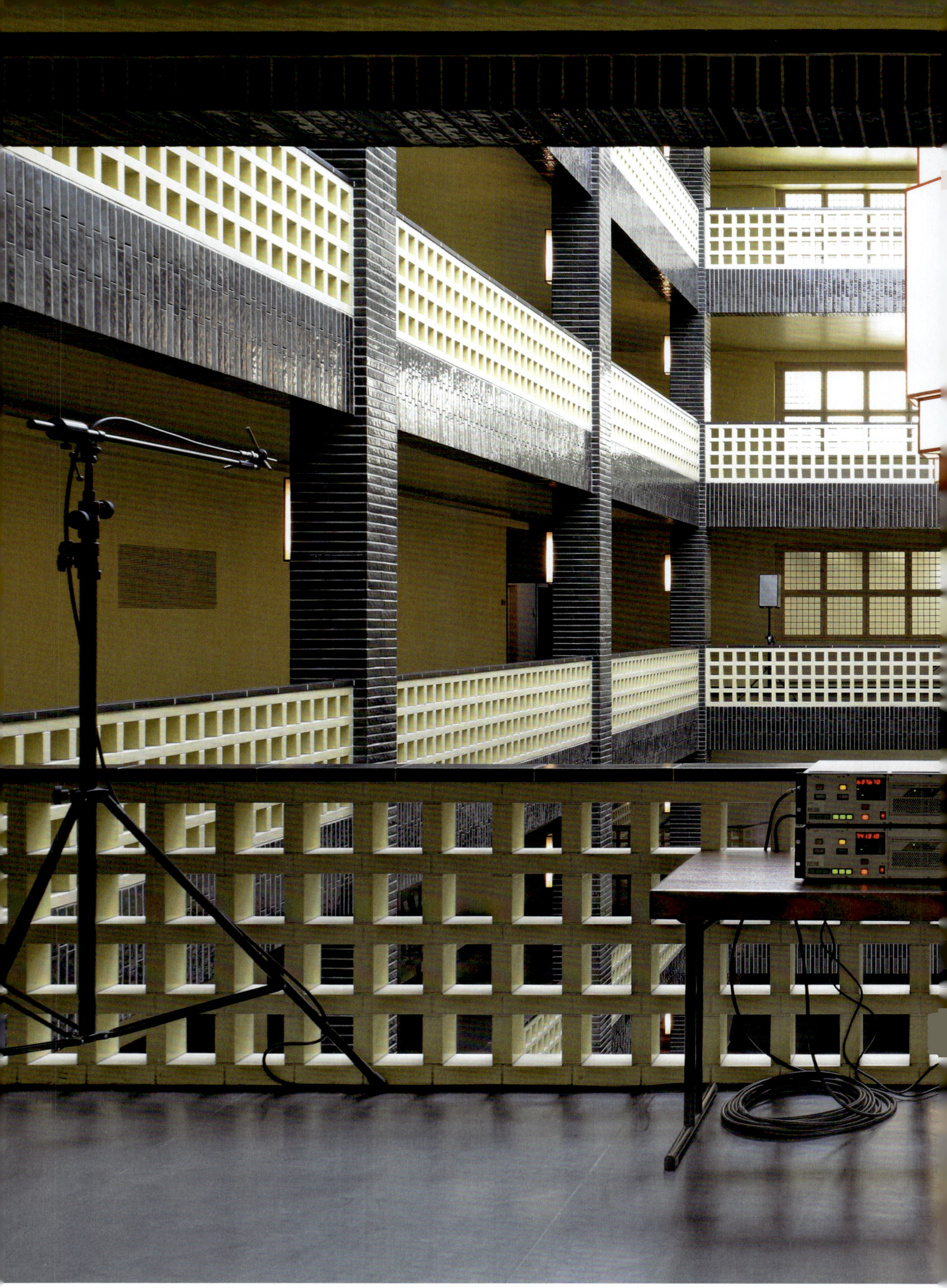

05 ——— *Radio Ceylon* ——— Sri Lanka ——— 1965
06 ——— *Murmansk Radio* ——— Russia ——— 1975

07 ——— *Korean Central Broadcasting Station* ——— North Korea ——— 1980
08 ——— *Mother Vietnam (clandestine)* ——— Vietnam ——— 1971

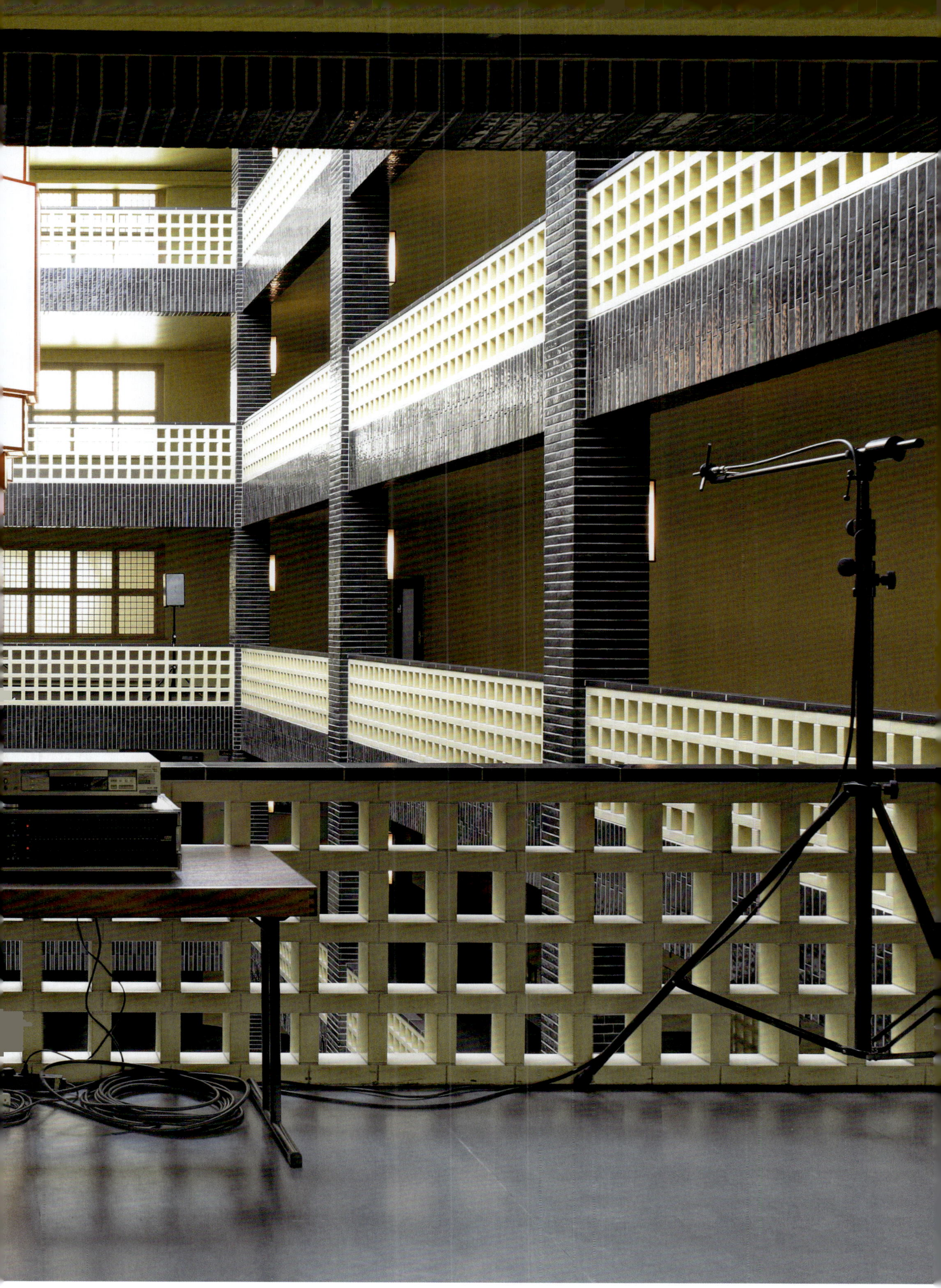

09 — *Hessischer Rundfunk* — Germany — 1975
10 — *Radio Greenland* — Greenland — 1961

11 — *Bizim Radio (clandestine)* — Turkey — 1989
12 — *Kasakh Radio* — Kazakhstan — 1978

Facade of the Haus des Rundfunks, 1931. Photograph: Max Krajewsky, Courtesy: rbb Radio Berlin Brandenburg.

Hans Poelzig, Drawing, Haus des Rundfunks, Signage, 1931. Courtesy: Institut für Architektur, TU Berlin.

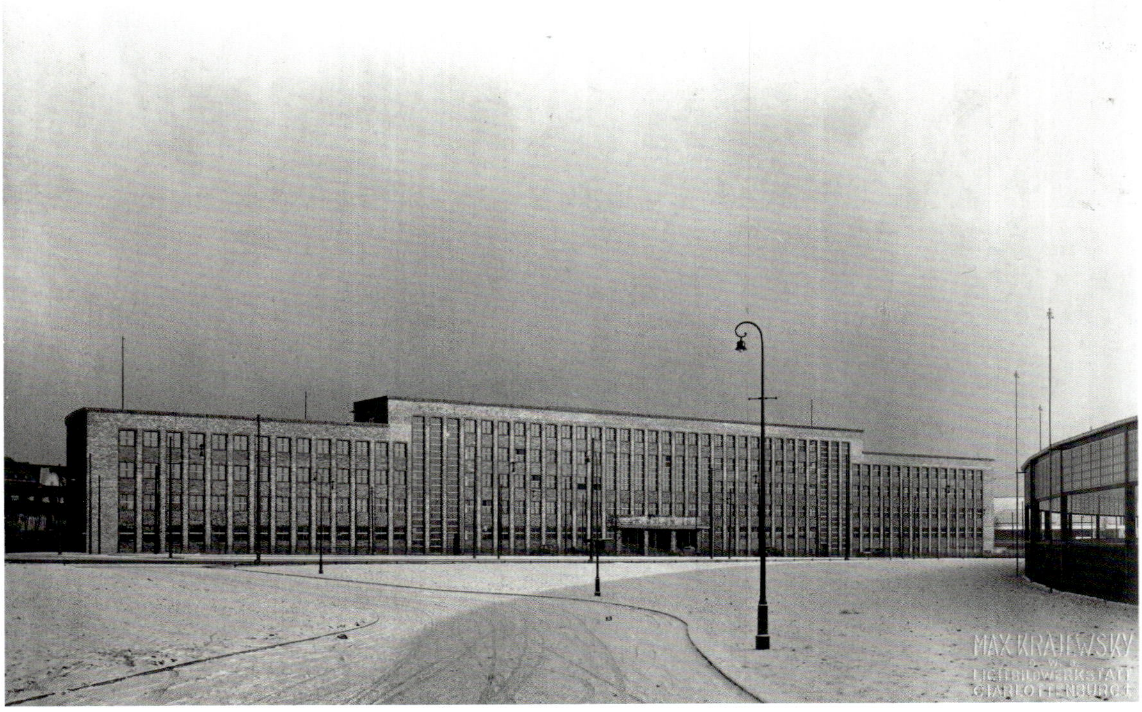

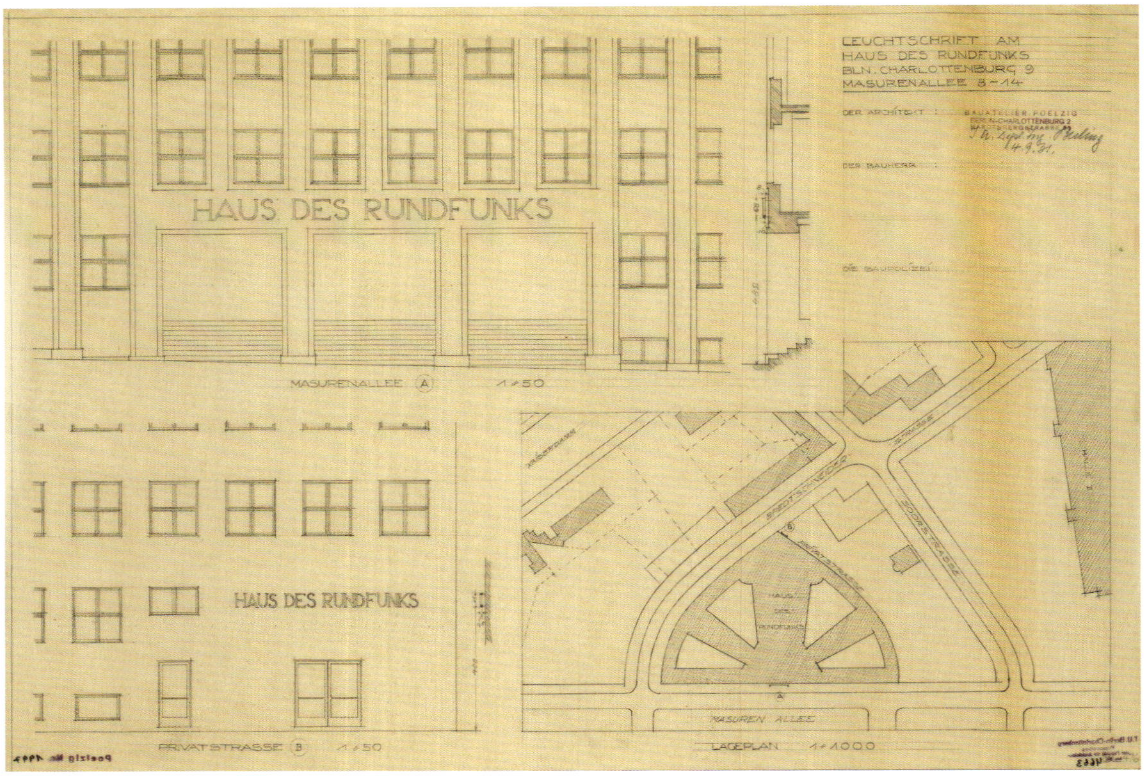

Funkstunde, Nr. 4, Berlin, 1931. Source: Funkstunde.

British officers patrolling the exterior of the Haus des Rundfunks, 1952. Courtesy: rbb Radio Berlin Brandenburg.

Hans Schellhorn sculpture in the atrium of the Haus des Rundfunks, 1936. Courtesy: rbb Radio Berlin Brandenburg.

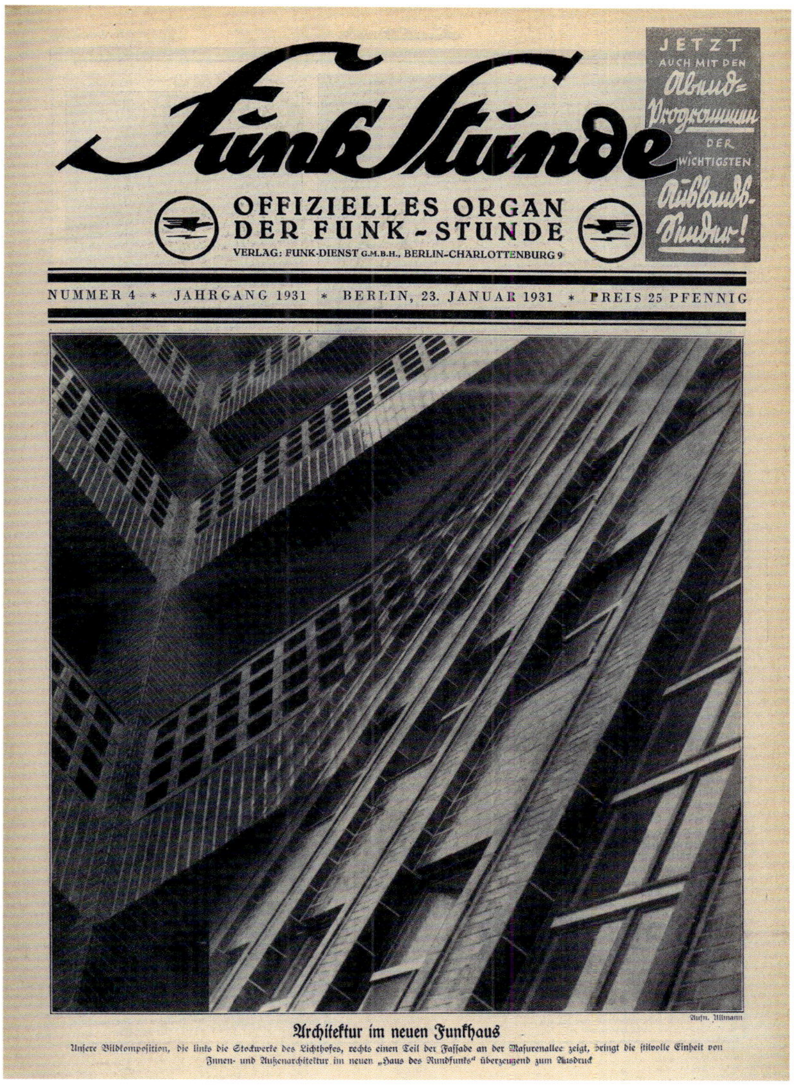

Funk Stunde

OFFIZIELLES ORGAN DER FUNK-STUNDE

VERLAG: FUNK-DIENST G.M.B.H., BERLIN-CHARLOTTENBURG 9

JETZT AUCH MIT DEN Abend-Programmen DER WICHTIGSTEN Auslands-Sender!

NUMMER 4 * JAHRGANG 1931 * BERLIN, 23. JANUAR 1931 * PREIS 25 PFENNIG

Aufn. Ullmann

Architektur im neuen Funkhaus

Unsere Bildkomposition, die links die Stockwerke des Lichthofes, rechts einen Teil der Fassade an der Masurenallee zeigt, bringt die stilvolle Einheit von Innen- und Außenarchitektur im neuen „Haus des Rundfunks" überzeugend zum Ausdruck

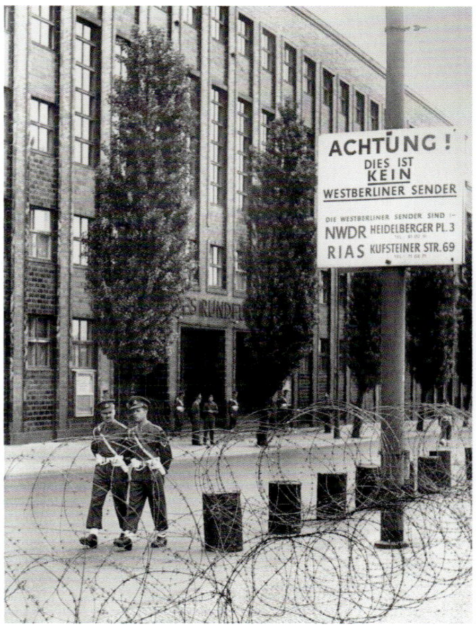

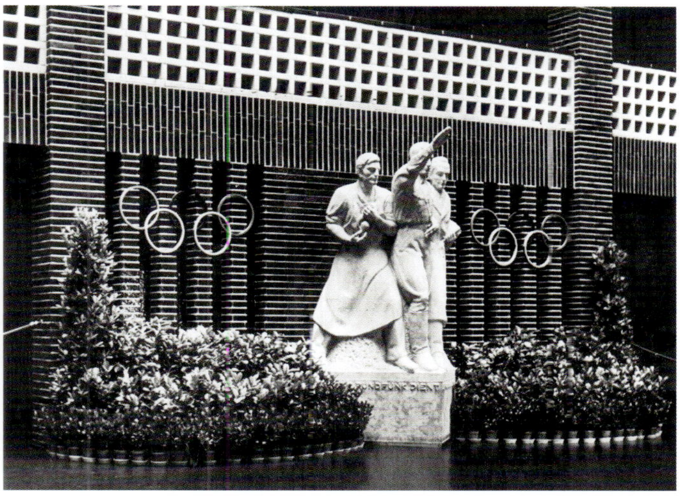

Haus des Rundfunks

When the Haus des Rundfunks, a leading example of Neue Sachlichkeit architecture, opened in 1931, it was one of the first self-contained broadcasting houses in the world. During the thirties the building came under the control of the NSDAP and it became known as the Broadcasting Headquarters of Greater Germany or Großdeutscher Rundfunk. After the war it was liberated by Russian troops and even though it was located in the British sector it was physically segregated from the rest of West Berlin and remained under Soviet control until it was handed over in 1956. From 1957 to 2003 it housed the broadcasting station Sender Freies Berlin, which had an important influence on the development of Stereophonic broadcasting.

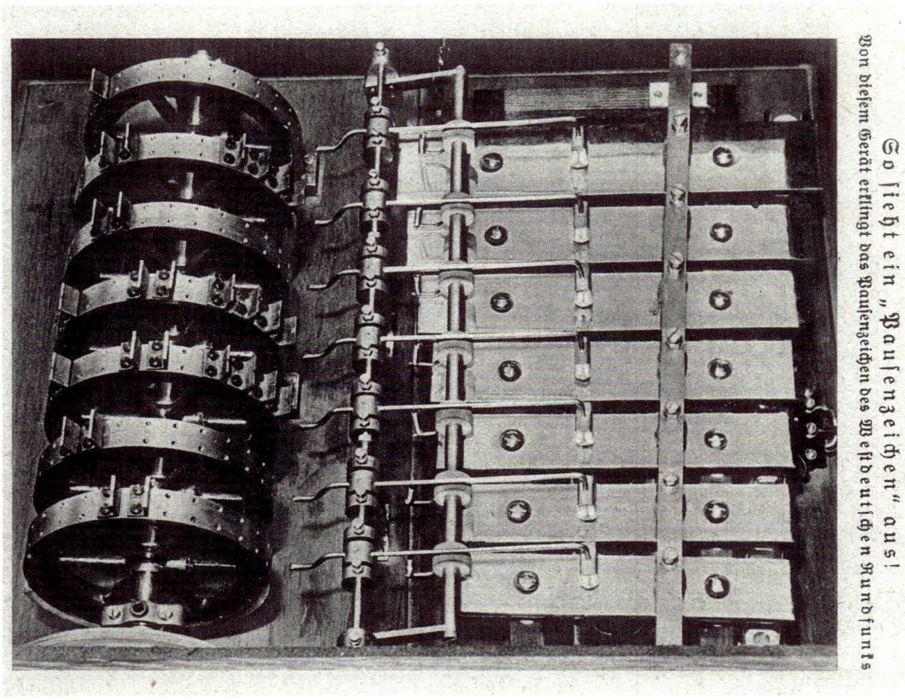

The interval signal generator for Westdeutscher Rundfunks. Source: Der Deutsche Rundfunk, Issue 26, 1933.

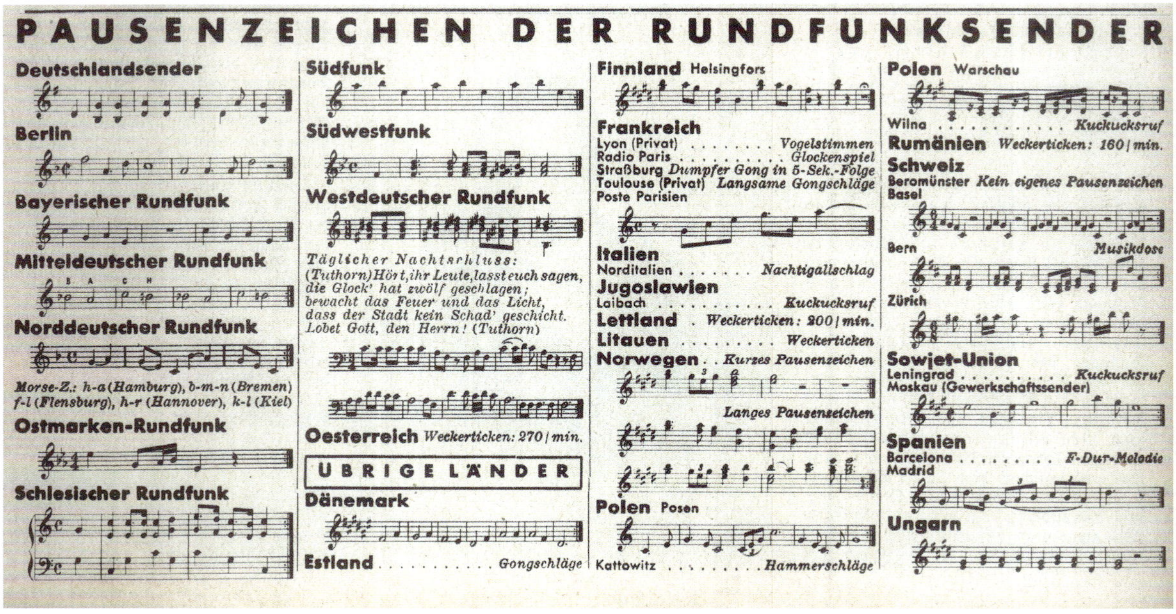

Interval signal notation Source: Der Deutsche Rundfunk, Issue 26, 1933.

Interval Signals

A radio interval signal is a brief musical notation played before commencement or during breaks in transmission that helps the viewer to identify the station being listened to. The most common form of signal is a brief musical sequence that is repeated three times. This is followed by an identification announcement, a voice announcing the name and the frequency of the station and then the interval signal is repeated again three times. While some interval signals have a special significance, being based on national anthems or traditional national tunes, most are based around a simple, abstract sequence of notes. www.intervalsignals.net

The interval signal generator for Reichssender München. Funkschau Nr. 17, Munich, 1933. Courtesy: Funkschau.

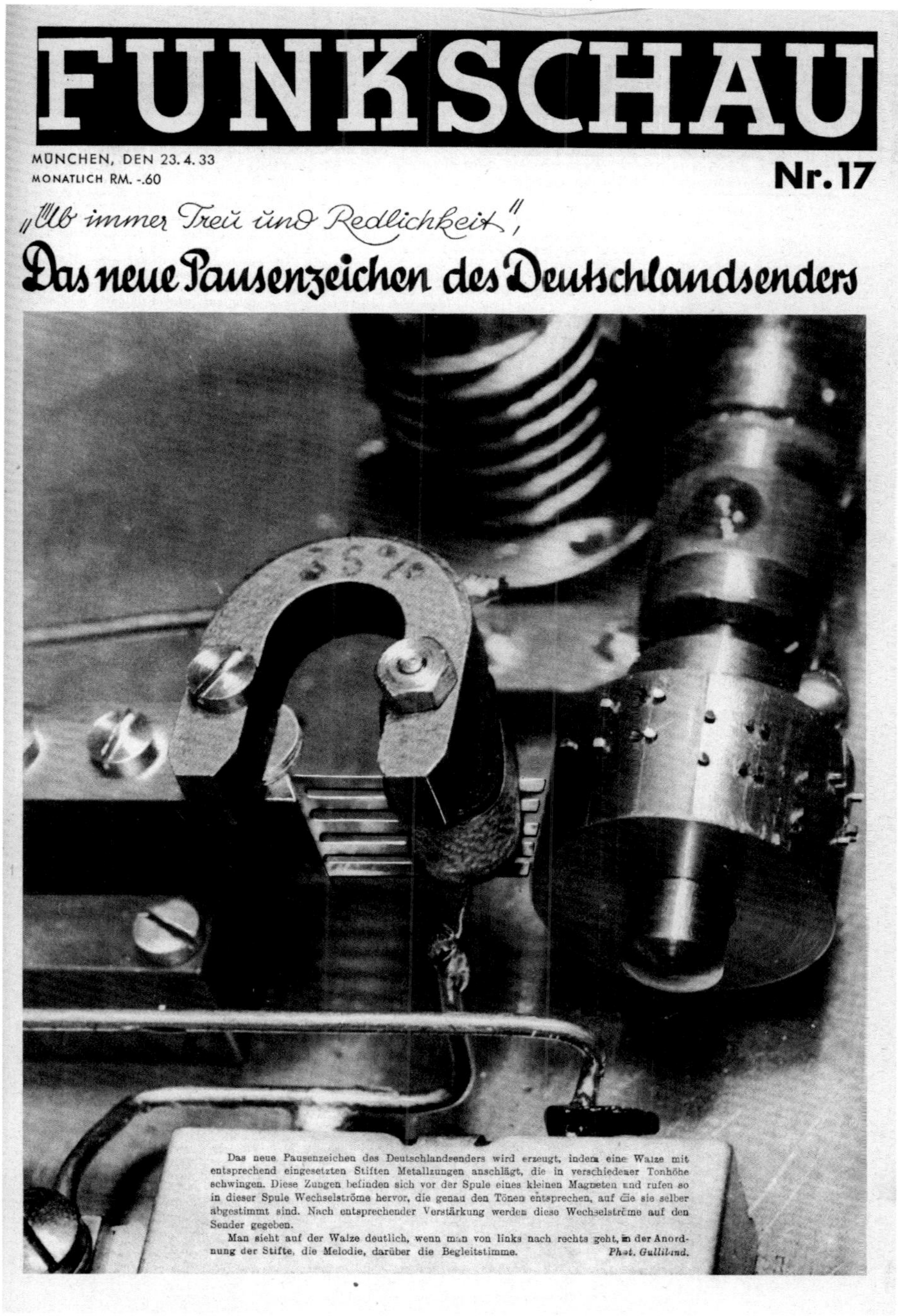

FUNKSCHAU

MÜNCHEN, DEN 23.4.33
MONATLICH RM. -.60

Nr. 17

„Üb immer Treu und Redlichkeit"

Das neue Pausenzeichen des Deutschlandsenders

Das neue Pausenzeichen des Deutschlandsenders wird erzeugt, indem eine Walze mit entsprechend eingesetzten Stiften Metallzungen anschlägt, die in verschiedener Tonhöhe schwingen. Diese Zungen befinden sich vor der Spule eines kleinen Magneten und rufen so in dieser Spule Wechselströme hervor, die genau den Tönen entsprechen, auf die sie selber abgestimmt sind. Nach entsprechender Verstärkung werden diese Wechselströme auf den Sender gegeben.

Man sieht auf der Walze deutlich, wenn man von links nach rechts geht, in der Anordnung der Stifte, die Melodie, darüber die Begleitstimme. *Phot. Gulliland.*

Interval Signal Generators

The new radio interval signal of the Deutschlandsender is generated when a cylinder, equipped with corresponding embedded pins, strikes narrow metal plates which vibrate on different pitch levels. Those metal plates are installed in front of the coil of a small magnet and thus create an alternating voltage in the coil that matches exactly the note which they themselves are set to.

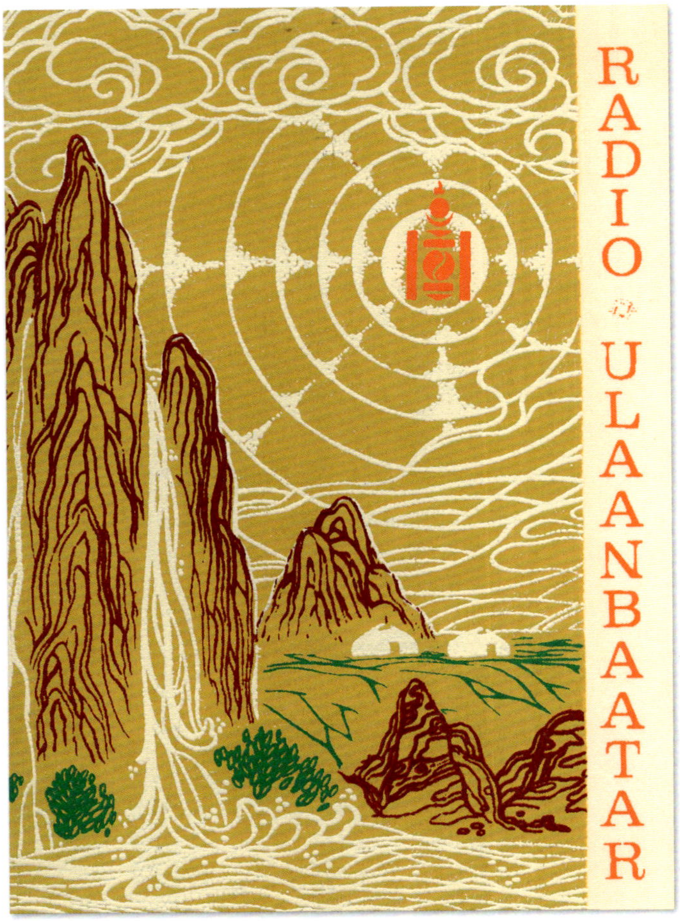

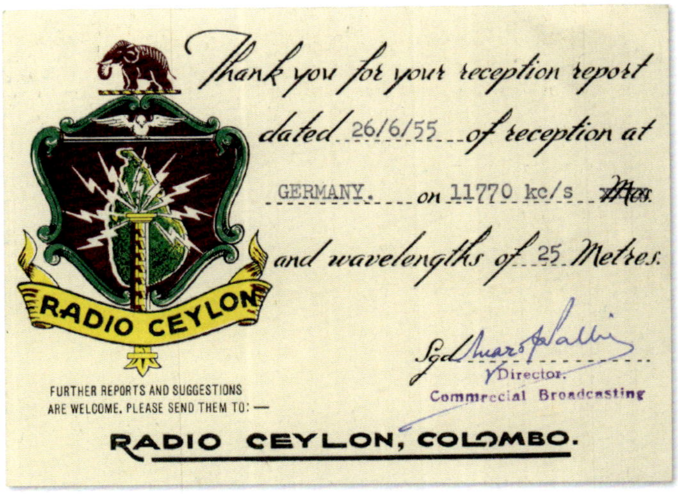

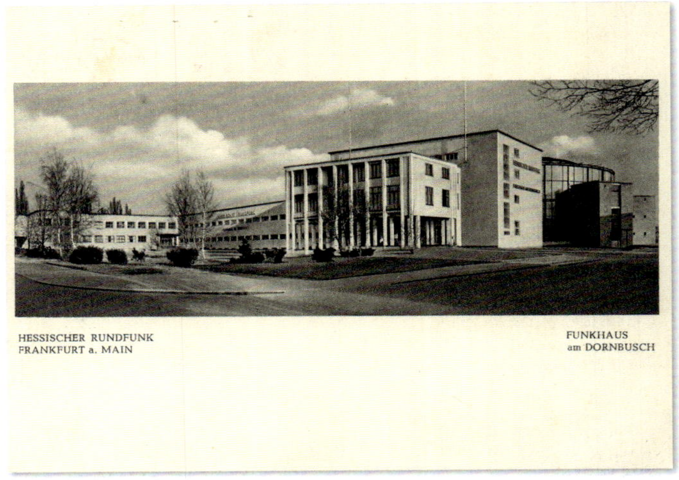

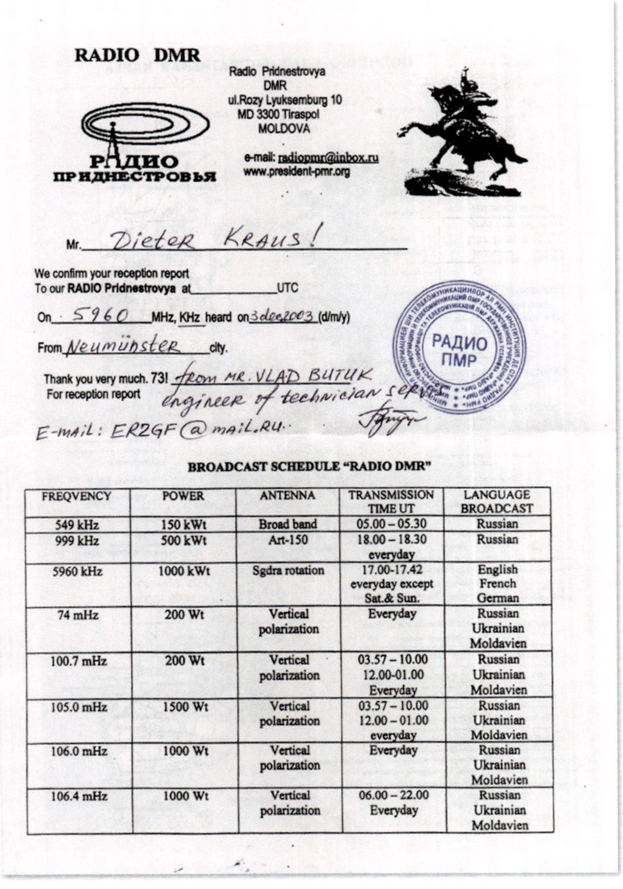

RADIO DMR

Radio Pridnestrovya
DMR
ul.Rozy Lyuksemburg 10
MD 3300 Tiraspol
MOLDOVA

РАДИО
ПРИДНЕСТРОВЬЯ

e-mail: radiopmr@inbox.ru
www.president-pmr.org

Mr. Dieter Kraus!

We confirm your reception report
To our **RADIO Pridnestrovya** at ______ UTC

On 5960 MHz, KHz heard on 3 dec 2003 (d/m/y)

From Neumünster city.

Thank you very much. 73! from Mr. Vlad Butuk
For reception report engineer of technician servis

E-mail: ER2GF@mail.ru

РАДИО
ПМР

BROADCAST SCHEDULE "RADIO DMR"

FREQVENCY	POWER	ANTENNA	TRANSMISSION TIME UT	LANGUAGE BROADCAST
549 kHz	150 kWt	Broad band	05.00 – 05.30	Russian
999 kHz	500 kWt	Art-150	18.00 – 18.30 everyday	Russian
5960 kHz	1000 kWt	Sgdra rotation	17.00-17.42 everyday except Sat.& Sun.	English French German
74 mHz	200 Wt	Vertical polarization	Everyday	Russian Ukrainian Moldavien
100.7 mHz	200 Wt	Vertical polarization	03.57 – 10.00 12.00-01.00 Everyday	Russian Ukrainian Moldavien
105.0 mHz	1500 Wt	Vertical polarization	03.57 – 10.00 12.00 – 01.00 everyday	Russian Ukrainian Moldavien
106.0 mHz	1000 Wt	Vertical polarization	Everyday	Russian Ukrainian Moldavien
106.4 mHz	1000 Wt	Vertical polarization	06.00 – 22.00 Everyday	Russian Ukrainian Moldavien

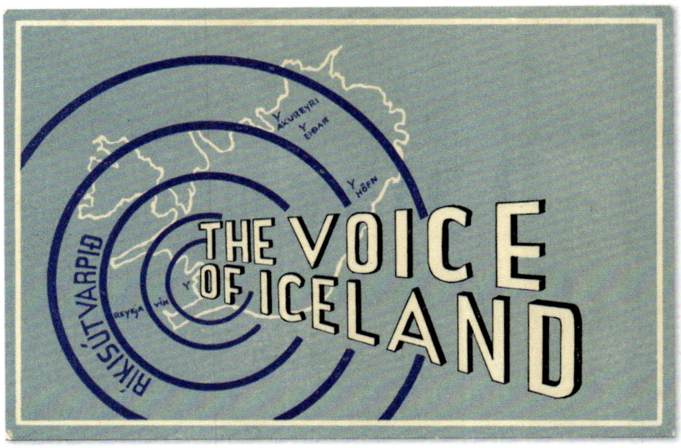

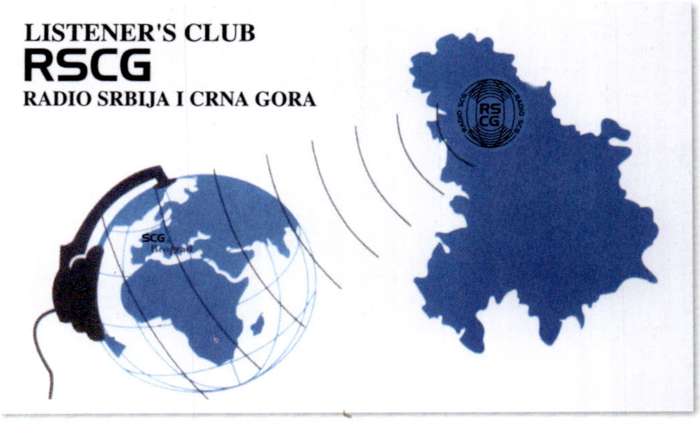

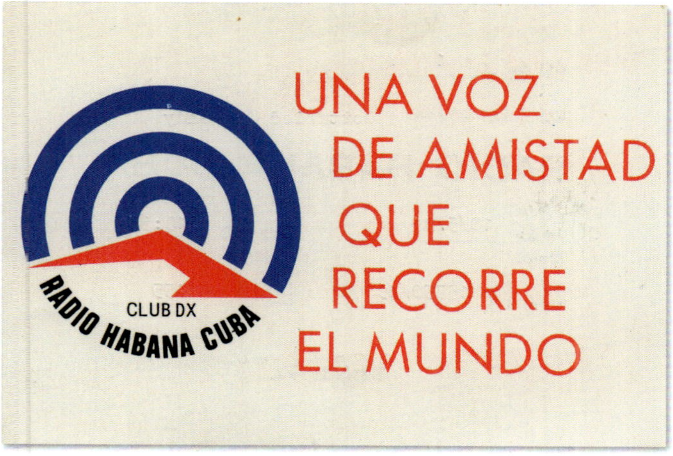

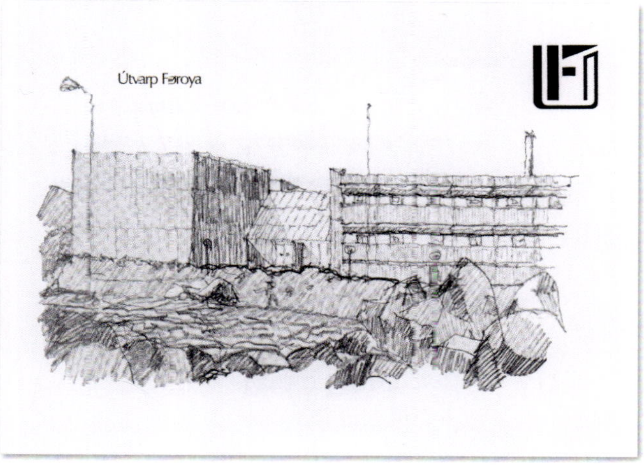

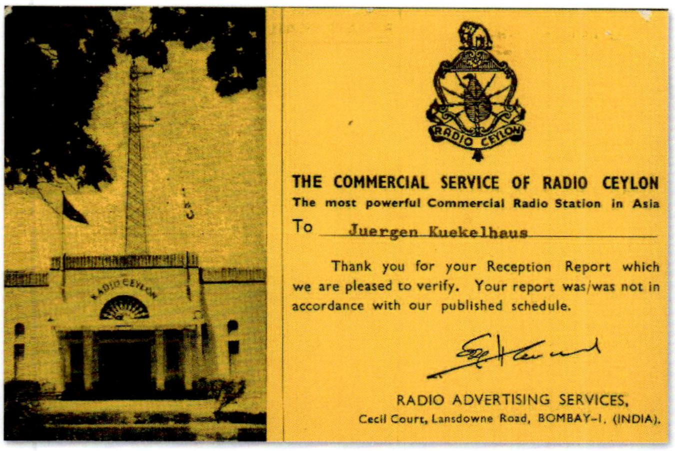

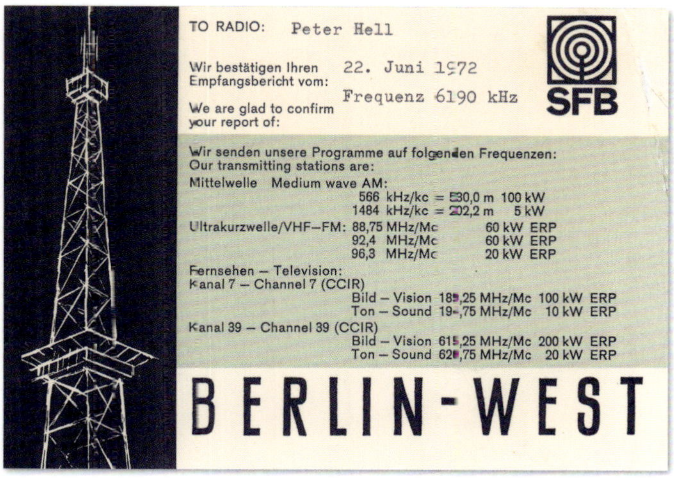

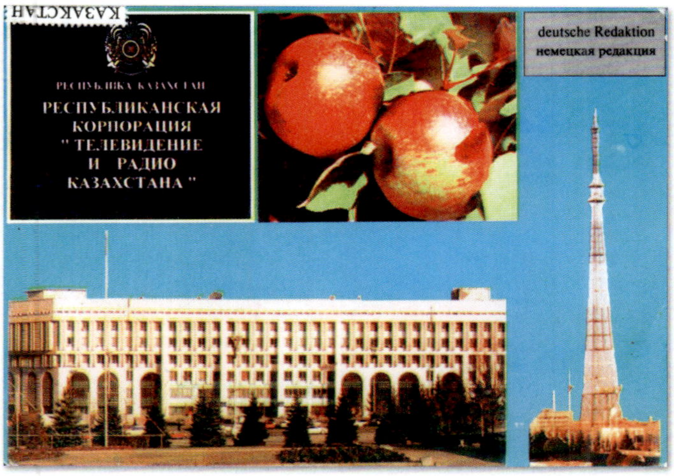

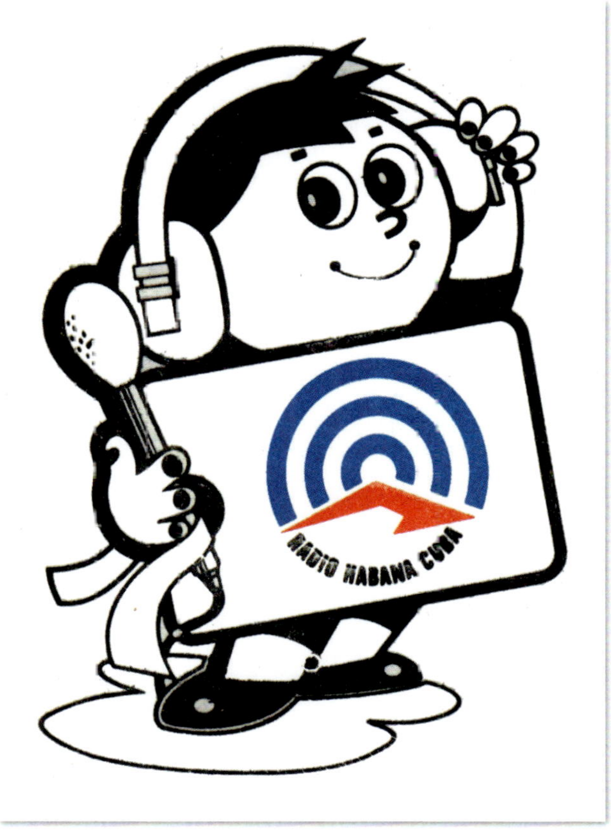

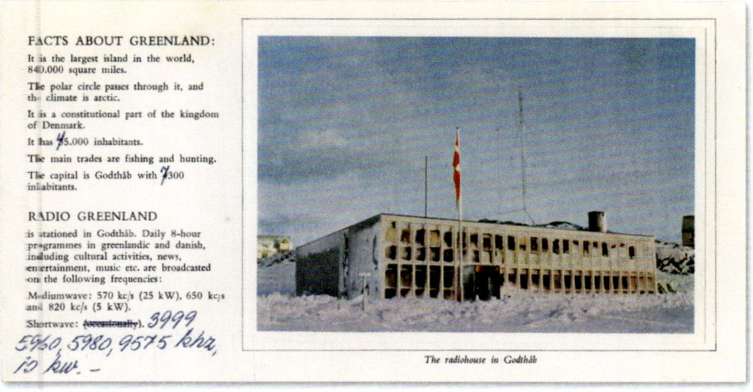

Reception Report Cards

I decided to name this project *You Are Not Alone* after learning about the existence of QSL or reception report cards. QSL cards are a broadcaster's written acknowledgement of a reception report confirmed by a listener. Like the interval signal generators, they are a reminder of the analogue nature of radio broadcasting. I imagined people sitting alone in their rooms, scanning the short wave frequency dial on their radio and picking up a signal that has travelled from afar and began to think of a community of listeners that were isolated and dispersed but at the same time connected. The reception report cards shown here illustrate the truly global nature of radio and the reach of some transmissions from remote places around the world. Reception report cards. Courtesy: ADDX e.V.

Reverberations in Time and Space

Maeve Connolly

Standing in the light-filled atrium of Haus des Rundfunks in Berlin, the site of Susan Philipsz's work *You Are Not Alone*, I found myself speculating upon the material and acoustic properties of this distinctive space, with its walls clad in small shiny ceramic tiles, and also remembering earlier encounters with Philipsz's work. I recalled moving through the everyday confusion of a bus station in Belfast, drawn by an unaccompanied female voice rising above the crowd and, some years later, hearing music as I climbed the stairs to the upper floor of a white-walled New York gallery, catching fragments of a 16th Century lament emanating from tall trees in the parkland of Kilkenny castle and, most recently, discerning a composition for strings as I approached the end of a platform in what was once the main train station of Kassel. As these disparate memories of Philipsz's work cohered, I was struck by the complex interplay between loss, longing and evocation — and between memory and history — in her practice.

In an article that reflects upon the relationship between history and memory in contemporary art, Peter Osborne proposes that concepts of 'trauma', 'melancholy' and 'mourning' have become prevalent in art discourse, reinstating a 'metaphorically expanded conception of memory as the medium of historical experience'.[1] Osborne also suggests that, by comparison with history, memory is 'temporally restricted' because it only enlivens the past in relation to the present.[2] In contrast, he argues, the 'ultimate object of history — the unity of the human' can only be thought from the standpoint of a particular future. Consequently history is characterised by a utopian dimension, which links it to art and finds expression in an extension beyond the present moment and in the 'projection of collectivity beyond all actually existing forms'. At the same time, he acknowledges that such acts of projection are never free from constraint, as the experience of the present both regulates the historical representation of the past and shapes the imagining of the future. Although Philipsz may be interested in the operations of memory, she is highly attuned to the role of the imagination in projecting collectivity at different moments in time. These concerns find expression in the complex temporality of *You Are Not Alone*, which was commissioned by Modern Art Oxford and first presented at the Radcliffe Observatory in 2009.

In this work, Philipsz draws attention to the persistence of sound in time through the form of the radio interval signal. These signals are short musical sequences, originating in the 1920s and 1930s when broadcast radio schedules often featured lengthy pauses. Intended to function as recognisable musical signatures enabling listeners to identify stations while tuning, interval signals were generally played before the commencement of transmission and during breaks. Although they have not vanished entirely, the majority of the sequences gathered by Philipsz during the course of her research were produced many decades ago. Some are also associated with cultural and political contexts that now resonate with historical significance, such as Radio Normandie in 1939, Mother Vietnam in 1971 and Serb Republic Radio in 1993. Yet rather than focusing her research on interval signals that seem historically significant by virtue of their source, Philipsz instead responded primarily to the musical qualities of these sequences. She noted that despite their varied form and origination, many were characterised by 'a sort of chime, like wind chimes, that can sound really beautiful — distant and melancholy'.[3]

Responding to these qualities, she recorded herself playing the selected interval sequences on a vibraphone. This percussive instrument is related to the xylophone but it incorporates motor-driven valves producing a vibrating effect that can be controlled and sustained. Transposed to the vibraphone, the already melancholy interval signals acquire an unearthly quality, which seems especially appropriate to the Radcliffe Observatory. This structure was conceived in response to a highly-anticipated astrological event, the Transit of Venus in 1769, which preceded its construction. Its form was also shaped by popular interest in the Tower of the Winds, an octagonal marble clock tower located in Athens, built in the 1st Century BC and incorporating sundials and a wind vane. This time-keeping device subsequently functioned both as a Christian bell-tower and a place of worship for dervishes, and its design and decoration were documented by James Stuart and Nicholas Revett's *Antiquities of Athens* (1762). James Wyatt was inspired by this source, so his design for the Radcliffe Observatory materialises an idea of the classical past that is specific to the moment of its construction. Consequently, this newly-built and highly advanced tool for scientific exploration was adorned with carvings of mythological figures. Images of ancient Greek wind deities and the twelve signs of the zodiac are still visible on the exterior of the building, which no longer functions as an observatory and now houses the common rooms of Green Templeton College at Oxford University.

This first presentation of *You Are Not Alone*, which took place in the autumn of 2009, involved a four-channel recording of interval signals drawn from over thirty different radio stations and arranged for the vibraphone. Broadcast from separate FM transmitters located in the tower of Modern Art Oxford, the recordings were transmitted across the city to receivers located in the Observing Room on the second floor of the Radcliffe Observatory. In this room, which once housed scientific machinery, the transmissions were relayed to visitors through four speakers, positioned beside the large windows that look out over the city. Experiencing the work in this context, Joerg Heiser was reminded of popular melodies but also prompted to speculate upon more sinister uses of radio technology, suggesting that secret code information might have been hidden within interval signals during the Cold War era.[4] In a practical sense, *You Are Not Alone* transformed the Observing Room into a kind of 'listening station', focused on sounds rather than distant images. But Philipsz also proposed a conceptual parallel between the telescope and radio, by invoking Marconi's notion of sound persisting in time: 'contemporary cosmologists say that telescopes are like time machines, the deeper they can see into the night sky the further back in time they allow us to travel. [...] Guglielmo Marconi suggested that sounds once generated never die, they fade but they continue to reverberate as sound waves across the universe. I began to think about radio as a medium to tune into the immense range of sounds echoing across the universe and also as a medium to transmit sounds to distant places'.[5] This quote is specifically concerned with telescopes and radio as technologies that enable enquiry in time and space. But Marconi's observation about the persistence of sound also makes it possible to think of the Radcliffe Observatory as a kind of time machine, enabling transport to earlier moments in the history of scientific thought.

The 'time machine' quality of *You Are Not Alone* was even more apparent at Haus des Rundfunks, where Philipsz's work was installed over a period of several days in April 2011. Although it remains in use as part of a complex belonging to Rundfunk Berlin-Brandenburg (RBB), this building has gradually acquired the role of an unofficial monument to broadcasting in Germany. Designed by Hans Poelzig, and opened in 1931 (a year before the completion of BBC Broadcasting House in London) the upper floors of the atrium now house architectural models and documentary panels detailing the building's central role in German social and political history. Early utopian aspirations for the medium of radio as a technology of public communication are suggested both by its luminous interior and its carefully crafted brick exterior, which suggests substance rather than spectacle. These aspirations were, however, rapidly overtaken by the rise of National Socialism and, following Hitler's ascent to power, 'Reichsender Berlin' acquired a new function, eventually becoming the wartime Broadcasting Headquarters of Greater Germany. At the end of the war Haus des Rundfunks was liberated by Russian troops and even though located in the British sector, it remained physically segregated from the rest of West Berlin, surrounded by barbed wire and manned by armed Soviet guards until 1956. It then housed the station Sender

Freies Berlin (from 1957 to 2003), which was to prove important in the early history of artists' television.[6] In response to this context, Philipsz reconfigured *You Are Not Alone* so that the sound sequence opened with a vibraphone version of the final signal transmitted in 1990 from Radio Berlin International (located in former East Berlin) and ended with a version of the Sender Freies Berlin signal from 1975. By locating both the transmitter and receiver within the same atrium space, Philipsz also hinted at the dual identity and purpose of Haus des Rundfunks, as both a site of transmission and a place in which music was frequently performed in front of a live audience. As demonstrated by the architectural models, the building was designed around a large auditorium, located immediately behind the atrium and images of live performances feature prominently in the documentary panels that detail its history. These images confirm the symbolic significance of Haus des Rundfunks as a space of public gathering in which crowds assembled, serving as audiences both for live entertainment and for political propaganda. The mediated presence of these crowds, audible to those listening at home, would have been integral to the experience of 'live broadcasting' during the 1930s and 1940s, and the creation of a sense of shared time and space. Interval signals were a way to maintain and extend this spatio-temporal bond between broadcaster and listener, in the absence of programming. Their vaguely disembodied sonic quality is appropriate to the articulation of cor-porate identity in broadcasting, pre-empting the graphic idents and logos that were to pervade television in a later era.[7] In *You Are Not Alone*, however, Philipsz emphasises the 'distant and melancholy' quality of the interval signal, as a hopeful and open-ended communication rather than an assertion of presence.

Philipsz's research also suggests that even if these musical sequences were designed partly to function as branding devices they could still be experienced in many different ways. The publication documenting the installation at Modern Art Oxford assembles relics of a specific, now somewhat arcane, form of correspondence that developed between radio broadcasters and dedicated listeners in relation to the interval signal. These radiophiles would scan frequencies for transmissions from distant stations, including services aimed at overseas audiences, submitting frequency reports to stations by post with the aim of receiving official acknowledgement postcards featuring the official logo.[8] It is possible that some of these listeners were expatriates or travellers seeking a connection with home, motivated by attachment to the seasonal, familial and national norms emphasised in radio programming.[9] But rather than focusing on the programme content they seem to have been specifically interested in the technology of radio, and in the formal properties of the signal.

By situating broadcasting in relation to ideas of temporal and spatial journeying that are found in scientific exploration, and by attending to the political and symbolic significance of structures such as the Haus des Rundfunks, Philipsz emphasises the multiple, and sometimes fraught, ways in which radio has shaped the formation of collectivity. But her engagement with these formations is not wholly constrained by reference to the past because she also uses the form of the interval signal to develop an exploration of the 'projection of collectivity beyond existing forms', recalling Osborne's account of the utopian dimension shared by art and history. So even though *You Are Not Alone* is integrally concerned with the evocative power of sound and music, and their capacity to communicate loss and longing, Philipsz's work nonetheless remains strongly oriented toward the future. As a result it becomes possible to conceive of the Radcliffe Observatory and Haus des Rundfunks as time machines, and to imagine that the vibraphone melodies heard in Oxford and in Berlin coexist and continue, endlessly reverberating in time and space.

1 — Peter Osborne, '"The Truth will be Known when the Last Witness is Dead": History not Memory', *After the Event: New Perspectives on Art History*, edited by Charles Merewether and John Potts (Manchester University Press, Manchester, 2010) p. 203.

2 — Osborne, 205. All subsequent references to this text are from Osborne, pp. 205–206.

3 — Susan Philipsz, 'You Are Not Alone,' in *Susan Philipsz: You Are Not Alone*, edited by Michael Stanley (Modern Art Oxford, Oxford, 2010) p. 7.

4 — Joerg Heiser, 'Lullabies for Strangers', *Susan Philipsz: You Are Not Alone*, edited by Michael Stanley (Modern Art Oxford, Oxford, 2010) p. 20.

5 — Philipsz, op. cit., p. 7.

6 — Sender Freies Berlin broadcast Gerry Schum's *Land Art* on April 15,1969. See Christine Mehring, 'TV Art's Abstract Starts: Europe, c.1944–1969', *October* 125 (2008): p. 62.

7 — For a discussion of television logos see Margaret Morse, 'Television Graphics and the Virtual Body: Words on the Move', *Virtualities: Television, Media Art, and Cyberculture*, Indiana University Press (Bloomington/Indiana, 1998) pp. 71–98.

8 — Some of these postcards, produced by Radio Peking, Radio Denmark, Rádio Nacional Brasília and 'The Voice of Indonesia' (The Overseas Service of Radio Republik Indonesia), are reprinted in *Susan Philipsz: You Are Not Alone*, edited by Michael Stanley (Modern Art Oxford, Oxford, 2010) p. 34, p. 37.

9 — These normative aspects of broadcasting are discussed in Paddy Scannell, *Radio, Television and Modern Life: A Phenomenological Approach* (Blackwell, Cambridge, Oxford, 1996).

When Day Closes

Helsinki, 2010

Central Railway Station, Helsinki, 2010. Single-channel sound installation. 1 minute, 58 seconds. Commissioned by Pro Arte Foundation, Finland.

When Day Closes was both a single-channel sound installation in the South Hall of Helsinki's Central Railway Station and a series of late night broadcasts on Finnish television. During my research I became interested in a particular tradition of Finnish lullabies, which are known as Tuonela lullabies. In this tradition the lullabies are divided between mourning songs where the death of the child is anticipated because of domestic hardship or threat songs where the child is threatened with violence or death if he or she does not go to sleep. In the railway station, recordings of my own voice singing the Tuonela lullaby *Sydämeni laulu* (Song of My Heart) could be heard through special hypersonic speakers that trained the sound around the curve of the vaulted ceiling.

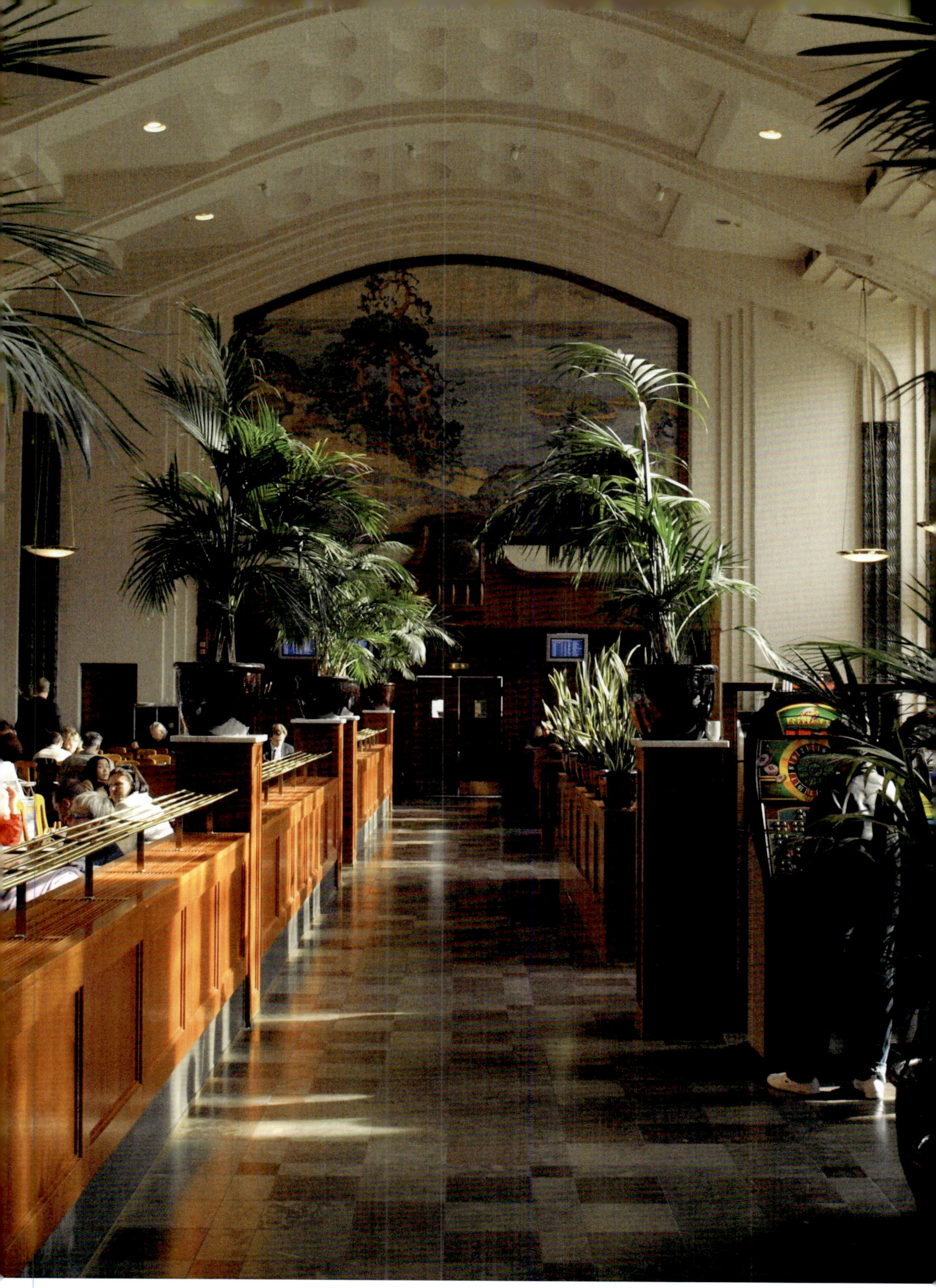

Grove of Tuoni, grove of night!——————————There thy bed of sand is light—————Thither my baby I lead

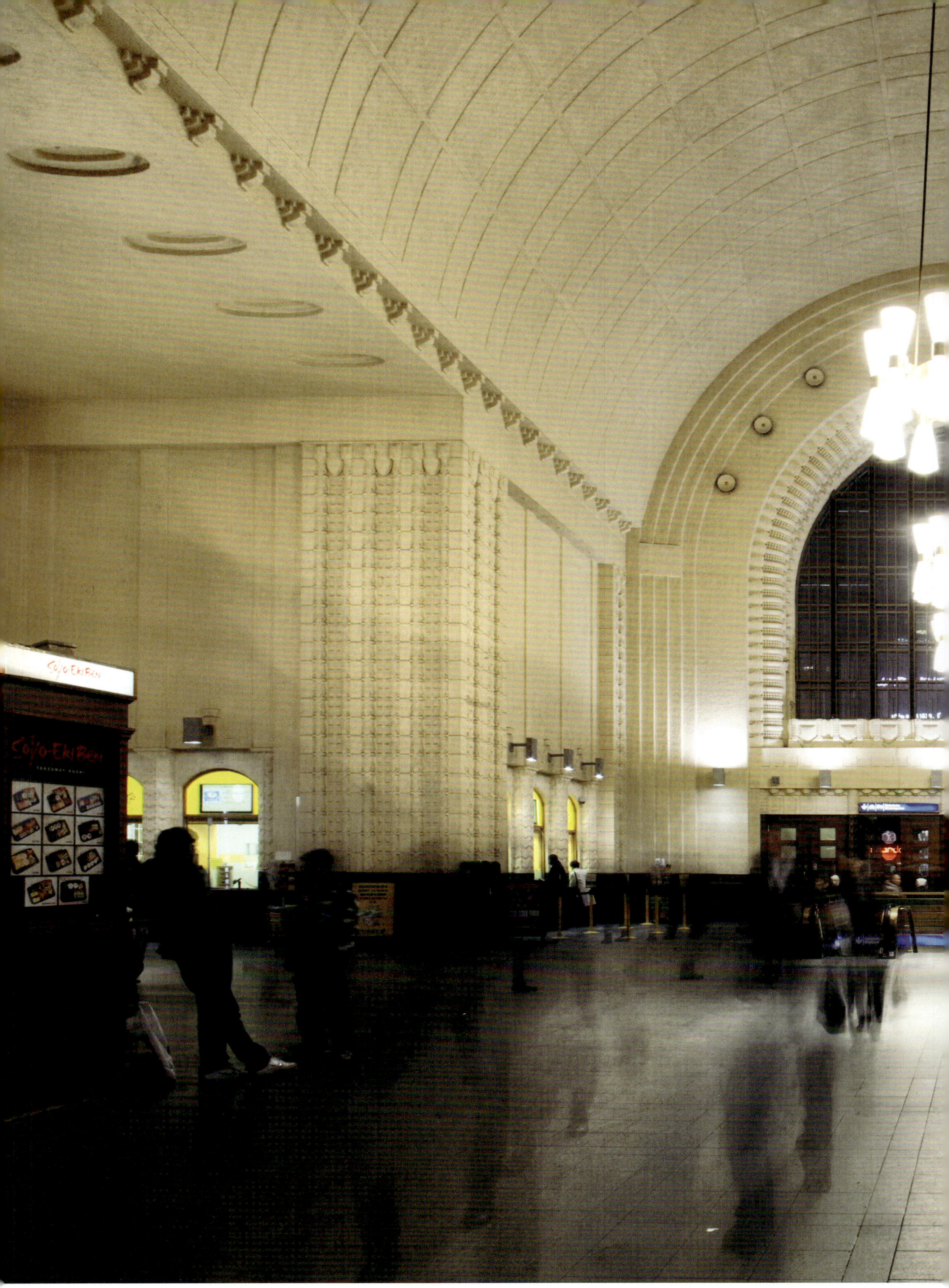

Mirth and joy———each long hour yields———In the Prince of Tuoni's fields———Tending the Tuonela cattle-

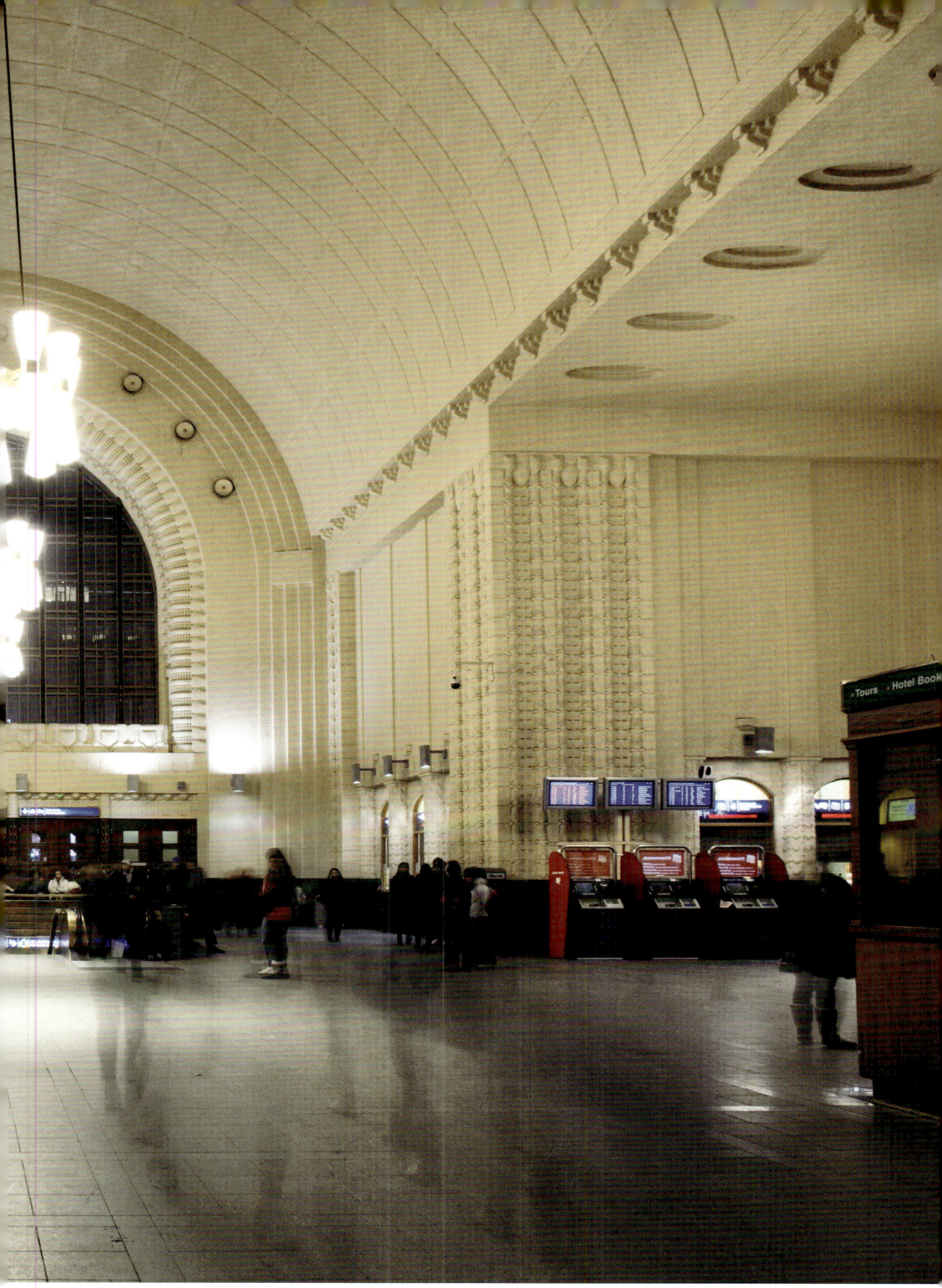

—Mirth and joy my babe will know——Lulled to sleep at evening glow——By the pale Tuonela maiden

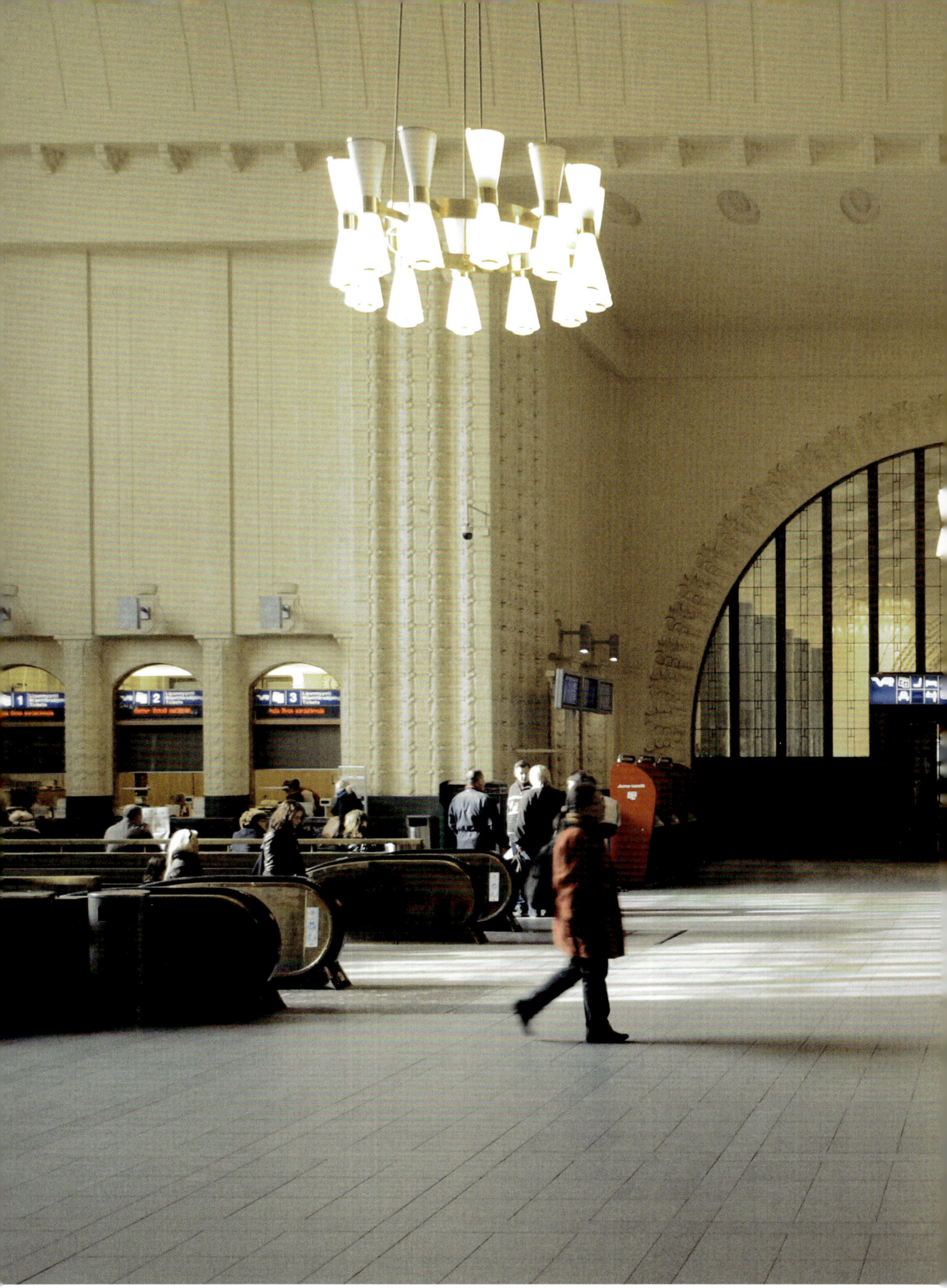

Surely joy hours will hold ——— Lying in thy cot of gold ——— Hearing the nightjar singing –

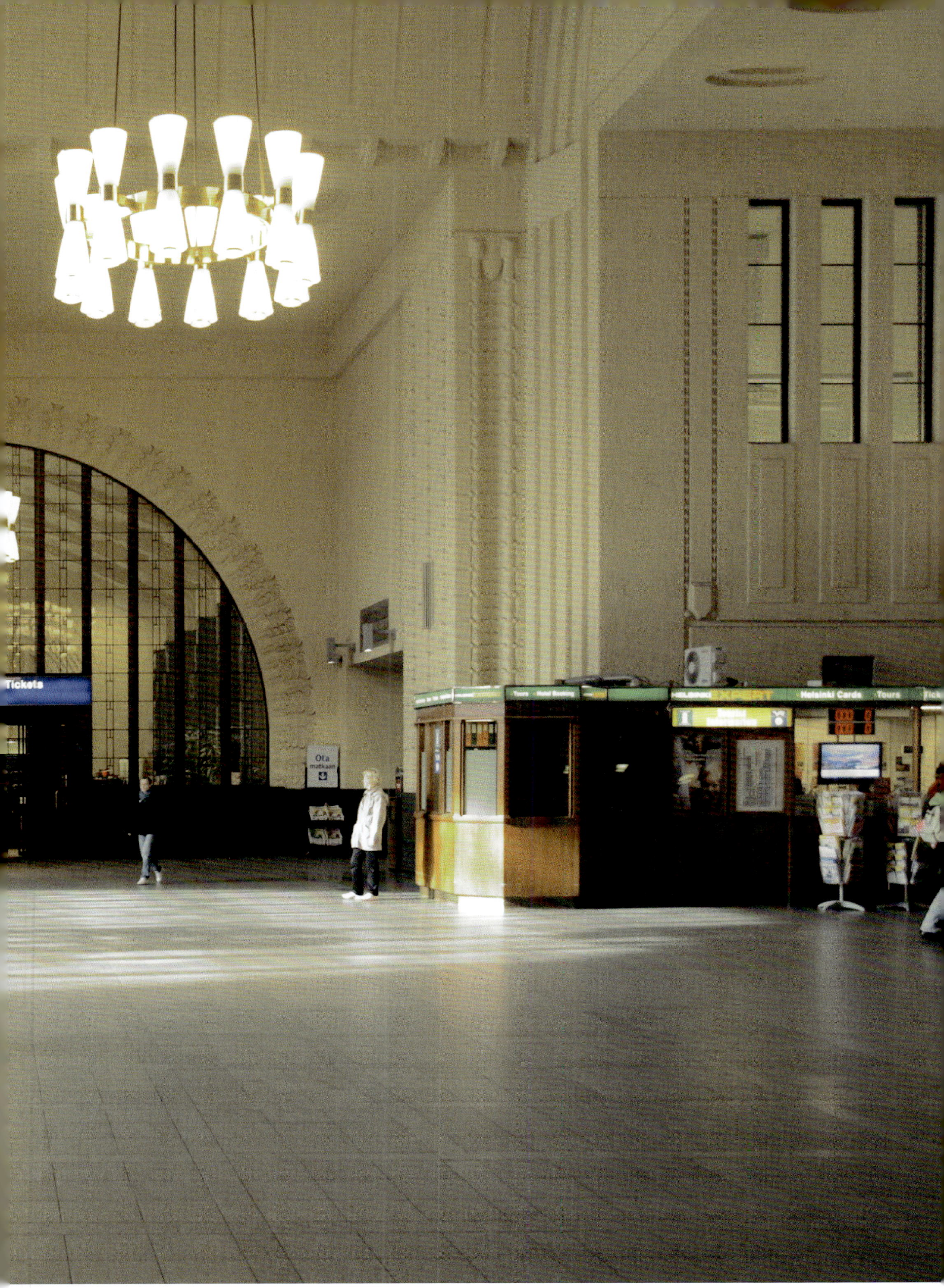

—Grove of Tuoni, grove of peace!——There all strife and passion cease——Distant the treacherous world.

Research photography
Suomenlinna sea
fortress, Helsinki, 2009.

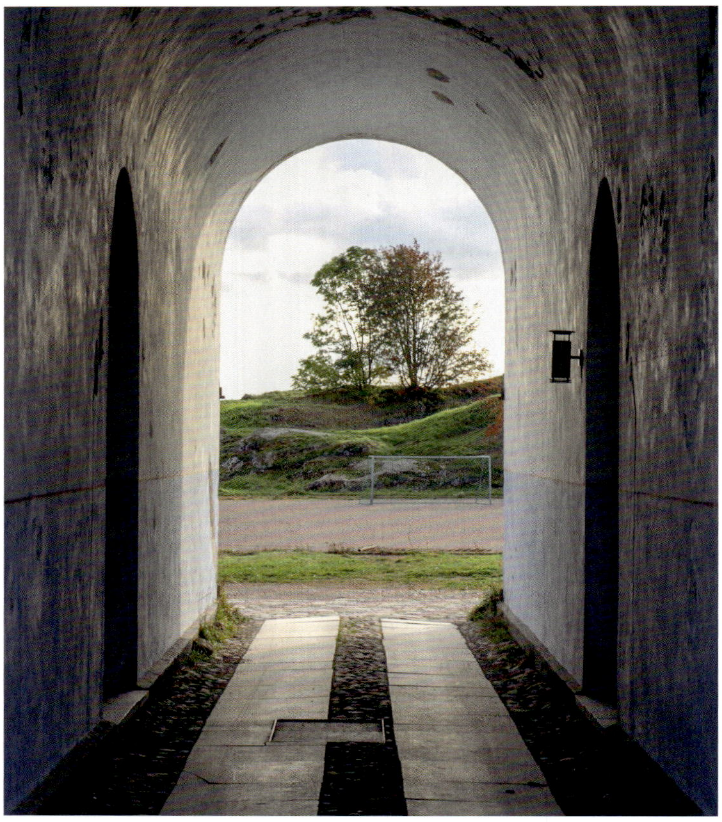

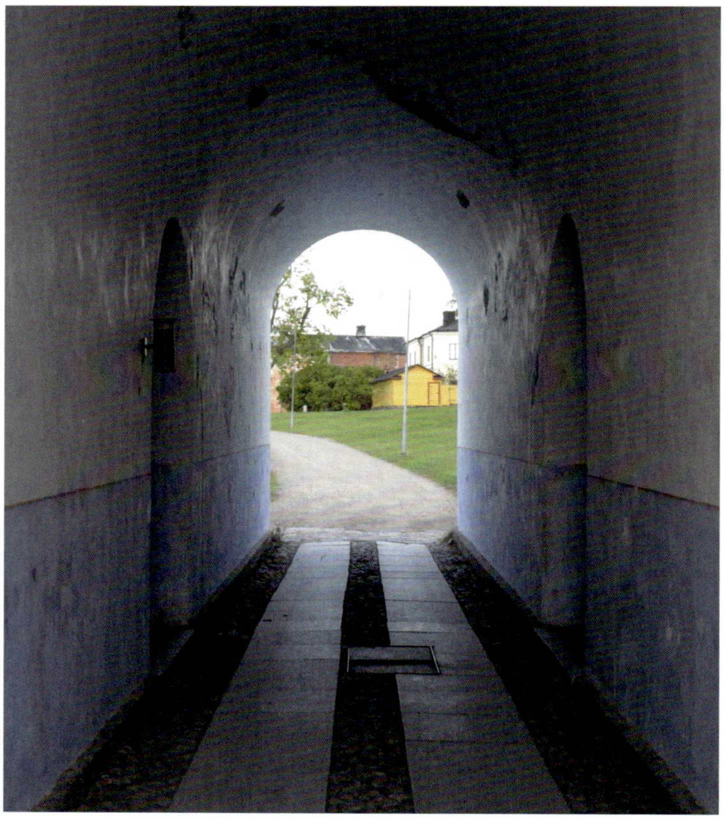

The Whispering Gallery

There was a story about the acoustics of a barrel-vaulted passageway on Suomenlinna Island in Helsinki that I always wanted to investigate. It was said that if two people stand at opposite ends of the passage way they can hear each other perfectly, but if the people take a step backwards and are standing just outside the passageway their voices are lost to each other. It is a phenomenon that occurs in circular or domed enclosures where whispering voices can be heard clearly over long distances. The South Hall of the Railway Station is one such space, the light streams through the arched windows creating dramatic silhouettes against the bright marble floor and the high barrel-vaulted ceiling that encloses the space creates a very special acoustic phenomenon.

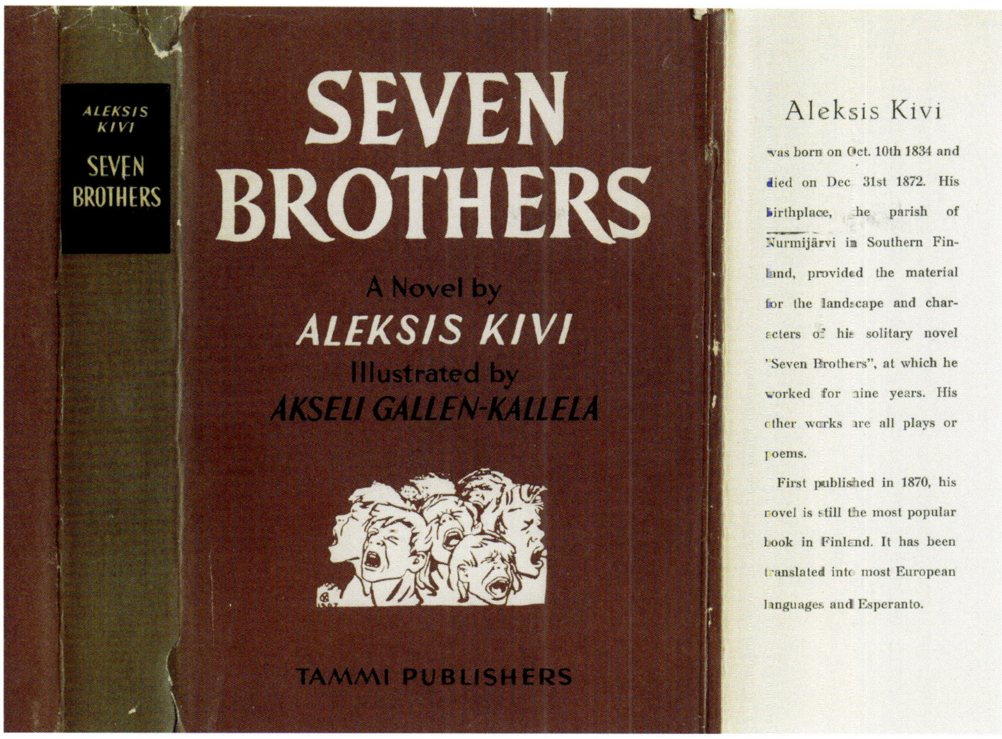

Cover and image from the artist's copy of *The Seven Brothers* by Alexis Kivi. Courtesy: Tammi Publications, Helsinki.

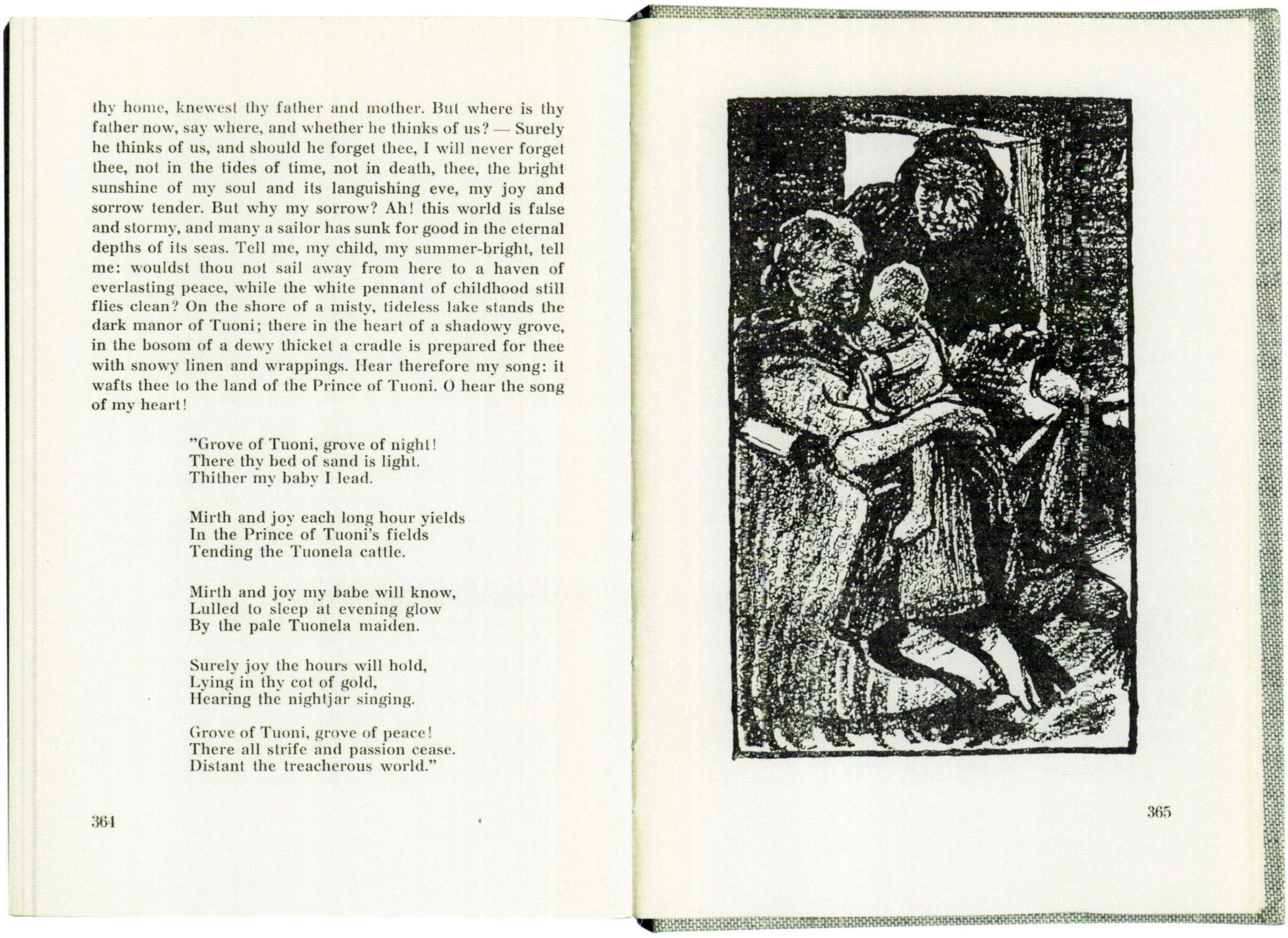

thy home, knewest thy father and mother. But where is thy father now, say where, and whether he thinks of us? — Surely he thinks of us, and should he forget thee, I will never forget thee, not in the tides of time, not in death, thee, the bright sunshine of my soul and its languishing eve, my joy and sorrow tender. But why my sorrow? Ah! this world is false and stormy, and many a sailor has sunk for good in the eternal depths of its seas. Tell me, my child, my summer-bright, tell me: wouldst thou not sail away from here to a haven of everlasting peace, while the white pennant of childhood still flies clean? On the shore of a misty, tideless lake stands the dark manor of Tuoni; there in the heart of a shadowy grove, in the bosom of a dewy thicket a cradle is prepared for thee with snowy linen and wrappings. Hear therefore my song: it wafts thee to the land of the Prince of Tuoni. O hear the song of my heart!

"Grove of Tuoni, grove of night!
There thy bed of sand is light.
Thither my baby I lead.

Mirth and joy each long hour yields
In the Prince of Tuoni's fields
Tending the Tuonela cattle.

Mirth and joy my babe will know,
Lulled to sleep at evening glow
By the pale Tuonela maiden.

Surely joy the hours will hold,
Lying in thy cot of gold,
Hearing the nightjar singing.

Grove of Tuoni, grove of peace!
There all strife and passion cease.
Distant the treacherous world."

364

365

Seven Brothers

The lullaby *Sydämeni laulu* (Song of My Heart) is taken from Aleksis Kivi's novel *Seven Brothers* (1870). Kivi's tale is one of hardship and redemption in the rugged Finnish countryside. In the midst of this hardship one brother's wife seems to wish her baby dead. 'Tell me my child, my summer-bright, tell me: wouldst thou not sail away from here to a haven of everlasting peace, while the white pennant of childhood still flies clean? On the shore of a misty, tideless lake stands the dark manor of Tuoni; there in the heart of a shadowy grove, in the bosom of a dewy thicket a cradle is prepared for thee with snowy linen and wrappings'. The lullaby was subsequently set to music by the Finnish composer Jean Sibelius.

To Watch, to Listen, to Sing a Lullaby

Carolyn Christov-Bakargiev

If you happened to be walking through the Central Hall of the Helsinki Railway station at the right moment in late March or early April 2010, you might have wondered why, across the Hall, people were gathering and for no visible reason looking upwards towards the empty vaulted ceiling. Slowing down to look at them, you might have approached them to understand why they were gathered together and what their shared experience, or vision, might have been. At the place where they were gathered, you would have heard a solitary woman's voice singing in her monotone voice a sad lullaby, without musical accompaniment.

The singing lasted about two minutes. Apparently coming from the vaulted ceiling above, the voice was clearly audible in that one spot in the city station and yet no singer — nor any speakers in lieu of a singer — were anywhere to be seen.

When Day Closes is Susan Philipsz's first work based on a children's lullaby. She recorded herself singing a cappella the Finnish *Sydämeni laulu* (*The Song of My Heart*), written in the tradition of the old Finnish *Tuonela* lullabies by Aleksis Kivi (1834–1872) in his novel *Seitsemän veljestä* (*The Seven Brothers*, 1870). The novel, in which a mother sings the *Tuonela* lullaby as she puts her baby to sleep, is almost a symbol of Finnish nationalism. It was later put to music by Jean Sibelius as a choral song rather than a solo in 1898.

Philipsz had her recording played back in the railway station in such a way that, as in a whispering gallery, one had the illusion that the voice was emanating from the ceiling above the spot where people gathered, that is, from a different place from where it was actually being transmitted at the other end of the Central Hall. That a private and intimate experience (the sudden penetration of a voice into our normal and routine life) could be a public artwork is characteristic of all of Philipsz's oeuvre to date. It perhaps points to the deep solitude we experience in crowds, or to the reversal of public and private space typical of our times — a symptom of the alienation experienced in a society characterized by the insistent exchange and exposure of the most minute personal information which in his book *The Fall of Public Man* (1977) Richard Sennett presciently called a 'tyranny of intimacy'. At the same time, listening to the a cappella voice offers a relief from that same condition of permanent 'publicness', of a private turned public, and a form of temporary withdrawal or retreat into one's self. As the artist has put it, 'Listening to something that is intimate or private in public can have an unsettling effect, making people more aware of their environment, appreciating the qualities of the here and now.'[1]

As in most of Philipsz's works, *When Day Closes* involves an appropriation of a found existing song and its insertion into a public space. But her works are not only appropriations, they are repetitions. Repeating rather than inventing a song is a form of re-enactment that instantiates two different times — a past moment of an 'original' song and the present one of her repetition. Repetition is a form of distancing, a deferral yet an affirmation of loss, separation and death. If you repeat a song, there must have been an original voice that sang it in the first place. By repeating the authorial voice of the song in the novel, by becoming the mother in that specific novel, a relationship (and thus a separation, an awareness of there being at least 'two' selves) is created. By repeating the song, we identify with a voice and in this case an imaginary body attached to the voice of the mother in the Kivi story). Technology has simultaneously provided us with a disembodied surrogate of that voice (through recordings, CDs, radio, mp3s, etc.) whilst removing the actual person singing. When experiencing Philipsz's works, we position ourselves within the authorial voice's persona, we 'act' and perform, we re-inscribe the voice in our own body. What's more, as we identify with the singer, we also identify with an absent collectivity of listeners from another time and place. The crowd falls away; we imagine the accompanying musicians, the absent chorus, the absent community. We are both singing to others and listening to ourselves, with imaginary others listening by our sides. In the station, those imaginary others became embodied, each listening to the lullaby mysteriously coming from nowhere.

Dating back centuries, the *Tuonela* lullabies are unique to Finland and some of its neighbouring countries. They have come down to us mainly through the Finnish epic poem Kalevala first published in 1835 but based on old Finnish and Karelian folklore and mythology. Unlike most lullabies (except perhaps for the well-known English 'Rock-a-bye-Baby' where a child is described swinging and falling from a tree), the *Tuonela* lullabies are connected with a psychic death-drive: the content of their lyrics either mourns the death of a child or threatens the child with violence and death if he or she does not fall asleep. In Finnish mythology, *Tuonela* is the kingdom of the dead, the place of the afterlife reached by crossing the river Tuoni, and in these lullabies it is described as a better world, a place of solace. Philipsz, whose work always carries a deep, yet not immediately recognizable, political dimension and empathy, was aware during her preliminary research and site visits to Finland in 2009, that these lullabies may have developed as modes of elaborating the fears caused by the high rate of children's deaths in the cold and harsh living conditions of Northern Europe before the 20th Century. These lullabies accompany the transition and passage from waking life to sleep—and waking up again the next day was never a given at the time Kivi wrote his novel.

Did the words of the song, almost soothing in their reference both to the peacefulness of sleep and to the wishful notion of the peacefulness of death as opposed to living in a 'treacherous world' (the last two words of the song) catch Philipsz's attention? There is a contrast between the choral singing of Sibelius's version, on the one hand, in which the loneliness of the lyrics is pacified by its being sung by many voices at once, and, on the other, the artist's imagination of the solitary mother, singing alone while she both protects her child and separates from her child every night, not knowing if the following day will bring her back from a night's rest or be the day of her child's burial? Philipsz's repetition is also therefore a restoration, a pulling back of the song from Sibelius's more popular choral version to the earlier solo version imagined in Kivi's novel.

The voice suggests a body, the presence of a body acting as a musical instrument on its own, and not an abstract song or a recording of a person singing. Yet, when you turned upwards to where the voice seemed to be coming from, there was no body, there was *nobody*. The voice was not ghostly or disembodied. Rather, *her* body was there somehow, more there it seemed than if our vision could have seen her or actually touched her. She is a girl, or a young woman, slightly uncertain about her own ability to sing the notes properly, and therefore carefully and slowly emitting them and moving from one to another as if a sense of fear, or fragility, caused her to focus on the notes lest the precarious balance of the song collapse. Most of the song is sung in a low key. However, there are three special moments when her voice has a very high pitch, held high up in her chest and she breaks a word in two, so that it might last longer, achieving a sense of suspension of the flow of life and a different duration. It is when Sibelius composed the notes for the second verse of the first, third and sixth strophes of the song, and it occurs when pronouncing the words 'Li-ight' in the verse 'There thy bed of sand is light', 'Glo-ow' in 'Lulled to sleep at evening glow', and 'Ce-ease' in 'There all strife and passion cease'.

When Philipsz traveled to Finland for her site visit in 2009, she visited an exhibition of over three hundred paintings inspired by the Kalevala epic poem at the Ateneum Art Museum in Helsinki. Executed from the 1850s to the present day, many of these works depict the 'grove of Tuoni' or Tuonela/Hades of Finnish mythology. During her trip, Philipsz also became aware of the novel by Kivi.

On the same journey, she went to Suomenlinna island where NIFCA, the Nordic Institute for Contemporary Art, had hosted artists' residencies until 2010. The long flat island was well-known for dark tales of torture and death during the period of the Russian Revolution and Finnish Civil War. Its fortress and ramparts are today eerie, haunted and still, and the acoustics there are very specific to the architecture. There,

Philipsz stumbled upon a passageway with an arched ceiling that acted as a large whispering gallery. She initially suggested installing a recording of the *Tuonela* lullaby in this fortress on Suomenlinna as her commission for the IHME Contemporary Art Festival, but later she decided to place it instead in the bustling centre of the city, thus creating a complex counterpoint between the crowded space of the station and the solitude of the song, rather than the more simple initial idea which would have involved layering the solitary song over a visual field itself suggesting solitude inside the barren island fortress.

Philipsz actually created *When Day Closes* in the spring of 2010 as the second part of a public art project for Finland. The first part was produced in a series of IHME Editions of the festival titled *After Closedown* and was presented in Autumn 2009, shortly after visiting Suomenlinna, and this first artwork constitutes part of the inspiration for *When Day Closes*. While *When Day Closes* was installed in a busy public space of physical transit, *After Closedown* was experienced on television, in the privacy of homes in Helsinki and throughout Finland. In this first piece, a recording of Philipsz's own voice appeared unexpectedly, late at night, at the end of the regular television programming of the Finnish Broadcasting Company YLE on specific days and times in late September and early October 2009. Television viewers heard two songs from cult horror movies — Robin Hardy's *The Wicker Man* (1973) where the protagonist is sung a soothing lullaby before being burnt and killed, and the notorious lullaby theme tune from Roman Polanski's *Rosemary's Baby* (1968), in which the protagonist hums a tune to her unborn child.

If we consider that *After Closedown* and *When Day Closes* are two parts of a single project, both exploring condition of 'closure' between day and night, then the solo singing of *After Closedown* irrupting into peoples' bedrooms late at night over a blank television screen just before people turned their tv sets off before going to sleep, could be interpreted as a contemporary re-enactment of the earlier tradition of late night *Tuonela* lullaby singing, based on a leap of the imagination that might connect the stories of risks of death-by-night in hunger-stricken parts of Finland with the risks of a symbolic death-by-screen in media-stricken areas of today's society of communication and information.

The layering of Philipsz's physical research trips and journeys with further meandering through links on the Web, suggests an associative and intuitive process. It did not go unnoticed by the artist, for example, that the same train station where she installed her work still has today a café/restaurant with a painting of a wood where Sibelius would go for inspiration. What Philipsz finds through her research is not there to prove anything, her project is not some kind of historical discovery or recuperation with no other productive end. In this web of relations that Philipsz evokes and enacts around a semiotic field of associations involving childhood, singing, the political dimension of pain, poverty, child death in Northern Europe, she takes the position of the weeping, singing mother.

What is the mother? As a historical figure, the mother feels, has effects and emotions. She is a figure of empathy, different to the singing lover in many other of Philipsz's works. Motherly love, rather than being 'in love', or unrequited love, is played out in *When Day Closes*. Yet it is connected with helplessness, both because the child is helpless and because the mother feels helpless, unable to protect her child from death. To care for, and yet *not to be able to* care for another suggests a disempowered form of love, a condition of the self without power, without yearning and without desire.

1 — Conversation with the author, 2010

Surround Me

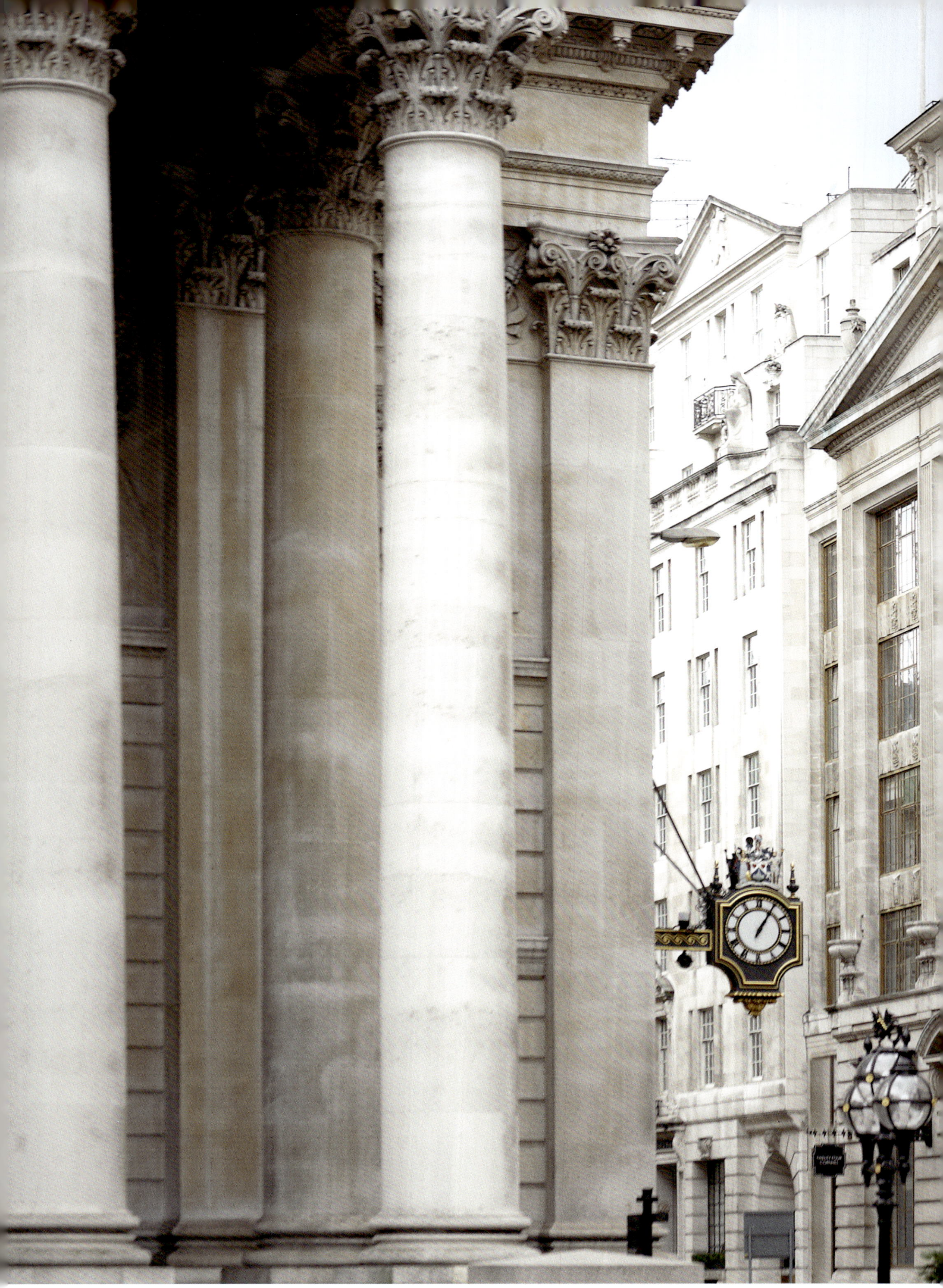

Surround Me. A Song Cycle for The City of London, 2010.
Six installations, various locations in the City of London.
Commissioned by Artangel

Surround Me; A Song Cycle for the City of London is a series of six sound works, arranged in a broad circle around the Royal Exchange designed to be experienced at the weekends. In contrast to the noise of the working week, over the weekend an eerie quiet descends on the public spaces of the City of London, broken only by the occasional sound of traffic, church bells and alarms. In the early modern city

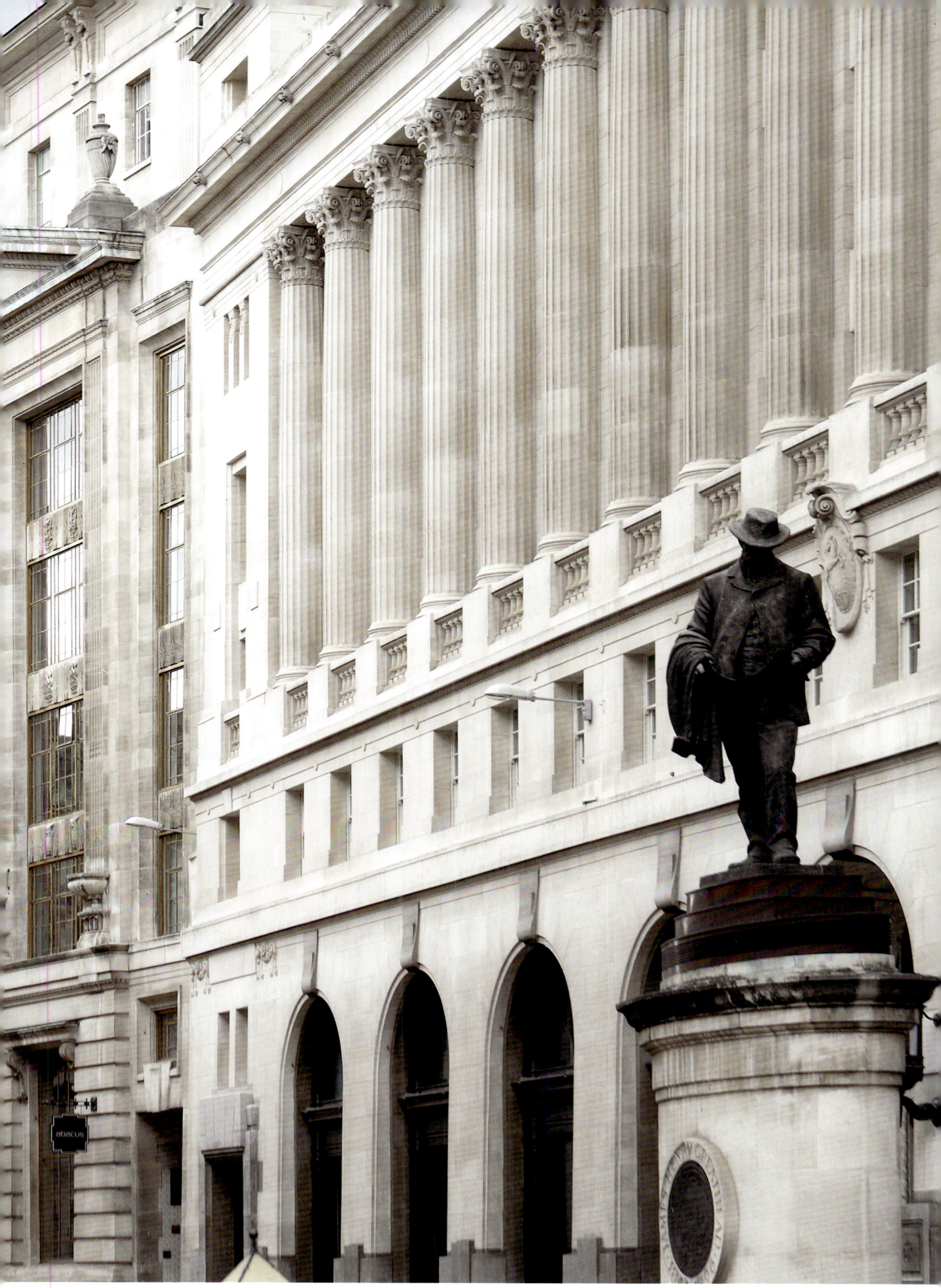

the voice had a much stronger role as an acoustic marker of civic space. To be heard over one another, a natural order and harmony evolved in the cries of the street traders which enthused composers, such as Thomas Ravenscroft, to write canons where one voice follows the other in a round. The madrigal, another popular song form for several voices, emerged in Italy in the 16th Century and soon travelled to England where it flowered as the English Madrigal School. *Surround Me; A Song Cycle for the City of London* embraces the vocal traditions of the City of London connecting themes of love and loss with those of fluidity, circulation and immersion; the flood of tears, the swelling tide and the ebb and flow of the river, to convey a poignant sense of absence and loss in contemporary London.

New Oysters

Change Alley, London,
2010. Three channel
sound installation.
56 seconds.

Change Alley is a network of interlocking alleyways situated near the Royal Exchange and the Bank of England. For this location I chose a very simple round by Thomas Ravenscroft called *New Oysters*, based on the cries of street traders. The round is for three voices, one voice following the other in a layered cycle of singing. I had the speakers placed at the end of each alleyway with the sound directed towards the centre. Once named the Kingdom of Change Alley, the place is famous as the precursor to the London Stock Exchange, with the trading conducted in the Alley's coffee houses. The idea of the trade in stocks and commodities spilling out on to the alleyway contrasts with the street traders selling oysters for more uncomplicated pleasures.

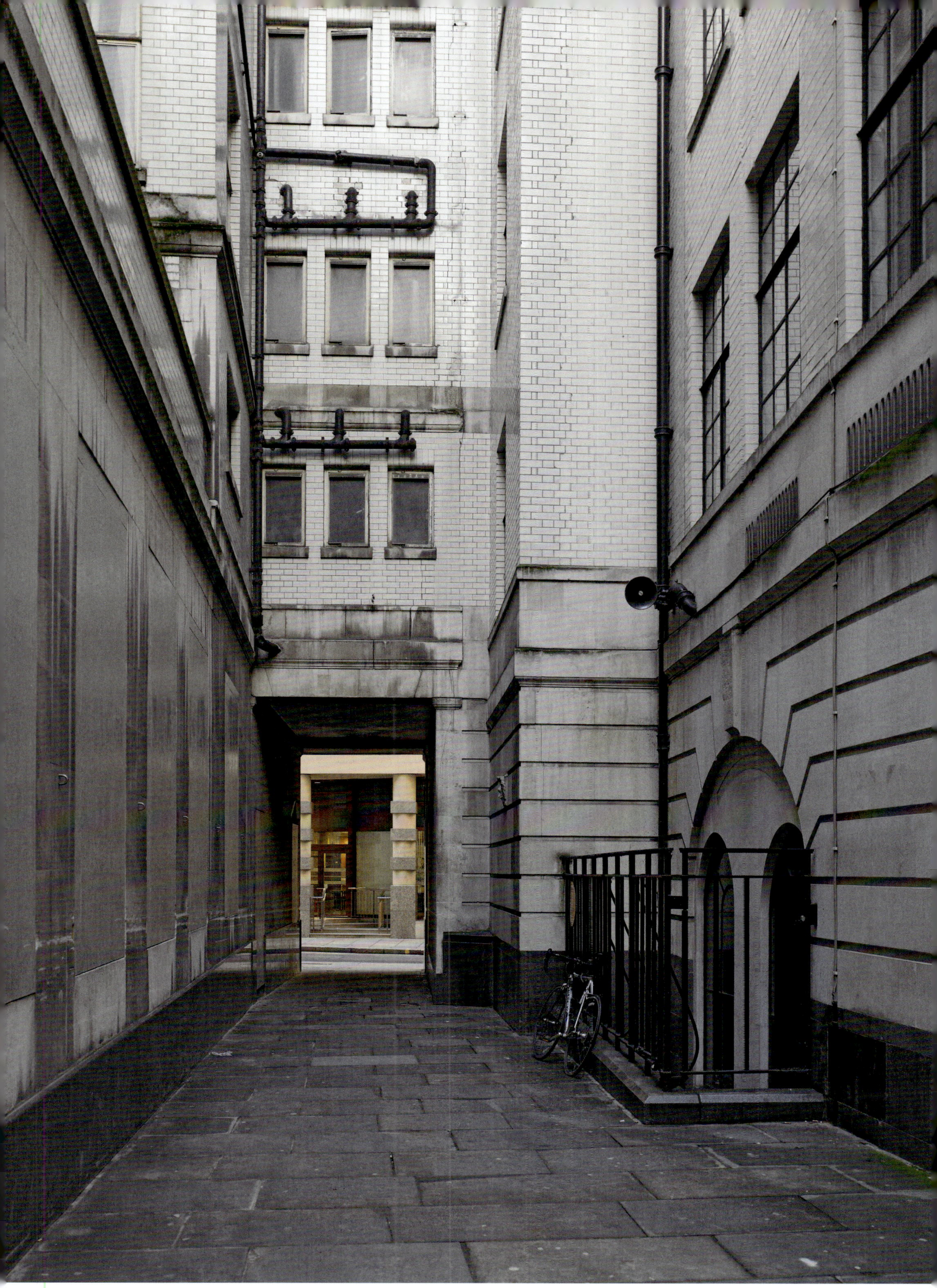

New oys-ters———new oys-ters———new Wale fleet———oys — ters———at——a groat a peck,

New———oys — ters,

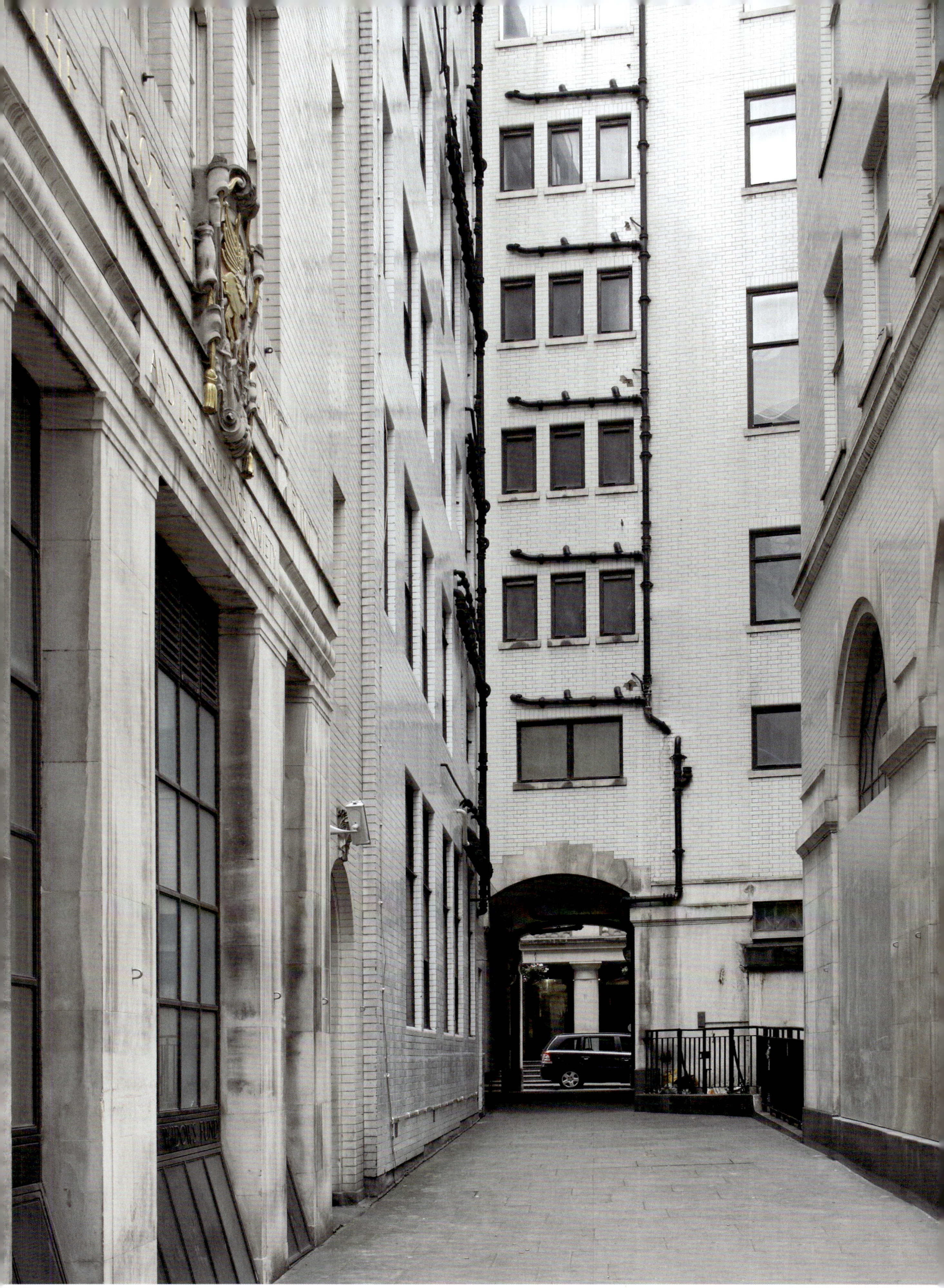

at a groat a peck, each——oys–ter——worth two pence——fetch us bread and wine that we may eat,–

new oys–ters,——new——Wale——fleet——oys — ters,——at——a groat——a——peck,–

New——oys — ters,–

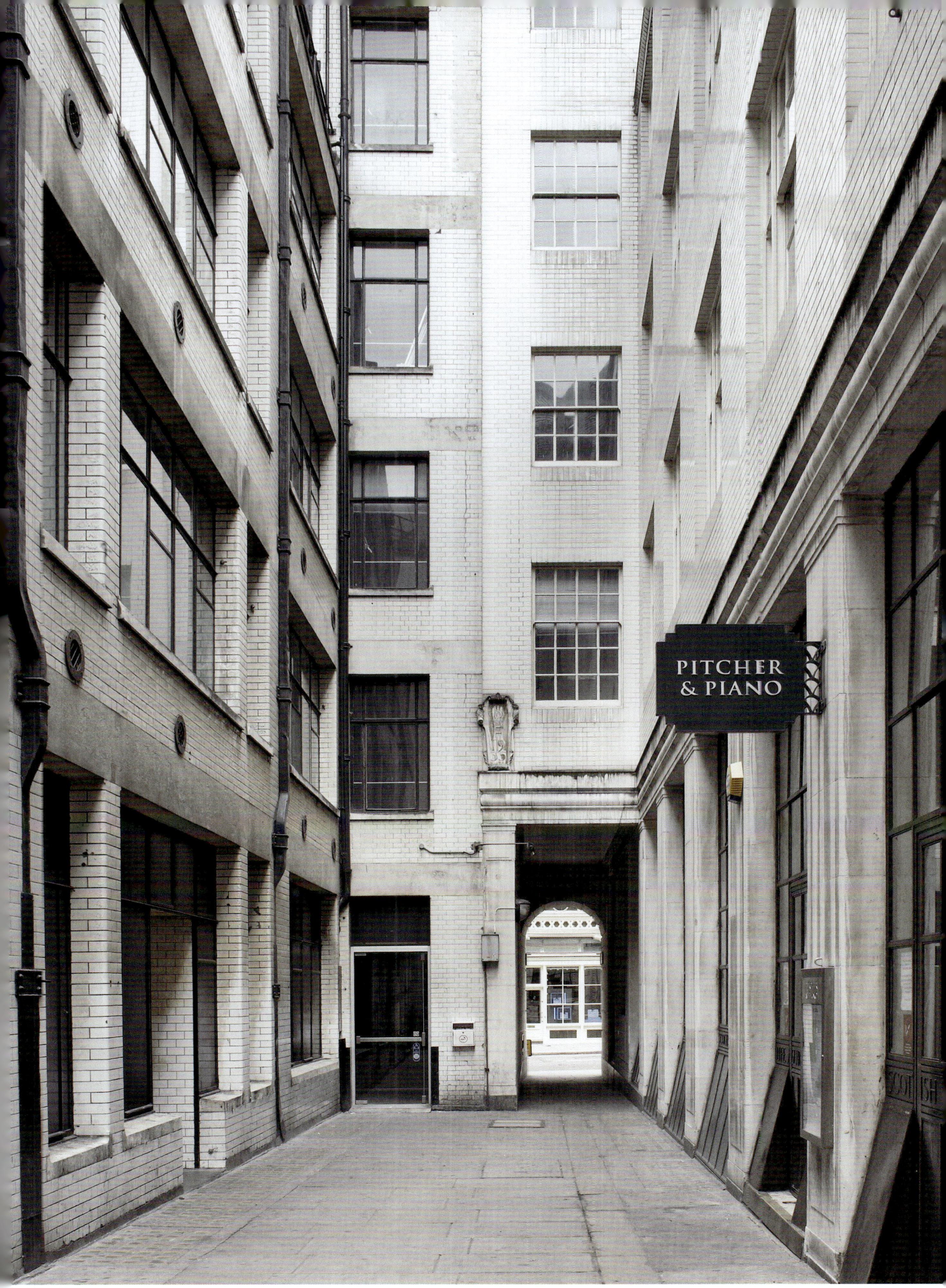

—Let us——lose no time with such good meat——a——ban — qɹet——for——a prince.

—at a——groat ——a——peck——each——oys — ter——worth two pence.

—new——oys — ters——new——Wale——fleet——oys — ters.

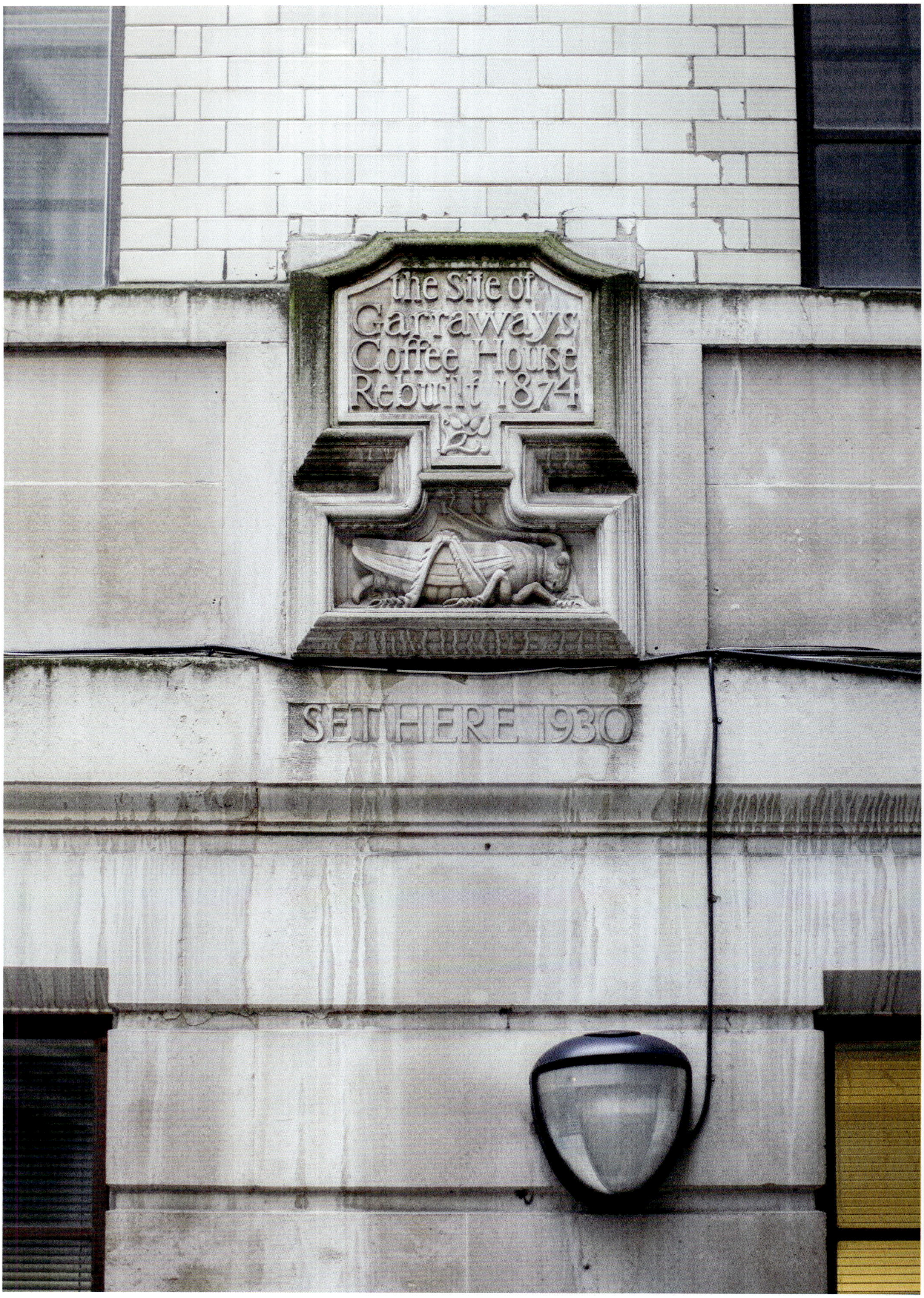
the Site of
Garraways
Coffee House
Rebuilt 1874
SET HERE 1930

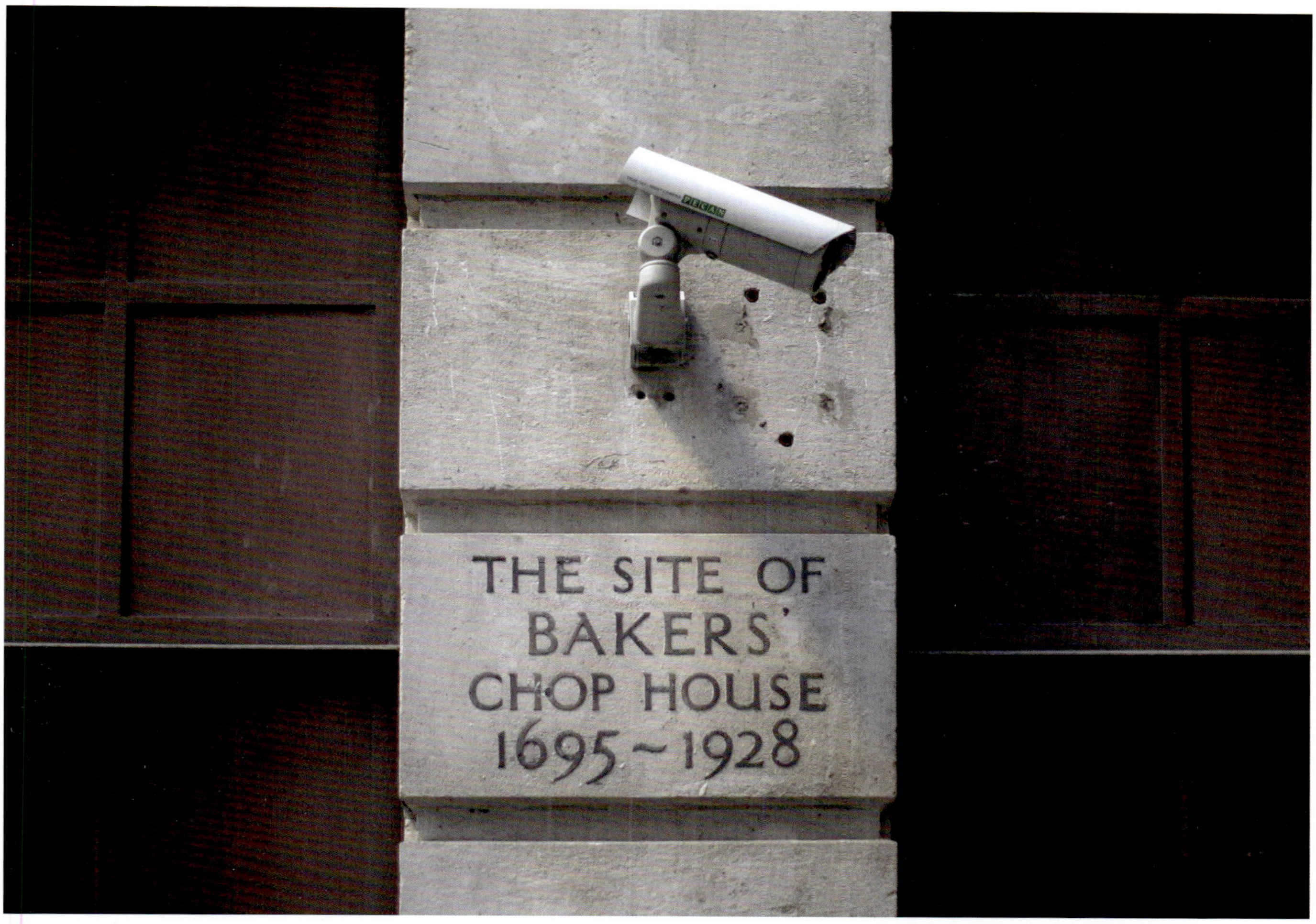

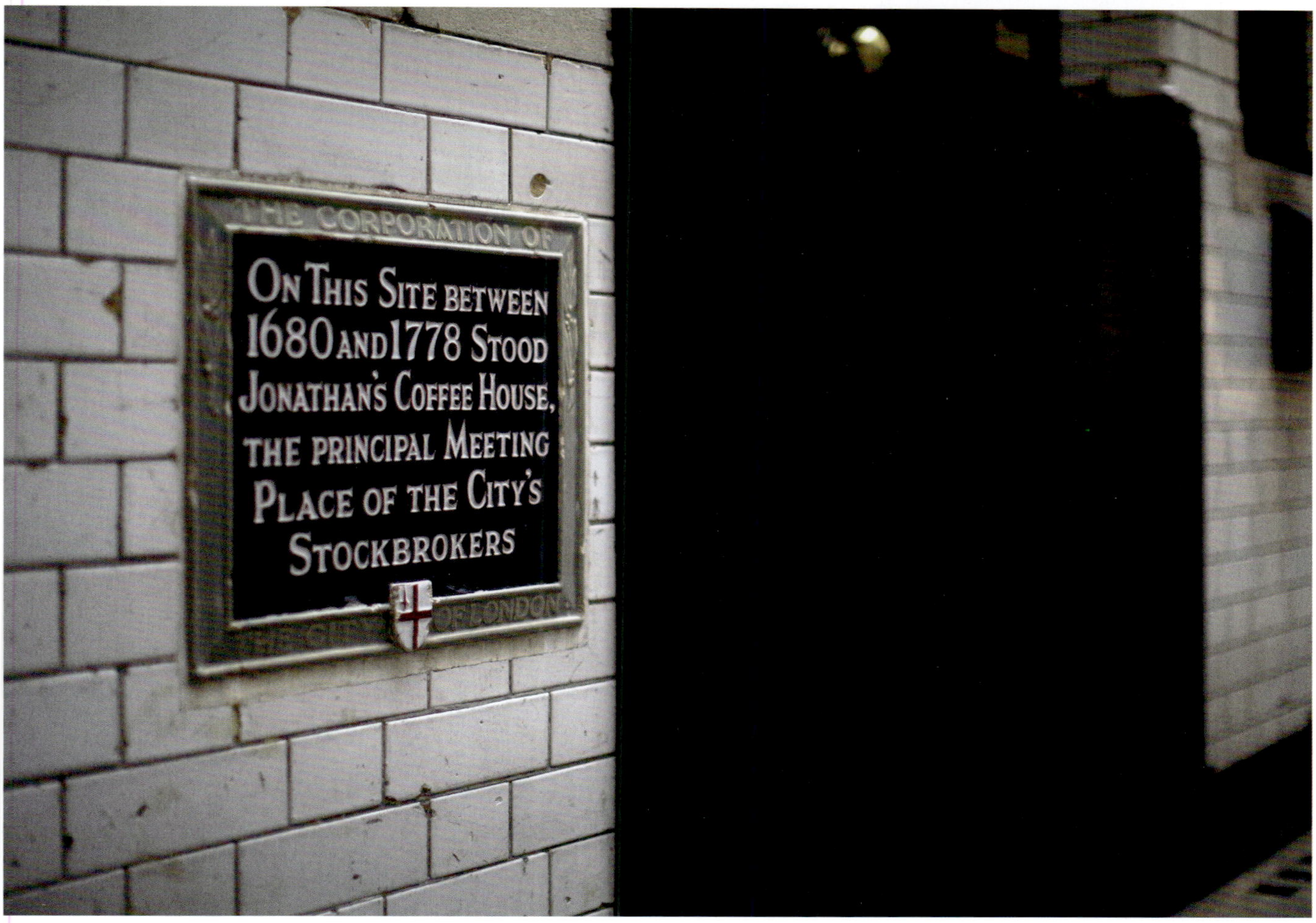

The Kingdom of Change Alley

'The centre of jobbing is in the kingdom of Change Alley. You may go over its limits in about a minute and a half. Stepping out of Jonathan's into the Alley, you turn your face full south; moving on a few paces, and then turning to the east, you advance to Garraway's; from thence, going out at the other door, you go on, still east, into Birchin Lane; and then, halting at the Sword-blade Bank, you immediately face to the north, enter Cornhill, visit two or three petty provinces there on your way to the west; and thus, having boxed your compass, and sailed round the stock-jobbing globe, you turn into Jonathan's again . Thornbury & Walford, *Old And New London. A Narrative Of Its History, Its People, and Its Places*, 1881.

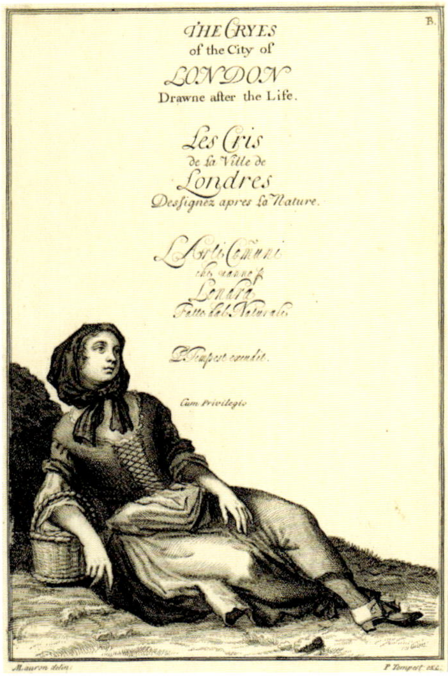

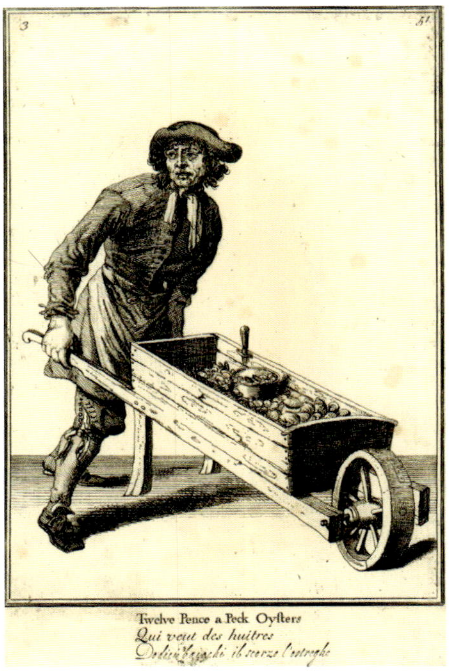

Title page and Twelve Pence a Peck Oysters, *The Cryes of the City of London Drawne after the Life. After Marcellus Laroon II*, 1688. Courtesy: Trustees of the British Museum.

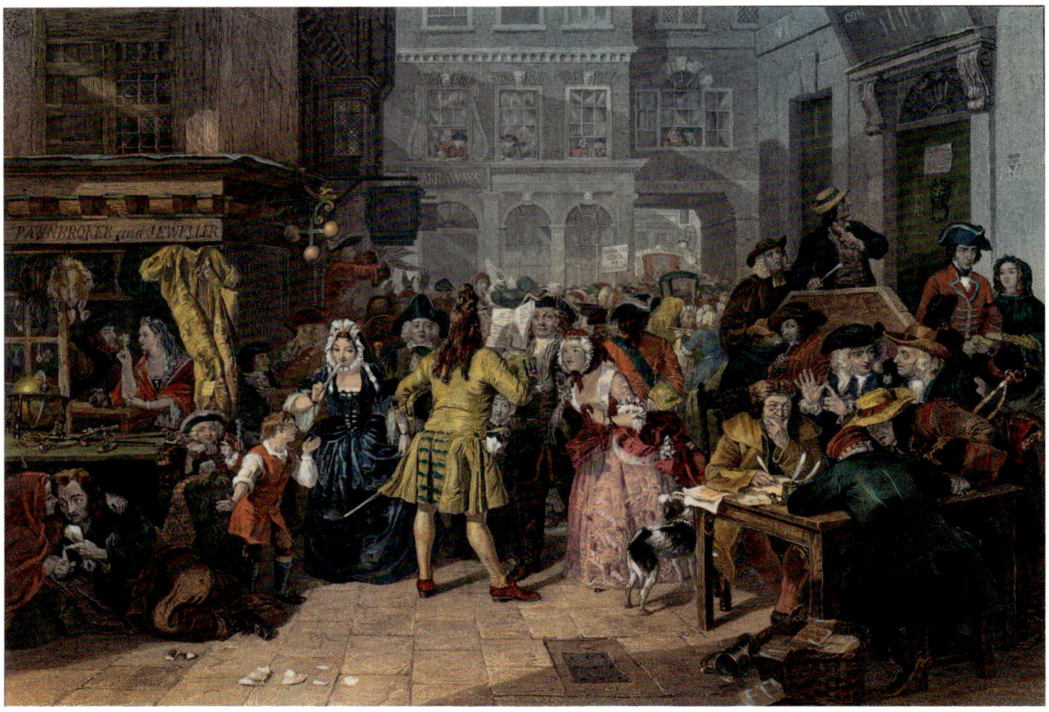

The South-Sea Bubble, James Carter, 1720. Courtesy: Baker Library of the Harvard Business School.

Jonathan Swift, The Bubble

'There is a Gulph where Thousands fell / Here all the bold Advent'rers came / A narrow Sound, though Deep as Hell / Change-Alley is the dreadful Name / Nine times a Day it Ebbs and Flows / Yet he that on the Surface lies / Without a Pilot seldom knows/ The time it Falls, or when 'twill Rise / Subscribers here by Thousands float / And justle one another down / Each paddling in his leaky Boat / And here they fish for Gold, and drown / Now bury'd in the Depth below / Now mounted up to Heaven again / They Reel and Stagger to and fro / At their Wits end, like Drunken Men / Mean time secure on Garr'way's Cliffs / A Savage Race by Shipwrecks fed / Lye waiting for the founder'd Skiffs / And Strip the Bodies of the Dead.'

Plan of all the Houses destroyed or damaged by the Great Fire, which begun in Exchange Alley Cornhill, on Friday, March 25, 1748. Jeffrey Thomas, 1748. Courtesy: British Library.

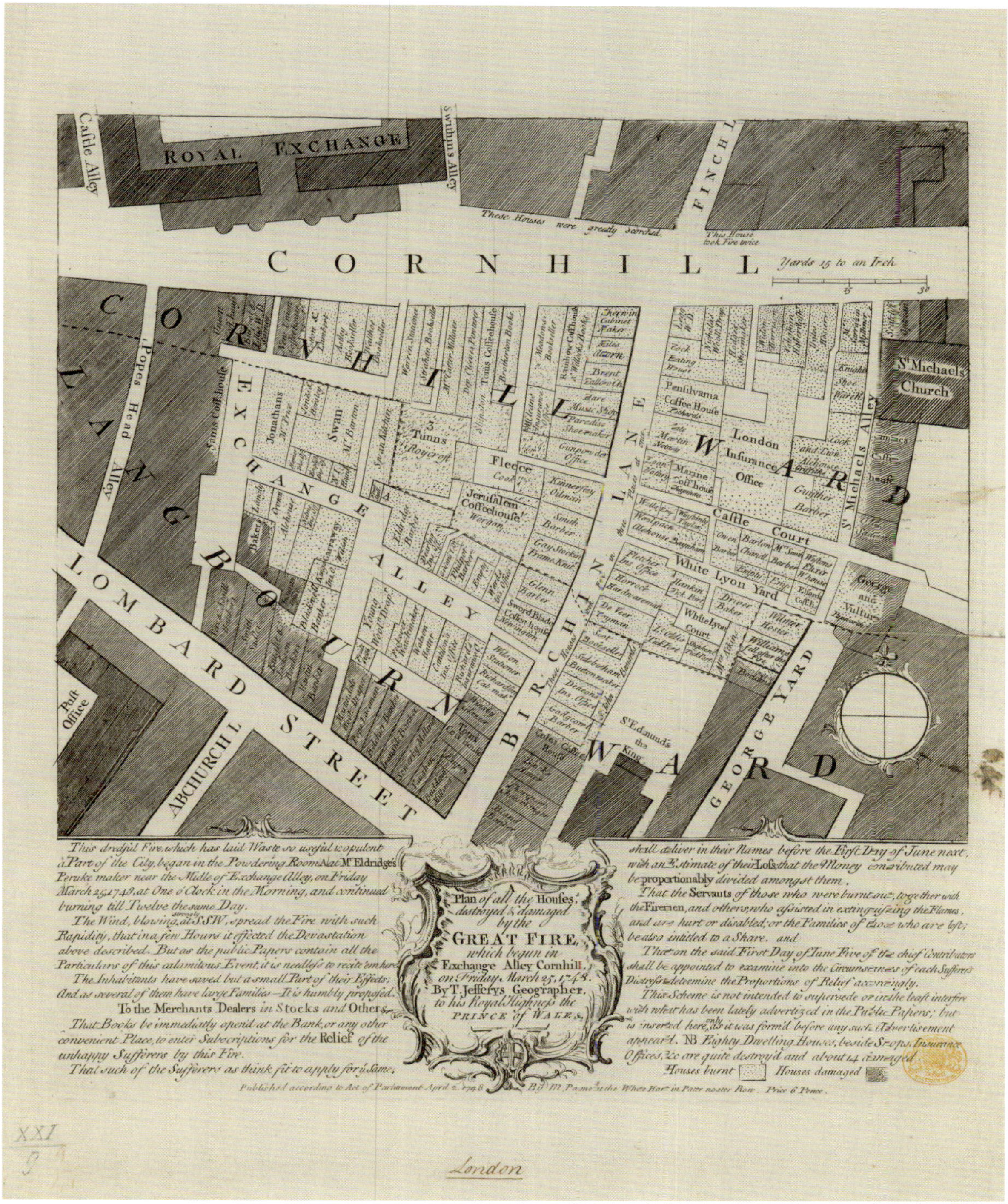

Diary of Samuel Pepys, 5th September 1666

'The Exchange a sad sight, nothing standing there, of all the statues or pillars, but Sir Thomas Gresham's picture in the corner. Walked into Moorefields (our feet ready to burn, walking through the towne among the hot coles), and find that full of people, and poor wretches carrying their good there, and every body keeping his goods together by themselves... Thence homeward, having passed through Cheapside and Newgate Market, all burned, and seen Anthony Joyce's House in fire. And took up a piece of glasse of Mercers' Chappell in the streete, where much more was, so melted and buckled with the heat of the fire like parchment. I also did see a poor cat taken out of a hole in the chimney, joyning to the wall of the Exchange; with, the hair all burned off the body, and yet alive.'

Lachrimae

Milk Street, London, 2010. Seven-channel sound installation. 36 minutes.

Lachrimae is a seven-part instrumental piece, composed by John Dowland in 1604 and based upon the image of a single falling tear. All seven *Lachrimae** were interpreted and played independently, with each of the seven notes coming from their own individual speakers. The speakers were arranged on the façade of a characterless building on Milk Street and for the most part the sound is abstract, with the tune coming together in parts only to separate again. The uniform surfaces of the glass facades at the junction of Milk Street and Russian Row created a series of visual and acoustic reflections that extended the piece into the streets around.

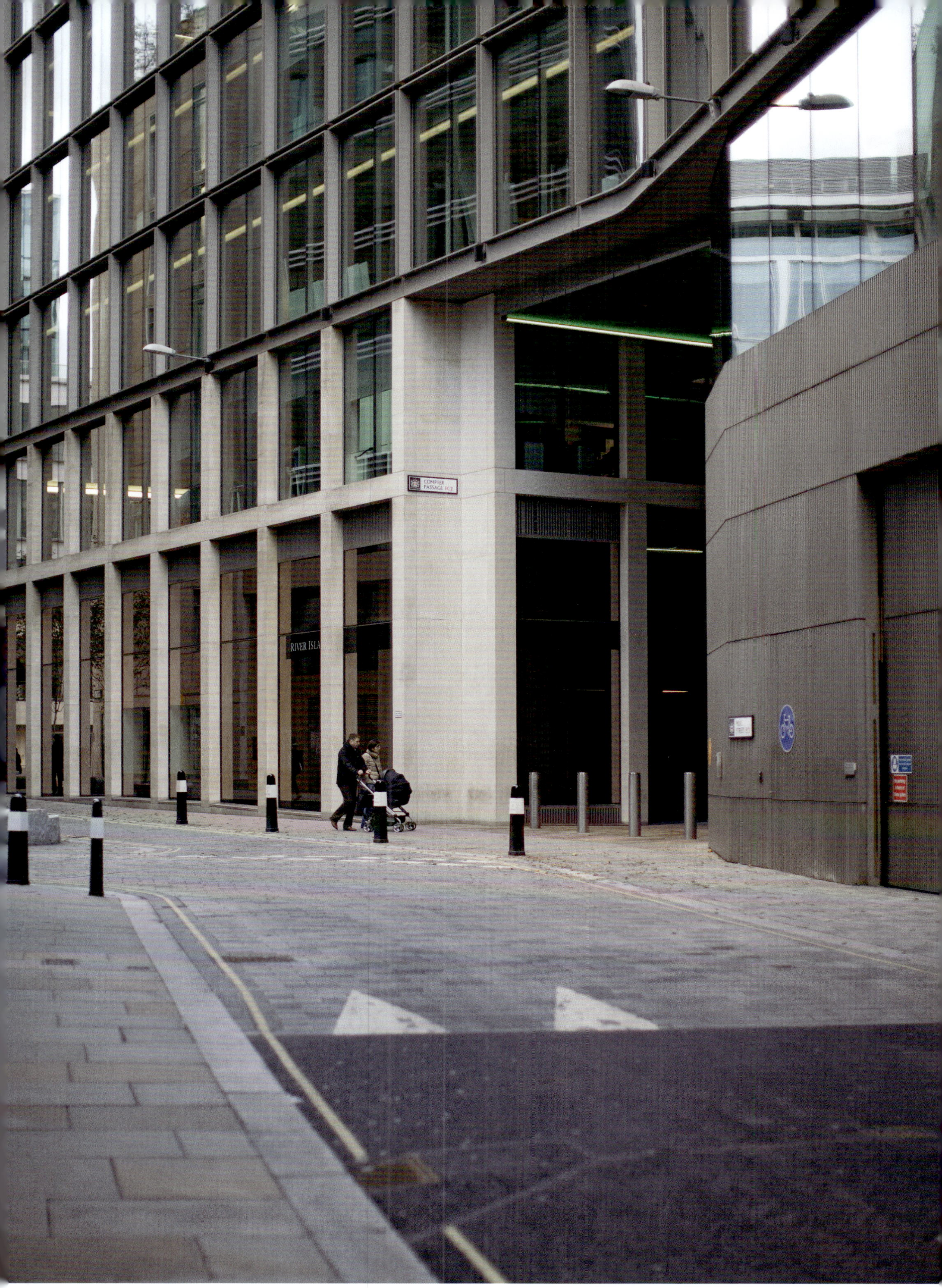

* Lachrimæ Antiquae ———— (lat. *Old tears*)
Lachrimæ Antiquae Novæ ——— (lat. *Old tears renewed*)
Lachrimæ Gementes ———— (lat. *Sighing tears*)
Lachrimæ Tristes ———— (lat. *Sad tears*)
Lachrimæ Coactae ———— (lat. *Forced tears*)
Lachrimæ Amantis ———— (lat. *A Lover's tears*)
Lachrimæ Veræ ———— (lat. *True tears*)

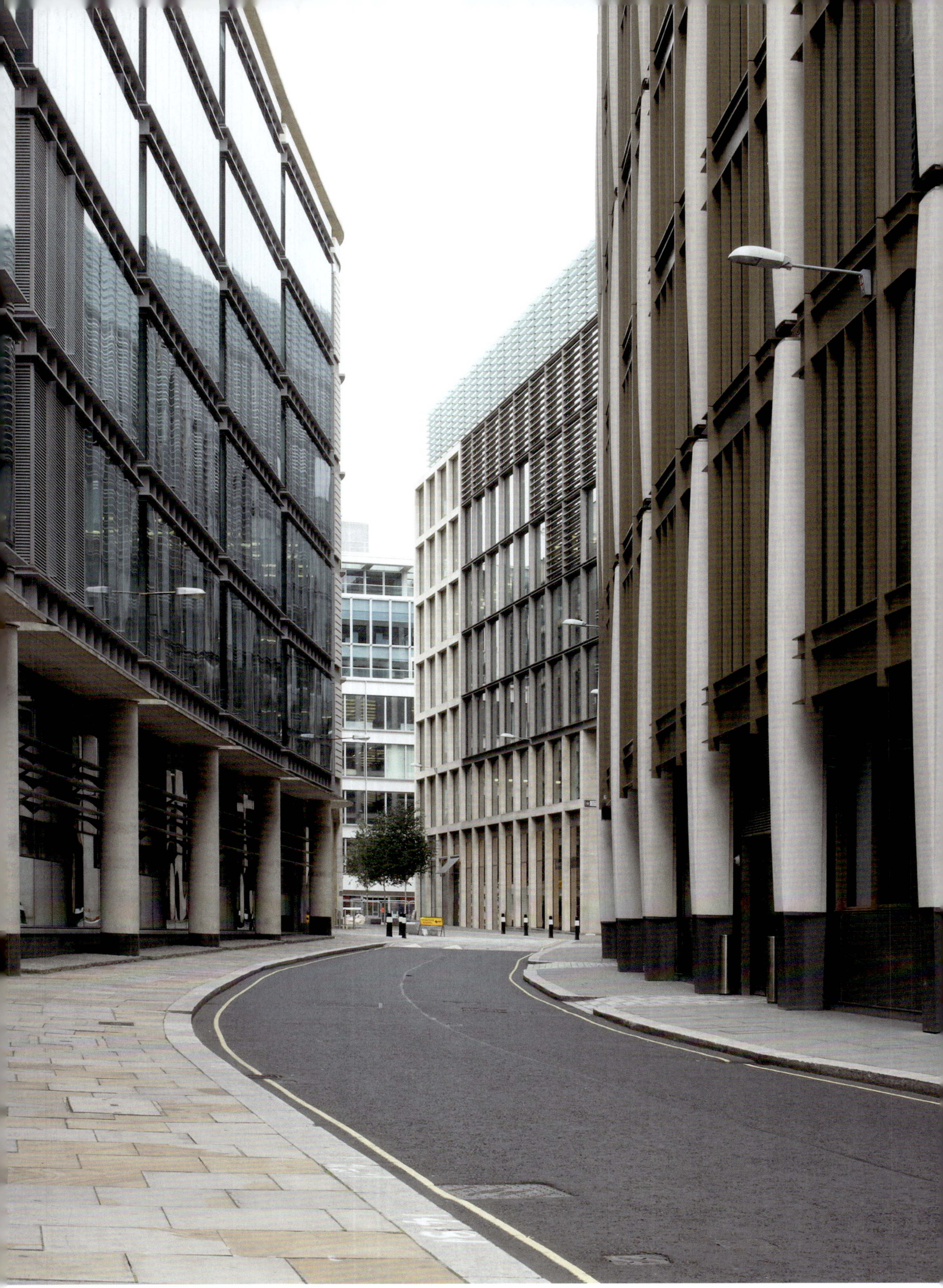

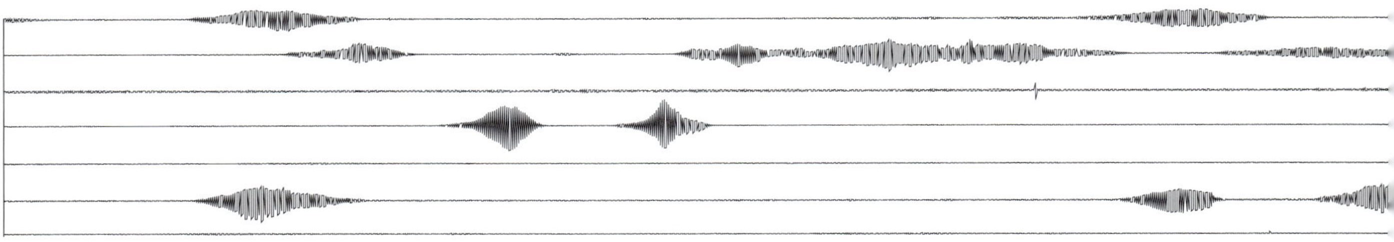

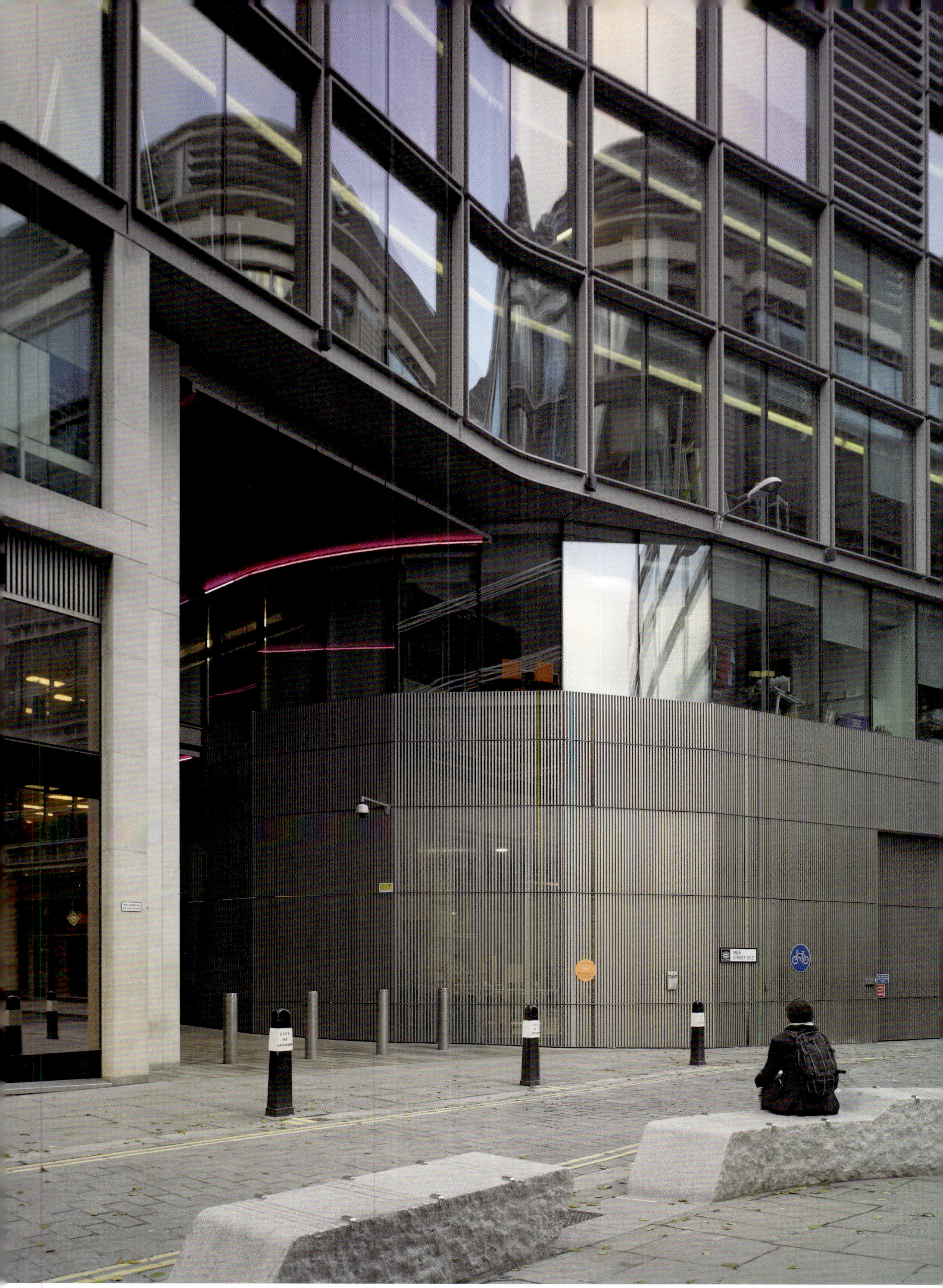
CITY OF LONDON
MILK STREET EC2

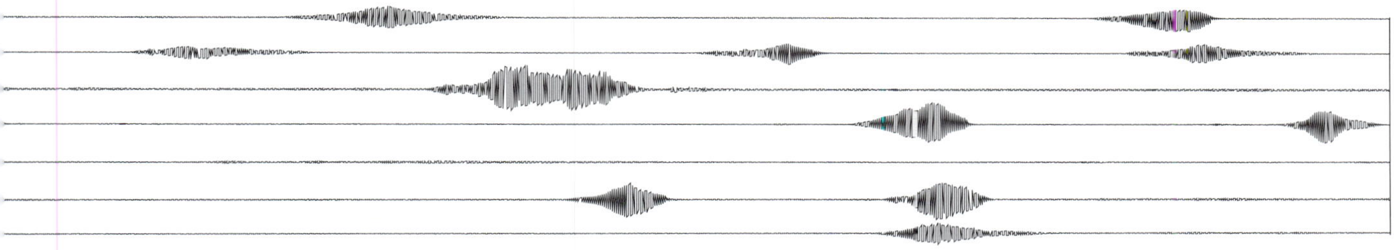

The Silver Swan

Tokenhouse Yard, London, 2010. Single-channel sound installation. 1 minute, 20 seconds.

Tokenhouse Yard derives its name from farthing pocket-pieces, or tokens, that were distributed from here and circulated among the London tradesmen in the Elizabethan era. The melancholy atmosphere of this long empty street behind the Bank of England offered a perfect setting for a version Orlando Gibbons' song *The Silver Swan*. The lyrics are a metaphor for the end of an era, the passing of the madrigal as a form of singing, perhaps the waning of the Elizabethan musical tradition. In the empty city it could be interpreted as evoking the end of other eras too. *The Silver Swan* was originally scored for five voices but I chose to record a single voice to accentuate the sense of absence and loss.

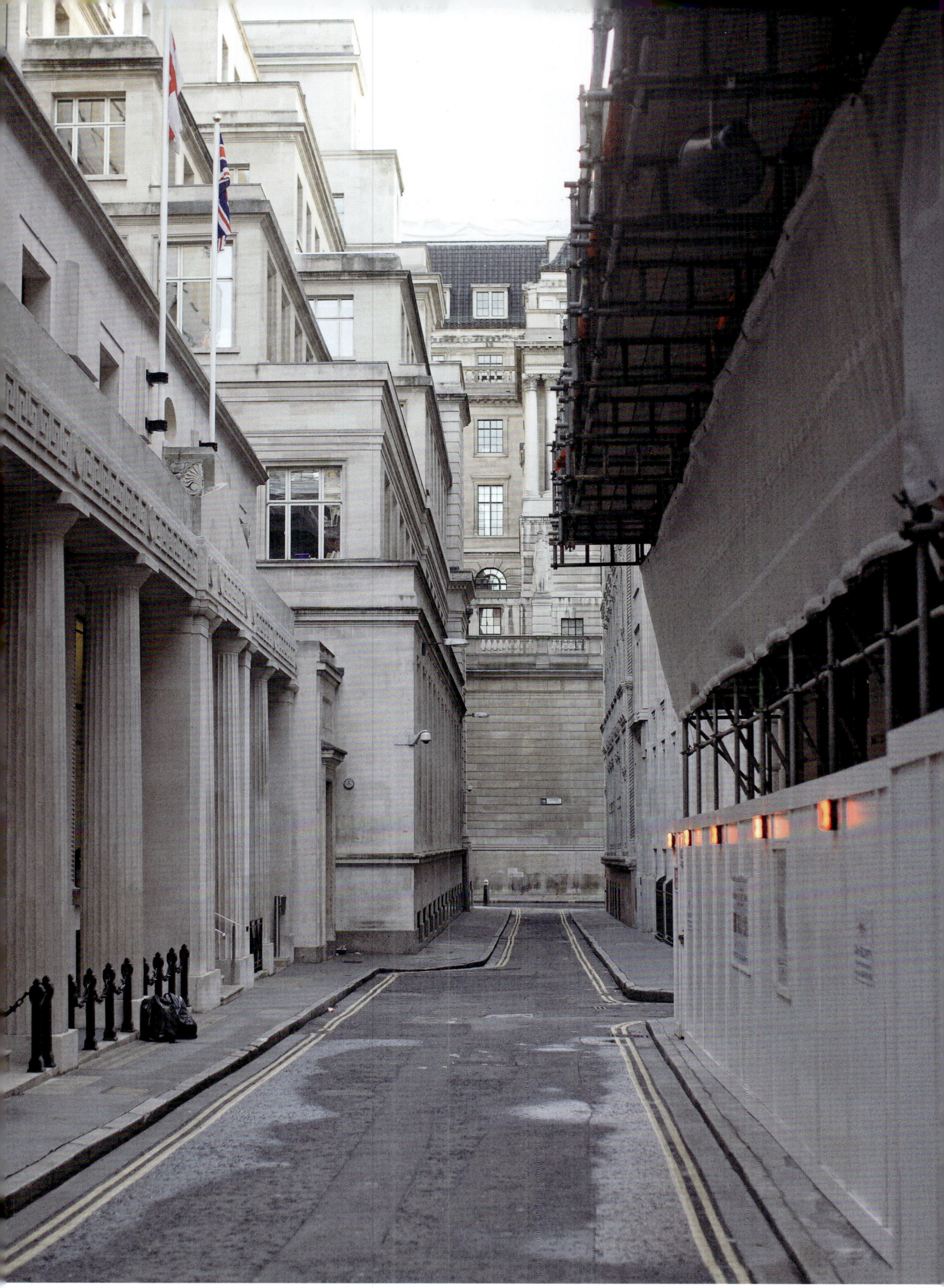

The sil – ver swan, who liv – ing had no ___ note, ——— When death ap – proached, un – locked her ___ si – lent throat;

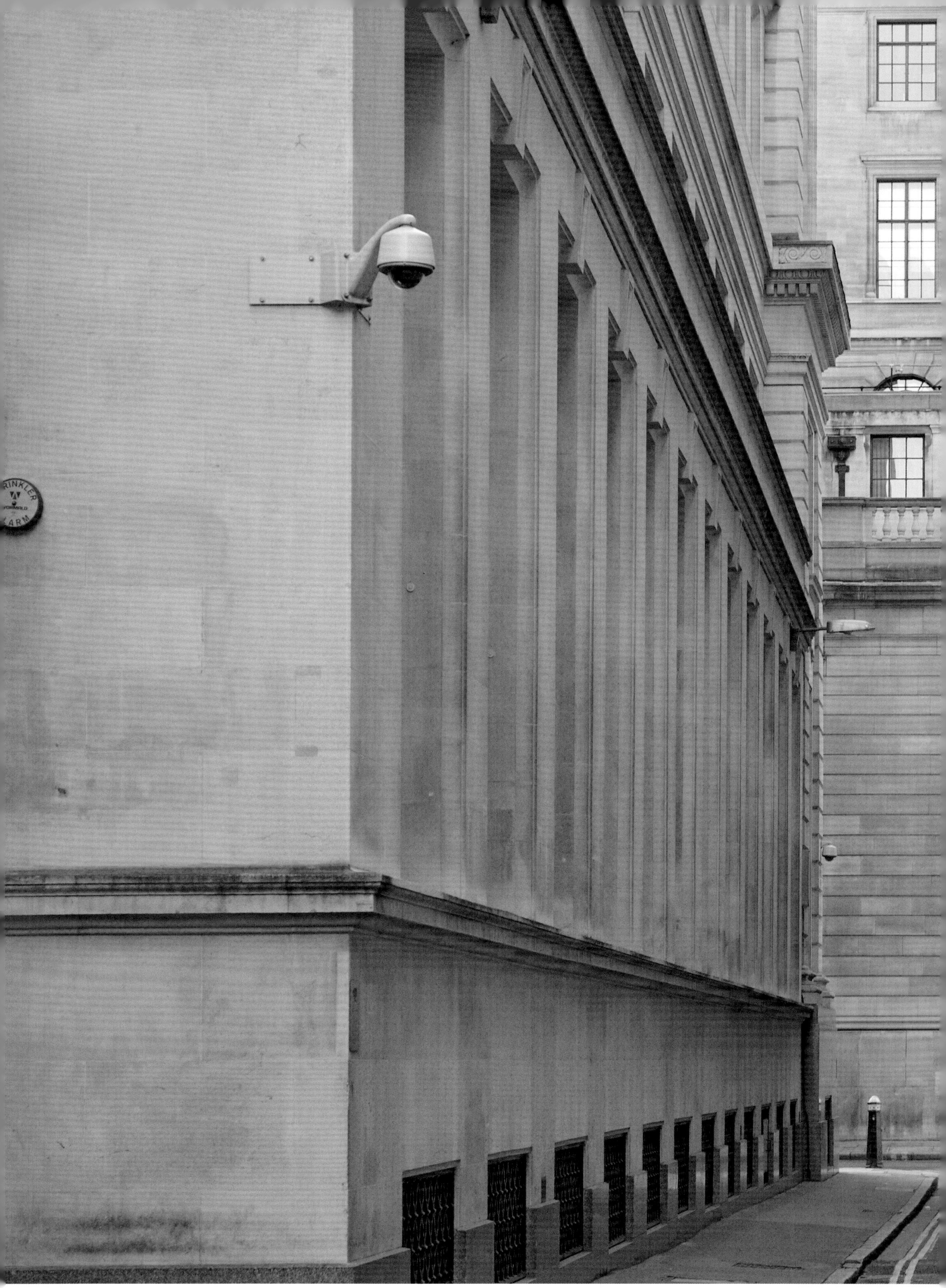

Lean–ing her breast up–on the reed ______y shore, thus sung her first and last, and sung no ______ more: Fare—

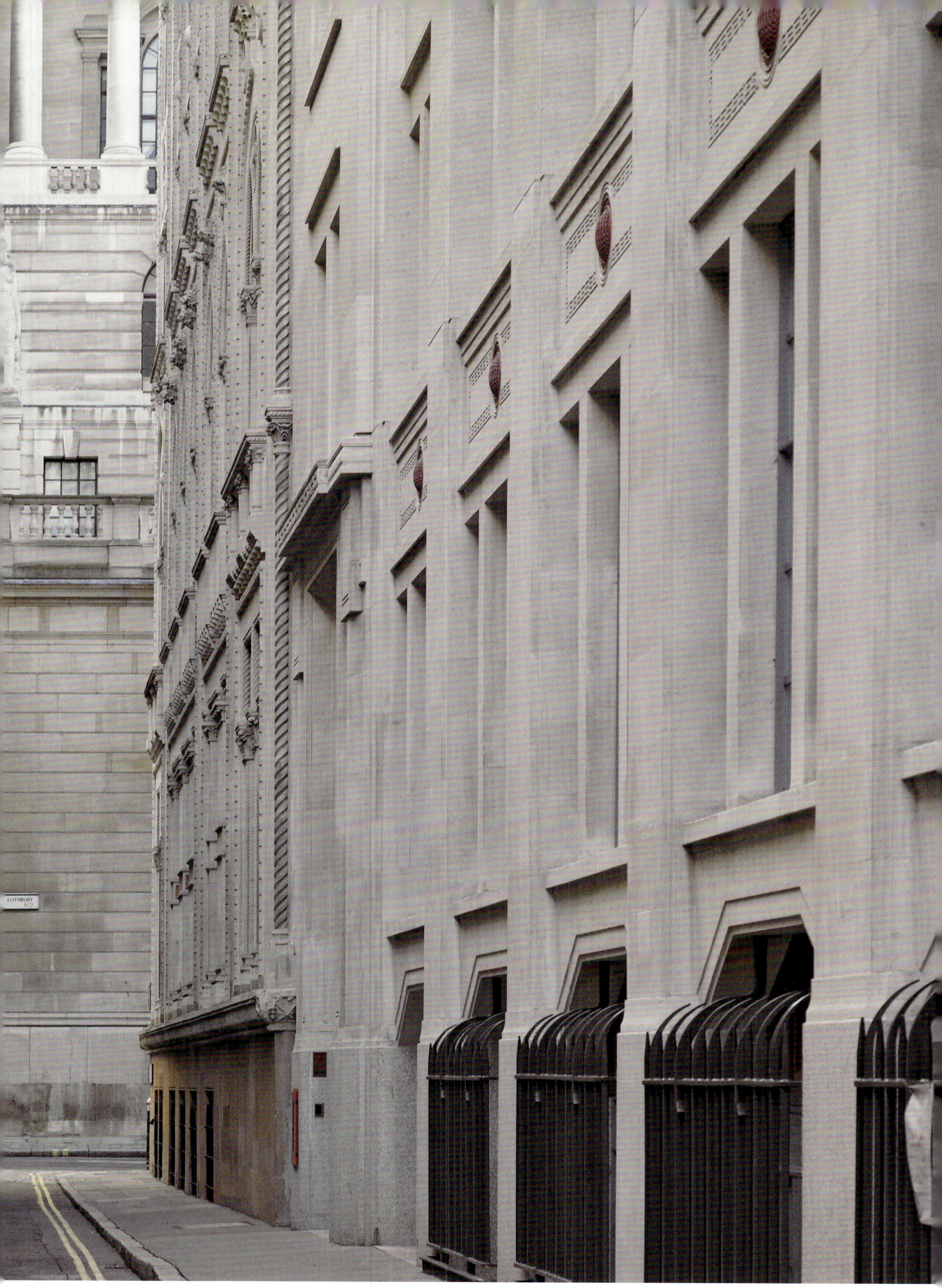

—we l, all joys! O—— Death, come close mine——eyes!——More geese than swans now live, mo-e fools than wise.

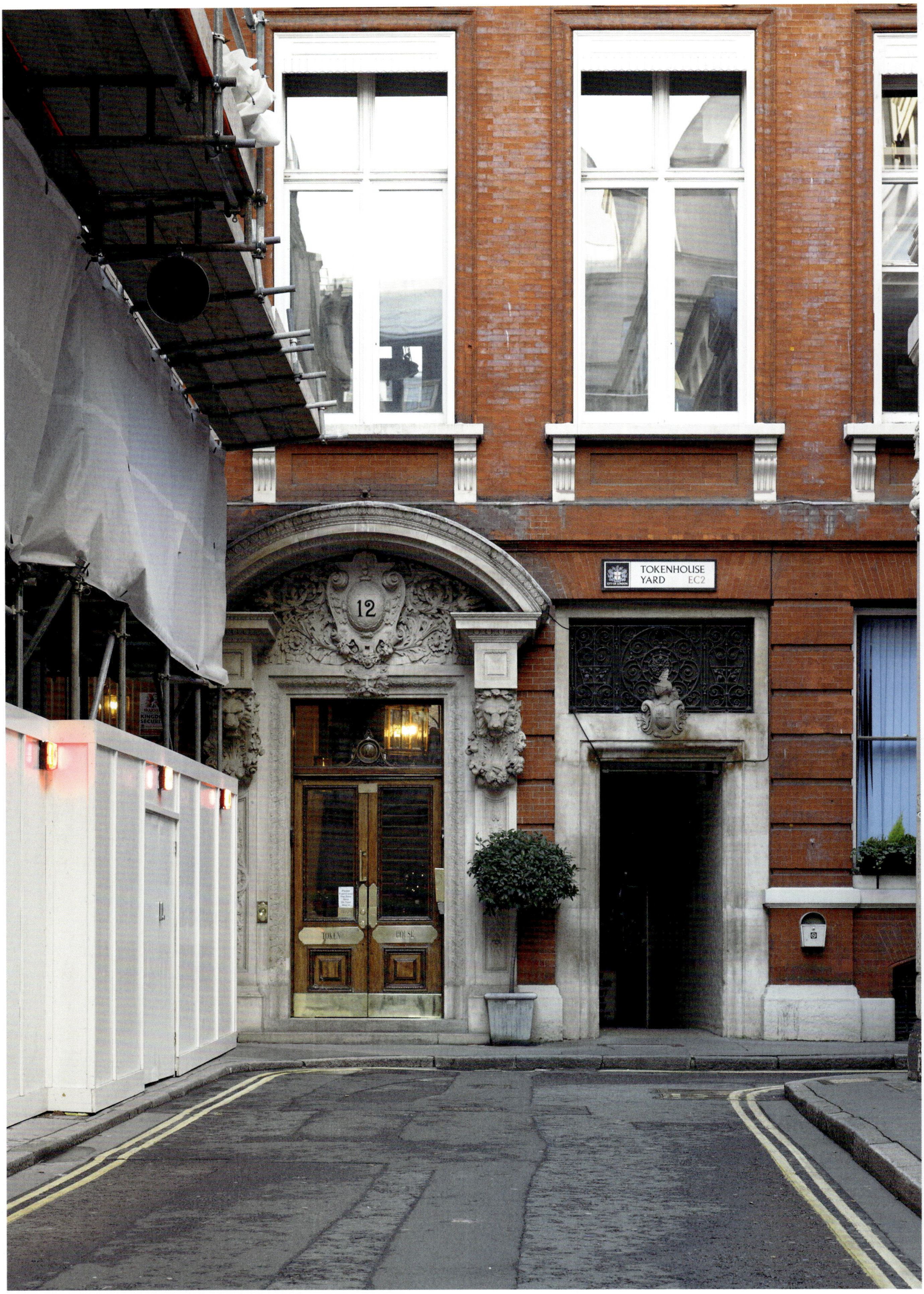
12
TOKENHOUSE
YARD EC2

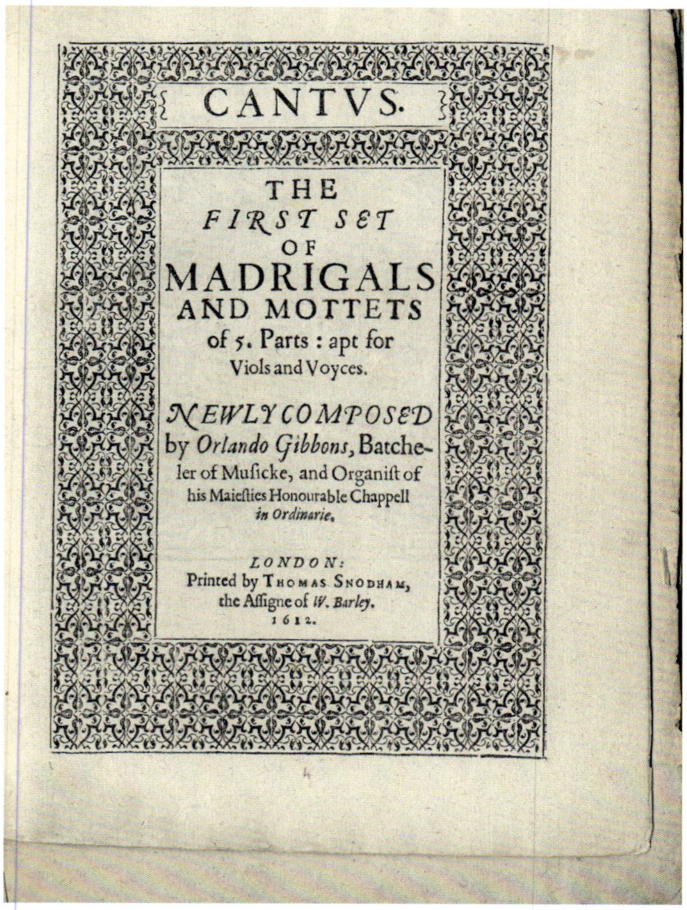
CANTVS.

THE
FIRST SET
OF
MADRIGALS
AND MOTTETS
of 5. Parts : apt for
Viols and Voyces.

NEWLY COMPOSED
by Orlando Gibbons, Batche-
ler of Musicke, and Organist of
his Maiesties Honourable Chappell
in Ordinarie.

LONDON:
Printed by THOMAS SNODHAM,
the Assigne of W. Barley.
1612.

Cantus title page, *Madrigals and Motettes*, Orlando Gibbons. London 1612. Courtesy: Folger Shakespeare Library.

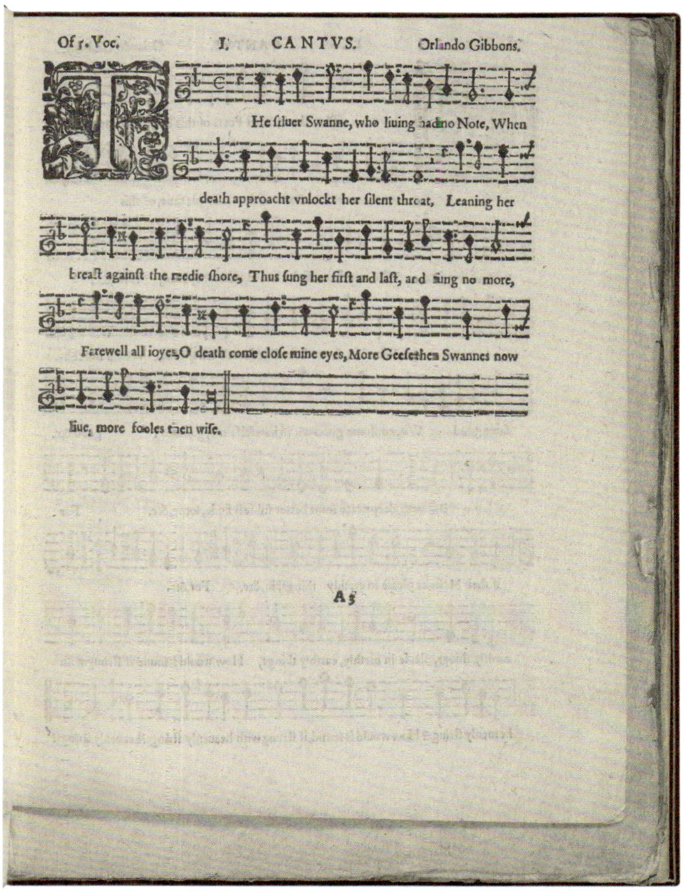

The Siluer Swanne, *Madrigals and Motettes*, Orlando Gibbons. London 1612. Courtesy: Folger Shakespeare Library.

A Journal of the Plague Year

'In my walks, I had many dismal scenes before my eyes, as particularly of persons falling dead in the streets, terrible shrieks and screeching of women, who in their agonies would throw open their chamber windows, and cry out in a dismal surprising manner. Passing through Tokenhouse Yard, in Lothbury, of a sudden a casement violently opened just over my head, and a woman gave three frightful screeches, and then cried, "Oh! death, death, death!" in a most inimitable tone, which struck me with horror, and a chilliness in my very blood. There was nobody to be seen in the whole street, neither did any other window open, for people had no curiosity now in any case, nor could anybody help one another'. Daniel Defoe, *A Journal of the Plague Year*, 1722.

Weep, O Mine Eyes

Moorfields Highwalk,
London, 2010.
Four-channel sound
installation. 1 minute
58 seconds.

The madrigal was said to be an attempt to imitate the sound of angels' voices, one voice replacing the other as breath was drawn, to convey the illusion of continuous singing. I recorded myself singing in turn the soprano, alto, tenor and bass parts of *Weep O Mine Eyes*, a madrigal written by John Bennet in homage to John Dowland's signature *Lachrimae*. The setting for this four-part madrigal is the elevated landscape of Moorfields Highwalk, a huge 1960s development of office buildings with open courts and connecting passageways. The area has a desolate feel, with empty office space and a derelict telephone exchange enclosing the open spaces. The rise and fall of the voices in the madrigal suggested an ocean of tears rising and falling on this concrete shore.

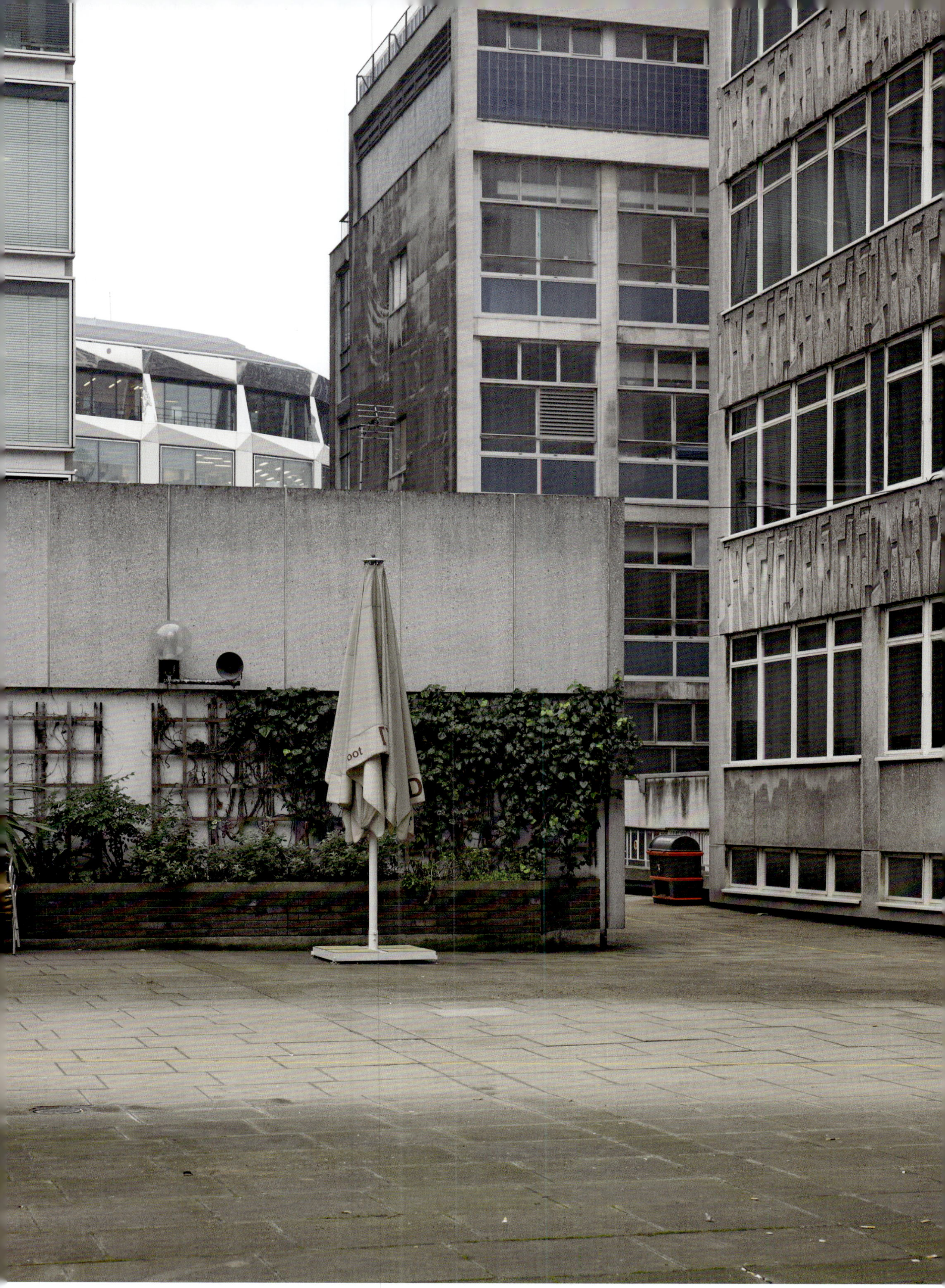

Weep, —— O mine eyes, —— weep,

Weep, —— O mine eyes, —— weep —— O mine eyes —— and —— cease ——

Weep, —— O mine eyes and —— cease —— not, —— weep —— O mine eyes and cease

Weep, —— O mine eyes, —— and —— cease —— not, weep, —— O —— mine

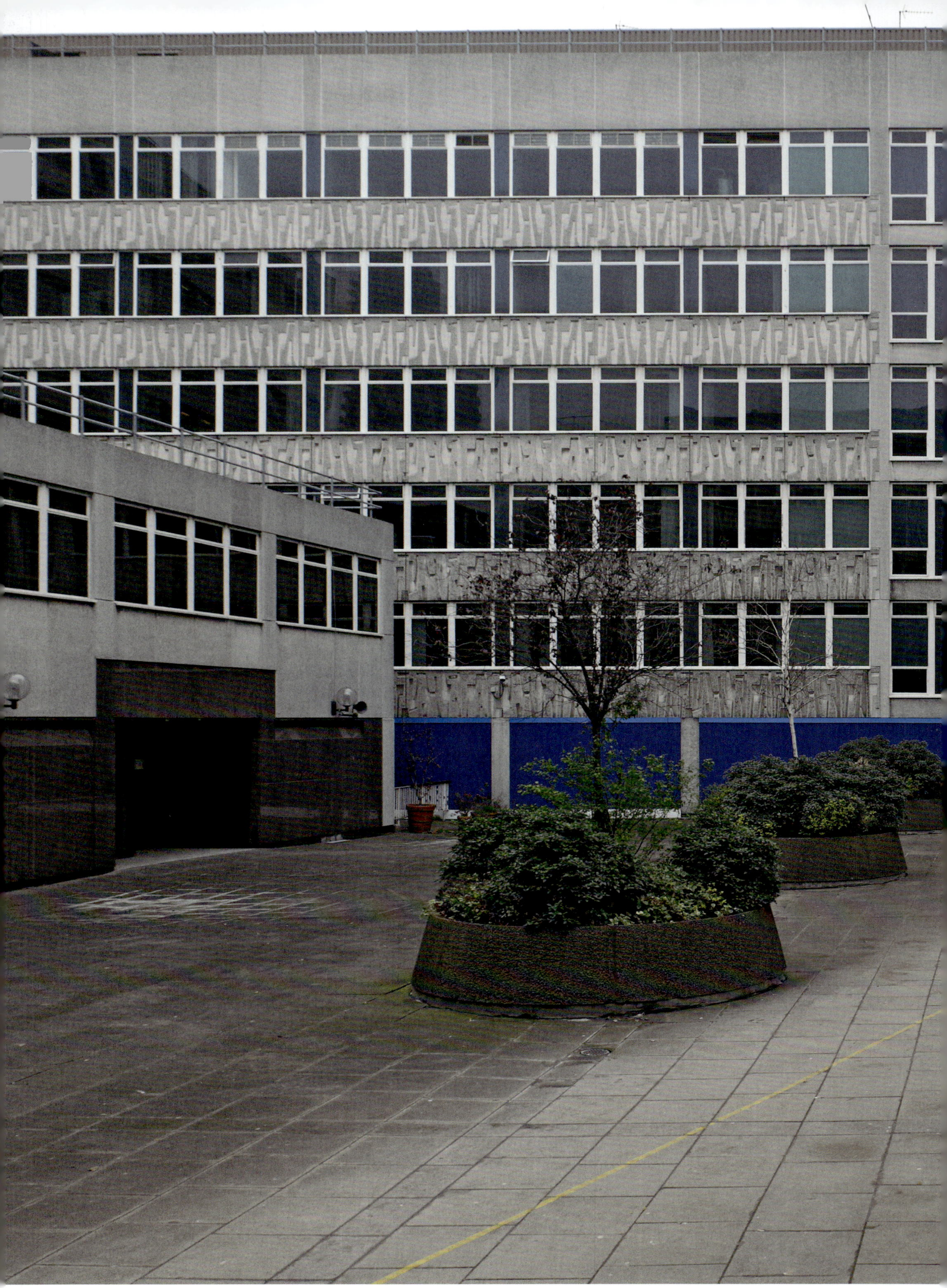

—O mine—eyes,—weep,—O mine eyes, and—cease—not,—

not,—and—cease—not,—weep,—O mine—eyes and cease—not,—

not,—weep—O mine eyes,—weep—O mine—eyes and—cease—not,—

eyes,—weep,—O—mine—eyes,—weep—and—cease—not,—

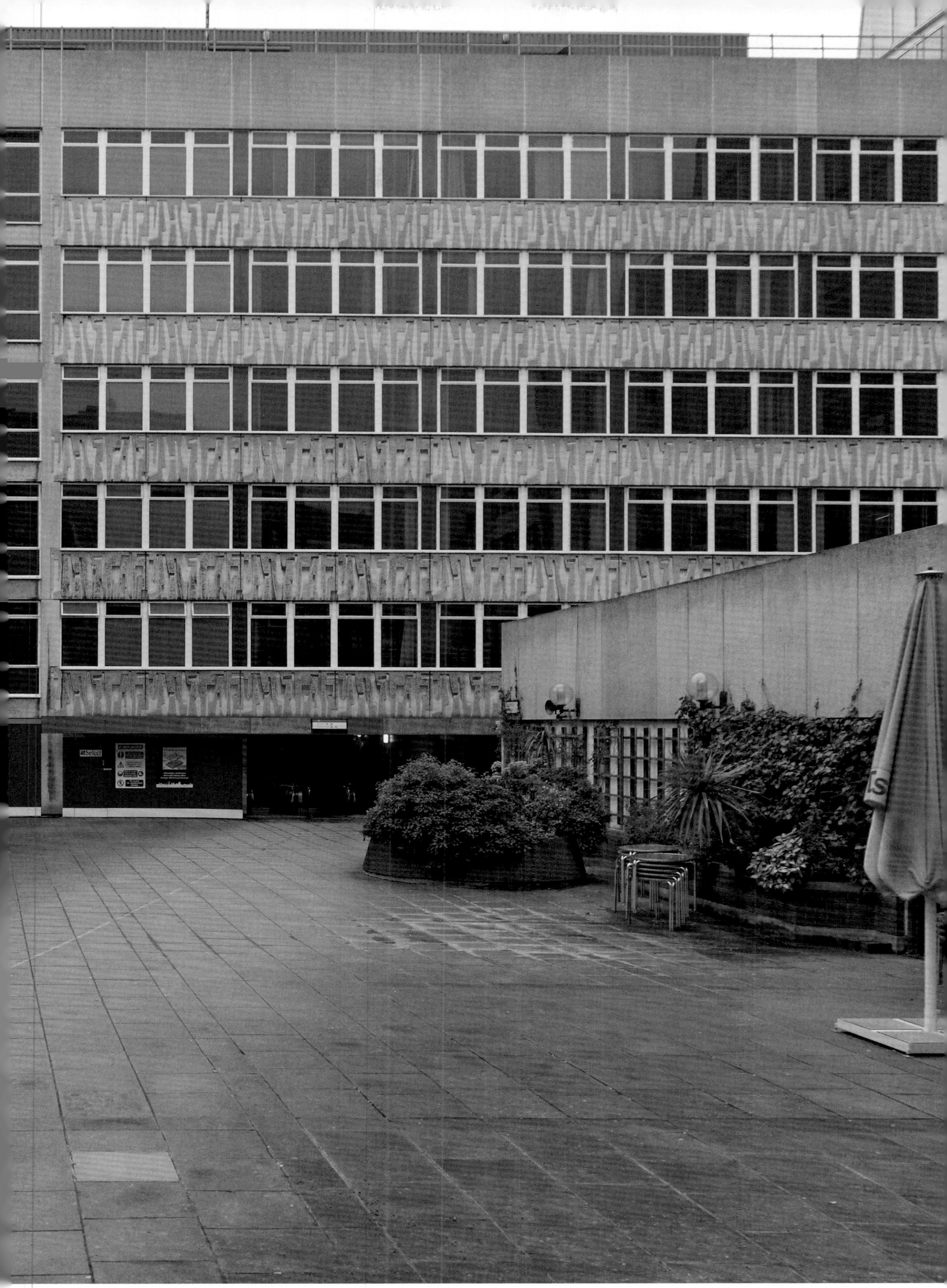

——————— A ———— las, ———— these your———— spring — tides ——————— a — las, your ——

– A ————— las, ———— these ———— your ————— spring — tices – a ——— las, ————— these your ——— spring

——————— A —— las, ———— these your —— spring ———— tides——————————— a ————— las ——

— and ——— cease — not, ——————————— A ———— las, ———— these your ———— spring —————

Barbican Redevelopment, 1959. Chamberlin, Powell & Bon (Architects), 1959. Source: London Metropolitan Archive.

Peter Chamberlin of Chamberlin, Powell and Bon with a model of the proposed Barbican redevelopment in the Guildhall, London, 1956. Courtesy: Keystone Press / ZUMAPress.com.

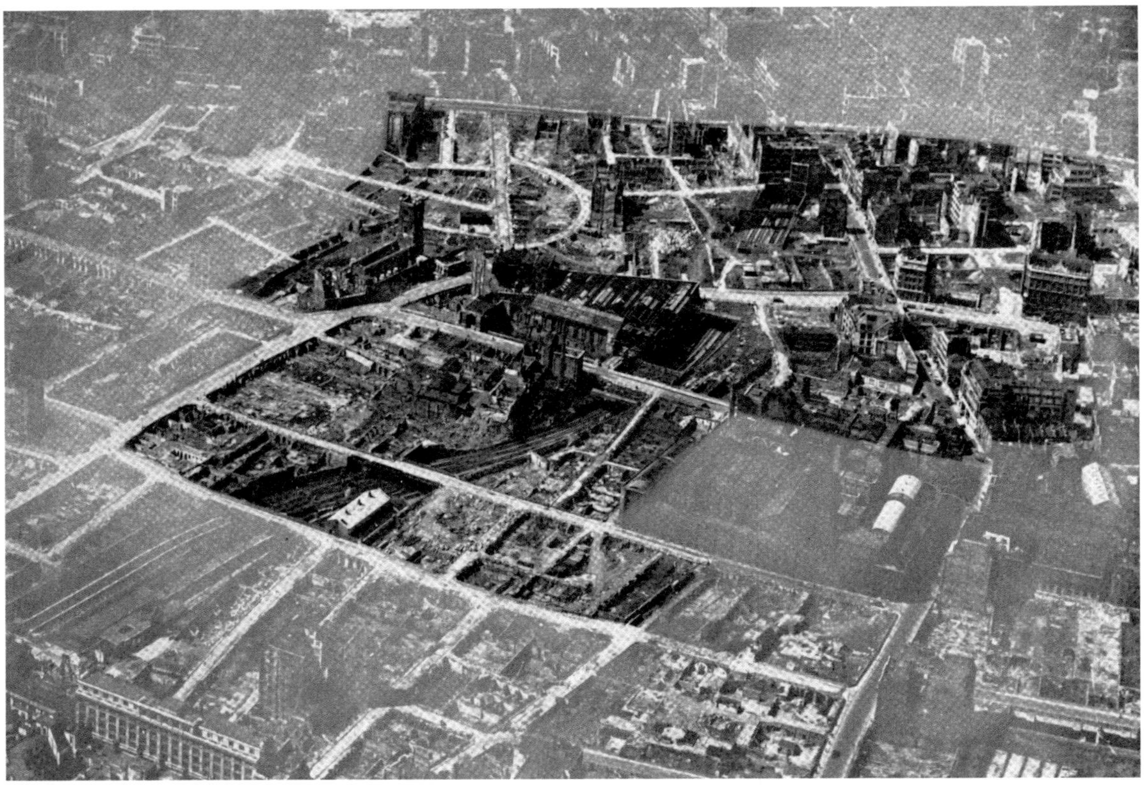

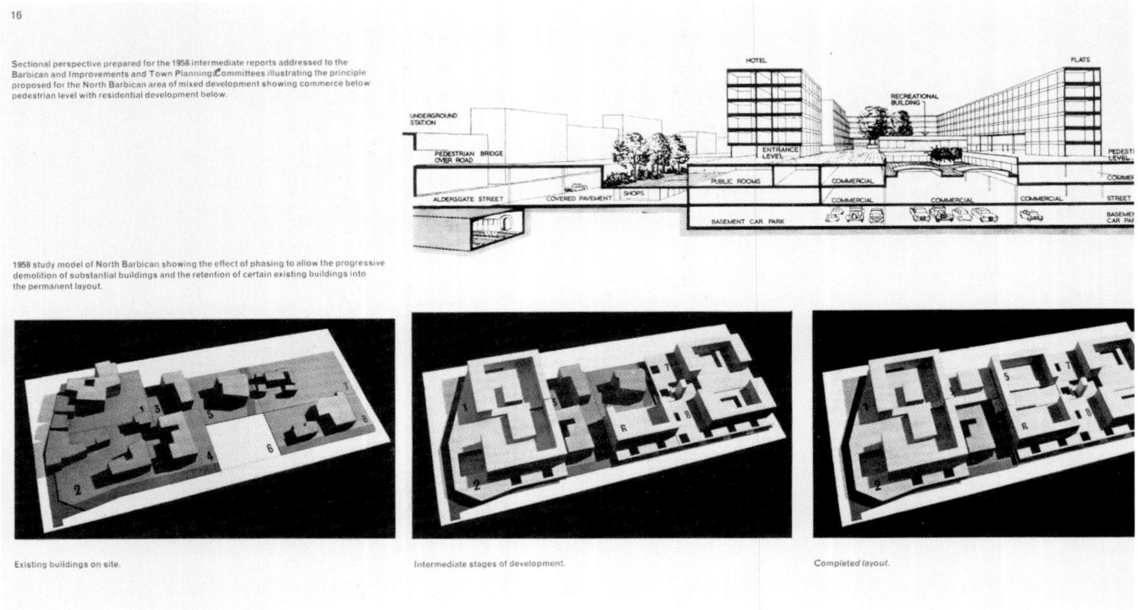
16

Sectional perspective prepared for the 1958 intermediate reports addressed to the Barbican and Improvements and Town Planning Committees illustrating the principle proposed for the North Barbican area of mixed development showing commerce below pedestrian level with residential development below.

1958 study model of North Barbican showing the effect of phasing to allow the progressive demolition of substantial buildings and the retention of certain existing buildings into the permanent layout.

Existing buildings on site.

Intermediate stages of development.

Completed layout.

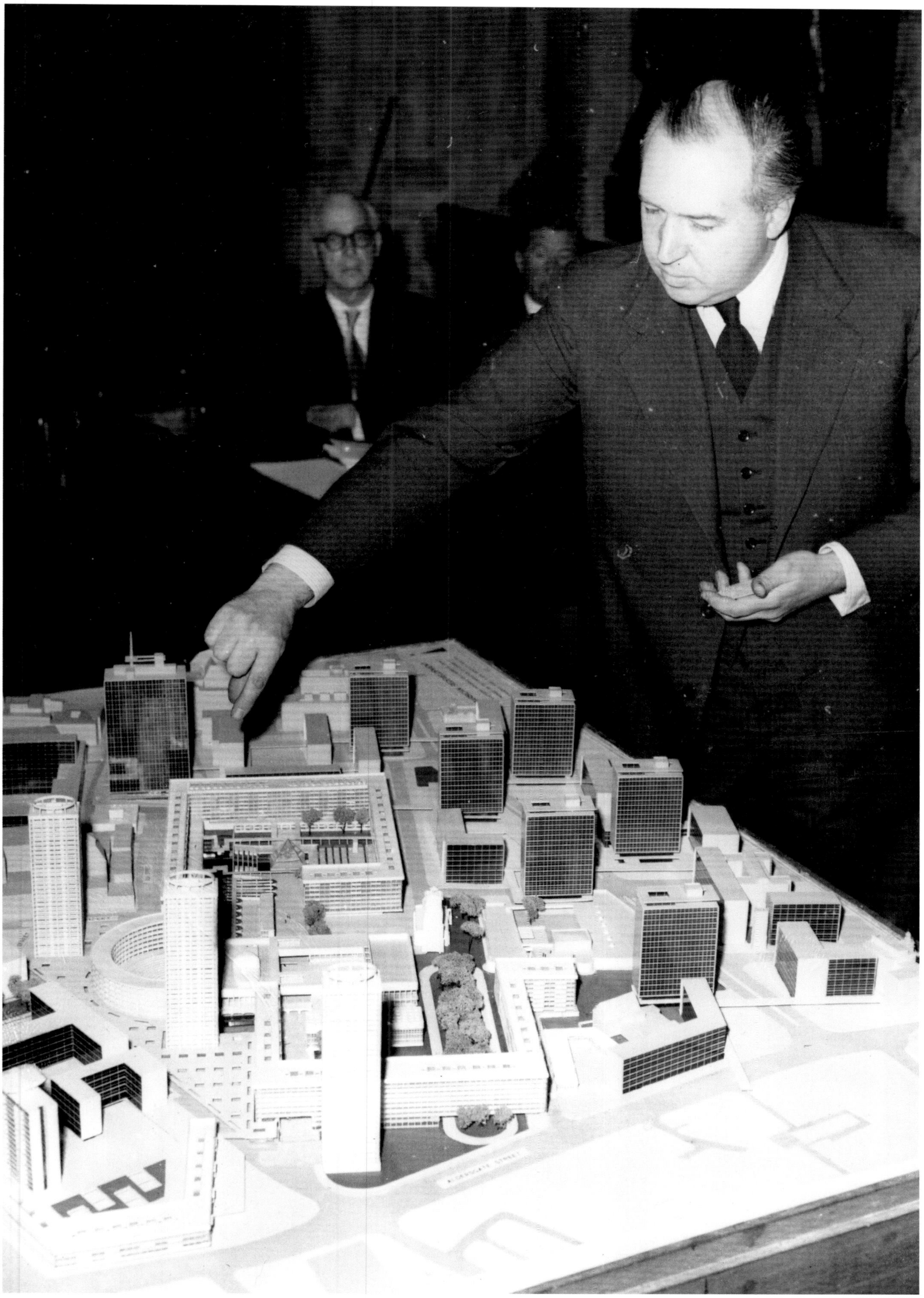

Venice in Concrete

'The intention underlying our design is to create a coherent residential precinct in which people can live both conveniently and with pleasure. Despite its high density the layout is spacious; the buildings and the space between them are composed in such a way as to create a clear sense of order without monotony. Uninterrupted by road traffic (which is kept separate from pedestrian circulation through and about the neighbourhood) a quiet precinct will be created in which people will be able to move about freely enjoying constantly changing perspectives of terraces, lawns, trees and flowers seen against the background of the new buildings or reflected in the ornamental lake. Chamberlin, Powell & Bon, Architects Barbican Redevelopment, 1959

Oh My Love

Mark Street / Star Alley,
London, 2010.
Four-channel sound
installation. 21 seconds.

Oh My Love, a simple round of unrequited love was scored by Thomas Ravenscroft for four voices to be performed in a seemingly endless loop. In the opening pages of *Deuteromelia*, 1609, Ravenscroft introduces a collection 'made truely Musicall with Art by my correction and yet plaine, and capable with ease, by my direction'. He also celebrates the songs simplicity. 'Now then the nature of these (call them as you will) in regard of their facilitie and so their capabilitie is more communicable, then any other kind of Musicke, and in this respect more commendable'. I thought this was a beautiful description and I recorded myself singing each part and the four parts played over and over again, echoing around the space.

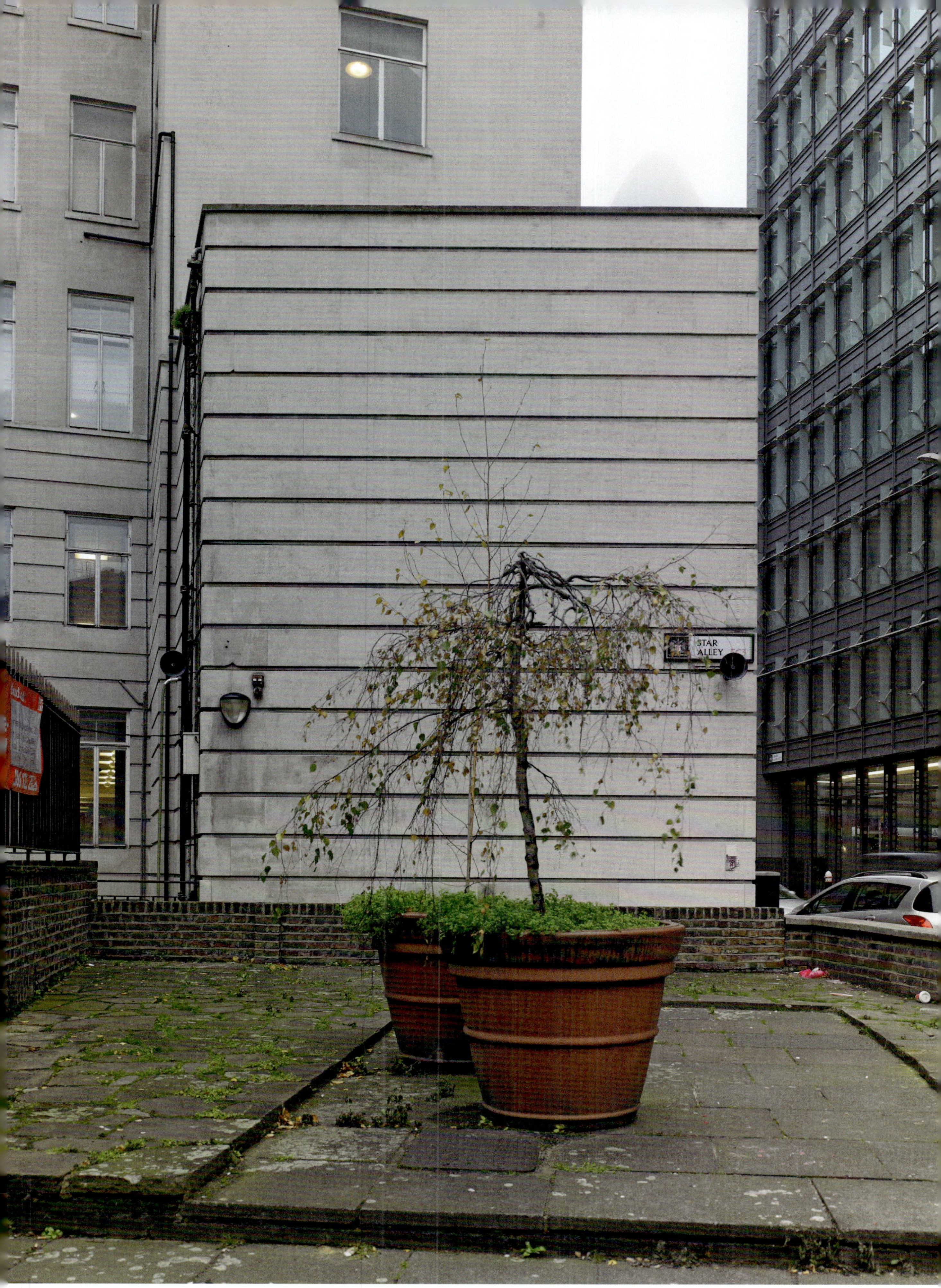

Oh My Love,——lov'st thou me?——then quick – ly come and save him——that——dies——for——thee

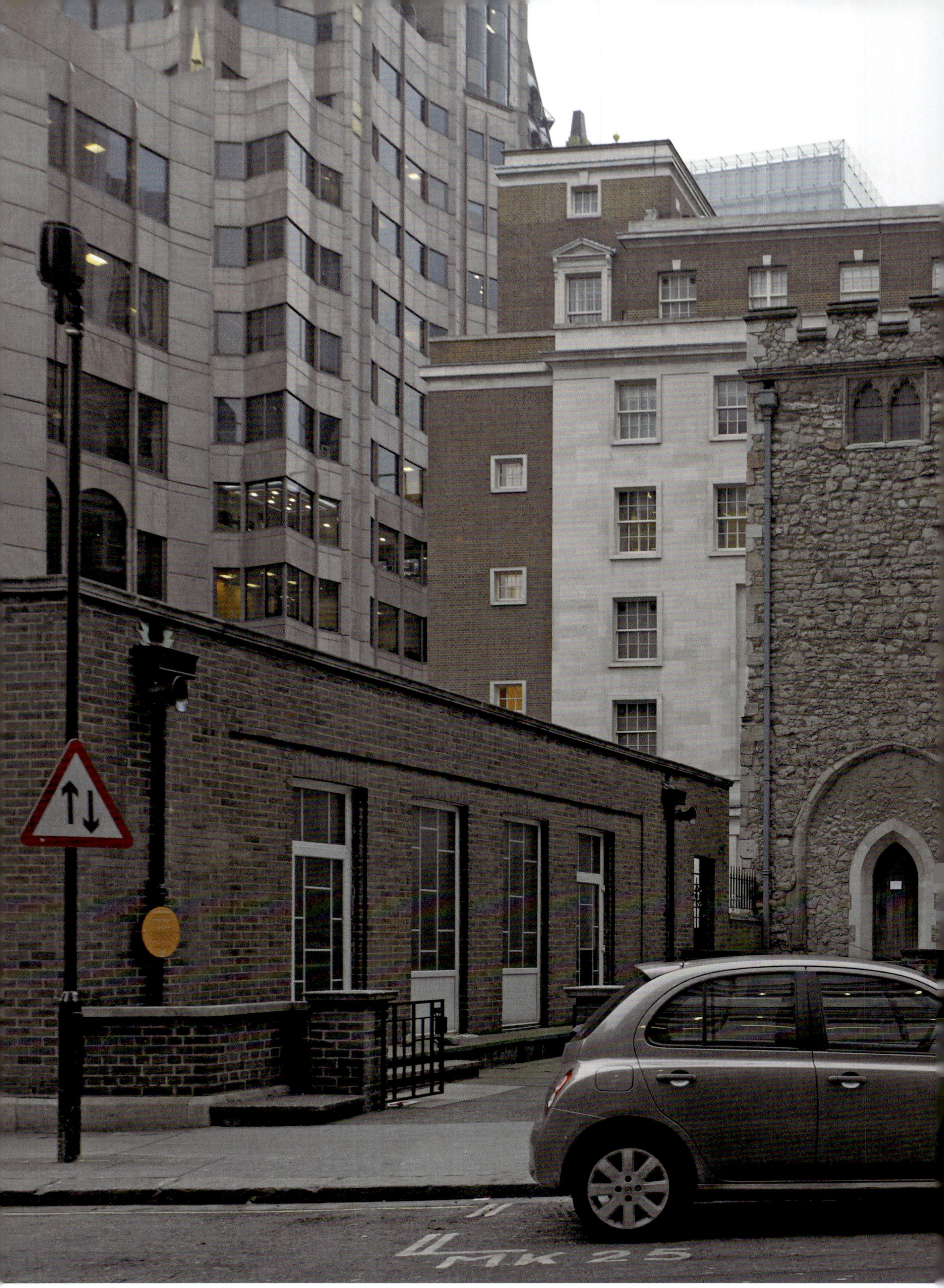

Oh My Love,—lov'st thou me?—then quick – ly come and save him that——dies—for——thee——

Oh My Love,——lov'st thou me?—then quick – ly come and save him—that——dies—for—

Oh My Love,——lov'st thou me?—then quick – ly come and save him—that—

Oh My Love,——lov'st thou me?—then quick – ly—come—

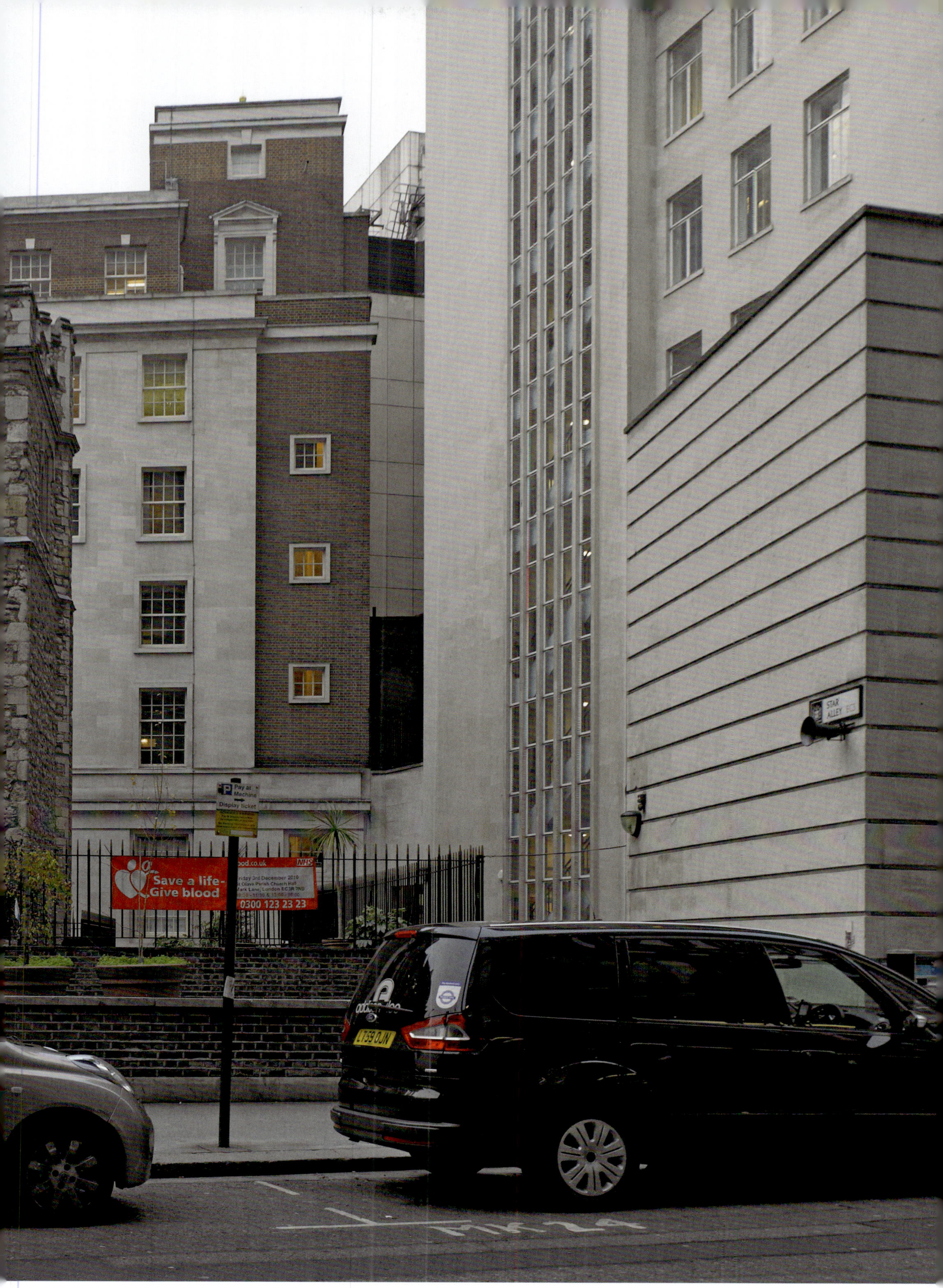

– Oh My Love, — lov'st thou me? — then quick – ly come and save him — that — dies — for — thee

– thee — Oh My Love, — lov'st thou me? — then quick – ly come and save him — that — dies

– dies — for — thee — Oh My Love, — lov'st thou me? — then quick – ly come and save — him

– him — that — dies for — thee — Oh My Love, — lov'st thou me? — then — quick – ly

Title page, *Deuteromelia*, Thomas Ravenscroft, 1609. Courtesy: The Royal College of Music, London.

Construction of the sixth Clothworkers' Hall looking west with the Tower of All Hallows Staining and the temporary church of St Olave, Hart Street in the right foreground. 1956. Photograph: E.J. Reed. Courtesy: The Clothworker's Company.

The remains of Clothworkers' Hall from Mark Lane with the Tower of All Hallows Staining in the right foreground, 1941. Photograph: Sydney W. Newbery. Source: The Clothworker's Company.

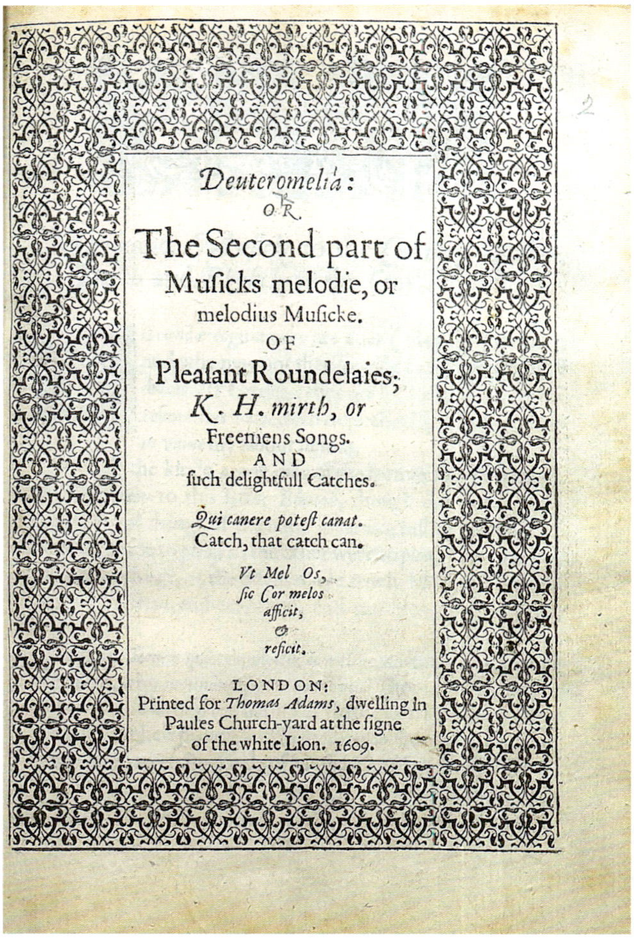

Deuteromelia:
OR
The Second part of
Muſicks melodie, or
melodius Muſicke.
OF
Pleaſant Roundelaies;
K. H. mirth, or
Freemens Songs.
AND
ſuch delightfull Catches.

Qui canere poteſt canat.
Catch, that catch can.

Vt Mel Os,
ſic Cor melos
afficit,
&
reficit.

LONDON:
Printed for *Thomas Adams*, dwelling in
Paules Church-yard at the ſigne
of the white Lion. 1609.

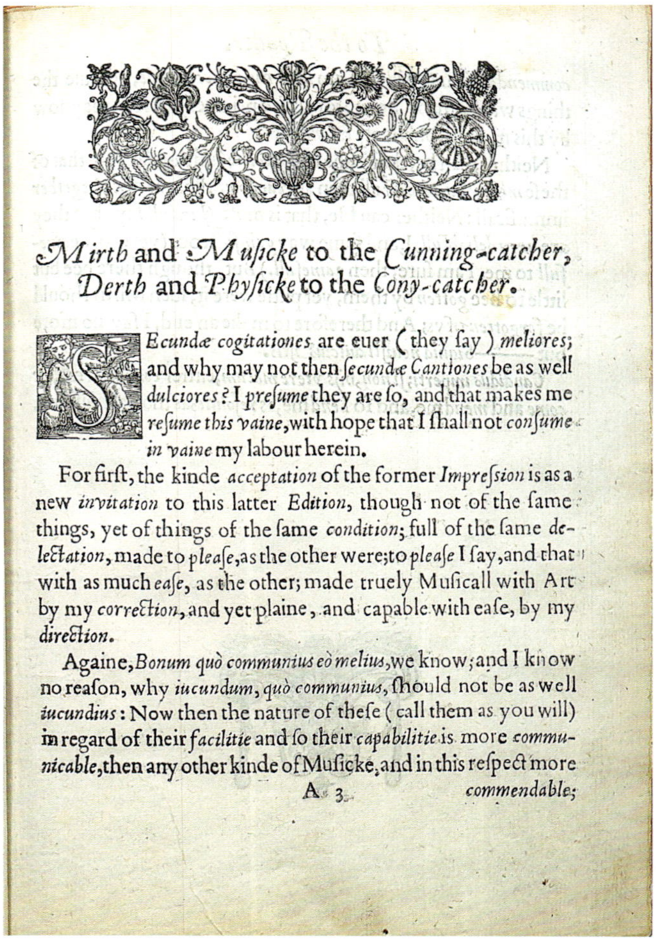

Mirth and *Muſicke* to the *Cunning-catcher*,
Derth and *Phyſicke* to the *Cony-catcher*.

S*Ecundæ cogitationes* are euer (they ſay) *meliores*; and why may not then *ſecundæ Cantiones* be as well *dulciores*? I *preſume* they are ſo, and that makes me *reſume this vaine*, with hope that I ſhall not *conſume in vaine* my labour herein.

For firſt, the kinde *acceptation* of the former *Impreſsion* is as a new *invitation* to this latter *Edition*, though not of the ſame things, yet of things of the ſame *condition*; full of the ſame *delectation*, made to *pleaſe*, as the other were; to *pleaſe* I ſay, and that with as much *eaſe*, as the other; made truely Muſicall with Art by my *correction*, and yet plaine, and capable with eaſe, by my *direction*.

Againe, *Bonum quò communius eò melius*, we know; and I know no reaſon, why *iucundum, quò communius*, ſhould not be as well *iucundius*: Now then the nature of theſe (call them as you will) in regard of their *facilitie* and ſo their *capabilitie* is more *communicable*, then any other kinde of Muſicke, and in this reſpect more
A 3 *commendable*;

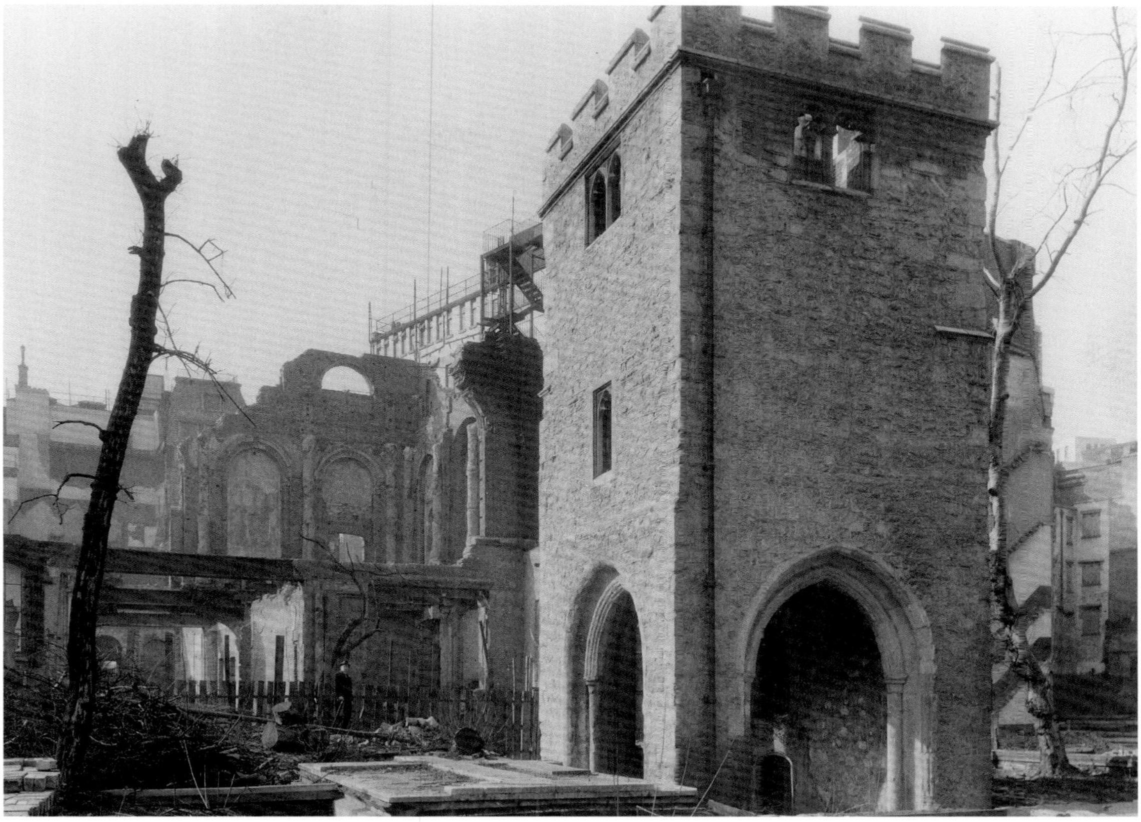

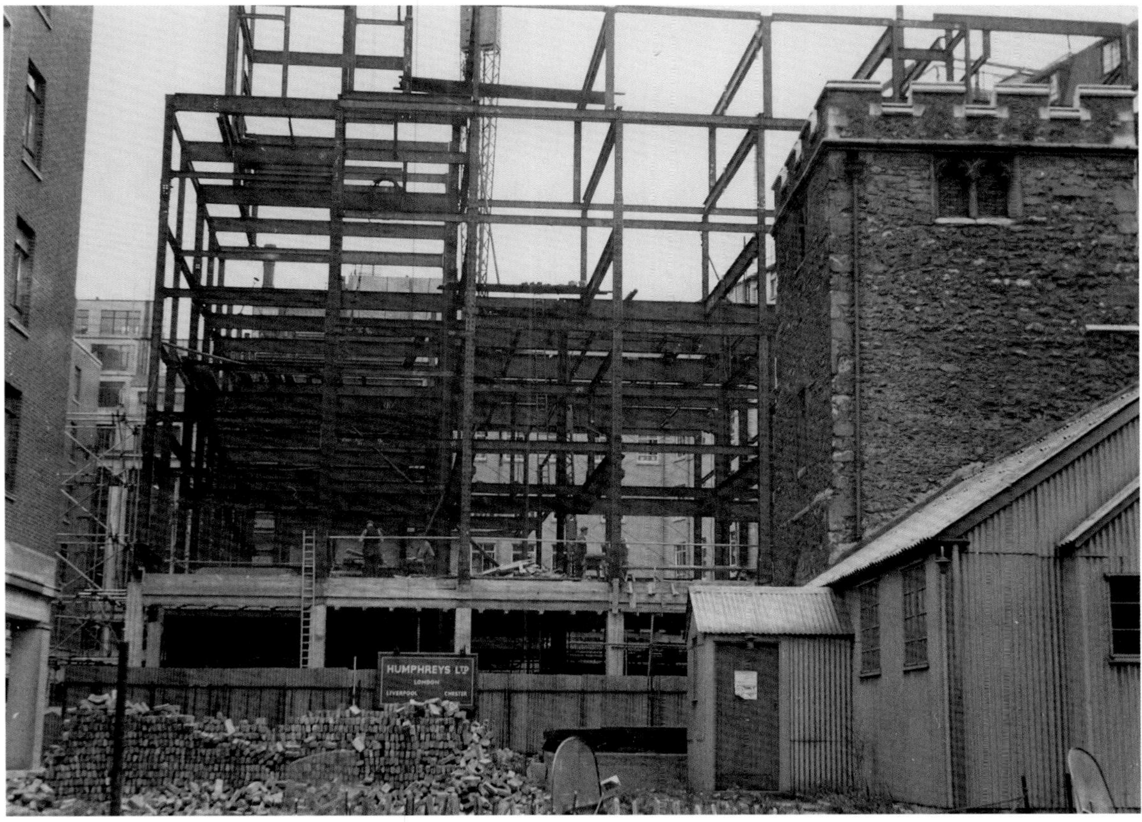

All Hallows Staining Church

The tower of All Hallows Staining Church, built in the 14th Century, stands as a remnant from a previous age, surrounded by more modern buildings. The tower has survived the Great Fire of 1666, bombing during the Second World War and, more importantly, it has survived successive waves of redevelopment over the years. These photographs show the area after a bombing raid, which destroyed the Clothworkers' Hall in 1941 and with a temporary church attached during the reconstruction of the Clothworkers' Hall in 1951. Seen alongside the Gherkin and the neo-Gothic architecture that engulfs it it reminds me of the layers of architecture and history in this part of the city.

Flow My Tears

London Bridge, London, 2010. Single-channel sound installation. 3 minutes 35 seconds.

I came to realise how important London Bridge was to the early modern city and to the cycle of works for the City of London. It enabled me to bring the river into *Surround Me*. The flow of water, which the river so powerfully evokes, is reflected in almost all the works around the City. The lyrics of John Dowland's song *Flow My Tears* resonate with the dark underside of the bridge and reflect a darker mood.

The River Thames is a notorious place for people to disappear. The lone voice was projected out across the water, and rebounded off the piers as if returning invisibly from the middle of the river. The work also rhymes with the instrumental *Lachrimae* to which it is intimately related and brings the song cycle around full circle.

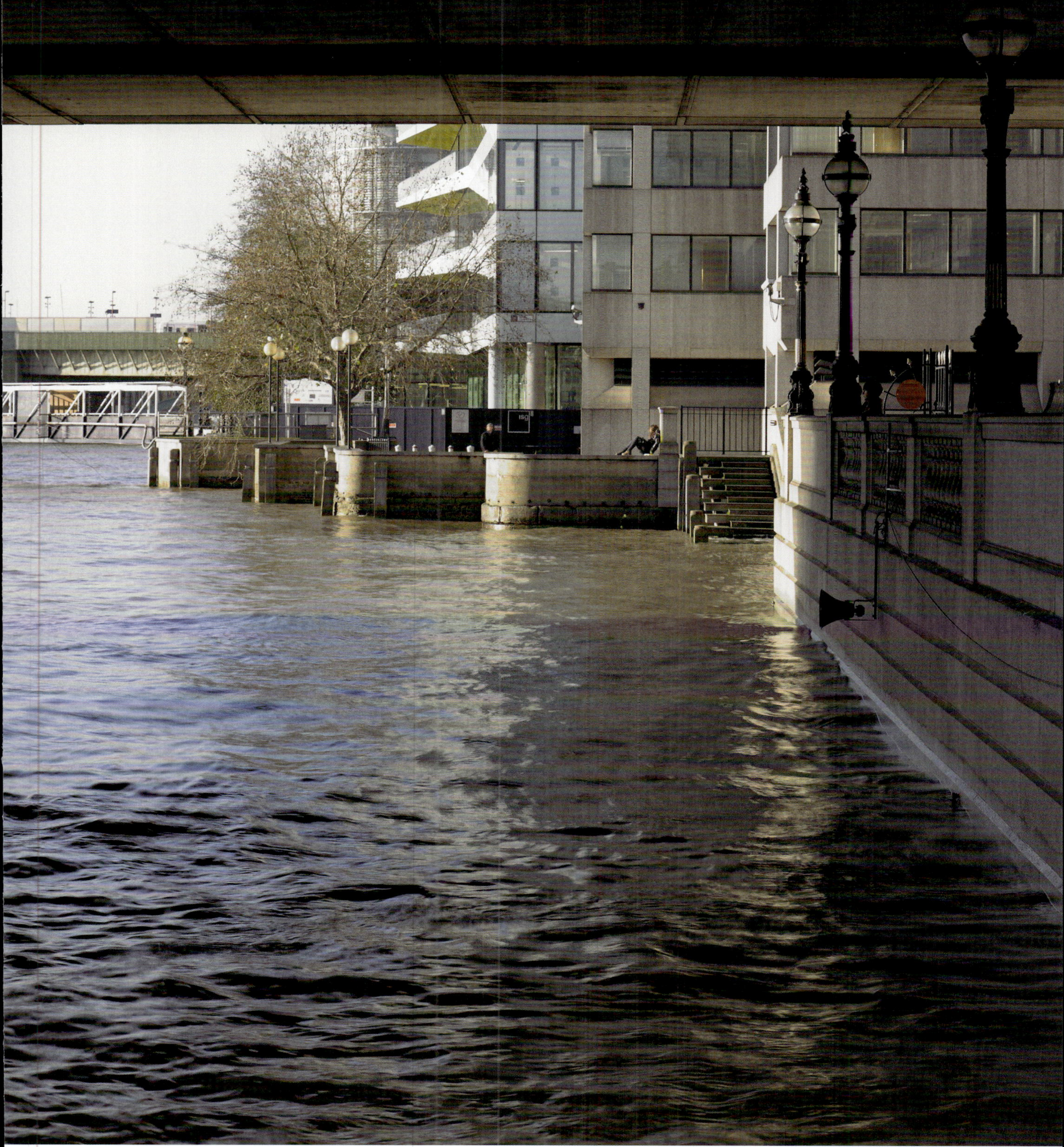

Flow, my ___ tears, fall ______ from your springs! ______ Ex – iled for ev – er, let me mourn; ____ Where night's black

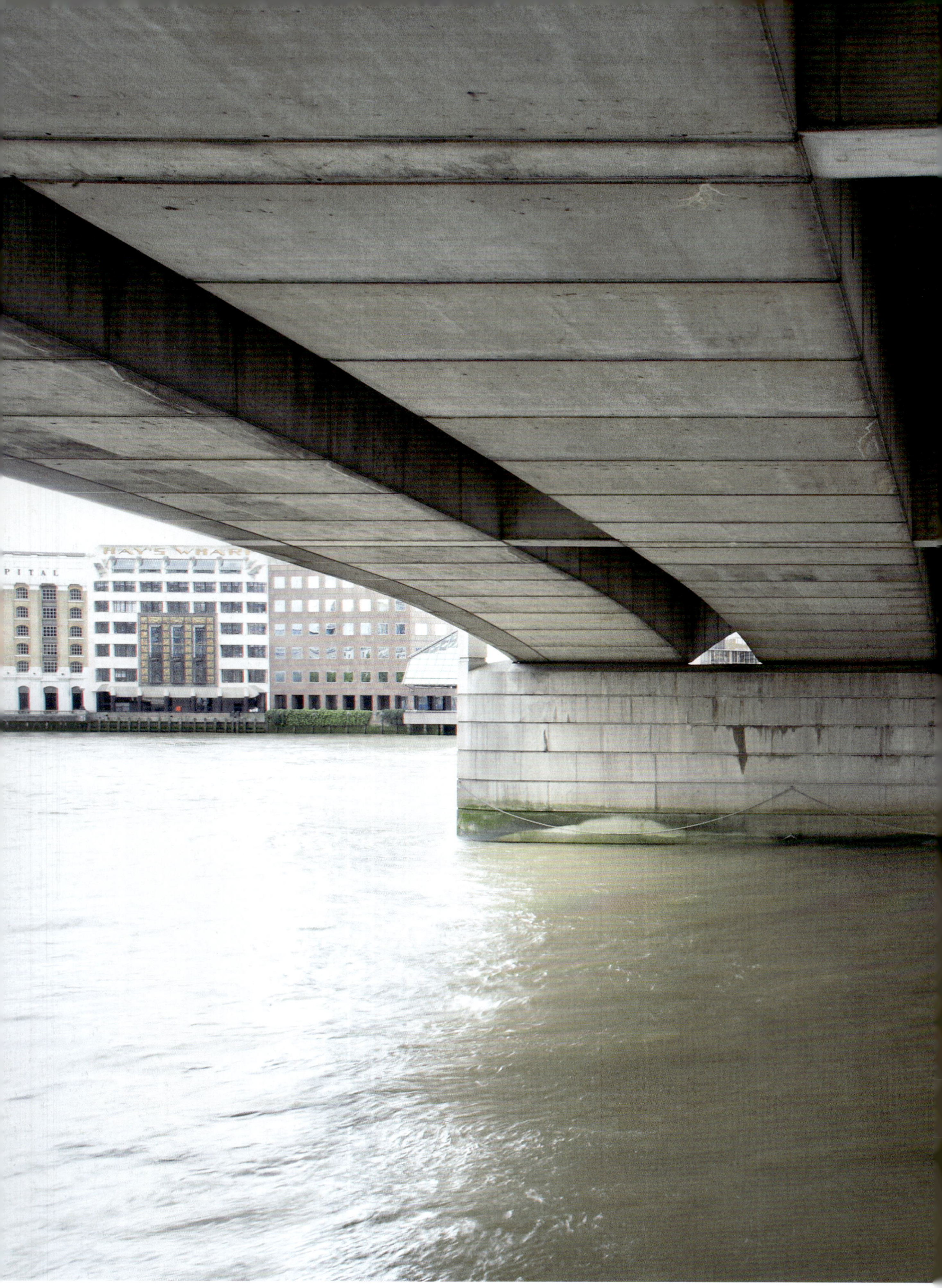

bird her sad in – fa – my sings——There let me live for – lorn.———Down vain——lights, shine———you no more!—

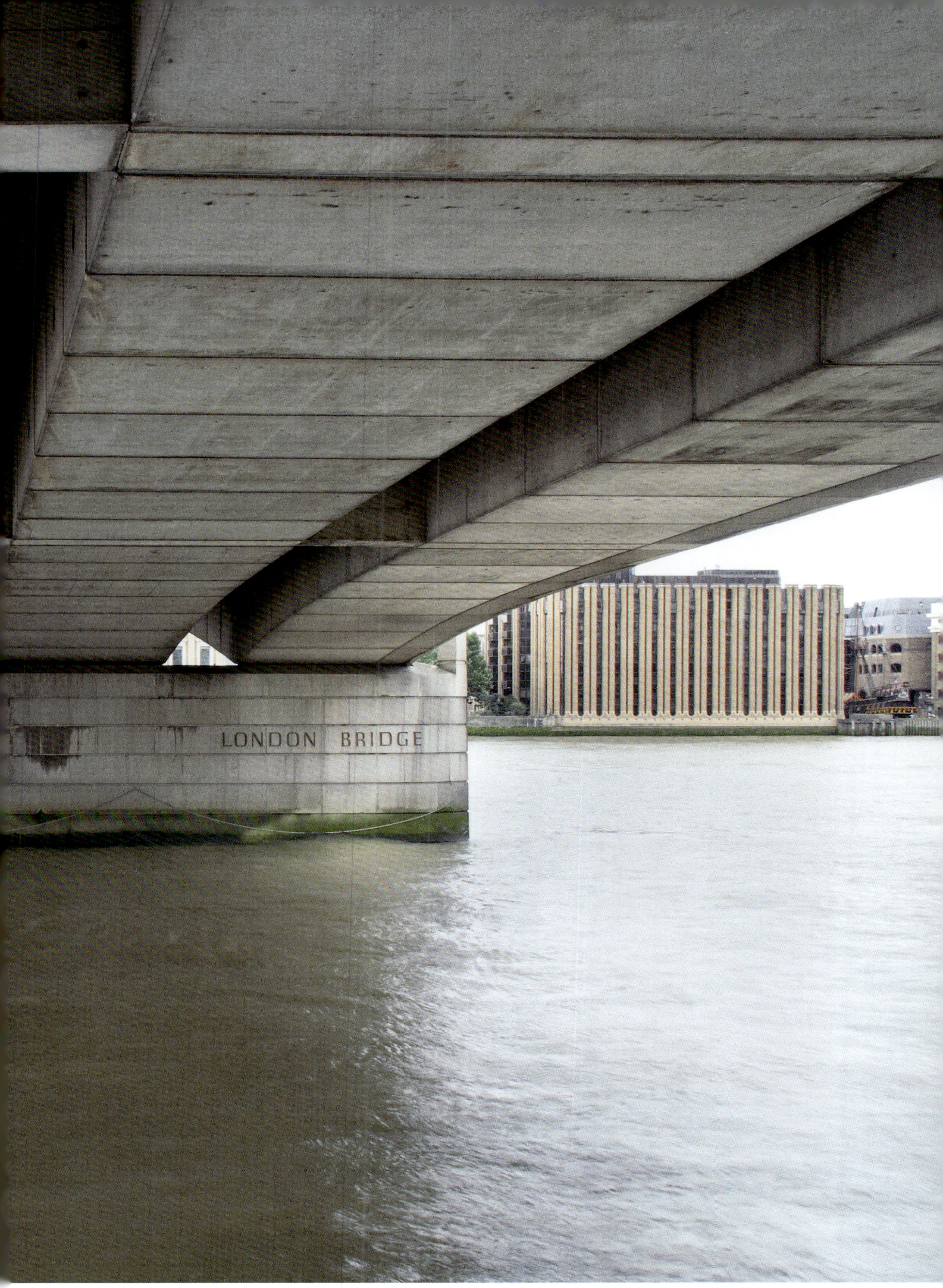

—No nights are dark ———— e – nough for those ———— That in de – spair their lost for – tunes de – plore

The view of London Bridge from East to West, John Norden, 1597. Courtesy: The Shakespeare Birthplace Trust, Stratford-upon-Avon.

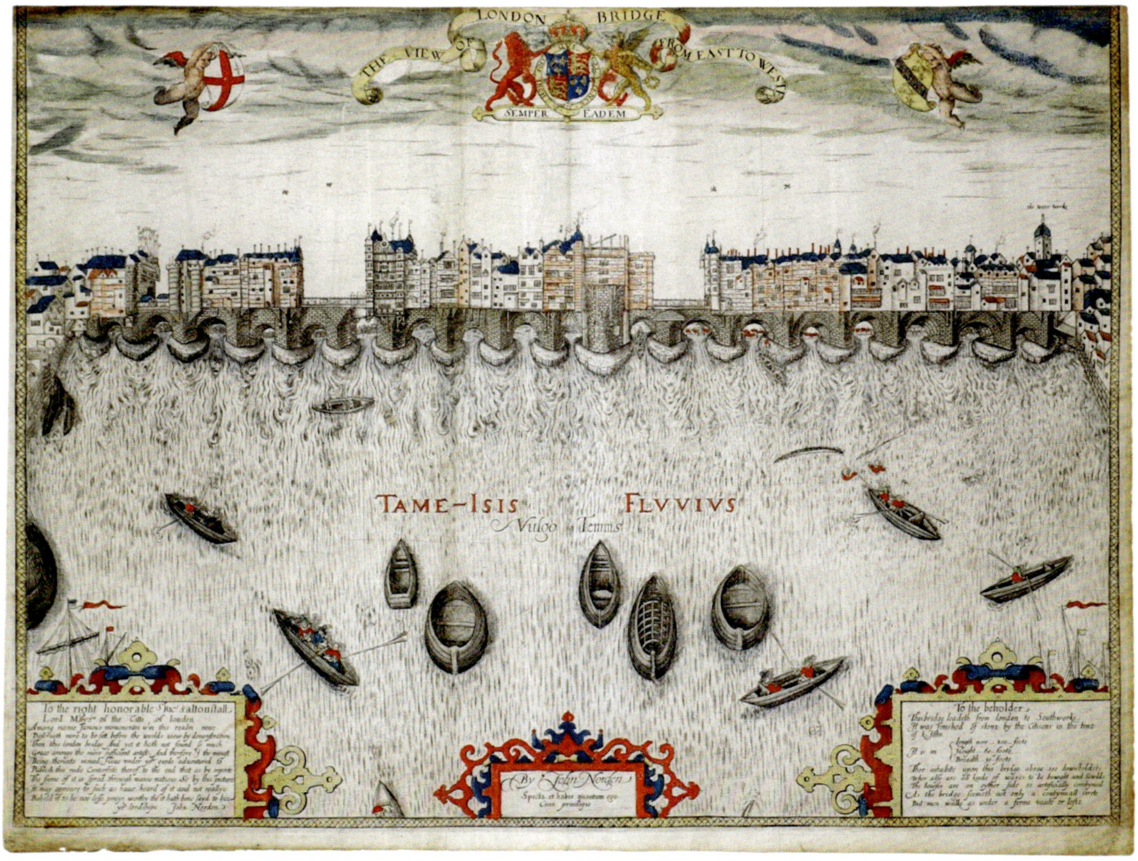

The Water Poet

'Braue London Bridge claimes right preheminence, / For strength and Architects magnificence / To be true None-such for no eye beheld / A bridge which it each way hath paralleld / The arches (Tame and Isis) shadie bowres / Through which both East and West in twice twelue houres, Twice Neptune greets it flowing from the Maine, / And twice the riuer fends it backe againe / And as the flouds or ebbes encrease or falls / They through the arches murmure Madrigals / Whilst th' Eddies divers wayes doth turne and trace / Tame doth with Isis dance the wilde goose chace.' John Taylor, *Taylor on Thame Isis* (John Haviland, London, 1632).

Civitas veri sive morum, Bartolommeo del Bene, 1609. Courtesy: Folger Shakespear Library, Washington.

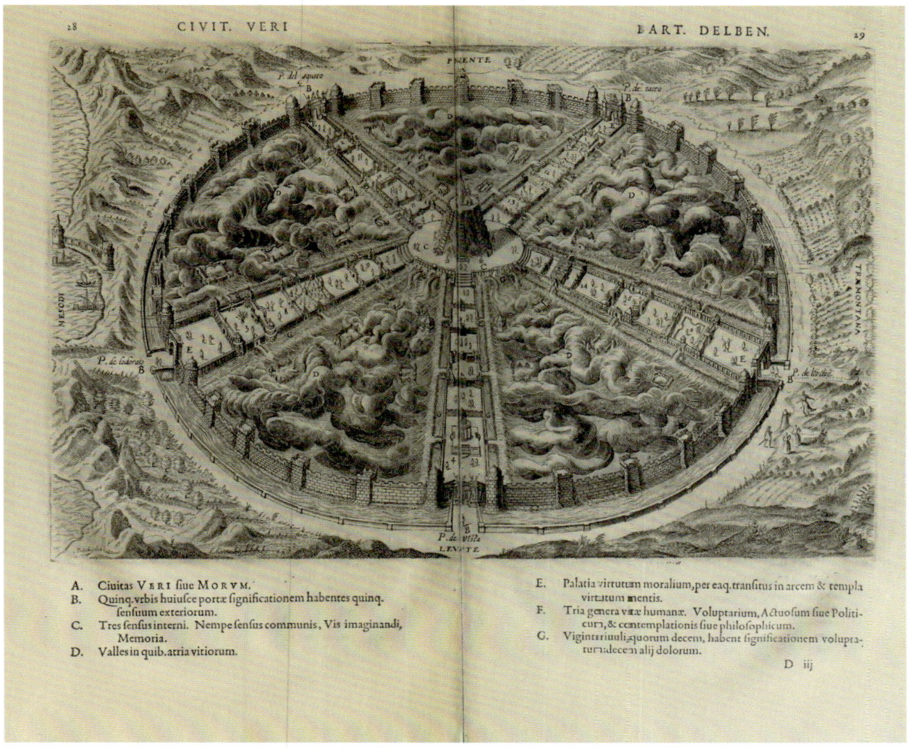

Civitas Veri

Classical and medieval thinkers sometimes give visual form to the functioning of the human mind by imagining it as a walled city—a city that is circular in shape. The topos is elaborated on an epic scale in Bartolomeo del Bene's philosophical poem *Civitas Veri sive Morum* (1609). Five gates in the city walls correspond to the five senses. The gate of hearing—creaking on copper hinges, adorned with musical instruments, presided over by Apollo and the Muses—stands to the right in del Bene's image, toward the north or tramontana, against the echo producing mountains that define the horizon of the Italian imagination. It is, in fact, through the gate of hearing that del Bene, his patron Queen Margaret of Savoie, and two of her ladies in waiting, along with the poem's reader, enter the city.

Surround Me

Steven Connor

Susan Philipsz sculpts in space, sound and time. This will only seem anomalous if we restrict sculpture to working with solid forms in space. But to sculpt is to carve out, engrave or scoop, and to shape, it has been suggested, may have as its root idea, as suggested by Dutch *scheppen* and Old High German *scephen*, to draw water, as in a scoop or ladle. So sculpture and the space it occupies, the solid and the hollow, the hard and the soft, are always in fact mingled in sculpture, which may be seen therefore as a meditation on the nature of the solid. Susan Philipsz's sculptures, formed out of what the 16th Century called 'airs', sing out this solidarity of the soft and the hard.

For her song-cycle *Surround Me*, which was in place from 9th October 2010 to 2nd January 2011, Susan Philipsz installed in six locations in the City of London recordings of herself singing English madrigals from the late 16th and the early 17th centuries. The work was mined with ellipsis and hiatus. Her voice, even when overdubbed, is so plain and piping, with all passion, dynamism or expressive intensity muted, that each harmonic line seemed to hold itself chastely apart from the others, making the intervals between them almost palpable. Intimate with distance, her voice seems always to stand slightly to the side of the song it is singing. It may be said to be disem-bodied in two, cooperating ways. First, it has no visible source; the loudspeakers which project the sound being placed so unobtrusively as not to be noticeable until the recordings start up. Secondly, the voice itself seems to be spectrally lacking in body, and almost to be appealing to the listener to supply in their audition the substance that would confirm its being. The largest of all the locations in *Surround Me*, was the square on Moorfields Highwalk, which left the listener free to move around as John Bennet's *Weep, O Mine Eyes* spilled out from four separate speakers, but also exposed one to dips and declivities in the sound texture, emphasising the articulation of volume and emptiness of which the piece is composed.

Visitors were encouraged to visit all six locations, which were arranged in a very rough circle around the Bank of England. To move between them recalled the ancient practice of Beating the Bounds, in which, at Rogationtide, members of a parish would process round its outer limits, singing and dancing, in what the historian of early modern sound culture, Bruce R. Smith, has called a 'choroloquy', or singing of place.[1] In fact, the word *choir* already intimates this link between singing and the setting in which it occurs — Greek χώρα (*chora*) means place, or landscape. The beating of the bounds is an attempt to assert the physical existence and continuity of a territory, though, inevitably, as one made one's way from one song-site to another in *Surround Me*, intervals interposed during which the memory of the song heard in one location would slowly decay, until revived by the song heard on arrival at the new location. But hesitation and holding back persisted even at the locations themselves. Sometimes one would be alerted that the spot was nearby by hearing the faint, fluting notes of Susan Philipsz's voice, eroded by echo, only to find that the air had finished before one arrived, so that there would be another expectant pause before it came round again. One of the madrigals, Orlando Gibbons's *The Silent Swan*, alludes in its opening lines to this emergence of sound from a silence suddenly disclosed as such by being broken: 'The silver swan, who living had no note, / When death approached, unlocked her silent throat'. Thomas Ravenscroft, the Elizabethan composer of many rounds and catches, two of which are featured in *Surround Me*, wrote that 'the perfection of Time (as growing out of Circular motion) is exprest by a Round Circle', but these gaps and suspensions in Susan Philipsz's work ensure that time never fully rounds out into this consummation.[2] The composer Thomas Morley observed in 1597 that achieving balance and reciprocity in six-part madrigals required a complex coordination of singing and refraining: 'in these compositions of sixe parts, you must haue an especiall care of causing your parts giue place one to another, which you cannot do without restings, nor can you (as you shall knowe more at large anon) cause them rest till they haue expressed that part of the dittying which they haue begun'.[2]

The origin of the word *madrigal* is not entirely clear, but it seems to indicate something matrical, that is, primary or original. A matrix is a womb, and, by extension, any enclosing or surrounding structure, or environment, especially one that provides a source or beginning (matriculation comes at the beginning of an academic career). A matrix can also signify a cement which binds together a more amorphous aggregate, as well as the mass or matter in which a jewel may be embedded. The matrix is primary, but, because of this, it is also copious, for it can be a source of replication, as, for example, in the mould from which type may be cast, or an original gramophone disc, from which innumerable copies may be printed off. So, in the madrigal, we have a conjuncture of elements that signify mass, materiality and also maternity, especially in the sense of that which encloses or surrounds. As a matrix, a madrigal is already a choir; both are settings—a musical as well as a topographic word. Once we know that a madrigal itself means an environment or surrounding, a musical setting in which things may take shape, the title of Susan Philipsz's piece, *Surround Me*, seems like a reprise or recycling of the very elements that comprise it.

More recently, the word matrix has come to signify, not a formless mass, but a lattice or grid of possibilities, a general array of elements from which a particular form may be drawn out. One may say that the matrix is a virtual form, which holds together in suspension parallel possibilities. This idea too seems to be anticipated in the ways in which madrigals were conceived, as the intricate weaving together of musical and emotive variations. As Thomas Morley explained:

'the more varietie of points bee shewed in one song, the more is the *Madrigal* esteemed, and withall you must bring in fine bindinges and strange closes according as the words of your Dittie shal moue you... the parts of a Madrigal either of fiue or sixe parts go somtimes full, sometimes very single, sometimes iumping together, and somtime quite contrarie waies, like vnto the passion which they expresse, for as you schollers say that loue is ful of hopes and feares, so is the Madrigall or louers musicke full of diuersitie of passions and ayres'.[4]

Even as the madrigal emerges from this matrix of abstract possibilities, it seems also to mimic or merge back into it. In this sense, it is at once in front of and behind itself, an oscillation between figure and ground. Susan Philipsz was prompted to set her song-cycle in the City of London, since it itself undergoes such remarkable alternations of sound. The sounds of *Surround Me* that would have simply dissolved in the humming, bustling surroundings during the working week stood out starkly beached against the sabbatarian hush of the weekend.

The locations that Philipsz chose were semi-permeable places of retreat or retirement, alcoves, angles and alleyways hollowed out of the hubbub of the city. These locations are settings, which surround and sustain the listener; but they are also themselves sunk, omphalos-like, into the larger setting of the City around them. In them, sound of the airs seemed to have been washed up, in the way that litter will be chivvied into corners by the wind. They were reminders of the chamberings or primal cavities in which sounding and listening occur—the sounding box of the lute, the throat, the ear. Thomas Ravenscroft's *New Oysters*, heard in Change Alley, whose coffee houses in the 18th Century were the setting for the exchange of goods and commodities that would grow into the Stock Exchange, hinted at the shell-like nature of all these aural settings. If, in a sense, the delicate, finely-combed filaments of Philipsz's singing depended for their audibility on such places of scalloped parenthesis, the sound also helped to scoop out the places themselves, giving them a sort of porous solidity that they would not have had without the lingering to listen enjoined by the sounds fitfully resident in them.

Madrigals are at once impassioned and curiously impersonal; they express the emotion of a single subject, but distributed between different voices. They are often associated with birdsong—for example, in Shakespeare's *Passionate Pilgrim*, in which 'shepherds feed their flocks / By shallow rivers, by whose falls / Melodious birds sing madrigals' — with their intermittent concord of melodies that sifts between singularity and plurality.[5] Orlando Gibbons's *The Silver Swan*, heard in a narrow alley in Tokenhouse Yard, gave voice to the dying song of the swan, which itself ventriloquised the plaint of a disappointed lover. The airs we hear seem strangely detached from the feeling that hums through them. The ambiguity of the title of the piece, which lies between urging and neutral indication — is *Surround Me* an appeal, imperative, or erotic incitement, or just a truncated end of a simple predication? — is in tune with this affective ambivalence.

Michel Serres has memorably described the difference between the hard and the soft as simply a matter of variable speeds. The hard is just matter moving very slowly; a time-lapse photograph of a rocky coast taken over millions of years would show it leaping and flickering like a candle-flame.[6] Heraclitus declared that πάντα ῥεϊ (*panta rhei*), everything flows; but that must include the river bank as well as the river, for stasis is only a slower form of rhesis, or a flow coiled back on itself, as in forms like the cochlea of the ear, or the intricate convolutions of horns and trumpets. *Surround Me* multiplies examples of this concretion of flows, and corresponding erosion of solids. In the most literal sense, there is the liquid lilting of the music, set in the sometimes bleak and unyielding concrete of the City's buildings. More figuratively, there is the way in which the music itself is caught up in this sculptural enterprise, for example in the circles of the round, in songs like *New Oysters*, or Thomas Ravenscroft's *O my love*, heard at the foot of All Hallows Staining Church in Mark Lane, which seemed to be trying through their overlappings to thicken time into space, or draw elapsing up into a kind of endurance.

And hence, too, the close similarity between the flow of melody and flow of tears, which are repeatedly pooled together in *Surround Me*. The teardrops torn from the grieving weeper are at once a wound and balsam, providing a refuge or remission from the very pain to which they give expression. The madrigal by John Bennet installed in the wind-scoured square of Moorfields Highwalk works round this very idea, that one's tears might build into the comfort of an aqueous body, in which one might both dwell and drown: Weep, O mine eyes, and cease not / Alas, these your spring tides me thinks increase not / O when begin you / To swell so high that I may drown me in you? / That I may drown me in you?

John Dowland's *Lachrimae*, found at the junction of Milk Street and Russia Row, is made up of starkly separated shards of sound, and based upon a falling melody which imitates the dropping of tears, which the act of listening heals or hardens into stalactite suspension. Dowland's *Flow My Tears*, encountered under London Bridge, similarly effects a confluence of singing, weeping and melodic dwelling: 'Flow, my tears, fall from your springs! / Exiled forever, let me mourn; / Where night's black bird her sad infamy sings, / There let me live forlorn'. Even the briny oysters evoked and perhaps in part themselves given voice in *New Oysters*, in Change Alley, ramified this economy of the hard and the soft, the salty interior of the shellfish seeming an enclave of ocean within a hard outside, that is itself set in turn to harden into pearl.

And this permeable economy of the hard and the soft, the actual and the imaginary, encompasses economy itself. Interviewed by BBC London about *Surround Me*, Susan Philipsz remarked that she came to realise that 'the centre point of my project Bank, is not named after the financial institutions but after the bank of the river'.[7] The river bank gives rise to the Bank of England, for the amassing of wealth depends upon the movement of goods that the river makes possible. Money is the metre and the matrix of the matter of the City, where the hard and the soft have their most paradoxical alloying; for nothing has harder, or more inescapable consequences, nor yet is more melting and fluid, than the strange, soft, immaterial matter that money is.

1 — Smith, Bruce R. *The Acoustic World of Early Modern England: Attending to the O-Factor*. (University of Chicago Press, Chicago, 1999) p. 33.

2 — Ravenscroft, Thomas. *A Briefe Discourse of the True (but Neglected) Vse of Charact'ring the Degrees*... Edwarde Allde for Thomas Adams (London, 1614) p. 63.

3, 4 — Morley, Thomas. *A Plaine and Easie Introduction to Practicall Musicke Set Downe in Forme of a Dialogue*... Peter Short (London, 1597) p. 171.

5 — Shakespeare, William. The Complete Sonnets and Poems. Ed. Colin Burrow. Oxford University Press (Oxford, 2002) p. 365.

6 — Serres, Michel. *Hermès V: Le Passage du nord-ouest*. Editions de Minuit (Paris, 1980) pp. 51–2.

7 — Cantopher, Will. *Sound Artist Susan Philipsz Unveils City Song Project*. Online at http://news.bbc.co.uk/local/london/hi/people_and_places/arts_and_culture/newsid_9064000/9064141.stm, (2010).

Seven Tears

Aachen, 2011

Ludwig Forum, Aachen, 2011. Seven multi-channel sound installations. 43 minutes.

The exhibition at the Ludwig Forum in Aachen was comprised of an installation of seven related sound works (*Lachrimae*, *New Oysters*, *Oh My Love*, *Weep, O Mine Eyes*, *The Silver Swan*, *Flow My Tears*, *To the Greenwood*) that played over and alongside one another in the main gallery space. The title of the exhibition refers directly to John Dowland's famous *Lachrimae* or *Seaven Teares* (1604), seven adaptations of his signature instrumental based upon the image of a single falling tear. The layering and sequencing of the works, combined with the movement of the audience through the space, created a fluid environment where sound and space came together to convey a sense of absence and loss in the present.

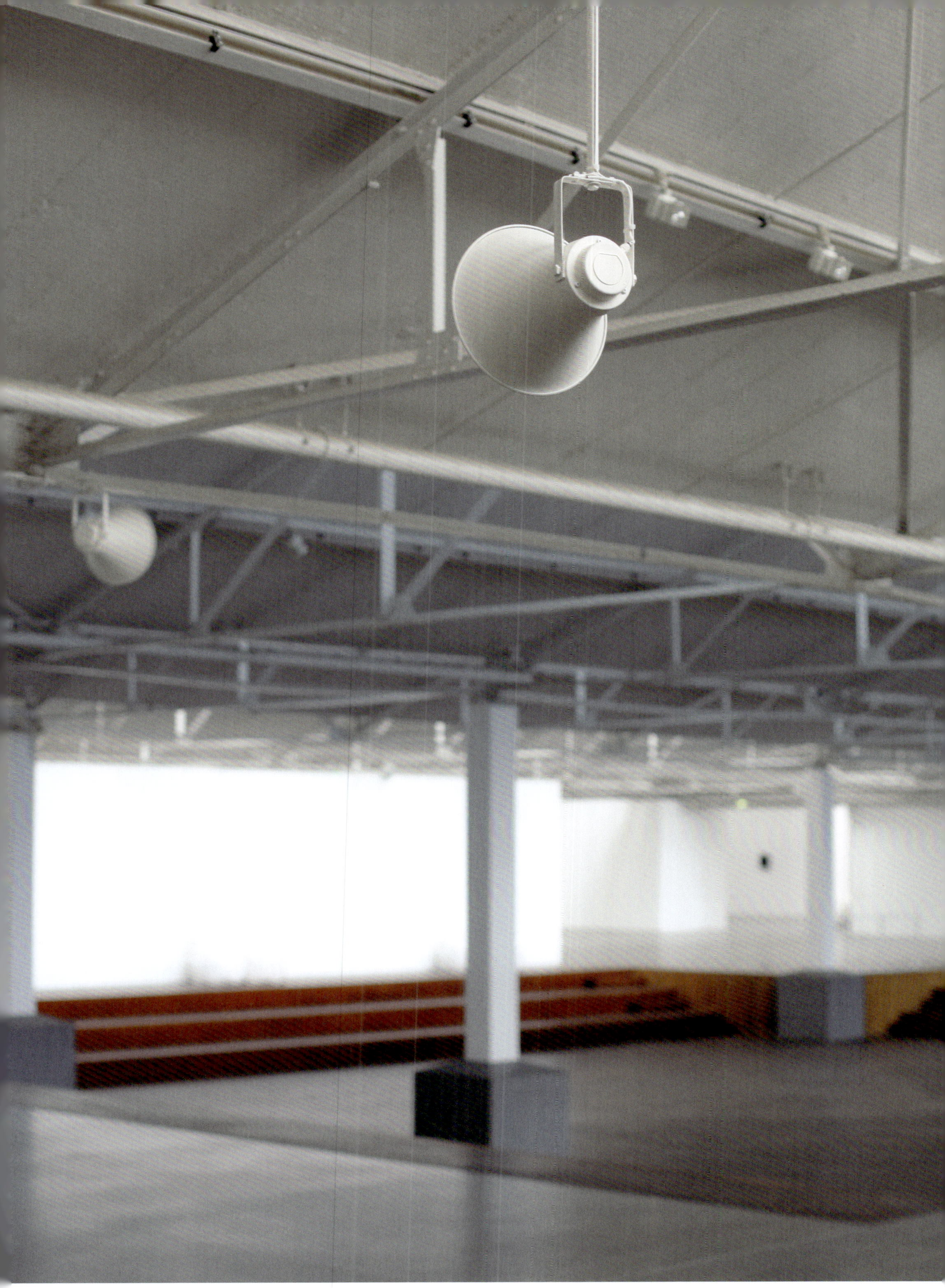

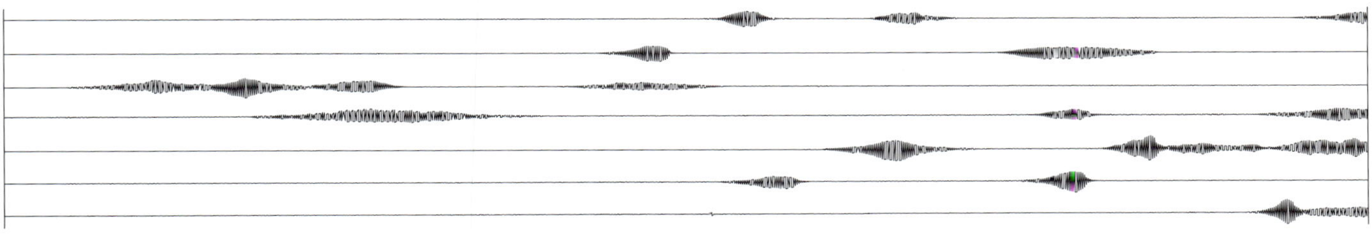

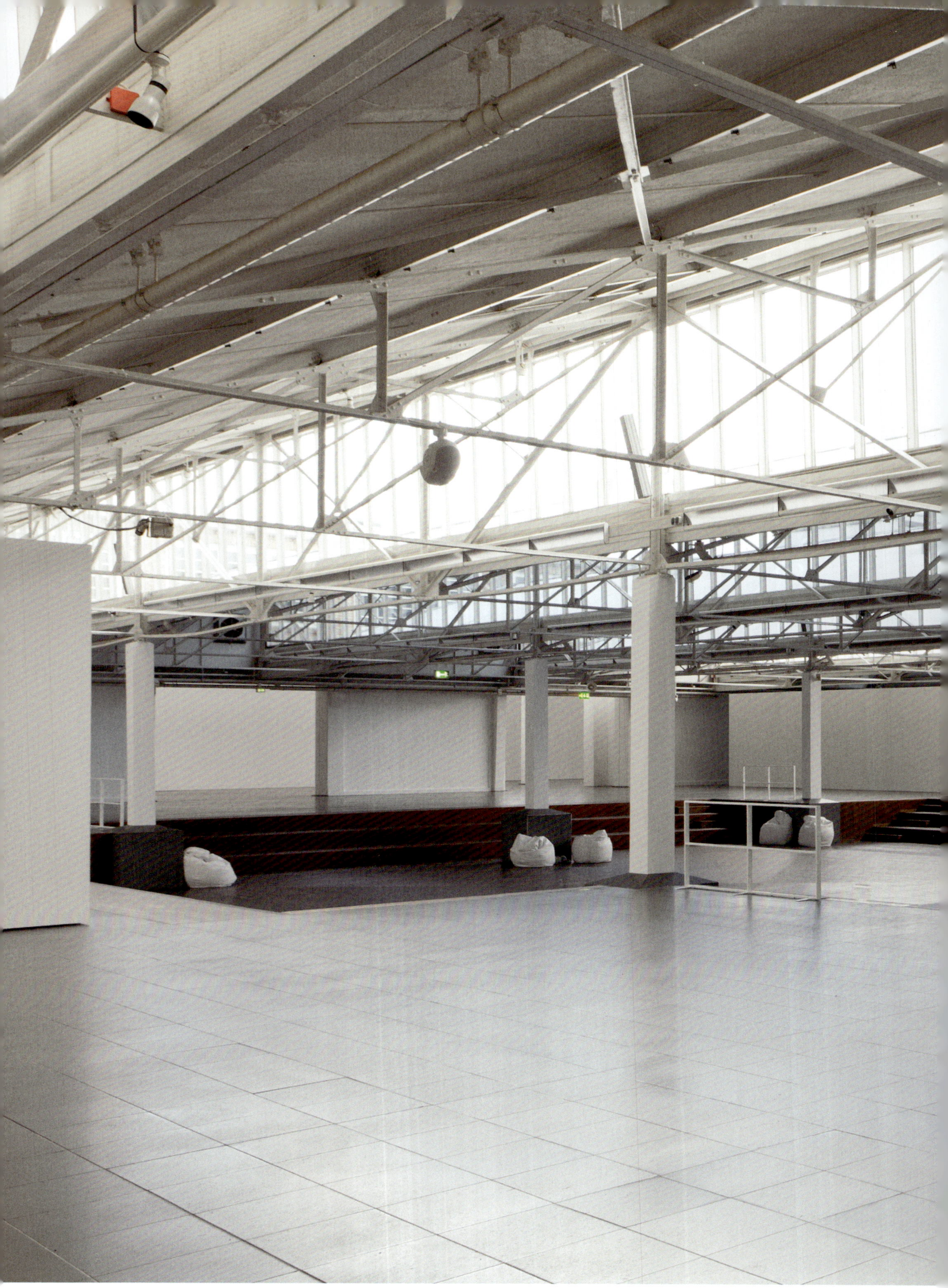

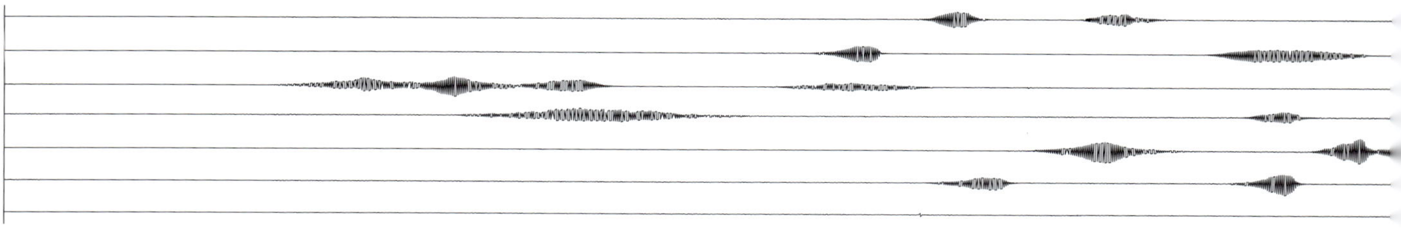

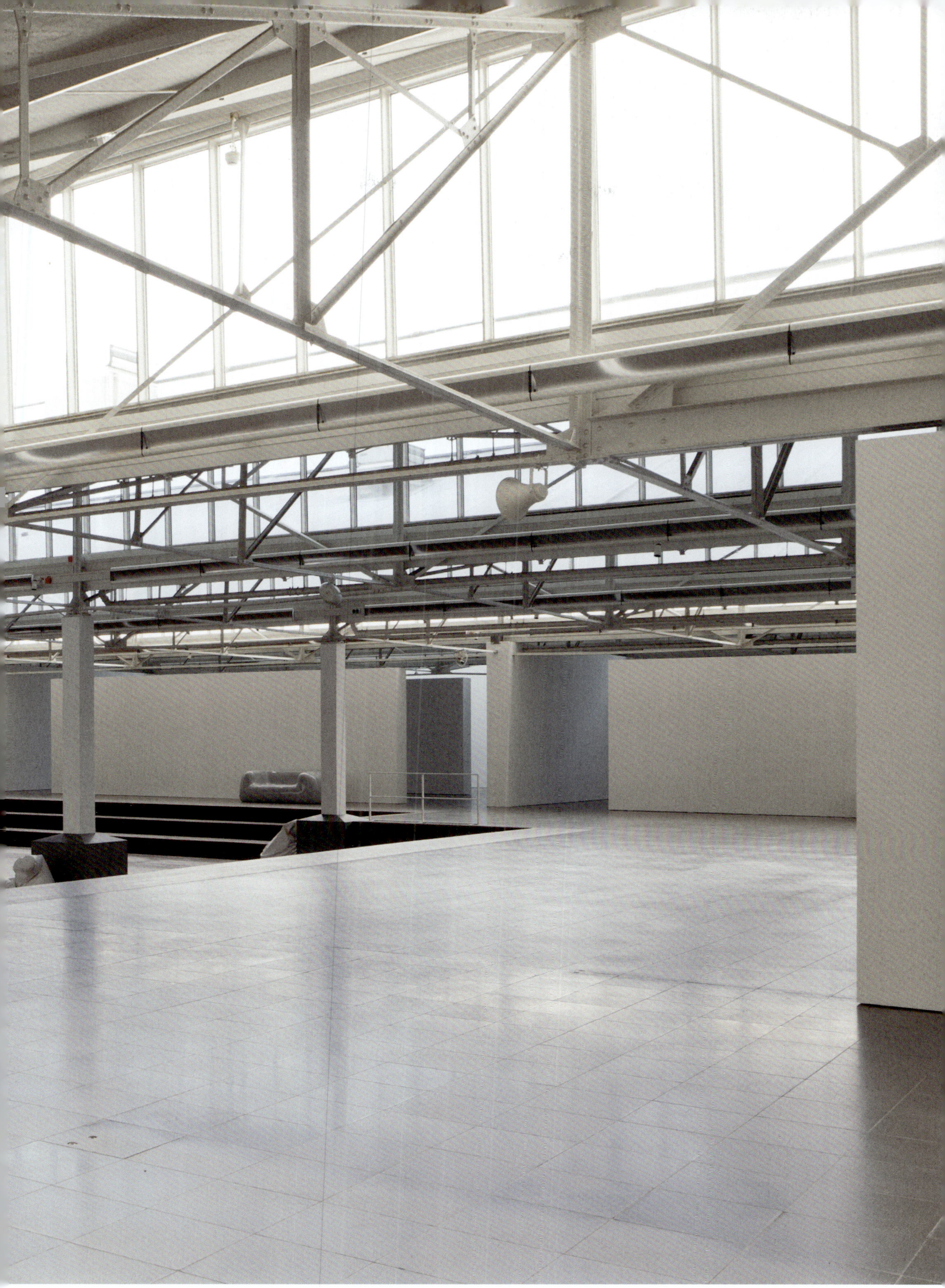
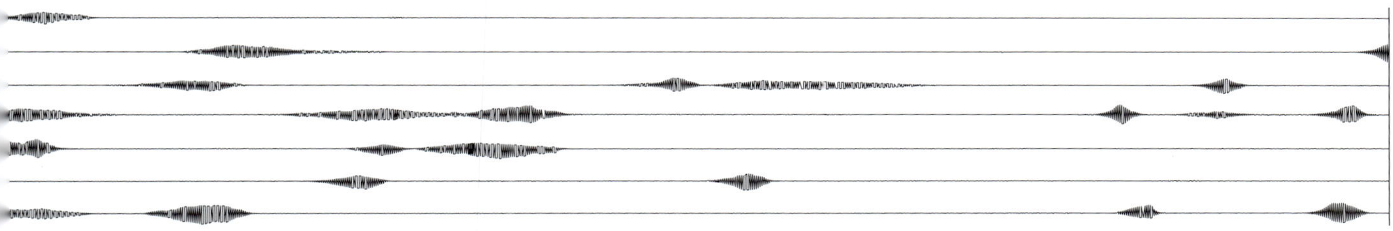

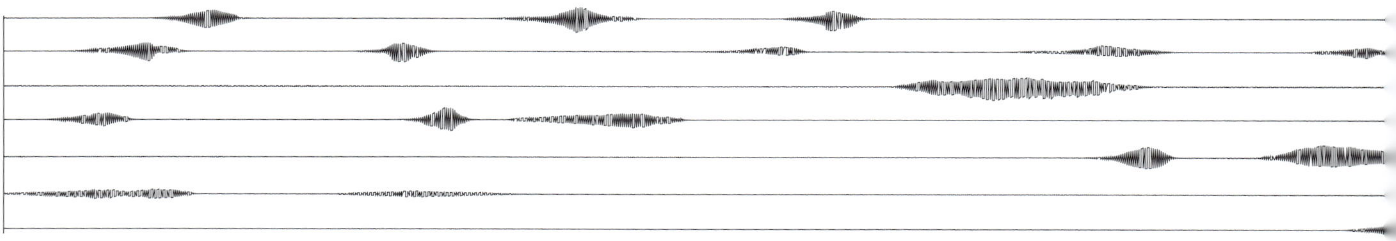

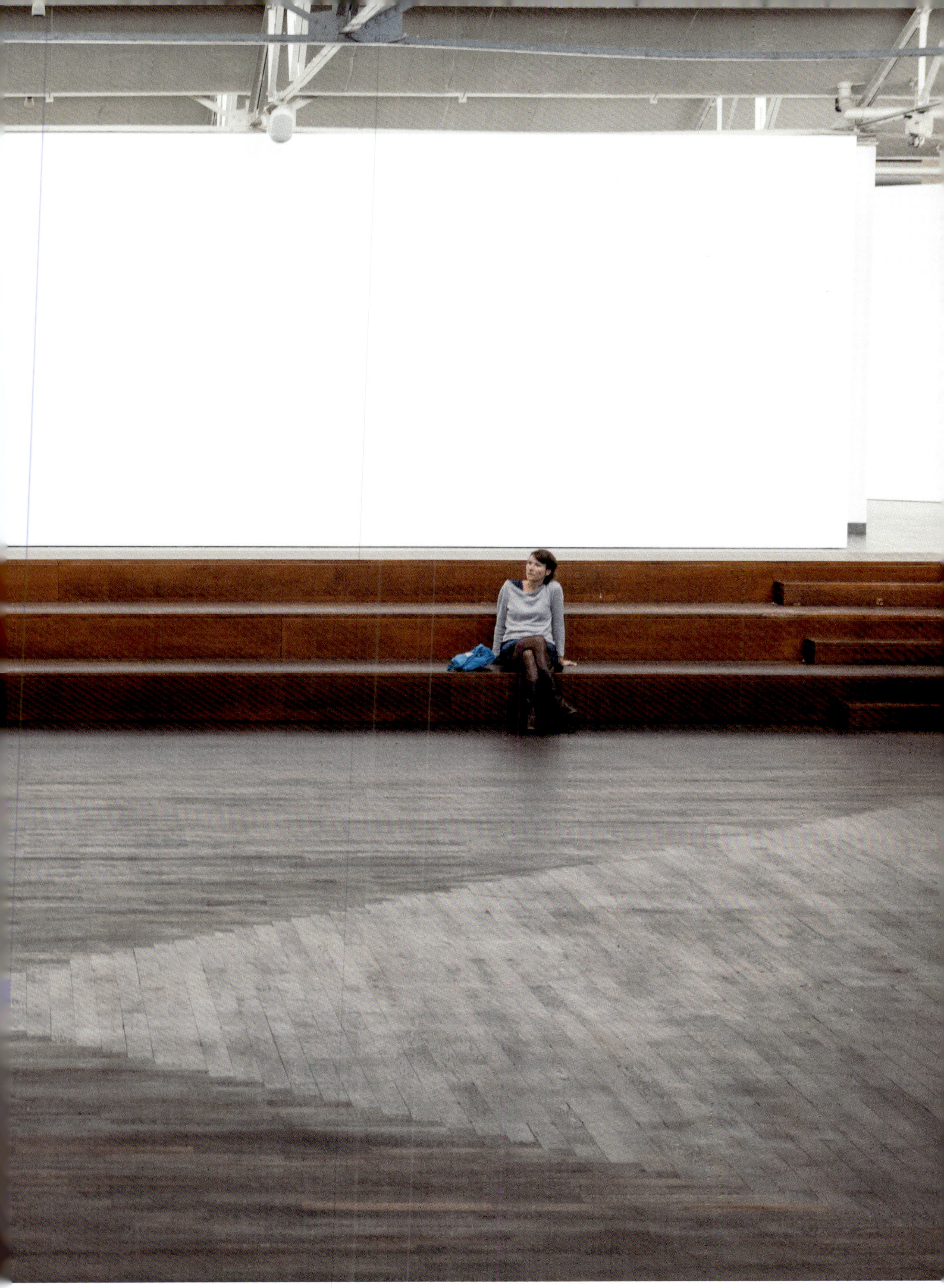

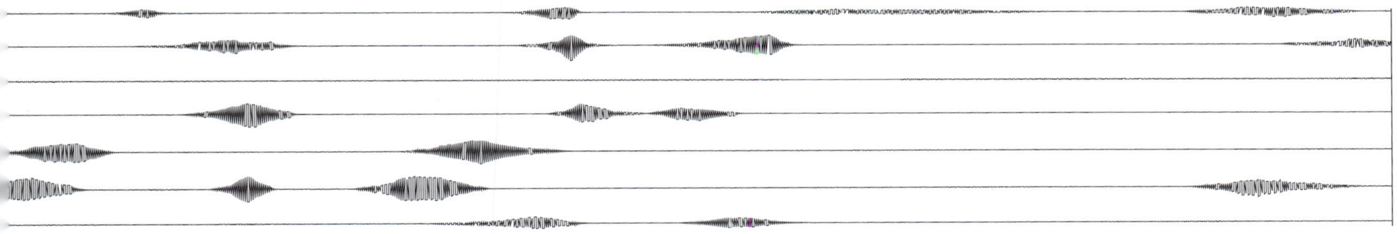

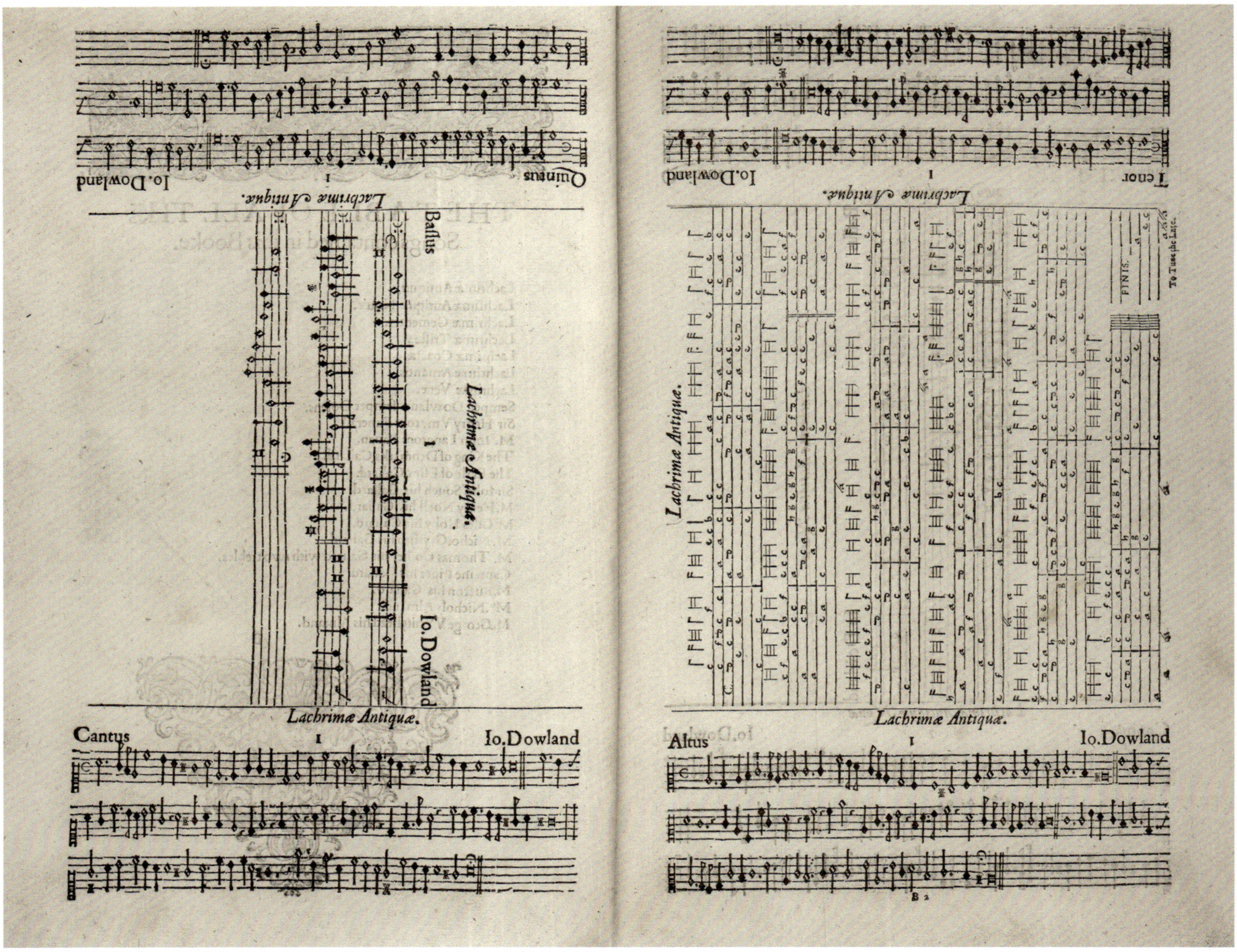
Lachrimæ Antiquæ.
Cantus
1
Io.Dowland
Lachrimæ Antiquæ.
Altus
1
Io.Dowland
Bassus
Lachrimæ Antiquæ.
1
Io.Dowland
Quintus
Lachrimæ Antiquæ.
1
Io.Dowland
Tenor
Lachrimæ Antiquæ.
1
Io.Dowland
Lachrimæ Antiquæ.
FINIS.
B 2

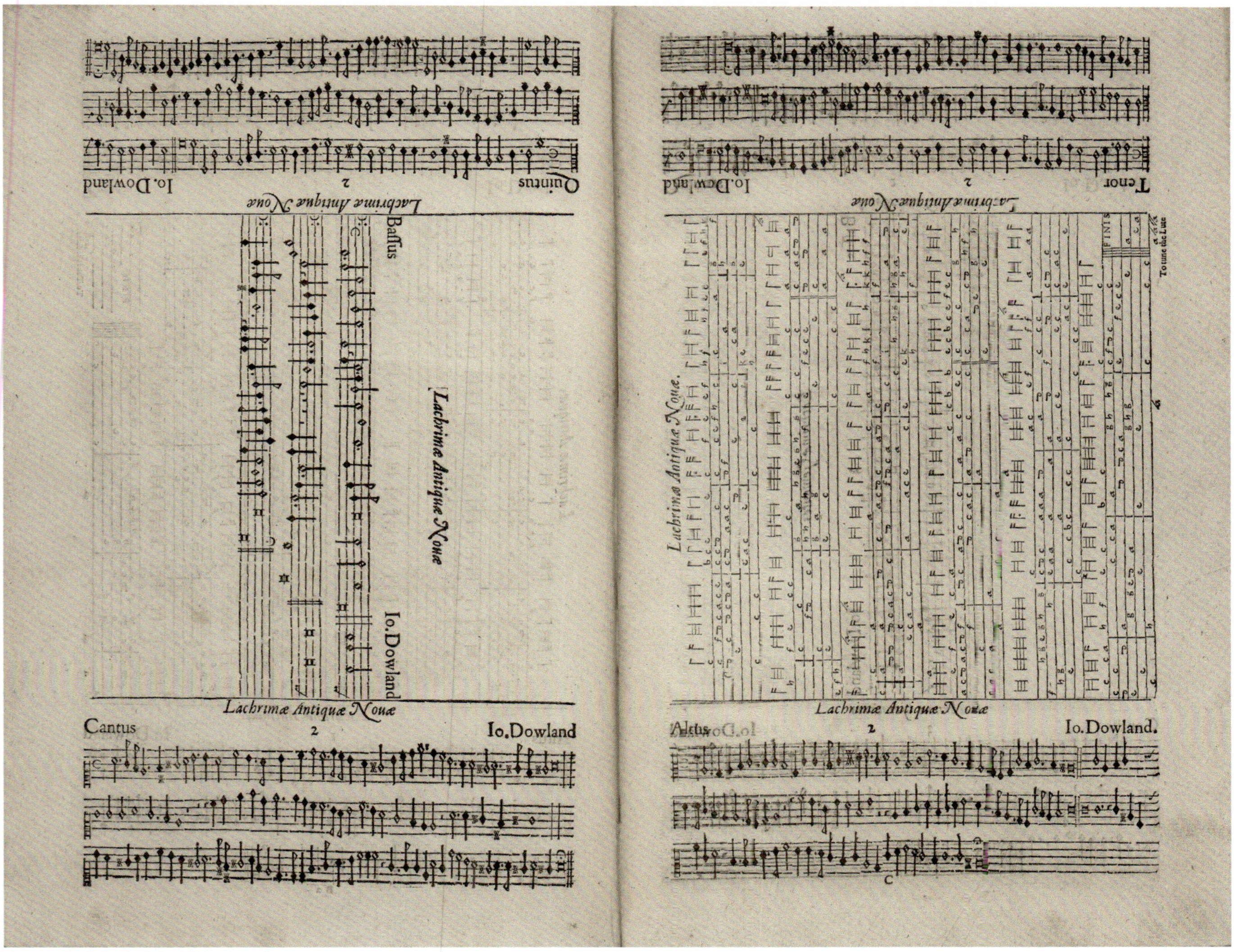

Lachrimae Antiquae, Lachrimæ or Seaven Teares Figured in Seaven Passionate Pavans (...), John Dowland, London, 1609. Courtesy: Royal Academy of Music, London.

Lachrimae

'The Lachrimae is published as a folio book intended to be placed on a small flat table, to be read by the performers grouped around it. Each piece is laid out on a single opening in the following order: *Cantus* (left bottom), *Bassus* (left middle facing outwards), *Quintus* (left top, upside down), *Tenor* (right top upside down), *the lute tablature* (right middle, opposite the Bassus), and *Altus* (right bottom) ... The table layout is related to the choirbook format, in which all the parts are spread around a single opening but face the same direction. Dowland's innovation was to apply the full table layout with parts laid around all four sides of the book'. Peter Holman, *Dowland Lachrimae*, 1604 (Cambridge University Press 1999).

Title page, *Lachrimæ or Seaven Teares Figured in Seaven Passionate Pavans* (...), John Dowland, London, 1609. Courtesy: Royal Academy of Music, London.

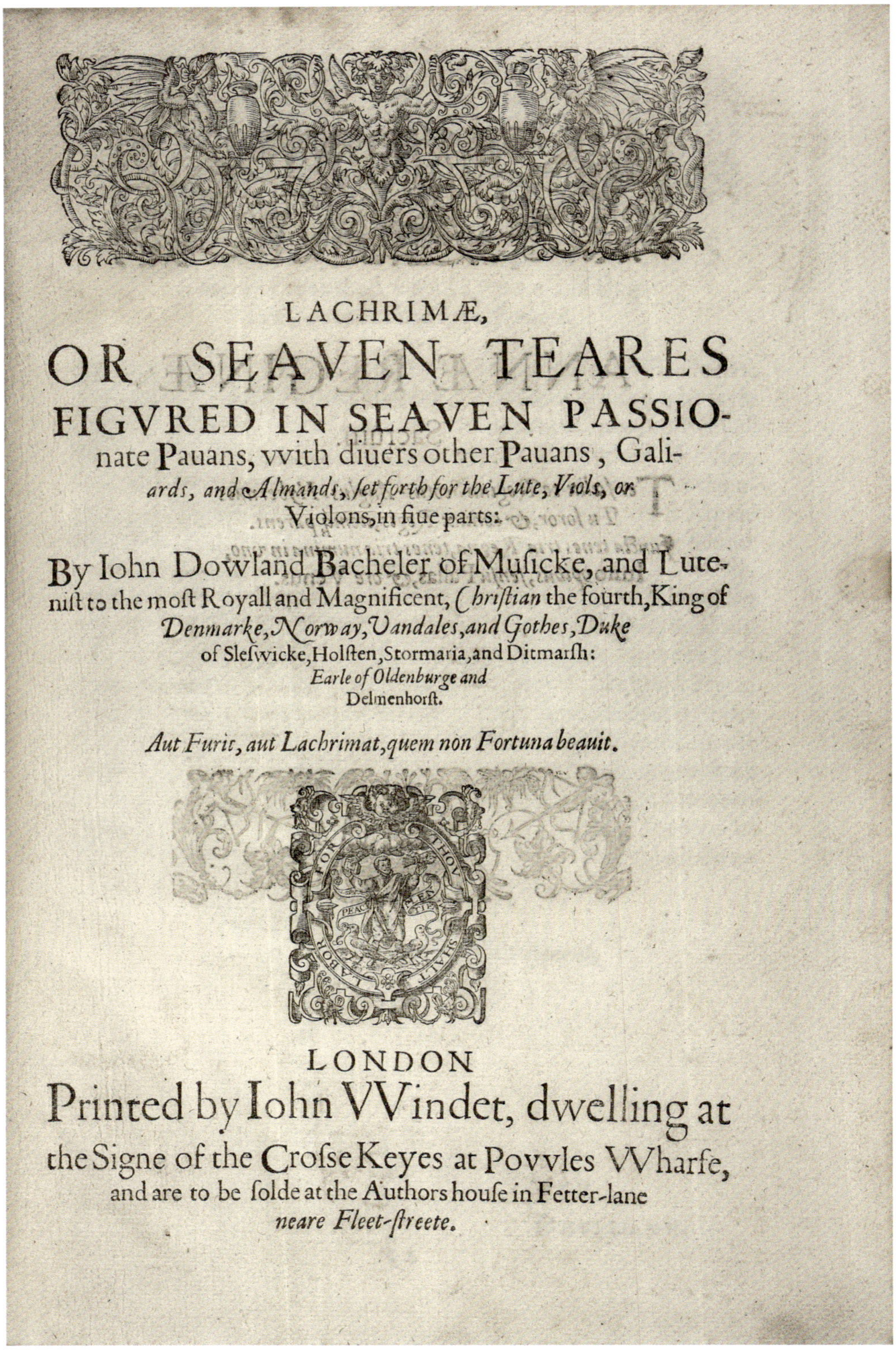

LACHRIMÆ,

OR SEAVEN TEARES FIGVRED IN SEAVEN PASSIO-nate Pauans, vvith diuers other Pauans, Gali-*ards, and Almands, set forth for the Lute, Viols, or* Violons, in fiue parts:

By Iohn Dowland Bacheler of Musicke, and Lute-nist to the most Royall and Magnificent, *Christian* the fourth, King of *Denmarke, Norway, Vandales, and Gothes, Duke* of Sleswicke, Holsten, Stormaria, and Ditmarsh: *Earle of Oldenburge and* Delmenhorst.

Aut Furit, aut Lachrimat, quem non Fortuna beauit.

LONDON

Printed by Iohn VVindet, dwelling at the Signe of the Crosse Keyes at Povvles Wharfe, and are to be solde at the Authors house in Fetter-lane *neare Fleet-streete.*

Thermal springs in Aachen, *Thermarum Aquisgranensium Et Porcetanarum Descriptio*, Francois Blondel, 1685. Courtesy: Crous Collection.

Badhuis te Aken, Jan Luyken, 1682. Courtesy: Crous Collection.

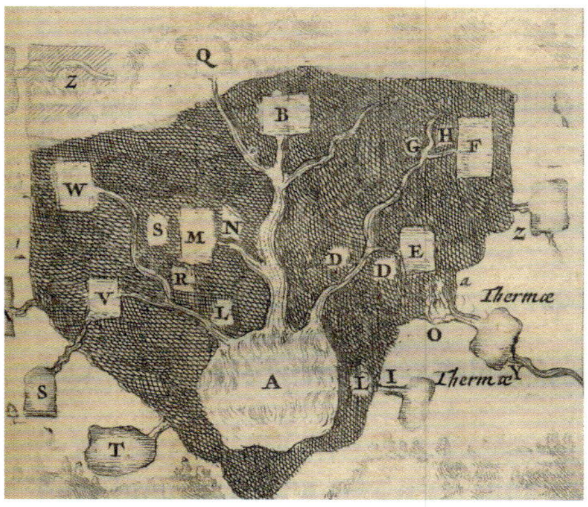

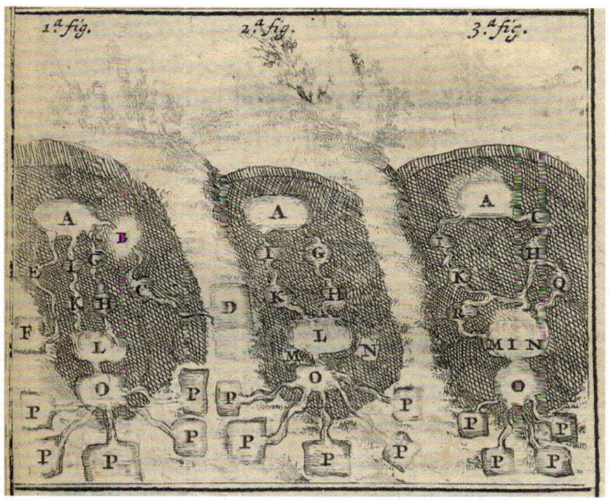

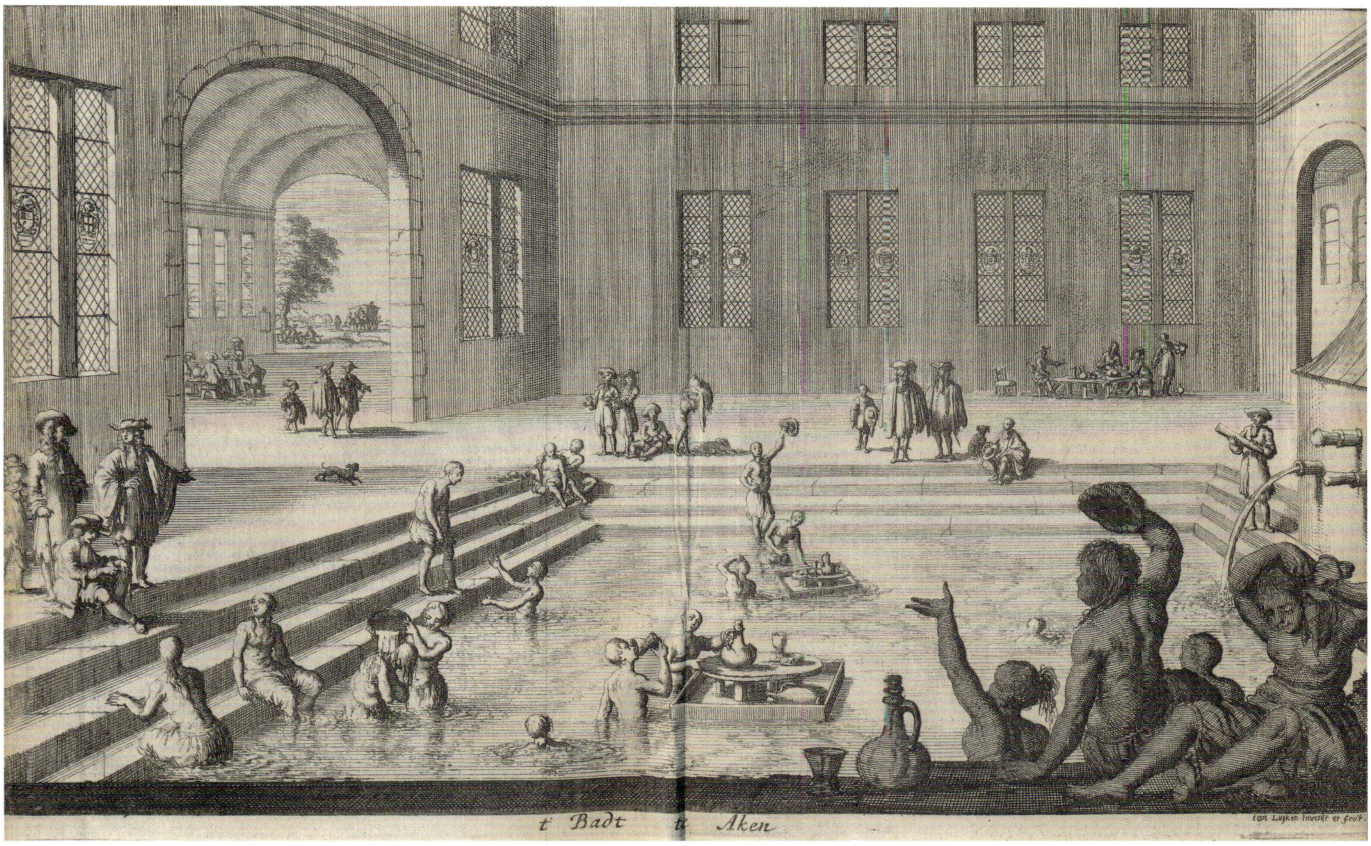

Aquae Granni

Aachen is a city renowned for its hot natural springs. Its name actually means 'waters of Grannus', derived from the Latin word for water 'Aquae' and the Celtic deity 'Grannus'. The Roman author Lucanus described the local scene: 'Water flowed out of dark springs, and there stood plainly and without any decorative elements carved wooden idols, spooky and half rotten'. Because of damage caused during the Second World War, and on account of a general change in taste most of these springs have since been covered over or abandoned. However there are traces remaining in different places throughout Aachen that link this historic moment with the contemporary city.

An Echo of Melancholy

Anna Sophia Schultz

Lachrimae or Seven Teares, a collection of instrumental ensemble music based on the image of a single falling teardrop, was published by the English composer John Dowland in 1604. It opens with seven pavans (a slow processional dance originating in Italy), each a variation of the famous *Lachrimae* motif (lachrima, Latin: tear). The sequence of four descending diatonic notes (A-G-F-E) describes the rise and fall of a tear, forming in the eye, swelling into full size, tipping out of the eyeball, and flowing down the cheek.[1]

The motif proved enormously popular in late Elizabethan England and was appropriated and adapted in numerous instrumental and vocal compositions by Dowland's English contemporaries.[2] John Bennet's four-part madrigal (*Weep, O Mine Eyes*, 1599) draws much of its material from the same vaunted four notes,[3] while Dowland himself had earlier used this sequence for his composition *Flow My Tears*, published in 1600 as part of the *Second Booke of Songs or Ayres*.[4] Its popularity derived not from its haunting musical quality alone; rather, the work resonated within a society enamoured by melancholy.[5] Along with Spain, England had become *the* domain for this 'specifically modern, deliberately cultivated melancholy',[6] which was also labeled a 'fashionable complaint' or, referring to its blossoming in England, as the 'Elizabethan' or 'English malady'.[7] Besides the 'inhospitable insular weather conditions'[8]—in particular the notorious English fog—social, political, cosmological and even national factors were called on to explain this phenomenon.[9] In his famous *Anatomy of Melancholy* Robert Burton produced the defining work of this early modern absorption with melancholy, at once mapping the obsession and lending it renewed impetus. Burton accords music a special rôle in melancholy, with its particular capacity of 'delivering from and sustaining this ambivalent, wistfully-sweet sentiment'.[10] The *Lachrimae* motif was considered 'the most succinctly formulated musical embodiment of the melancholy motif of the age',[11] complementing the musical realisation of the teardrop motif with an image for 'the *conditio humana*, for the fall of man from the divine sphere into the depths of earthly life'.[12] The motif became John Dowland's 'signature tune'[13] and it is no surprise that he—not least through the programmatic title of *Semper Dowland semper dolens* (always Dowland, always doleful) for an instrumental composition—came to epitomise the melancholic zeitgeist.[14] Composers and literati alike welcomed melancholy as 'inuencions food' [15], for it confronts the rediscovered objective of 'affective writing'[16] with the greatest possible challenge. Its basic vocabulary, which determined the tone of countless compositions, included tears, grief, pain, night, darkness, and death.[17] Melancholy was triggered by themes such as 'mutability and death'[18] and precisely here it preserves the peculiar ambivalence between sorrow and joy, expressed in phrases like the 'joy of grief', 'douce mélancholie', and 'Wonnen der Wehmut', which extend across different cultures and centuries.[19]

Susan Philipsz's sound installation[20] *Seven Tears*, exhibited over the summer months of 2011 in the Ludwig Forum für Internationale Kunst in Aachen, not only evokes the title of the famous instrumental collection by Dowland but also its profoundly melancholic tenor. Philipsz had al-

1—Christian Kelnberger, *Text und Musik bei John Dowland*, (Passau, 2010) p. 89.

2—Ibid. p. 103; see also Winfried Maynard, *Elizabethan lyric poetry and its music*, (Oxford, 1986) p. 116.

3—Christian Kelnberger, *Text und Musik bei John Dowland*, (Passau, 2010) p. 138.

4—Jean Clair characterizes *Flow My Tears* as the 'climax of the melancholic feeling'; see Jean Clair, *Musik und Melancholie*, in: *Melancholie. Genie und Wahnsinn in der Kunst*, ed. Jean Clair, Berlin / Paris 2006, p. 243.

5—Christian Kelnberger, *Text und Musik bei John Dowland*, (Passau, 2010) p. 88; Robin Headlam Wells, *Elizabethan Mythologies. Studies in poetry, drama and music*, (Cambridge, 1994) p. 196.

6—Raymond Klibansky, Erwin Panofsky und Fritz Saxl, *Saturn und Melancholie—Studien zur Geschichte der Naturphilosophie und Medizin, der Religion und der Kunst*, 1990, pp. 341–342.

7—Werner Braun, *Die Musik des 17. Jahrhunderts*, (Wiesbaden, 1981) p. 134; see also Ludger Heidbrink, *Melancholie und Moderne. Zur Kritik der Historischen Verzweiflung*, (Munich, 1994) p. 30; H. Flashar, in: *Historisches Wörterbuch der Philosophie*, (Basel, 1980) p. 1040. George Cheyne described it as the 'English Malady' in a tract of the same name from 1733.

8—Ute Mohr, *Melancholie und Melancholiekritik im England des 18. Jahrhunderts*, (Frankfurt a. M., 1990) p. 57.

9—Ibid., p. 48 ff.; Olivier Meslay speaks of 'melancholy as a national trait'. Olivier Meslay, *Die Melancholie elisabethanischer Mörder*, in: *Melancholie. Genie und Wahnsinn in der Kunst*, ed. Jean Clair, (Berlin / Paris, 2006) p. 129.

10—Raymond Klibansky, Erwin Panofsky und Fritz Saxl, *Saturn und Melancholie. Studien zur Geschichte der Naturphilosophie und Medizin, der Religion und der Kunst*, 1990, p. 338–339; see also Jacomien Prins, *A philosophic music therapy for melancholy* in Marsilio Ficino's 'Timaeus', in: *Melancholie — zwischen Attitüde und Diskurs*, eds. Andrea Sieber and Antje Wittstock, (Göttingen, 2009) p. 119–143.

11—Christian Kelnberger, *Text und Musik bei John Dowland*, (Passau, 2010) p. 108.

12—Ibid., p. 89; see also Robin Headlam Wells, *Elizabethan Mythologies. Studies in poetry, drama and music*, (Cambridge, 1994) p. 195.

13—Christian Kelnberger, *Text und Musik bei John Dowland*, (Passau, 2010) p. 180.

14—Robin Headlam Wells, *Elizabethan Mythologies. Studies in poetry, drama and music*, (Cambridge, 1994) p. 20, 190.

15—Ibid., p. 203.

16—Ibid., p. 198.

17—Christian Kelnberger, *Text und Musik bei John Dowland*, (Passau, 2010) p. 62.

18—Robin Headlam Wells, *Elizabethan Mythologies. Studies in poetry, drama and music*, (Cambridge, 1994) p. 189. Gottfried Boehm characterizes an 'experience of time and dealing with death' as the 'horizon of every conception of melancholy'; Gottfried Boehm, *Augenblick und Ewigkeit. Bemerkungen zur Zeiterfahrung in der Kunst der Moderne*, in: *Allegorie und Melancholie*, ed. Willem van Reijen, (Frankfurt a. M., 1992) p. 109.

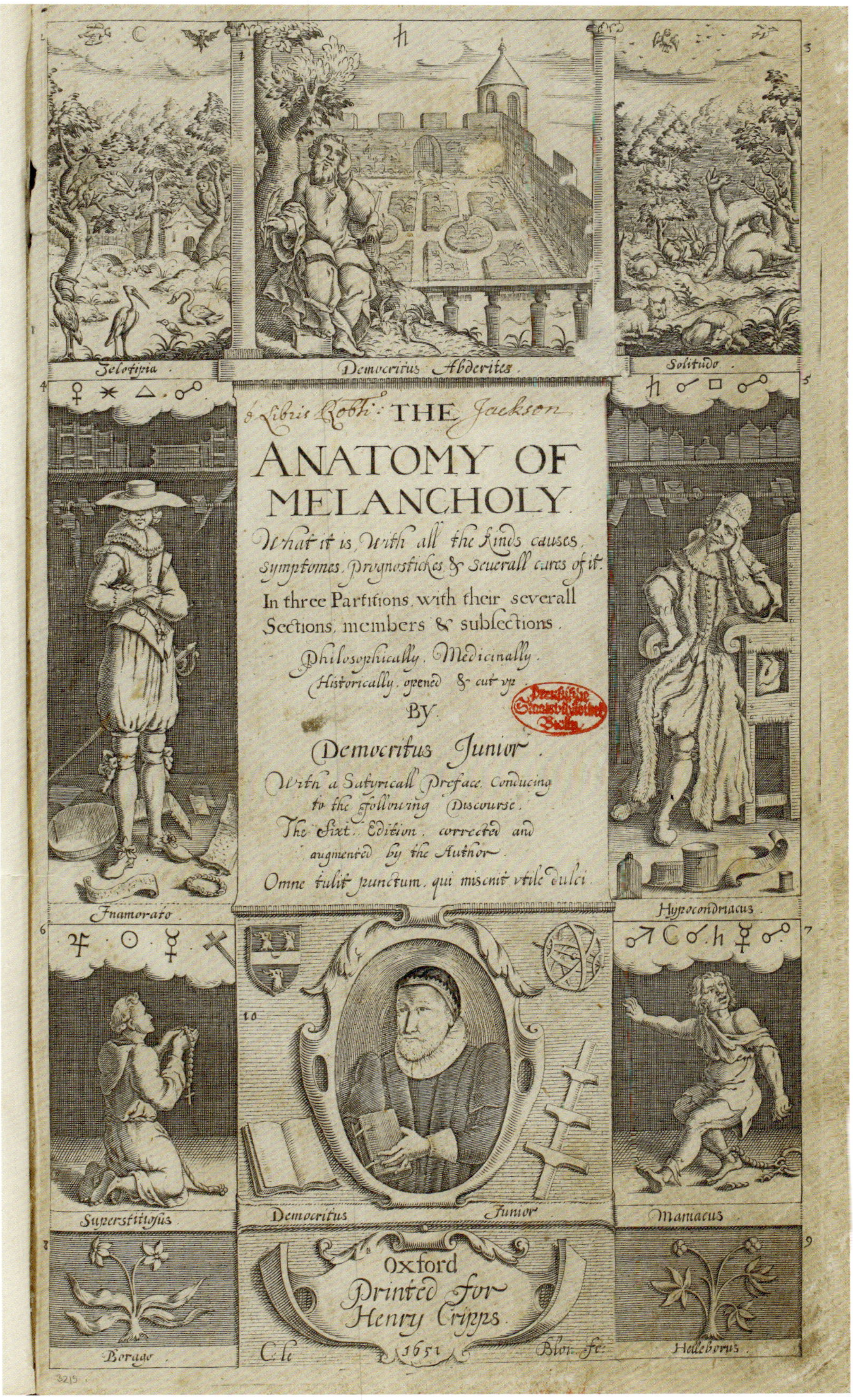

Title page, *The Anatomy of Melancholy*, Robert Burton, 1651. Courtesy: bpk Bildagentur für Kunst, Kultur und Geschichte, Berlin.

ready presented six of the seven pieces she brought together at the Ludwig Forum the previous year in her project *Surround Me; A Song Cycle for the City of London*.[21] She had been intrigued to read about the ubiquitous presence of the human voice in the public spaces of the early modern City of London at the time of Dowland's compositions, at the turn from the 16th to the 17th Century.

'...the voice was so prevalent that it is said the city's traders would modulate their cries to harmonise and remain distinctive from one another as they called out across the city streets. This created a polyphonic layered vocal which inspired the likes of Shakespeare and composers such as Thomas Ravenscroft to set the cries to music and arrange them in rounds and canons.'

With *Surround Me* Philipsz brought to attention the peculiar stillness that descends today upon parts of the City on weekends and brought back the human voice to the City in two ways. In a form which reached back to the historical soundscape, recordings of Philipsz singing several songs from the late Elizabethan period were played back via loudspeakers at six selected sites around the City.[22] The polyphonic texture of the songs evoked, along with their notably melancholic tenor, the London of the Elizabethan era, whilst the specific urban and architectural setting of the six sites in the cycle created particular frames of reference for each composition in turn.[23]

Surround Me was clearly a site-specific work in London and *Seven Tears* can be understood as an exceptional form of variation[24]—which restaged an almost identical selection of musical pieces in a space that could scarcely have been more different in both spatial and typological terms from the original sites in the City of London. Without abandoning the connection to its prototype, this dislocation and relocation brought forth a substantially new composition—and in doing so raised the question of how the relationship between the work and the site had changed.

Seven Tears gathered six pieces from London in the main hall of the Ludwig Forum and added a seventh, *To the Greenwood* by Thomas Ravenscroft. The central space of the former umbrella factory built in the late 1920s was cleared out completely, including the exhibition rooms opening on to the hall in the surrounding corona, and transformed into a monumental sound box. Due to the alterations made to the building in the 1990s, its spaces now constitute a hybrid between industrial architecture and the white cube. The wide, relatively low-ceilinged hall (once the workplace of hundreds of seamstresses) the characteristic structure of the shed roof and the prominent support structures in the high spaces to the side—all these features connect the clear architectural lines of the exhibition rooms to the original function. Within this single architectonic space the seven musical pieces form new spaces, exploiting its openness and spaciousness.[25] Whereas the urban setting of *Surround Me* was used as a referent for the pieces, the white walls of the museum's interior function like projection surfaces, off which the thematic of the pieces bounced back to the listener.[26] The connection of the industrial past to the texts and sounds of the pieces was somewhat too tenuous to suggest any direct link. Instead, in this new topographical compression, in the merging of the pieces into a single sweeping space, recurring motifs crystallised. These are the same motifs about which Susan Philipsz has written in another context: 'I use a simple vibraphone melody and voice to explore how repetition and metaphor can be used to reflect themes of life, death and transcendence'.[27] Brought together at the Ludwig Forum,

19—Ludger Heidbrink, *Melancholie und Moderne. Zur Kritik der Historischen Verzweiflung*, (Munich, 1994) p. 30.

20—Defined by Volker Straebel as 'sculptural emitted sound that is experienced by the listener spatially in their own movement'; Volker Straebel, *Vom Verschwinden der Klangkunst—Der Begriff Klangkunst als wissenschaftsgeschichtliches Konstrukt*, in: Klangräume der Kunst, (Heidelberg, 2010) p. 55.

21—The six pieces are: *Weep, O Mine Eyes* (John Bennet, 1599), *Flow My Tears* (John Dowland, 1600), *Lachrimae* (John Dowland, 1604), *New Oysters* (Thomas Ravenscroft, 1609), *Oh My Love* (Thomas Ravenscroft, 1609), and *The Silver Swan* (Orlando Gibbons, 1612).

22—The six sites were located within the banking district sufficiently distanced so that the pieces could only be experienced successively, by moving from one site to another; their integration into a 'whole' was thus only possible in the mind.

23—See: www.artangel.org.uk//projects/2010/surround_me/about_the_project/surround_me

24—The concept of variation is selected here because, despite all the changes to the staging and reception parameters as well as the addition of a seventh piece, the other six present an explicit reference to the London project, one that poses the question as to the work's impact in a museum space.

25—*Weep, O Mine Eyes*, *To the Greenwood* and *New Oysters* take hold of the hall in its entirety, while *Flow My Tears, Oh My Love* and *The Silver Swan* play with the intimacy and enclosed nature of the side areas. The seven-channel work *Lachrimae* forms the basic motif embracing all the other works and weaving a tapestry of sound which the other pieces successively join in. During the total time of 40 minutes the pieces are repeated in varying sequence, in part with slight, dissonant overlapping, in part with pauses.

26—Beyond the museum space, Aachen's hot springs are an indirect referent for the sound installation. They have decisively shaped the history of the city, and yet today are barely perceptible in the cityscape and reveal signs of their presence only to the initiated in special markings, escaping vapors and the characteristic sulfuric odor recalling bad eggs. Susan Philipsz became particularly interested in these underground watercourses. The flowing of thermal waters and circulation as the cause of its warming form an analogy to the specific tear metaphoric ('spring tides', 'Flow, my tears, fall from your springs!') of some pieces and the formal structure of the canon as well as to the Thames, regarding which Susan Philipsz writes: 'It helped me to bring in the river [Thames] to the project and the flow of water, which the river so powerfully evokes, is reflected in almost all the sound works.' www.artangel.org.uk//projects/2010/surround_me/bbc_interview/interview. The brochure to the exhibition featured a selection of Aachen springs with visual and text material, while guided bike tours to the springs were included in the accompanying program, creating a relationship their antagonism operated as a motor of melancholy.[28] It is in the juxtaposition between the depictions of transience, loss and death in *Weep, O Mine Eyes*, *Flow My Tears*, and *The Silver Swan* and the pieces celebrating life, *To the Greenwood* and *New Oysters*, that the constitutive ambivalence of the 'bonneur d'être triste'[29] finds its equivalent.[30] The life-affirming tenor of the latter pieces loses none of its élan when contrasted with the former; indeed, it coalesces with them to form exactly 'the ambivalent, wistfully-sweet sentiment' which is distinctive of melancholy. The melancholic impetus inherent to the music is duplicated in the carefully choreographed staging of the work.

Beyond this spatialising of melancholic ambivalence, the specific staging of the sound installation also corresponded in other ways to the essence of a melancholy which, for all the 'semantic vagueness'[31] of the term, always implies a conflict: between what is and its inevitable passing, and something unattainable and the yearning for it.[32] In the exhibition space (and in another form in London's urban space) this conflict corresponded to the tension between the immediate presence of a voice, which emphatically foregrounded what was textually and tonally evoked, and a staged visual emptiness in the gallery (or the experience of the past in the spaces of the city).

With the interior space of the museum[33] Susan Philipsz chose a site which was conventionally given over for presentations of visual artifacts and representations and hence always generates a corresponding visual expectation. It is in the very disappointing of this expectation that the potential lies to intensify the emptiness into a contrasting, projective foil for the resonating sound. This intensification makes us aware of how the white cube also has the quality of a *silent cube*, possessing its own, albeit much reduced soundscape. The silence as an acoustic blank space existing side by side with its visual counterpart is emphatically perceptible in the incisive pauses Philipsz leaves between the pieces.[34] The particular presence of the voice derives both from the specific nature of the recording and its staging in space. Although most of the pieces were composed for many voices, Philipsz sings all the parts herself and without musical accompaniment. Her untrained voice is recorded in real time, so that the recording also includes her breathing, intervals, and imperfections. The audible drawing of breath brings the physical act of singing closer, while the choreography and technical realisation create a very full volume of sound in space. The human sound box (the chest of the singer) is superimposed with the architectural one (the space of the gallery), generating an experience of being directly addressed physically. With the usual separation between performance and reception space nullified, the listener, now situated *inside* the sound box, is deprived of the possibility to gain any distance to the work.

Shed of any visible works, the exhibition space is transformed into a stage upon which whoever enters must (re-)act. The interplay between the loudspeakers withholds from the visitor any directions for movement through space, while their gaze is thrown back to the totality of the architectonic form. By addressing different levels of perception, this superimposing of space and sound enables presence and absence to be experienced simultaneously.[35]

The embodied-disembodied voice, which precisely through its distinctive presence emphasizes the singer's absence, continues the elaboration of the melancholic conflict, to which the appropriation of existing song lore also contrib-

between the museum and the urban space. Taking up a poem by Charles d'Orléans from the 14th Century, Jean Starobinski links the melancholy thematic to the motif of the spring, while Vincent Pomarède points out the relationship between melancholy and water: Jean Starobinski, *Die Tinte der Melancholie* and Vincent Pomarède, *Die Lust an der Melancholie* (Senancour), both in: *Melancholie. Genie und Wahnsinn in der Kunst*, ed. Jean Clair, (Berlin / Paris, 2006) p. 28–29 and p. 320, 323.

27 — Susan Philipsz on her work *From the Beginning* (2007) in: Susan Philipsz. *There is Nothing Left Here*, Centro Galego de Arte Contemporanea, (Santiago de Compostela, 2008) p. 51.

28 — The concept of melancholy is originally medical in provenance and goes back to the humoral pathology of Ancient Greece, the four temperaments. From this origin melancholy is variously described in different epochs and disciplines as a psychological or psychosomatic illness (depression), a character trait, a prevailing mood, or a mindset. It can be a characteristic of the individual, a period or even a society; it can be constitutive or temporary. In the present text we are employing it in the sense of a prevailing mood. A representative overview of the conceptions of melancholy is to be found in the standard work by Raymond Klibansky (*Saturn und Melancholie. Studien zur Geschichte der Naturphilosophie und Medizin, der Religion und der Kunst*, 1990) and the publication accompanying the exhibition *Melancholie. Genie und Wahnsinn in der Kunst*, (Paris / Berlin, 2005 / 2006).

29 — Victor Hugo, *Les Travailleurs de la Mer*, (Vienna, 1924).

30 — On the aspect of ambivalence, see: Ludger Heidbrink, *Melancholie und Moderne. Zur Kritik der Historischen Verzweiflung*, (Munich, 1994) p. 50; Andrea Sieber and Antje Wittstock, Einleitung, in: *Melancholie — zwischen Attitüde und Diskurs*, eds. Andrea Sieber and Antje Wittstock, (Göttingen, 2009) p. 7; Yves Bonnefoy, *Melancholie, Wahnsinn, Genie — Poesie*, in: *Melancholie. Genie und Wahnsinn in der Kunst*, ed. Jean Clair, (Berlin / Paris, 2006) p. 15.

31 — Ludger Heidbrink, *Melancholie und Moderne. Zur Kritik der Historischen Verzweiflung*, (Munich, 1994) p. 49. See also Jean Clair: 'In the interaction between the soul and the body, between fleeting mood and enduring temperament, melancholy truly remains ungraspable: man has sought to comprehend it for over 2500 years in the Occident.' Jean Clair, *Ein Museum der Melancholie*, in: *Melancholie. Genie und Wahnsinn in der Kunst*, ed. Jean Clair, (Berlin / Paris, 2006) p. 82.

32 — Yves Bonnefoy describes melancholy as the result of a 'fracture between existence and conceptual thinking'. His definition shares with the aspect of the suffering felt when confronted with the unreachable, mentioned above and the basis of the following argumentation, the discrepancy opening up between actual existence with the longed-for difference or wanting to be elsewhere. Yves Bonnefoy, Melancholie, Wahnsinn, Genie — Poesie, in: *Melancholie. Genie und Wahnsinn in der Kunst*,

utes. Singing known works from film, pop, opera, and folk music, or political or historical pieces, where the deviation from the original emphasizes the personal dimension of appropriation, means a subjective actualization in which the present presence and the recalled merge.[36] The work *Company* (2000) shows just how pivotal this moment of appropriation is: Susan Philipsz plays a piano sequence from the film *Don't Look Now* (Nicholas Roeg, 1973), although she has never learnt the piano. The ten-minute sound recording documents a tentative emulation of the prototype and ends with achieving a recognizable melody. The lack of technical perfection in the performance (in both playing the piano and singing) is not some kind of concession the artist makes in order to present what interests her, but rather a device for conveying the process of an audible appropriation, enabling her to relate the themes of the pieces to her own person while, through the manner of the recording and staging, also opening up this relationship for the listener. In the short texts she frequently writes on her works in accompanying publications, Philipsz describes music pieces and films as the expression and bearer of fundamental human experiences and emotions.[37] Through the filter of her appropriation and the specific conditions of reception in a museum she makes available the distillate of these themes anew.

Through this form of appropriation and the audible distance it generates to the prototype, Philipsz is furthermore able to tangibly render melancholy as a salient historical-cultural idea, one which can be *contemplated* (especially as to its current relevance). With the act of appropriation and the use of loudspeakers taking on a mediating role in the exhibition space, a double distance is created between the listener and the historical source material, which itself is already a reflection of a melancholic zeitgeist. The multiple refraction and estrangement deliberately staged in space turns the melancholy itself into a substrate. The self-contained, circular structure of canon and loop forms the framework for this mediation on melancholy, a structure that suspends time and affirms the museum as a site of exemplary contemplation.

ed. Jean Clair, (Berlin/Paris, 2006) p. 14 ff.

33 — The same applies for the auditorium of the Museum of Modern Art in Busan, where *There is Nothing Left Here* (2006) was shown.

34 — The interplay between fullness and emptiness is a key moment in the work *There is Nothing Left Here*, in which, besides her voice, Susan Philipsz uses a vibraphone that is played in the gallery room during the pauses, 'emphasizing the emptiness of the space as they [the vibraphone chimes] fill it' (Susan Philipsz in: Susan Philipsz. *There is Nothing Left Here*, Centro Galego de Arte Contemporanea, p. 33).

35 — The 'spectral' in her works, which Susan Philipsz repeatedly alludes to in her texts, corresponds to this invisible presence: Susan Philipsz. *There is Nothing Left Here*, Centro Galego de Arte Contemporanea, (Santiago de Compostela, 2008) p. 13, 33, 43.

36 — Francis Mckee, *The Secret Sign*, in: *Susan Philipsz*, ed. Malmö Konsthall, Malmö 2005, p. 30–34. The overcoming of the temporal distance in the appropriation finds a spatial correlation in the works *Let It Breathe* (2007) and *The Lost Reflection* (2007), where two voices or organs meet one another across the distance of a room or a river.

37 — Susan Philipsz in: *Susan Philipsz. There is Nothing Left Here*, Centro Galego de Arte Contemporanea, (Santiago de Compostela, 2008) p. 27, 33, 51, 63.

We Shall Be All

Chicago, 2011

Museum of Contemporary Art, Chicago, 2011.
35mm film transferred to DVD and four-channel sound installation.
8 minutes.

The title *We Shall Be All* comes from the American version of *The Internationale* adapted by Charles H. Kerr for the International Workers of the World songbook. The exhibition consisted of three parts. A version of *The Internationale*, originally made in 1999 was installed in the atrium of the museum. In an adjoining darkened space a black film projection titled *We Shall Be All* (2011), could be heard.

In the Jane Addam's Hull House Museum on South Halsted Street, I installed *Pledge*, a sound work from 2002. The first element of the 35mm film work is a single voice rendition of me singing the Scottish ballad Annie Laurie. It was reported that one of the Haymarket martyrs A.R. Parsons sung this song to a rapt prison audience the night before he was executed. The second element is the projection of a

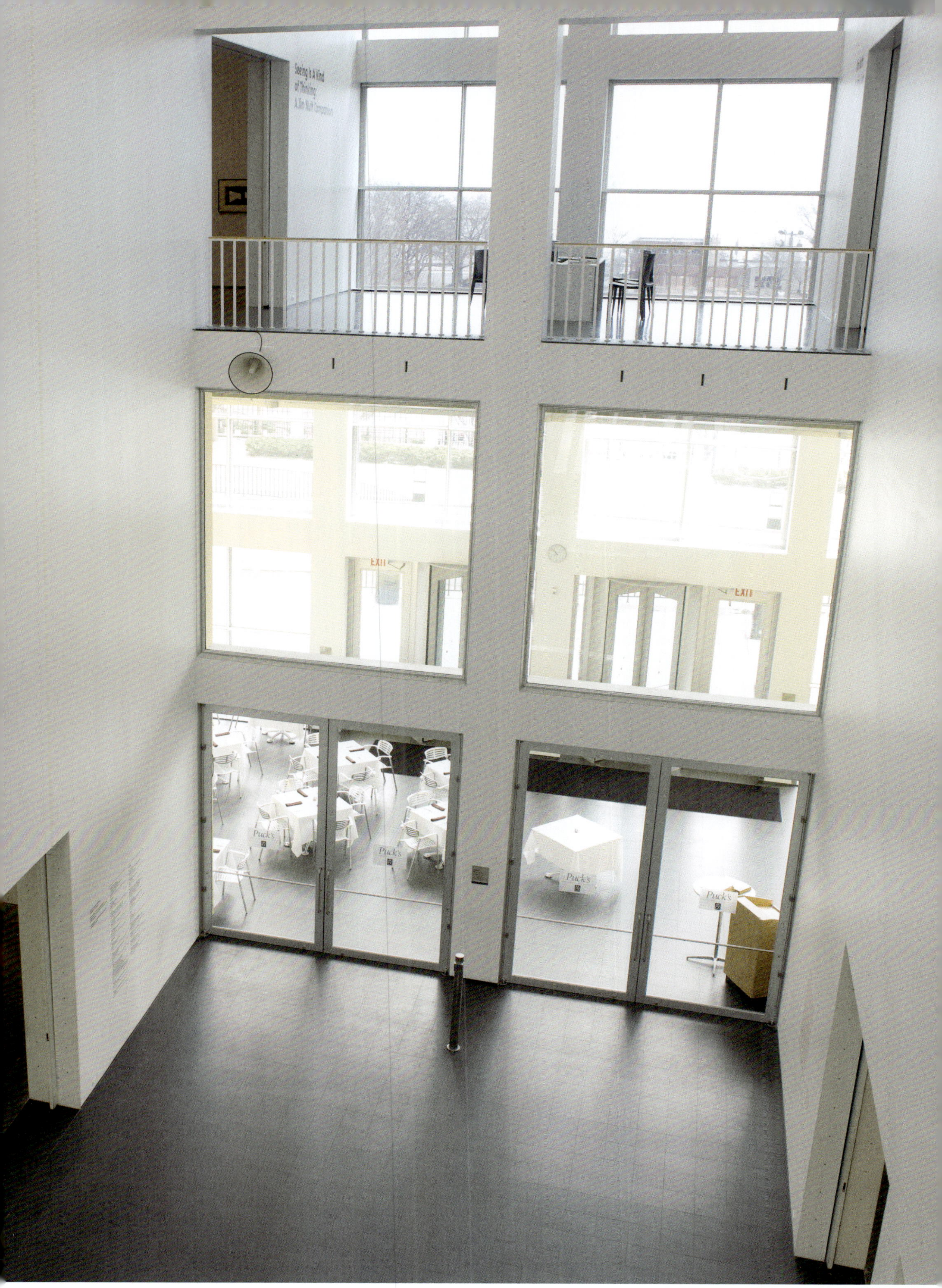

short extract from a poem, which originated in the Paris Commune of 1871 but was often repeated in speeches by Voltairine de Cleyre in memory of the Haymarket martyrs. The work samples the beginning of Godspeed You! Black Emperor's *East Hastings* as it features on their debut album *F# A# ∞*, with rhythmic bagpipe playing over-layered with the sounds of traffic noise and a street preacher. The samples were arranged in a round moving the sound through four speakers in the space. The final part features four separate recordings of me singing Leonard Cohen's song *Who By Fire* in unison.

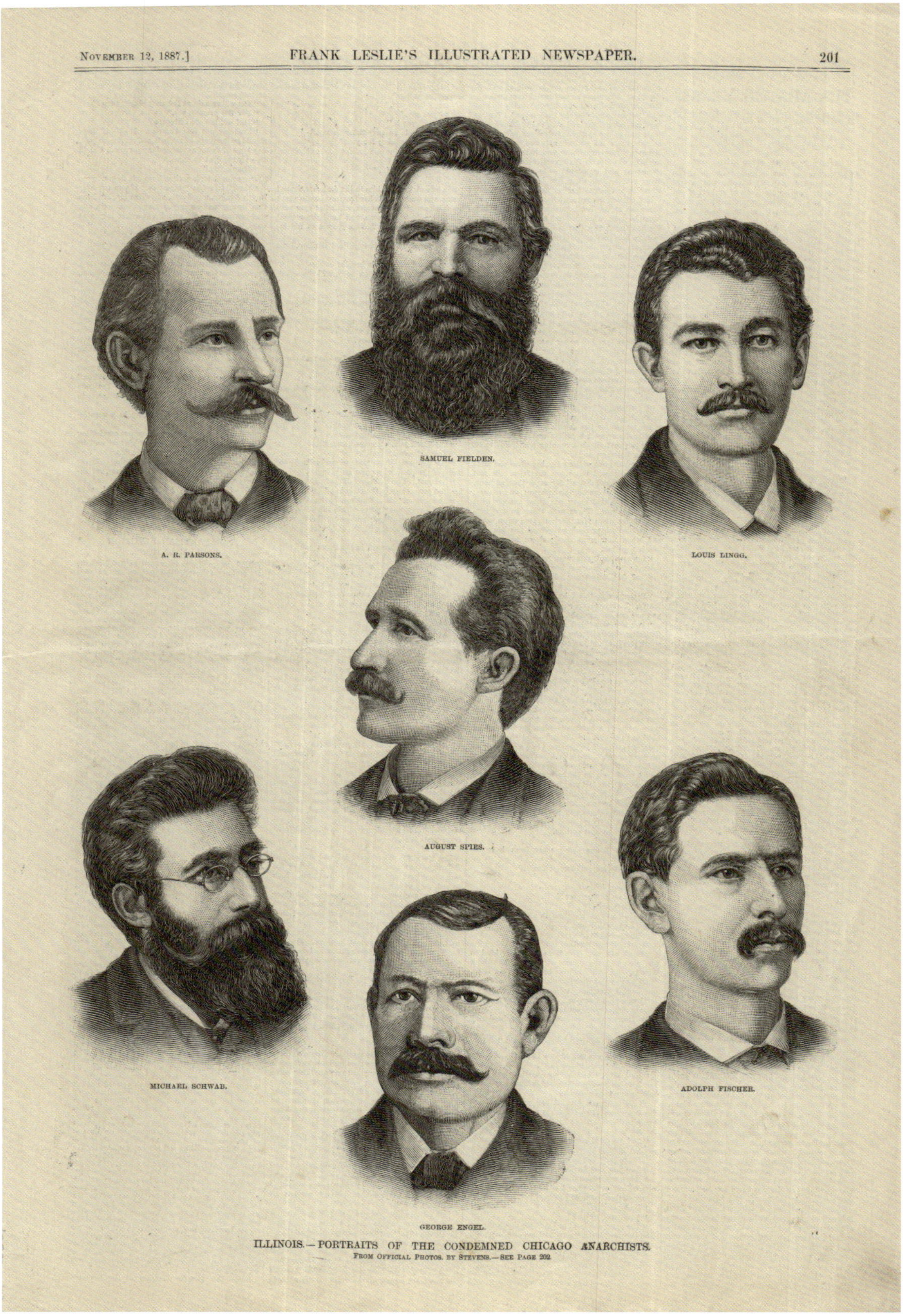

The Haymarket Martyrs

'Before morning he (Parsons) broke the stillness of his surroundings by singing a favourite song of his earlier days, *Annie Laurie*. The clear tones echoing down the corridor startled all then awake, and prisoners and deathwatch eagerly inclined their heads to catch every word and note. When Parsons drew near the closing stanza, his voice tripped and hesitated, unmistakably showing that his feelings were giving way to the recollections of former times.' Michael J. Schaack, *Anarchy and Anarchists. A History of the Red Terror and the Social Revolution in America and Europe. Communism, Socialism, and Nihilism in Doctrine and in Deed. The Chicago Haymarket Conspiracy, and the Detection and Trial of the Conspirators.* (Chicago, 1889)

Engraving of the Haymarket Martyrs reproduced in Frank Leslie's Illustrated Newspaper, November 12th 1887. Source: Library of Congress.

Voltairine de Cleyre in Philadelphia, aged 35, 1901. Photographer unknown. Source: Wiki Commons.

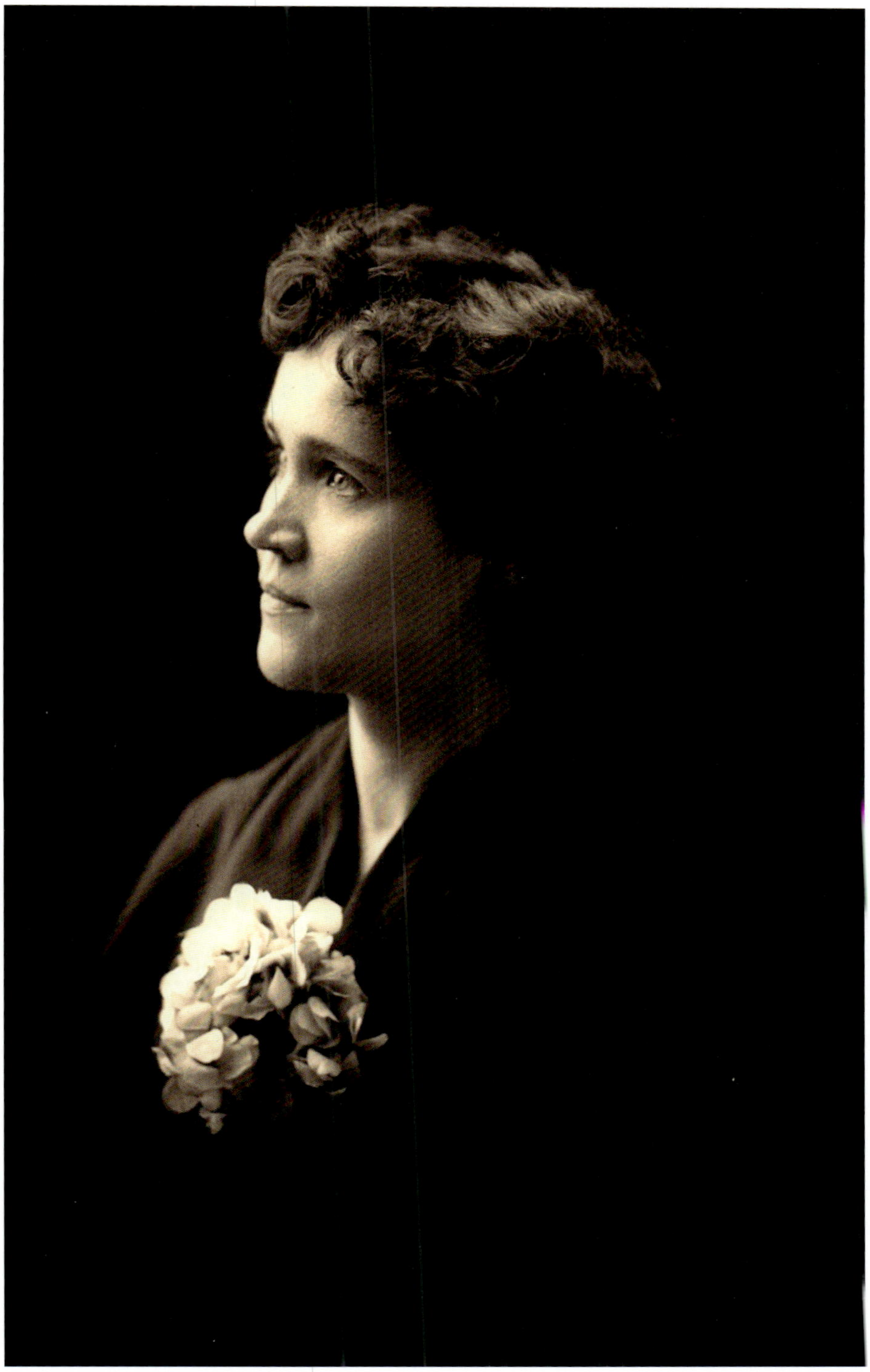

Glasgow and Chicago

During my teens and early twenties I was very politically active. I had grown up during the recession and the miners' strike in the UK and those events politicized a lot of people. During that time I heard a lot about the labour movement in Chicago, The International Workers of the World, Voltairine de Cleyre and the Haymarket Martyrs. I'd also read *The Jungle* (1906) by Upton Sinclair. This coloured my perception of how Chicago would look, which is why I was so surprised by all the gleaming towers of steel and glass. To my mind it seemed to have an affinity with Glasgow, which is also an industrial city with a very rich labour history and somehow I thought it would look the same.

Who By Song

Dieter Roelstraete

It is one of the many ironies typical of Chicago —arguably America's most American city, and justifiably proud of its long blue-collar and big-shoulders history—that Labor Day, one of the world's most widely observed non-religious holidays, is not celebrated in the city that, way back in 1886, became the scene of the primordial political event that would lead to the institution of International Worker's Day, commemorated every year around the world on 1 May.

The story is well known, but worth reiterating nonetheless (in forgetful Chicago in particular!) In the spring of 1886, Chicago unionists, reformers, socialists, anarchists, and ordinary workers joined forces to make the city the centre of the national movement for an eight-hour working day. Between 25 April and 4 May, countless meetings were held across town, many resulting in impromptu street protests. On Saturday 1 May, 35,000 workers walked off their jobs; tens of thousands more, both skilled and unskilled, joined them on 3 and 4 May, triggering a snowball effect of panic-stricken police responses. The bloodiest of these took place on 4 May at Haymarket Square, in what is today known as the West Loop, when a bomb was hurled into a police battalion, leading the latter to shoot indiscriminately into a crowd of overwhelmingly peaceful protesters. An undetermined number of workers were killed on the spot along with eight police officers, and hundreds of people were arrested in the event's frantic aftermath. The bomb-thrower himself was never identified, but eight prominent labour activists who clearly had no links whatsoever to the bombing were tried for murder, and seven were sentenced to death in what was eventually (but only much later) revised as one of the worst miscarriages of justice in American history, casting a shadow of suspicion and debt over the affair's protagonists and their families that still has not been wholly cancelled. (During the Cold War, Labor Day was demonised as a communist holiday. In 1955, President Eisenhower even went so far as to proclaim 1 May 'Loyalty Day' instead—a day meant to celebrate America's heritage of freedom.)[1] It is this story of willful forgetfulness, in part, that Susan Philipsz sought to memorialise in *We Shall Be All*, a site-specific project realised at Chicago's Museum of Contemporary Art in the spring of 2011, a mere half-hour walk away from the original site of the Haymarket protests. The title itself is a direct allusion to Chicago native Charles Hope Kerr's adaptation of the workers' anthem *L'Internationale*, which includes the immortal lines 'arise ye slaves, no more in thrall / the earth shall rise on new foundations / we have been naught, we shall be all'.

We Shall Be All—both the title of the exhibition and of one of the works in that exhibition, a 35 mm film transferred to DVD—consisted of four parts. In the first part, Philipsz, a native of Glasgow, could be heard singing the Scottish ballad *Annie Laurie* on a single-channel recording inside the exhibition space; it was rumoured that one of the Haymarket martyrs, socialist newspaper man Albert Parsons, sung this song to a rapt prison audience the night before his execution (his last words on the gallows were said to have been, rather fittingly, 'Let the voice of the people be heard'). In the second part, a scattering of fragments from a poem associated with both the Paris Commune and the speeches of the American anarchist and feminist Voltarine de Cleyre—who lies buried in Waldheim Cemetery in a Chicago suburb next to the Haymarket Seven and her better-known compagnon de route Emma Goldman—appeared on a projection screen, the only glimpses of light in an otherwise black film. The fragment read thus: 'I am not dead, I am not dead / I live a life intense, divine / Yours be the days forever fled / But all the morrows shall be mine'—the voice speaking in these verses was said to belong to the Commune herself. The third part recycled a sample taken from the debut album of Canadian cult heroes Godspeed You! Black Emperor containing droning bagpipe music and the raving and ranting of a pavement preacher struggling to make himself heard above ambient traffic noise. In the fourth

Rally at Haymarket Square. Courtesy: Library of Congress, Rare Book and Special Collections Division.

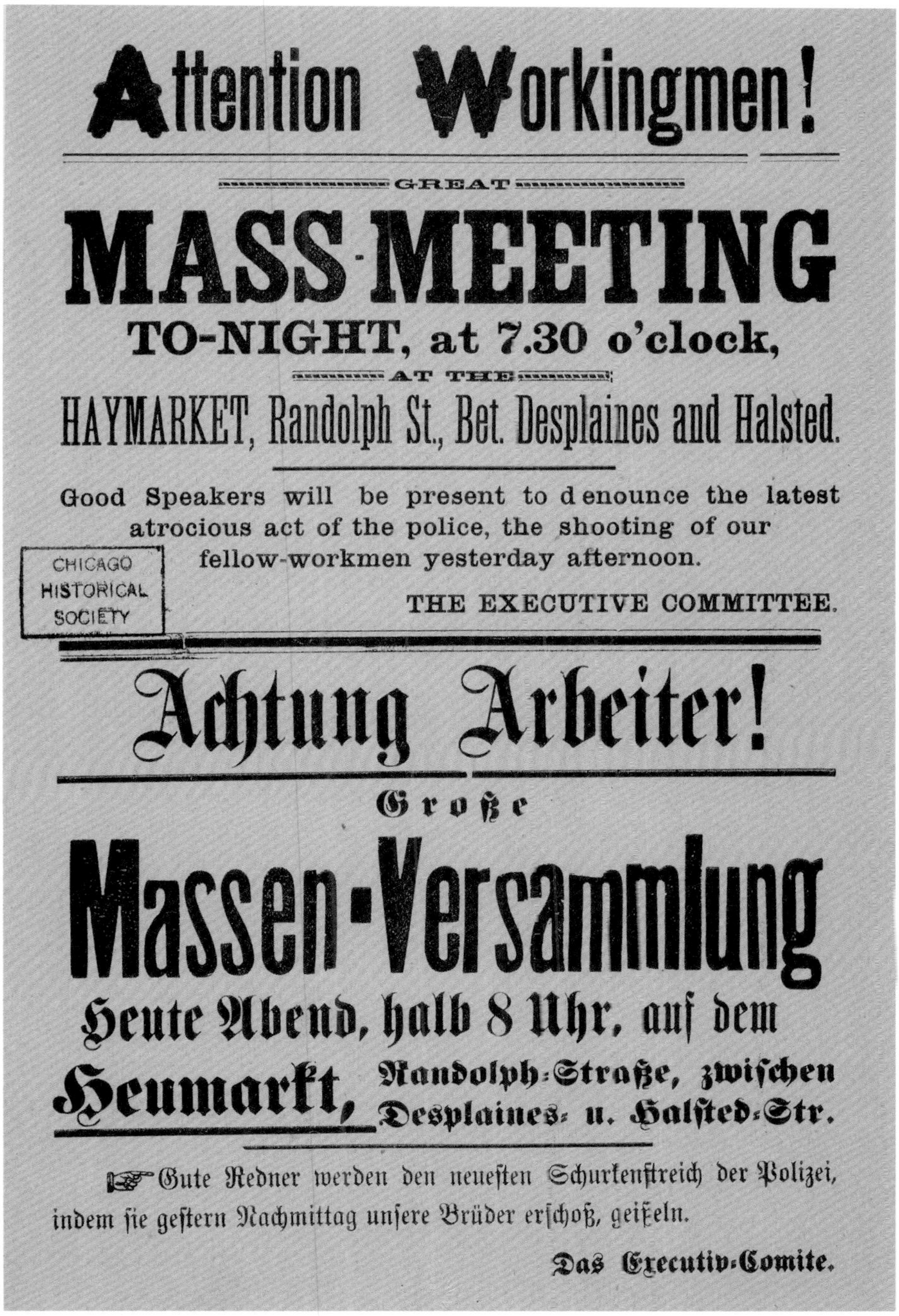

and final part, Philipsz herself could be heard again (this time in fourfold) as she performed a rendition of Leonard Cohen's classic *Who By Fire?*, listing a myriad of ways in which we might die and appear before God (it is one of Cohen's few songs to explicitly reference Jewish liturgy, as it is based on a prayer recited on both Rosh Hashanah and Yom Kippur). Both the third and fourth part of *We Shall Be All* made compelling use of the four speakers installed inside the exhibition space in distinctive ways, the third jumping, as it were, from one speaker to the next, the fourth sounding forth from all four speakers in chilling unison. The resultant eight-minute soundscape enacted a spiraling sensation of disorientation, and Philipsz's disembodied, unaccompanied voice was particularly effective in conveying the alienating sense of feeling all alone in an (imaginary) crowd which the artist is so often interested in triggering in her haunting use of institutional sites and spaces.

Indeed, 'haunting' is very much the operative term here. This project in particular, with its elegiac political overtones and portents of irretrievable utopias, certainly reminded this listener of the notion of hauntology—the smart neologism coined by Jacques Derrida in his landmark study *Spectres of Marx*, published in 1993, to evoke the phantom nature of Marx's gospel ('a spectre is haunting Europe, the spectre of Communism') after the fall of Soviet-style communism. It is worth remembering here that Derrida's book was very much written 'in the wake of the orgy of self-congratulations which followed the 1989 crumbling of the Berlin Wall,' and as a warning against a 'contagious optimism (...) best exemplified by the confidence and popularity of Francis Fukuyama's claim that the end of history was at hand, that the future—if that word could still be said to have the same meaning—was to become the global triumph of free market economies'.[2] *Spectres of Marx*, in short, was aimed at remembering precisely that which, back in the early nineties, too many of us were in a delirious rush to forget—shades, here, of America's own institutionalised forgetfulness with regards to its radical political past—and it is to this effect that Derrida emphasized the Marxian spectre as a revenant ('a question of repetition: a spectre is always a revenant'[3]), something that does not simply go away because we are so keen to forget it or put it aside as fully historicised fact, but rather always promises to come back, to move in circles: 'at bottom, the spectre is the future, it is always to come, it presents itself only as that which could come or come back.'[4] And so this very spectre continues to haunt, conjure and hang around, and refuses to fully disappear in thin air, much like the swirling echo of a disembodied, unaccompanied voice inside a museum that we are sure to take home with us. To quote Derrida again: 'haunting belongs to the structure of every hegemony'.[5] And *mutatis mutandis*, with regards to Philipsz's *We Shall Be All*, one could rephrase this passage as such: haunting belongs to the architecture of every hegemony—for it is in architecture first and foremost, and in museums as much as anywhere else, that such hegemonies materially and physically persist.

Ambling through the eerie dark or around the hushed nave of a museum with only angelic song to keep us company, one French philosopher inevitably leads to another—in fact, two. Here is what Gilles Deleuze and Félix Guattari have to say on the subject of song in the '1837: Of the Refrain' chapter of their delirious magnum opus *A Thousand Plateaus*: 'A child in the dark, gripped with fear, comforts himself by singing under his breath. He walks and halts to his song. (...) The song is like a rough sketch of a calming and stabilizing, calm and stable, centre in the heart of chaos'. Furthermore, 'a child hums to summon the strength for the schoolwork she has to hand in. A housewife sings to herself, or listens to the radio, as she marshals the antichaos forces of her work. (...) For sublime deeds like the foundation of a city or the fabrication of a golem, one draws a circle, or better yet walks in a circle as in a children's dance, combining rhythmic vowels and consonants that correspond to the interior forces of creation'.[6] These are all hallmarks, Deleuze and Guattari assert, of a single thing, the Refrain—and as the original French term, *ritournelle*, so clearly suggests—the refrain, too, is a revenant, something that comes back, possibly even eternally so. Indeed, 'let us recall Nietzsche's idea of the eternal return as a little ditty, a refrain,' the philosopher twins enjoin[7]

—but let us also recall the rather more innocuous example of a simple tune stuck in our mind, unwilling to go away or be dislodged, much like the ghosts and phantoms and spectre that 21st-Century politics, no matter how hegemonic and monolithic, is somehow unable to shake off. (Example given: the Haymarket refrain.) Though admittedly, at this point it is easier to conjure the languid melody of Leonard Cohen's *Who By Fire?* than the boisterous *Internationale*, whose marching-band magnanimity seems so tragically out of tune with our times, in which a very different idea of internationalism has come to dominate. *We Shall Be All*, a lonely voice timorously assures us—shall all of us be mere loners in the crowd?

1 — This account is based on the information gathered in the *Haymarket and May Day* entry (authored by Christopher Thale) in: James R. Grossman, Ann Durkin Keating & Janice L. Reiff (ed.), *Encyclopaedia of Chicago*, (University of Chicago Press, Chicago, 2004).

2 — Bernd Magnus and Stephen Cullenberg, *Editors' Introduction*, in: Jacques Derrida, *Specters of Marx* (trans. Peggy Kamuf)(Routledge, London, 1994) p.VII. The conflation of haunting and ontology in the Derridean concept of hauntology obviously chimes rather well with the radically immaterial nature of much of Philipsz's work.

3 — Jacques Derrida, op. cit., p. 11.

4 — Ibid., p. 48.

5 — Ibid., p. 46.

6 — Gilles Deleuze and Félix Guattari, *A Thousand Plateaus* (trans. Brian Massumi)(University of Minnesota Press, Minneapolis, 1987) p. 311.

7 — Ibid., p. 343.

Timeline

Edinburgh, 2012

Various locations,
Edinburgh, 2012.
Six three-channel sound installations, 8 seconds each. Commissioned by Edinburgh Art Festival.

Timeline was based on a series of recordings of my own voice sounding three harmonising notes around the key of 'G#', played simultaneously from six sites across the city at one o'clock. The sound was very short, lasting just under ten seconds, but it cut across all of the ambient sounds, like an aural clock. The sound was synchronised to travel from the first site at Calton Hill to the next at Calton Cemetery and on through North Bridge and Waverley Bridge and across the roof of the National Galleries of Scotland and on to Edinburgh Castle. There was a slight delay between the recordings so it seemed as if there was a domino effect of the sound travelling across the city.

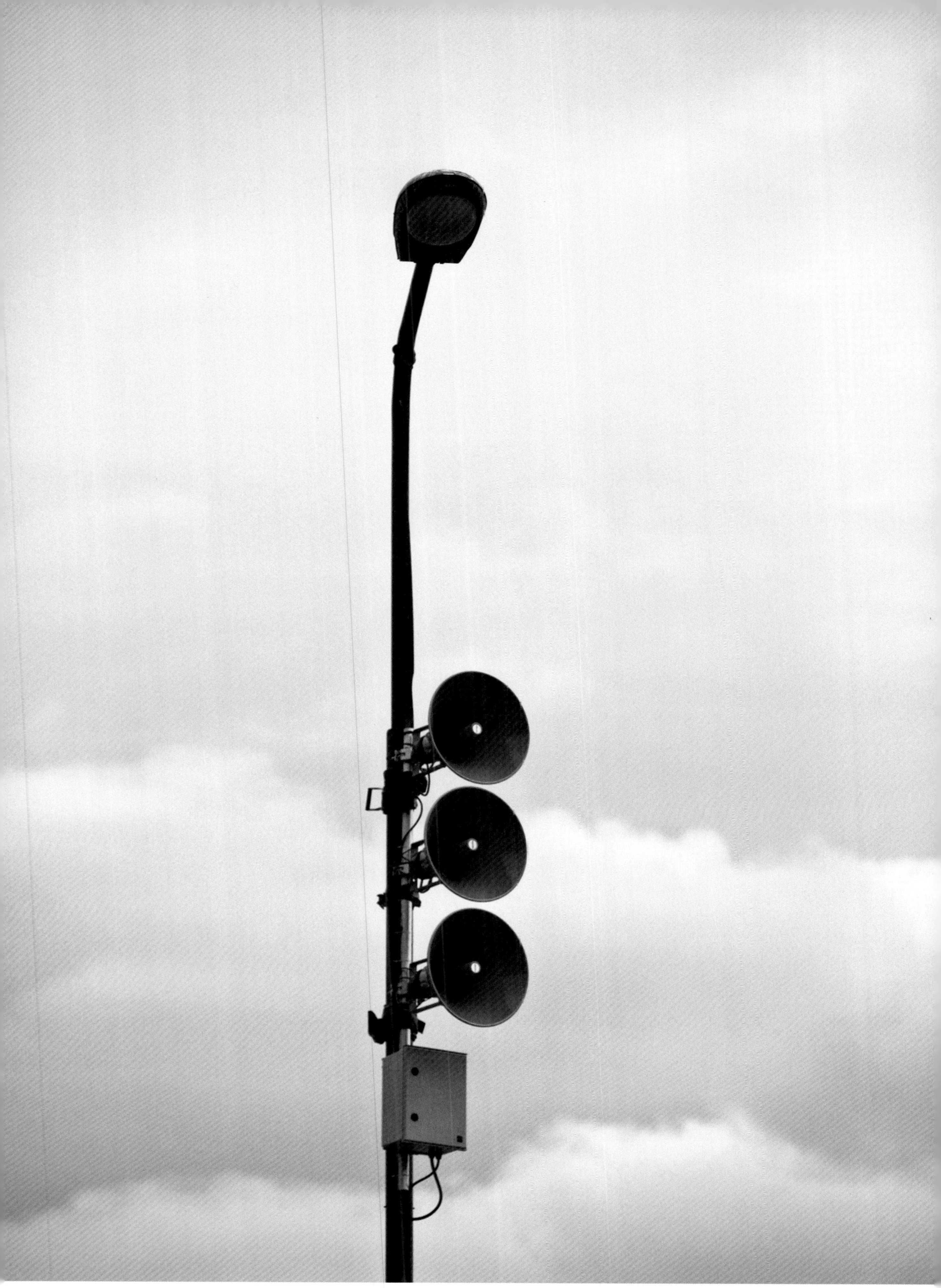
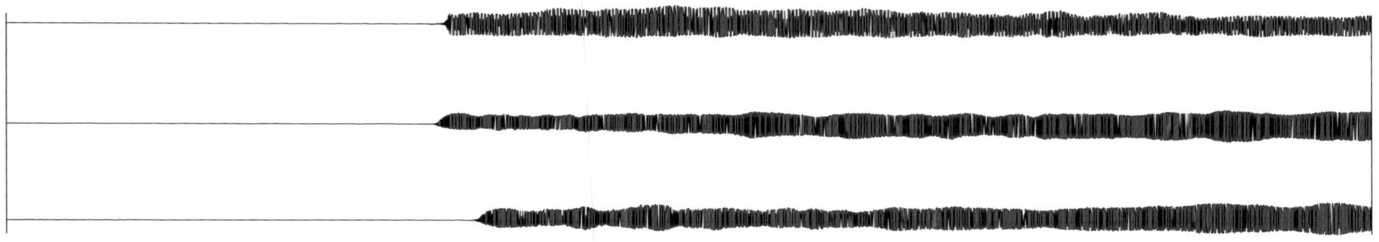

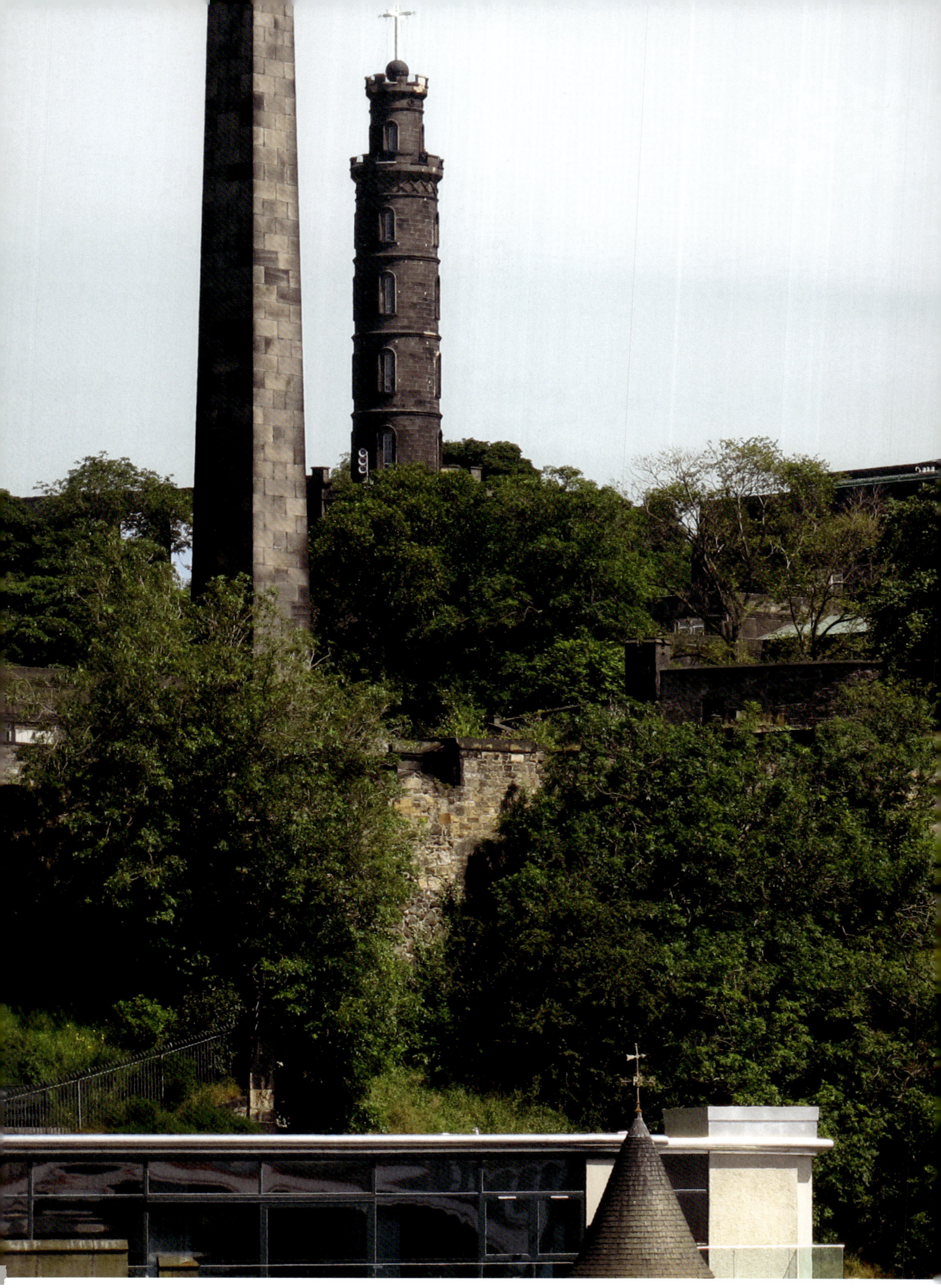

[redacted]

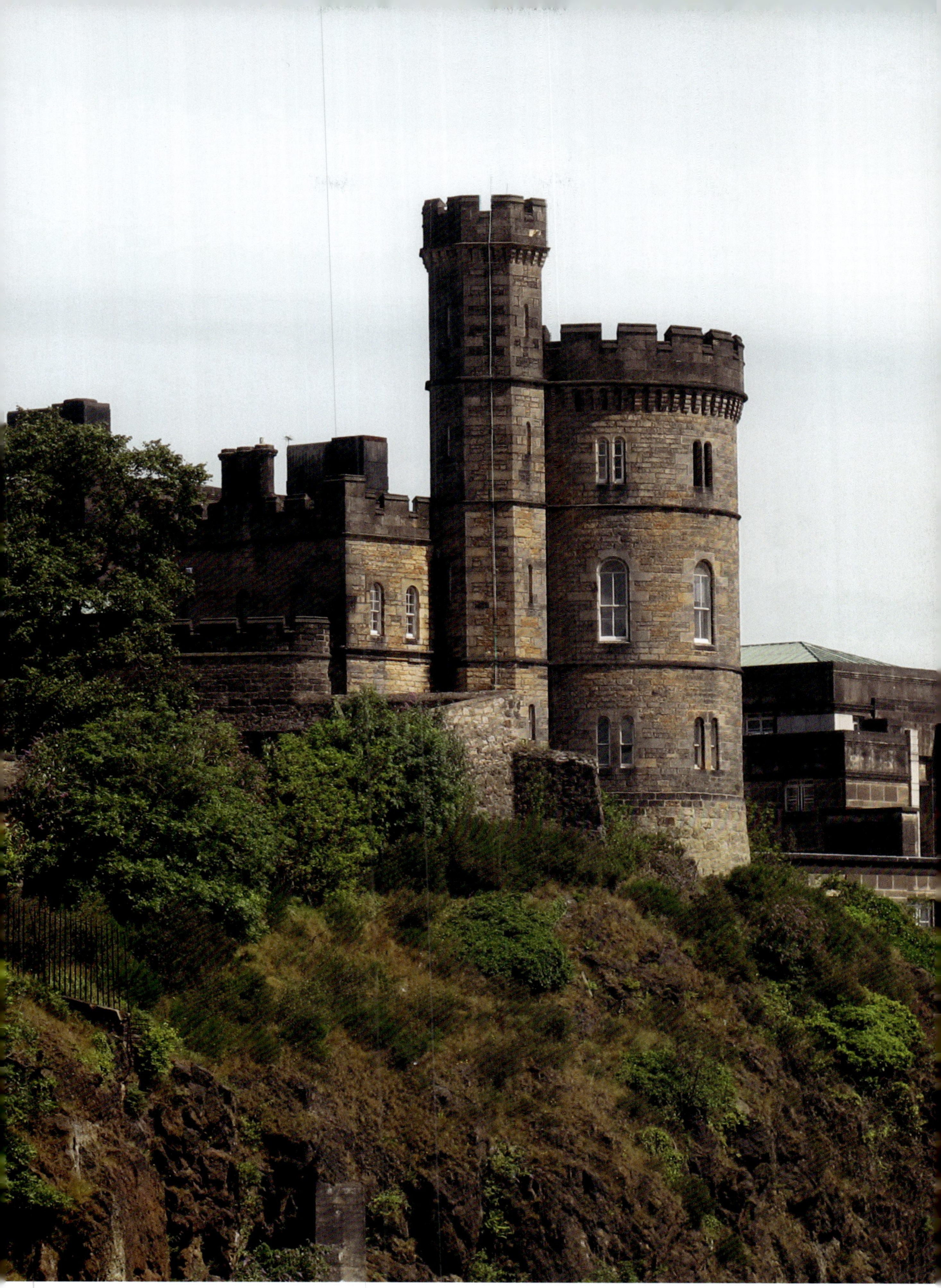

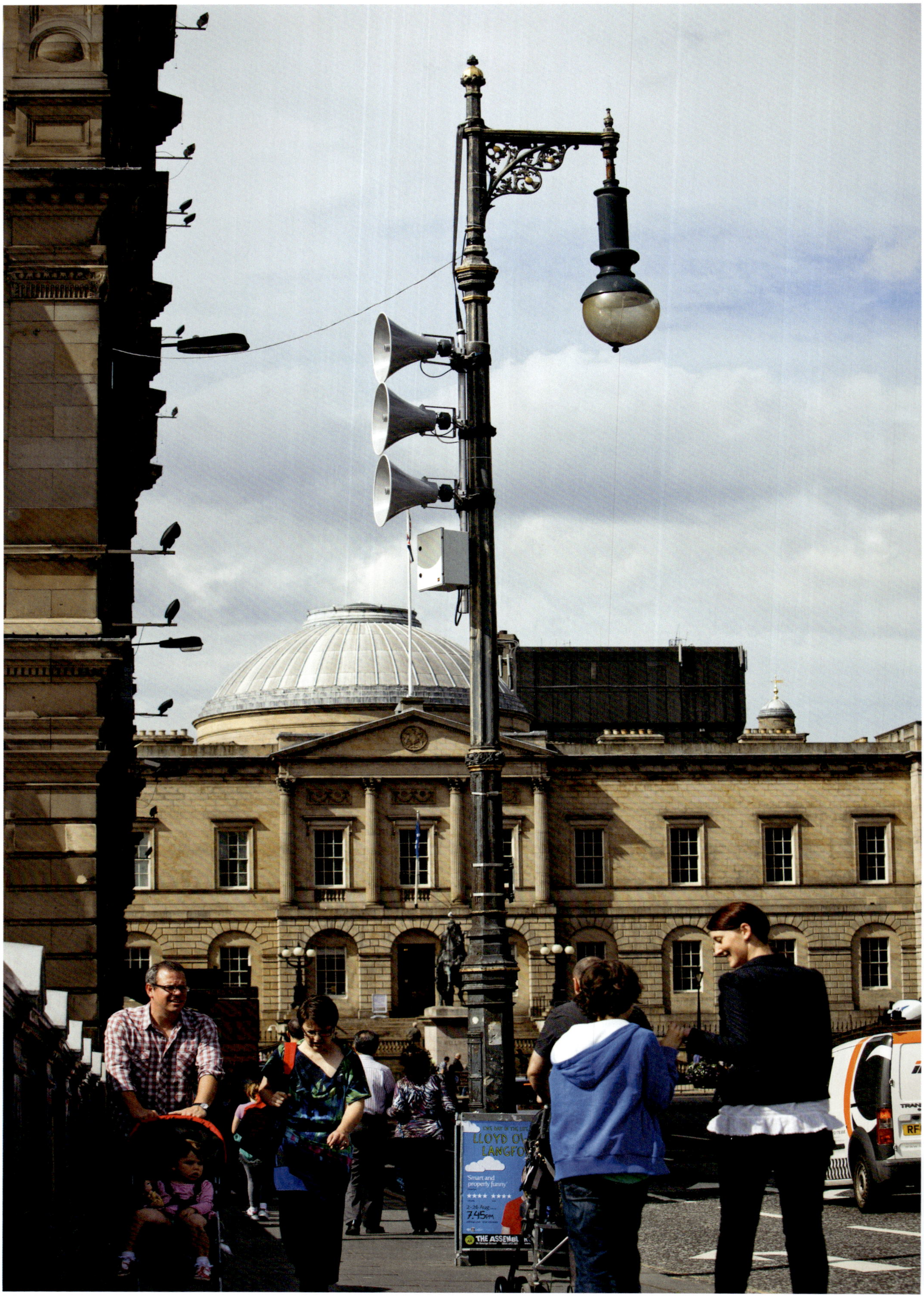
'Smart and properly funny'
2-26 Aug
7.45PM

Hermann von Helmholtz, Die Lehre von den Tonempfindungen als physiologische Grundlage für die Theorie der Musik. (Braunschweig, Friedrich Vieweg & Sohn, 1870).

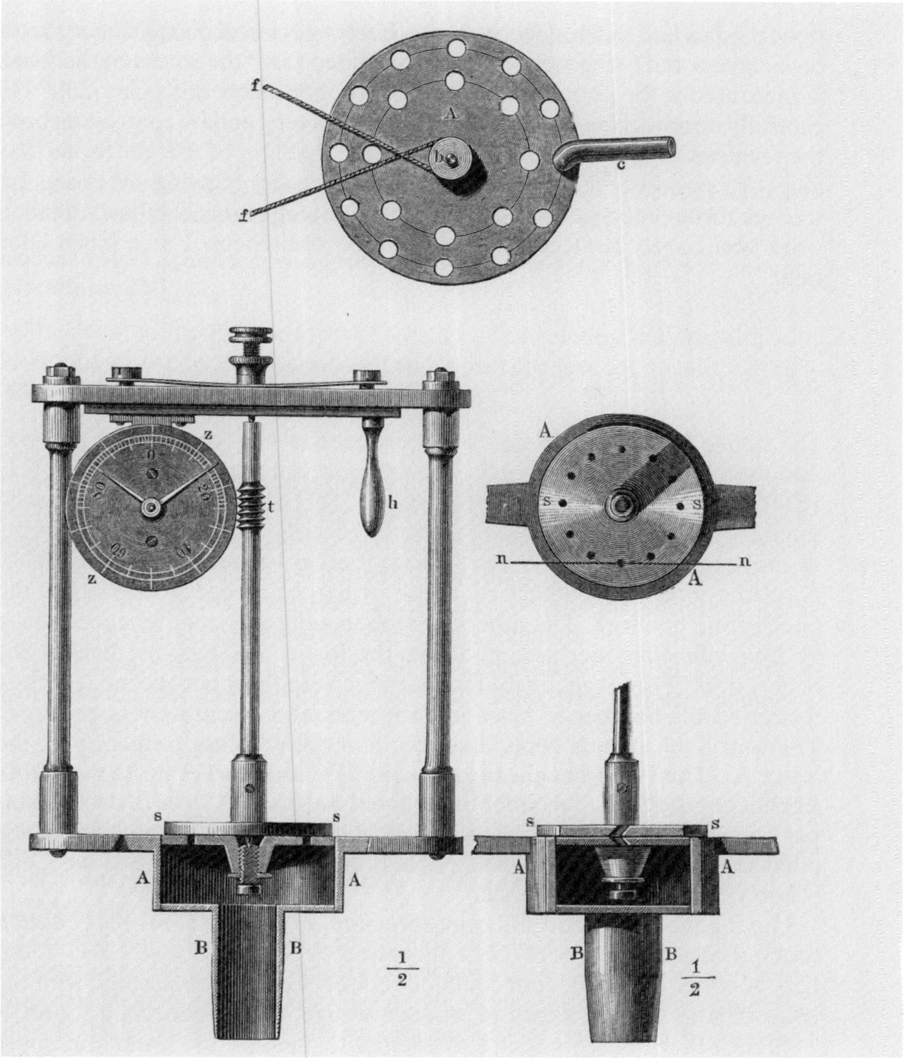

John Robison's Siren

'Professor Robison's device was the first form of an instrument, which will soon be introduced to you under the name of the syren. Robison describes his experiment in the following words: "A stop-cock was so constructed that it opened and shut the passage of a pipe 720 times in a second. The apparatus was fitted to the pipe of a conduit leading from the bellows to the wind-chest of an organ. The air was simply allowed to pass gently along this pipe by the opening of the cock. When this was repeated 720 times in a second, the sound g in alt was most smoothly uttered, equal in sweetness to a clear female voice".'
John Tyndall, *Sound: A course of eight lectures delivered at the Royal institution of Great Britain* (London Longmans, Green and Co., 1867), p. 55.

W&AK Johnston,
Time Gun Map, 1879,
Courtesy: The Trustees of the National Library of Scotland.

The view from Calton Hill looking towards Edinburgh Castle.

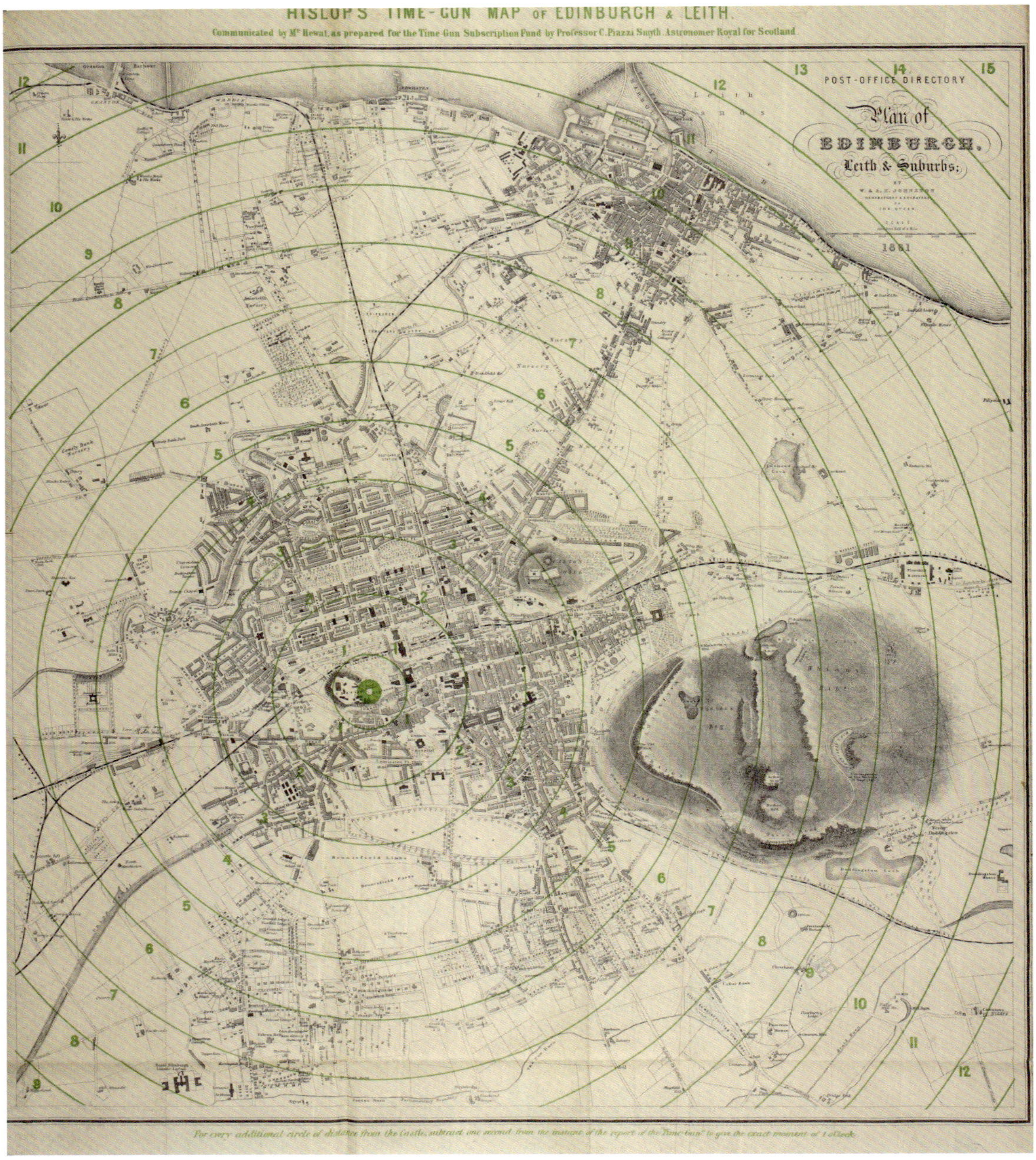

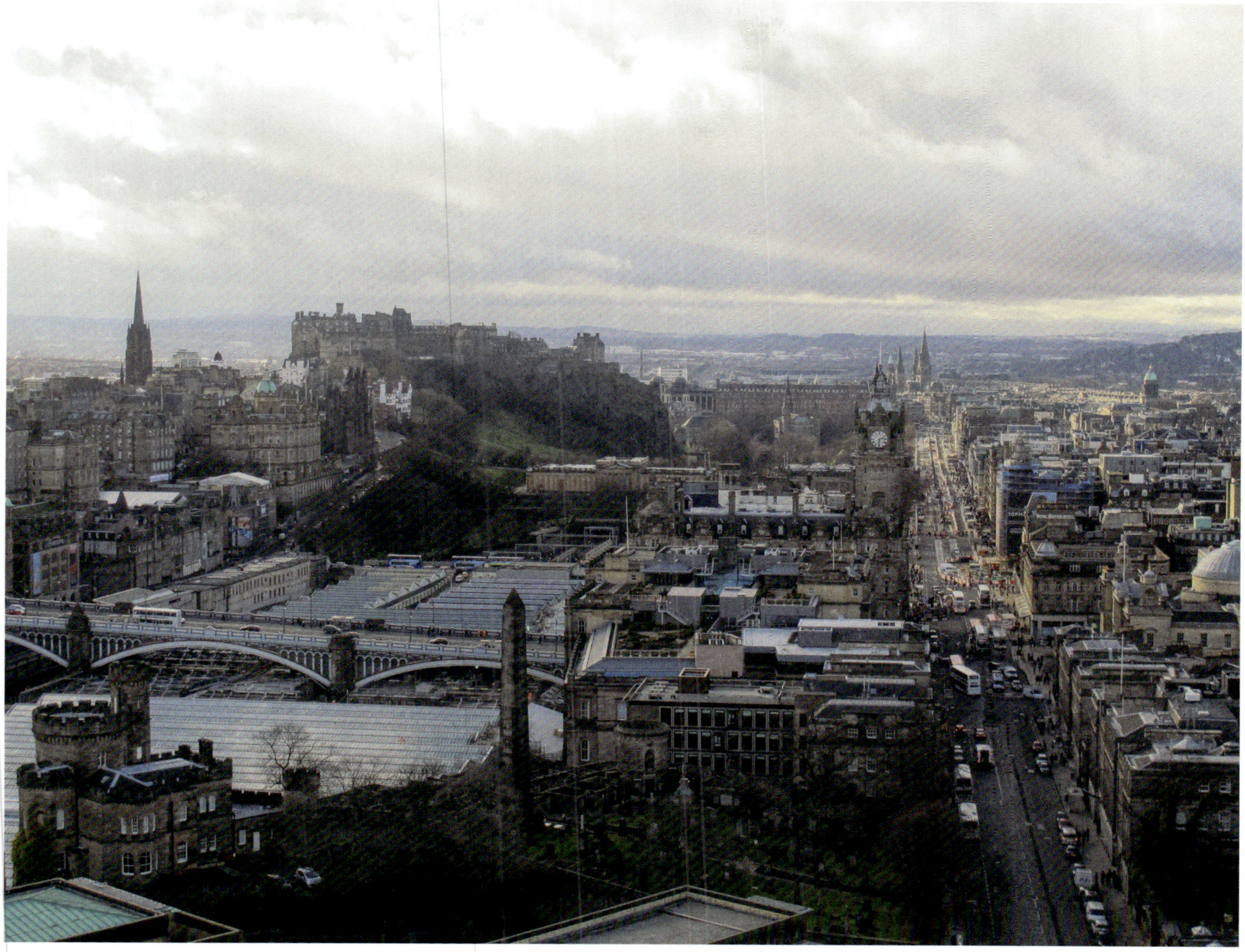

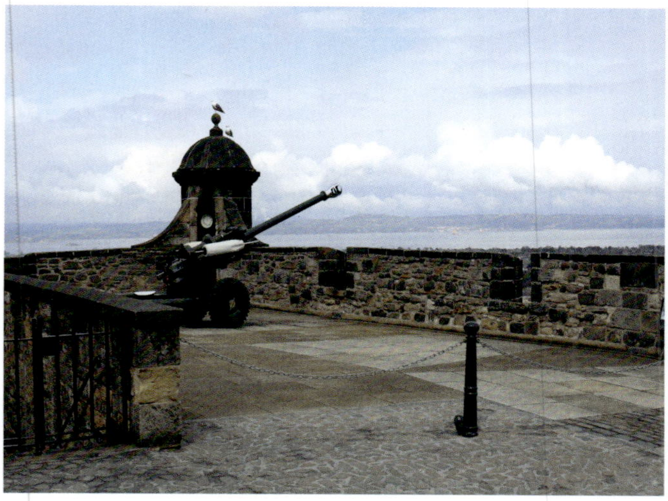

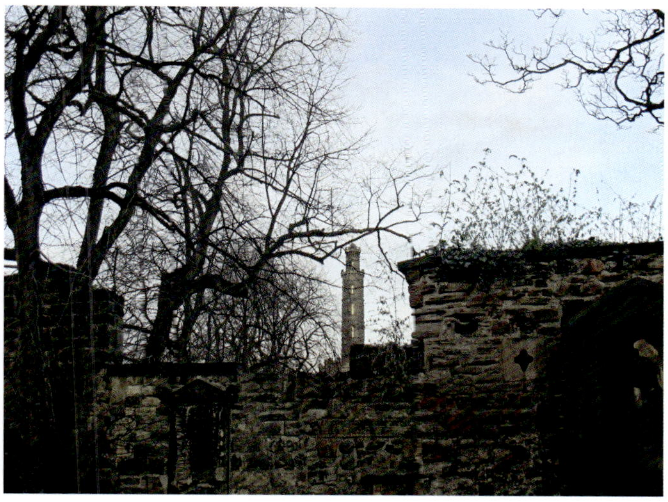

The Time Gun Map

In 1852, Edinburgh installed a time ball at the top of Nelson's Monument on Calton Hill, to enable the sailors in Leith docks and the Firth of Forth to adjust their chronometers. In 1861, a master clock on Calton Hill was linked by an overhead electric cable to a clock at Edinburgh Castle. This enabled the one o'clock gun at the castle to be fired automatically at exactly one o'clock. The electric cable linking the castle and Calton Hill was 1,225 metres long. It passed over Waverley Valley, without any support, at the height of 73 metres. In the 1860s, Time Gun Maps were published in the Edinburgh & Leith Post Office Directories to show the time taken for the sound of gunfire to travel across Edinburgh.

Socialism in her Heart: A Melodic Reverie in the Key of G. The Seven Harmonies of the Timeline

Ross Sinclair

C Major — When is Now?

I'm running along Princes St. It's the summer and the drained Nor-loch is on my right, a fetid swamp flooded by King James 3rd in 1460 to strengthen the defences of Edinburgh Castle. By the 19th Century it's been filled again to accommodate the demands of the expanding new town. Ebb and flow. Now it's called Princes St Gardens and I look beyond its trees and flowers and all the people lying on its rolling lawns towards the Castle above. It's nearly one o'clock. I anticipate a sound, I can almost see it floating there, hanging in the air, waiting in readiness, but something's missing. I'm still running, still dreaming. Calton Hill is directly in front of me, but flying far away and high above, the strange jumble of *world heritage*, monument and folly rising up from the East end of Princes St, high above the heads of the thousands of people swarming in between me and it. I know there is a connection between one of the monuments there and the sound I'm keening to hear. I'm listening, still running, late, late, past the broken tram works and their stupid everyday traffic jams towards the mound of Royal Scottish Academy and The National Galleries of Scotland. This place hasn't changed much since 1781 when one and a half million cartloads of earth excavated from the new town excavations were dumped on the nor-loch to make this ersatz hill on which the city's grandest art institutions were constructed. I'm still heading towards them where I know something is happening. I see a flash of red through the crowd, I think I can see her sisters. Suddenly the one o'clock gun fires, exploding in my right ear. I immediately understand that this something is happening right here, right now and that I am in the middle of it. There's an echo. A response. It has changed. A new sound. A woman's voice. I hear it again, in the gardens, on the bridges, in the air. Far away on Calton Hill. I think back, the direction is not clear. The sound is all around. In her *Timeline,* nothing is carved in stone. Geography, history and the relative position of people in-between are open and fluid. It might still be the 19th Century, and maybe the now famous one o'clock gun is about to fire for the first time. And a voice responds, echoing, falling across the city in an uncertain harmony. A peculiar siren, coming and going, breathing. No, not yet.

D Major — Empirical Evidence

Edinburgh Castle. The Old Town / New Town shuffle. Politics and parliament, education and knowledge, culture, democracy and 900 years of history punctuated every day by the now famous tradition of the one o'clock gun, still anachronistically keeping time for long dead sailors from the 19th Century. This is the Capital City of somewhere and the *Timeline* is currently pointing us to the epicentre of the exact moment of now. It feels like home for her but only because she hasn't lived here for years. This is a Sunday best image of a nation's home. Too good to be true, a dream, an unknown place, like the past — a reverie, a *foreign country.* It looks the part, more than most, but what's underneath? There are no foundations to these places, nothing fixed. Tectonic plates have become separated from their core and float around aimlessly, the people milling around on top, confused. Nothing is certain in the *Timeline* of the past or future of this damp northern European country. A nation's identity forged on myths and stories, literature and fiction, defining moments that never really existed in the first place — it's perfect for this *Timeline*. Everything could change forever, simply by answering one question on a ballot paper. The only authentic moment is right now, and her *Timeline* illuminates it momentarily before it evaporates. She's never really worked here before, but she's working now. It's one o'clock. Again I hear a woman's voice.

E Major — Sing History Changed

The *Timeline* grinds forward. We jump from the 15th to the 18th to the 21st Century. It's later now and everything has been transformed. The date is now 2015 or perhaps 2020. The Citizens of Edinburgh are living in 'The Pan-National All Inclusive Free Artists and Peoples Independent Socialist Republic of Neo-Scotia'. After Scotland became a sovereign nation state in the independence referendum of 2014 (answering one simple question), the leaders of the ruling Party sold off all current and future rights to all the oil in the North Sea for the people. It was worth trillions. And the people owned it all. Fired by the success of this socialist vision employing wisdom and foresight, the politicians handed over the running of the country to the nation's artists. Thus the new cultural custodians, with only the promise of good for all and joy ringing in their hearts, were able to immediately disband the military, sell off all the banks and turn over all the major infrastructures and the hundreds of billions now available in the peoples' reserve to the citizens of the new republic. Artists, writers, and philosophers, poets and musicians, playwrights, thinkers and dreamers would run the country now. And as Beuys said, everyone is an artist so everyone could be in charge. This new reading of the *Timeline* was very popular, and everyone was welcome to come from around the world, because all kinds of people are needed for all sorts of important jobs running things in this culture country.

So things are done differently, in this new Republic of Artists. For instance the *one o'clock gun* which inspired her *Timeline* no longer exists. There is no one o'clock gun here in Edinburgh anymore, no guns at all in the new *Timeline*, no shells, no explosion, no military barking and shouts, no men up here at all, no army and no navy and certainly no nuclear submarines and no nuclear weapons. All of these things have been de-materialised. Like all the objects which ceased long ago to be important in the *Timeline* of her artworks.

Replacing the one o'clock gun is a series of sounds which emerge from the high ramparts of this fortified structure previously called Edinburgh Castle. Echoing in a series of stages up from Calton Hill to the famous volcanic plug, this rock of ages, we hear a woman's voice, a harmony of voices — tremulous, yearning, travelling, and seeking out the company of other voices, a choir of a people, mapping a territory, constructing a constituency. This is the thing the tourists come to hear now. The one o'clock shout. This is her *Timeline*. First experienced in 2012 as part of the Edinburgh Art Festival in response to the gun, it has now totally replaced it. Objects de-materialised by the sound of her individual voice. This *Timeline* needs no gun, no bullets. There are no leftovers, no waste. Only the mechanics of the transfer of the sound into the air. Hers is a lean economy. One voice, amateur, idiosyncratic, individual and glorious.

F Major — Patterns of History in the Timeline

The Nelson Monument on Calton Hill, overlooking the city was originally designed by Alexander Nasmyth in 1807, though this scheme was deemed too expensive and eventually an alternative design of an 'upside-down telescope' was obtained from the architect Robert Burn. In 1853, the Astronomer Royal for Scotland, Charles Piazzi Smyth, invented the time ball, still seen today on top of the monument, made of wood and covered in zinc, after a version at Greenwich, home of time. This clock mechanism is raised everyday just before one o clock and at one pm exactly... it falls. It's strange to celebrate Nelson in this small country. The Napoleonic wars for which he became a martyr at Trafalgar were one of the prime motivations for the Highland Clearances in which the poor people were forced off the land in favour of better paying tenants, sheep for example, because the landed gentry were being squeezed for more taxes from their masters in the south-east to fund the war. This forced population removal produced a lively Scottish Diaspora, handy for future *'Years of Homecoming'* and touristic visits to Edinburgh in a genealogical grave-robbing frenzy to eclipse that even of Burke and Hare. Though in reality this changed the land and the people and the history of the 'half-nation' forever. That's why, on our peripatetic sojourns into deepest Scotland, we don't see anybody actually living in all the fertile hills and glens of this picturesque country, of which Edinburgh is the shining, gaudy bauble, as Dr. Johnson probably never said.

G Major — It's Always One O'Clock Somewhere

So on Calton Hill at one o'clock exactly every day since the middle of the 18th Century the ball drops on this monument to Lord Nelson, 561 feet above sea level. It gives the signal to sailors, enabling ships in the Firth of Forth and Port of Leith to check and reset their chronometers and watches since the days before accurate timepieces were available. However this rudimentary method of time keeping meant that someone would have to be looking out for the ball and it often couldn't be seen in foggy or inclement weather, of which there is a good deal in this damp country. So to augment this visual timepiece a gun began to be fired in tandem. The one o'clock gun was positioned on the highest vantage point, the castle, fired simultaneously to the time ball dropping. The gun could easily be heard by ships two miles away in Leith Harbour whatever the weather. Originally an 18-pound muzzle loading cannon that needed four men to load and activate was fired from the Half Moon Battery at the Castle. The cannon was eventually replaced with a 25-pound Howitzer in 1953 and was subsequently fired from Mill's Mount Battery on the North face of the Castle.

In 1861, to ensure the timing of the gun was perfectly accurate, a 1225 metre cable was installed between the eight-year-old clock on Calton Hill and the battery in Edinburgh Castle. At the same time the *Time Gun Map* was produced showing the time it took for the sound from the gun to reach different parts of the city out towards the ports and the sea, enabling compensation to be made for the time it took the sound to travel. Mapping time. In *Timeline* her voice retraces this now invisible connection, building a harmony in response from 'the clock' on the monument on Calton Hill to the gun, back to the Castle, different parts bonding, coalescing in the key of G. These singular voices radiate around the city, exploring, harmonized tones, coming together, falling apart.

A Major — The Timeline seen from Different Angles

The form of the sound created in *Timeline* is her voice emulating the noise of a ship's siren. In some ways this squares the circle, provides an essence of the original audience on the ships at sea for whom the whole complicated signal is intended, which now becomes an integral part of its own construction. This siren is not one tone, but is made up of different sounds heard together, an insistent harmony in three voices in our *Timeline*, constructed from sounds emanating from different points across the city, mirroring the Time Gun Map. Multiple voices, coming together. The mathematician and philosopher John Robison invented the first siren in Edinburgh in 1799. Designed as a musical instrument, the apparatus was first fitted to the wind-chest of an organ and was thus described, *The sound in G alt was most smoothly uttered, equal in sweetness to a clear female voice.* It was later proven that these sirens worked equally well under the water and had in any case been named after the classical Siren of Greek mythology, *femmes fatales* who lured sailors to their deaths with their enchanting music and voices. Since the Scottish Enlightenment, Edinburgh has been known as *The Athens of the North*, its neo-classical architecture the backdrop to a new way of ordering the shape of the world into existence and now serves as a rich context for her evocation of its sirens of mythology. Maybe the artist's feminine voice is here symbolically projected back from the sea, drawing listeners in, imploring, seducing, exploring a new topography across the neo-classical vista's of this peacock of a city. Bouncing from Calton Hill to the Castle to the sea and back, it oscillates, a critical frequency — a harmony in the key of G. This woman's voice.

B Major — A Tough Kind of Love... a Virtuous Circle

A Militant Tendency exists at the core of her work. This has been in her heart since the experience of her formative years conjured a landscape of politics populated by the passionate voices of its irascible inhabitants. With this paradigm, in this manner, she has been singing in the high world for many years but at the same time she sings a hymn to the low world and its fractured and frightened constituents, dismantling their barricades, piecing together the shards of experience, smoothing the edges. She will re-imagine the space where people will live yesterday and tomorrow using only the air that comes from inside her body, born out of her lungs, today. She has been pioneering new relationships, growing new rhizomatic networks – high – low – hi – lo – hello. Often we don't even know we are part of a conversation — we think it's all about us, the sounds inside our head, an indistinct voice of anaesthesia — we are opened up. This represents a rare victory. It's a tough kind of love... to make us part of the *Timeline.* Perhaps this need for dialogue is something to do with where she comes from, and where her *Timeline* might lead us.

High C — Finding the Correct Key that best suits your Voice

She told me recently that when she meets people they are often very excited to convey to her their unique experience of the work. They tell her about the specific meteorological conditions that were in place at the precise moment they found the work - what the weather was like, what time of day, the light, what they felt, what they thought, what they knew. And even in the summer, harmonising across the width and breadth of the city in the key of G, the weather of the Edinburgh *Timeline* is far from reliable. Still her listeners can believe their experience of the work is the only real and authentic one and yet one which she herself could never know, never experience. The work can be experienced without art always being the framing device. So people discuss the work as if it were lost and they, alone, had discovered it. They have the idea that the work doesn't actually exist until their experience of it gives it a shape. This articulates an odd paradox that although the audience can be in literal dialogue with the artist herself about her work, they can have the feeling that it is they, themselves, who have constructed it, authored it, whether in Edinburgh or Kassel, Berlin or Beijing, New York or Tokyo.

We listen to her voice and dream of the *Timelines* that articulate this precarious kind of socialism.

Study for Strings

Kassel, 2012

Kassel Hauptbahnhof, 2012. Eight-channel sound installation. 13 minutes. Commissioned by Documenta (13).

Study for Strings was installed at the end of the platforms at Kassel Hauptbahnhof as part of Documenta (13). The thing that struck me initially about Kassel Hauptbahnhof was how the station was large but quiet. There used to be a lot of rail traffic here but it has since been relocated. During my research I found out that Kassel Hauptbahnhof was the site of three major transportations organised to deport Jewish families to ghettos and concen-tration camps. In 1941, the composer Pavel Haas was deported to Theresienstadt where he wrote and performed his *Studie für Streichorchester*. I recorded a viola and a cello player playing their parts of the composition but I asked them to play each note separately. The recordings were spread across eight channels and installed on the tracks.

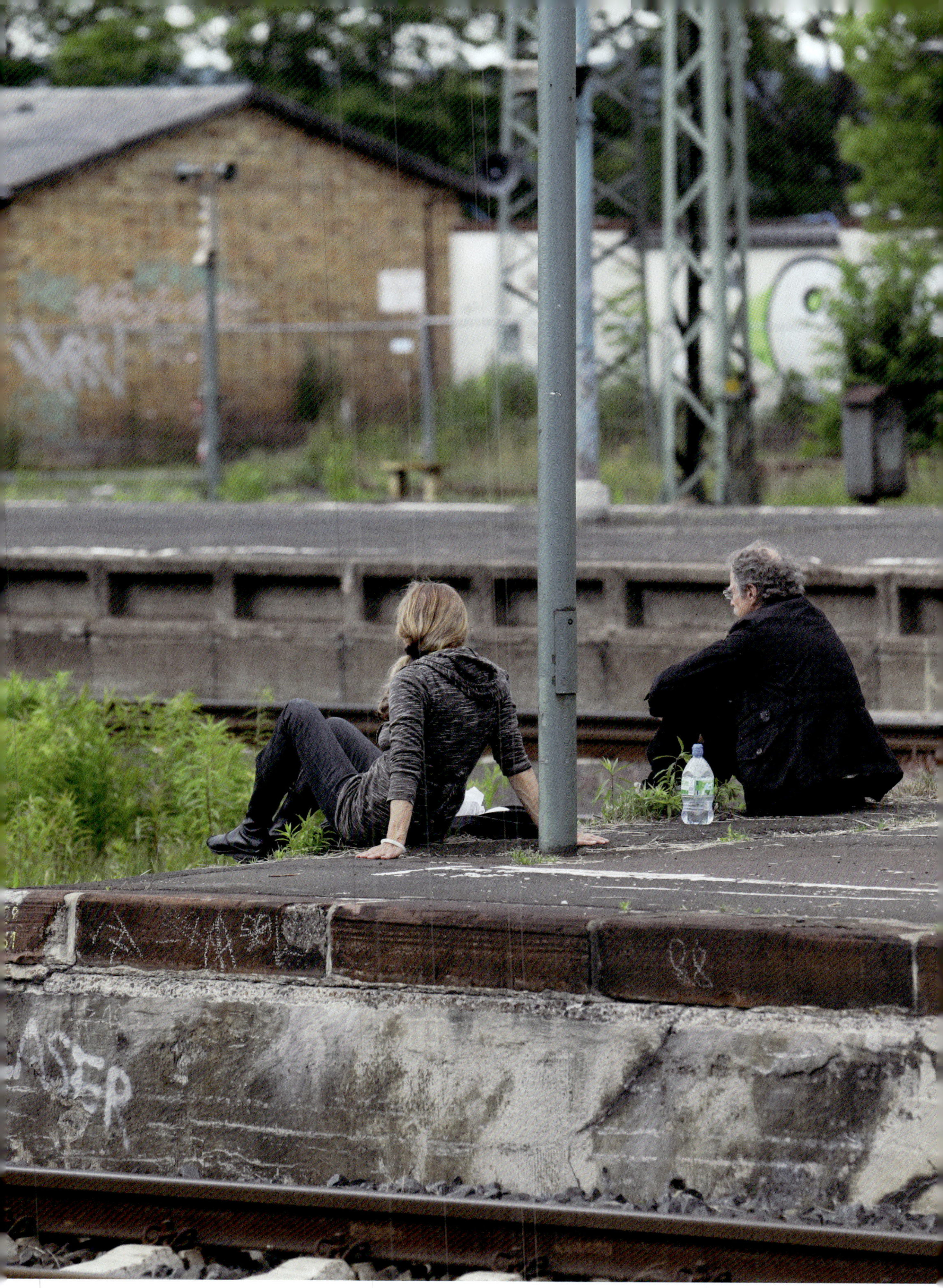

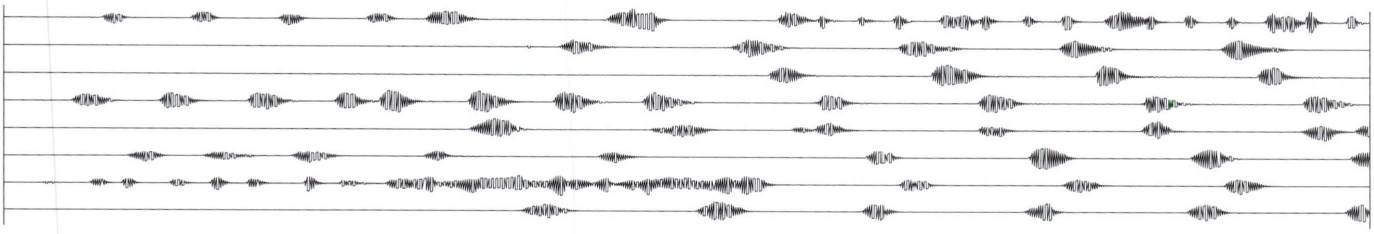

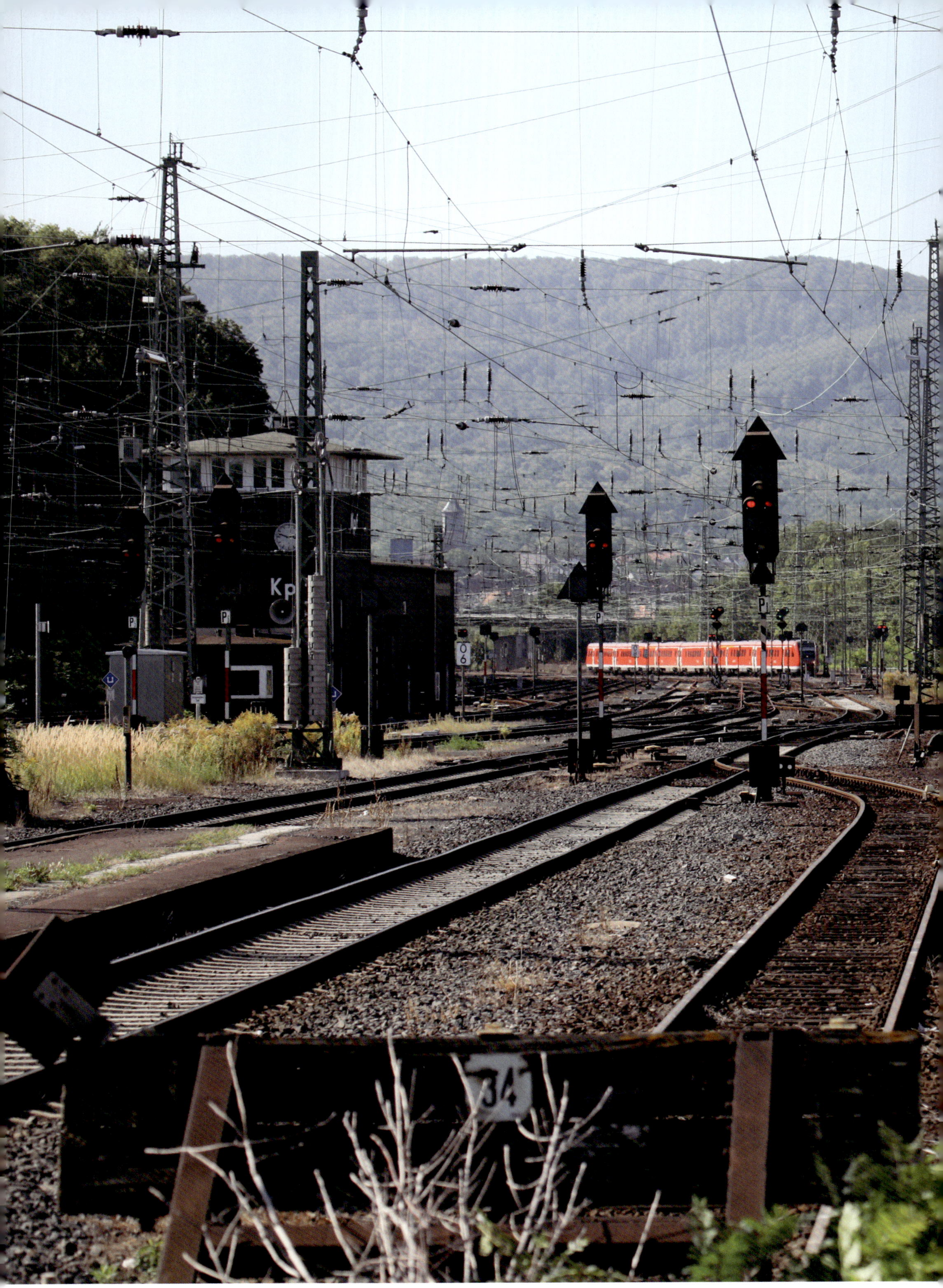
Kp
34

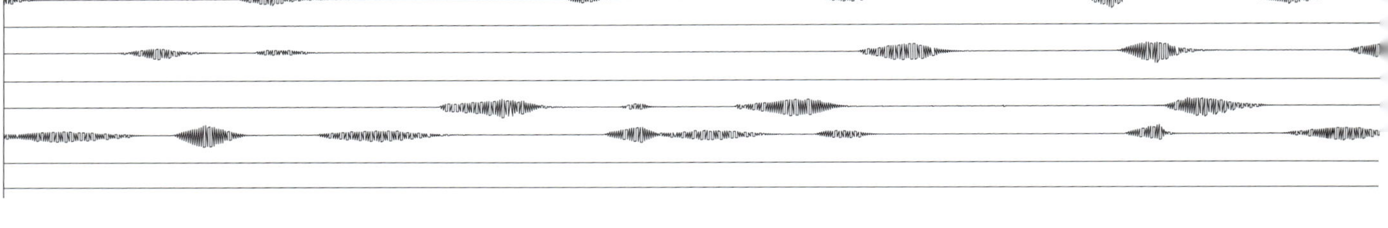

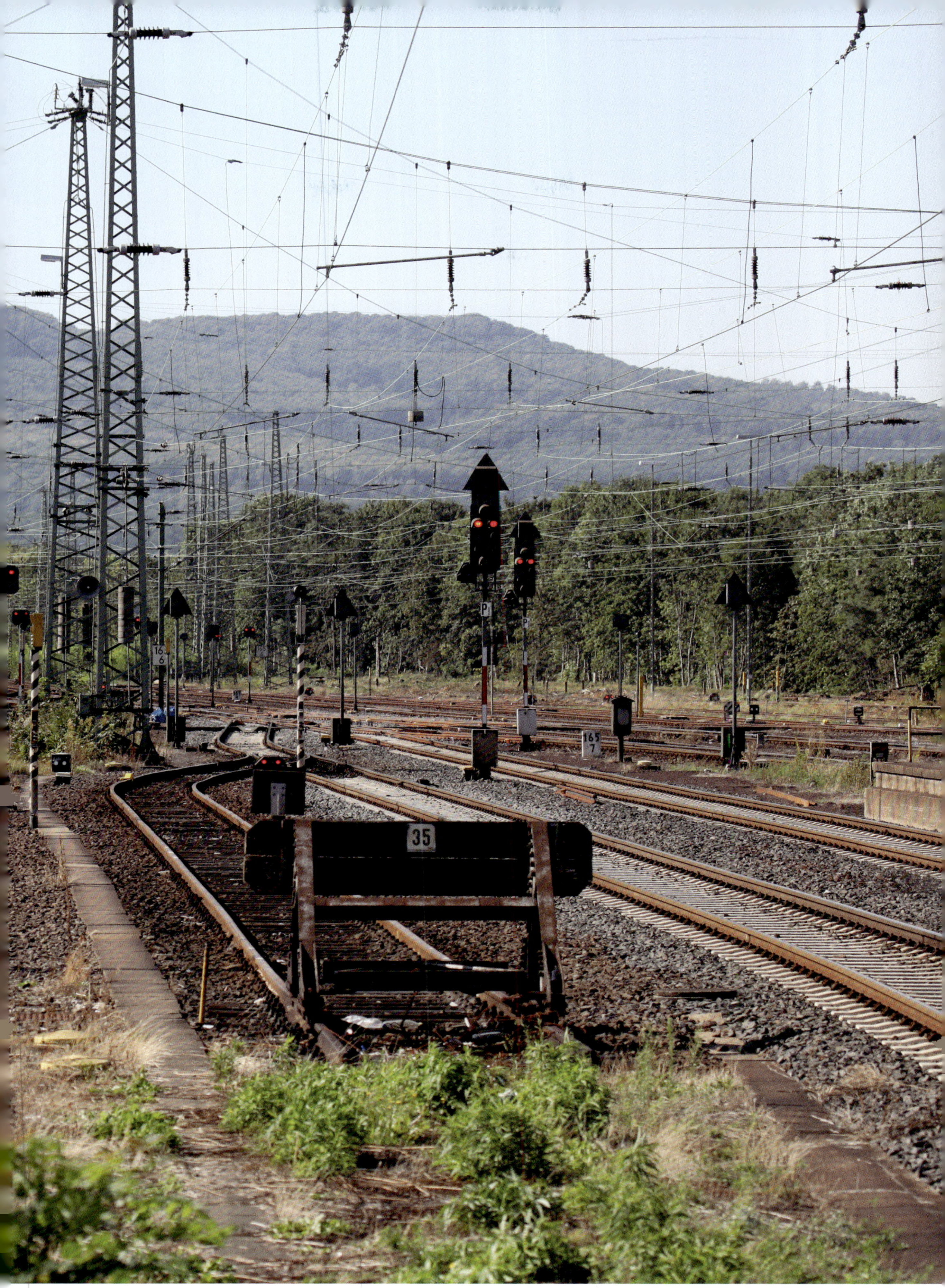
35

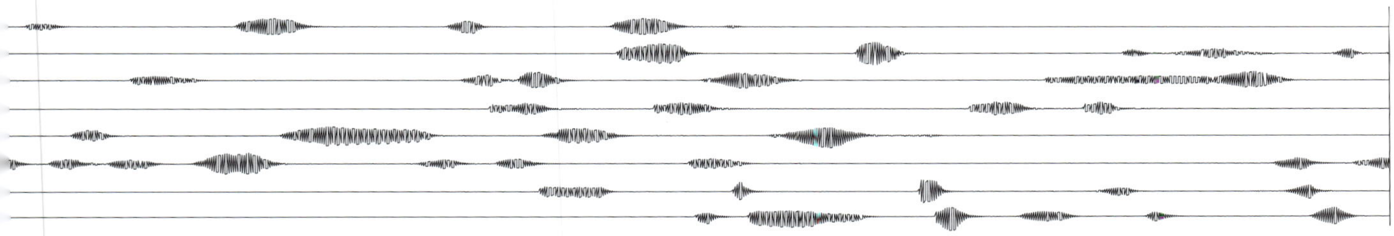

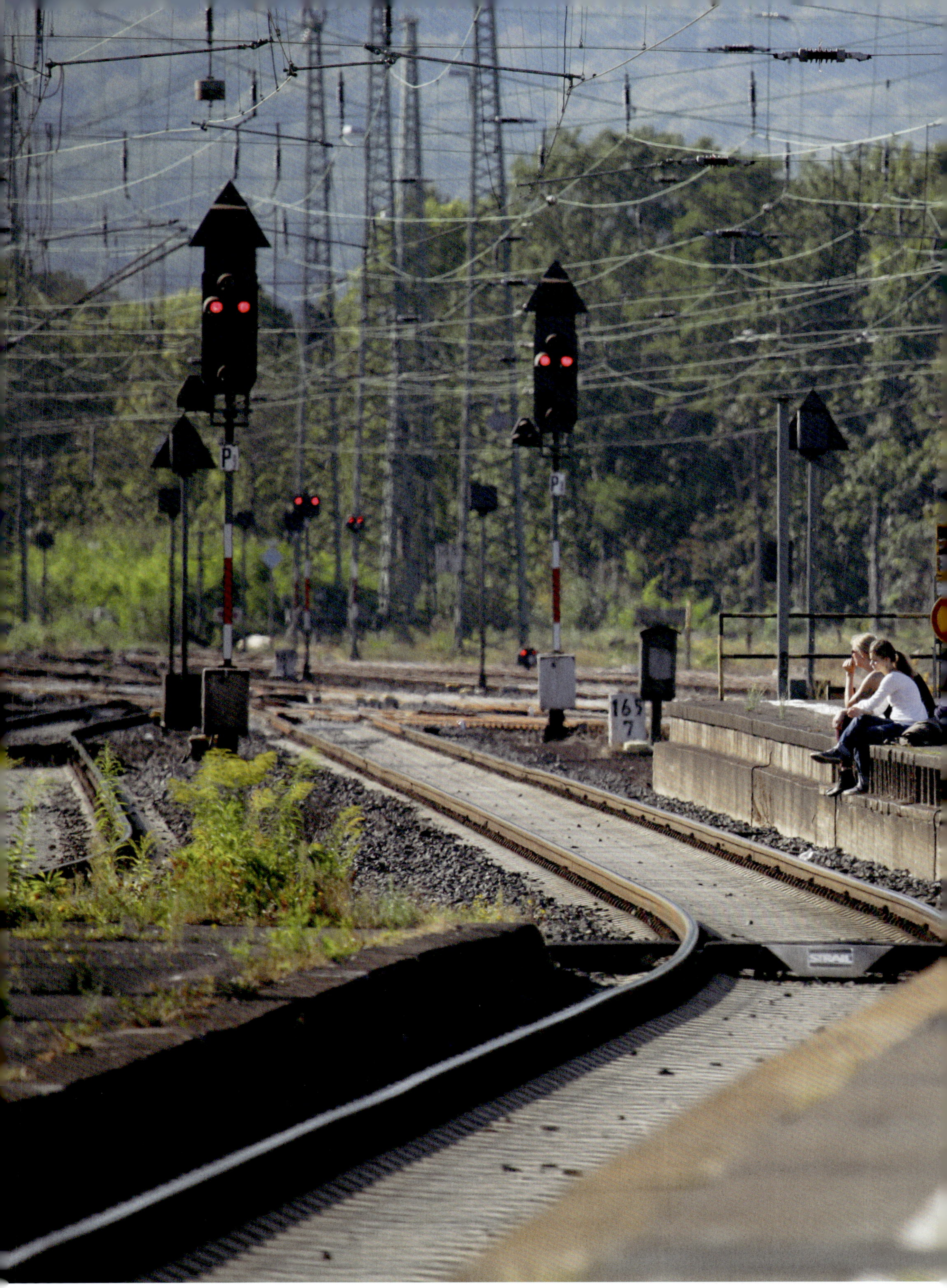
165
7
STRAIL

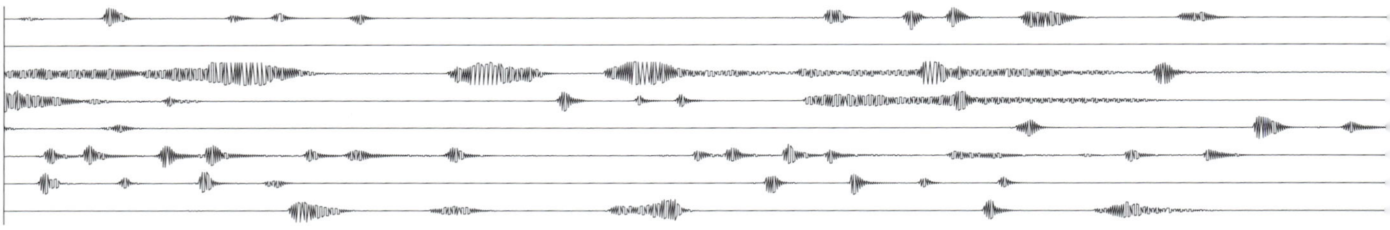

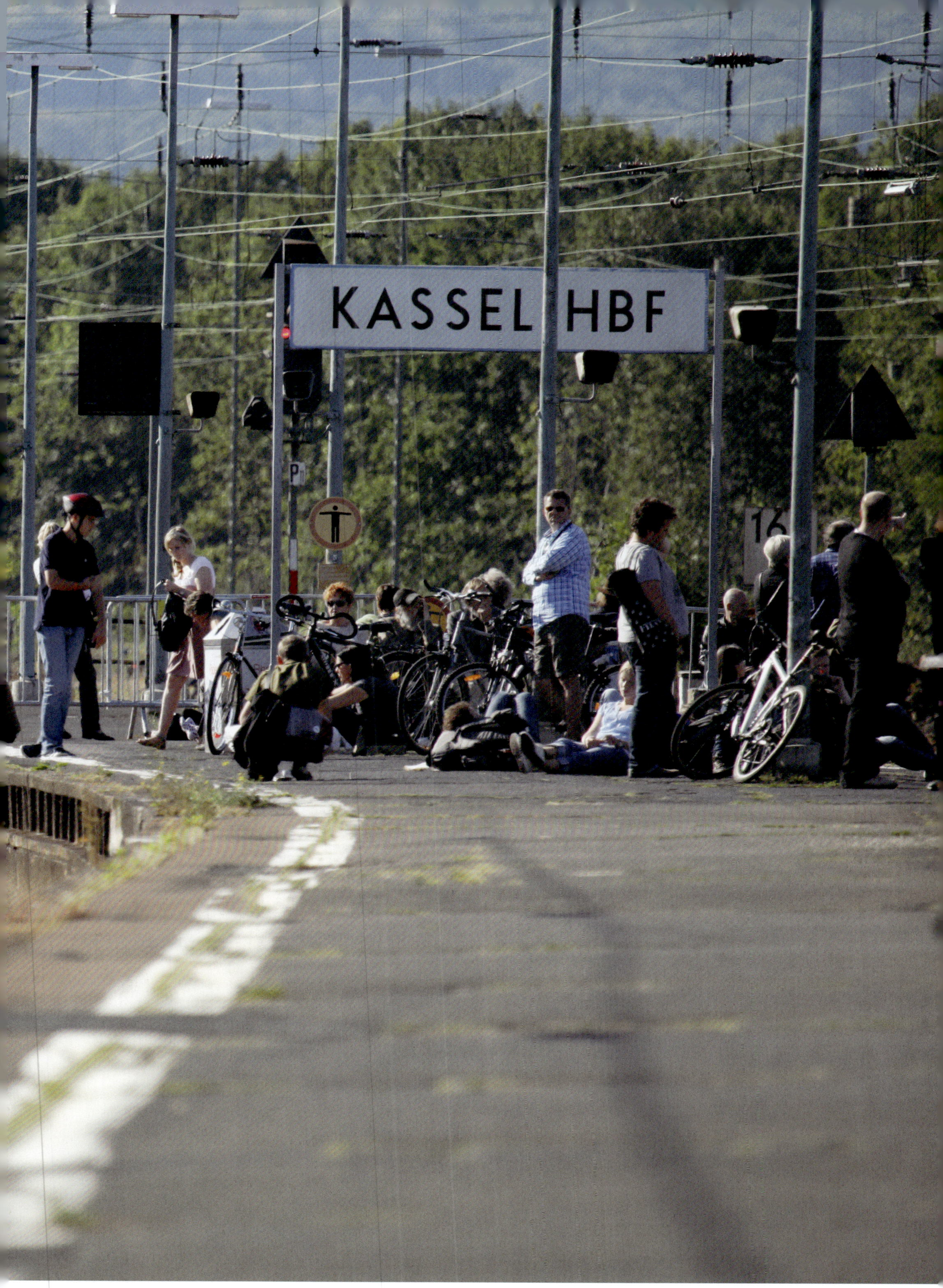
KASSEL HBF

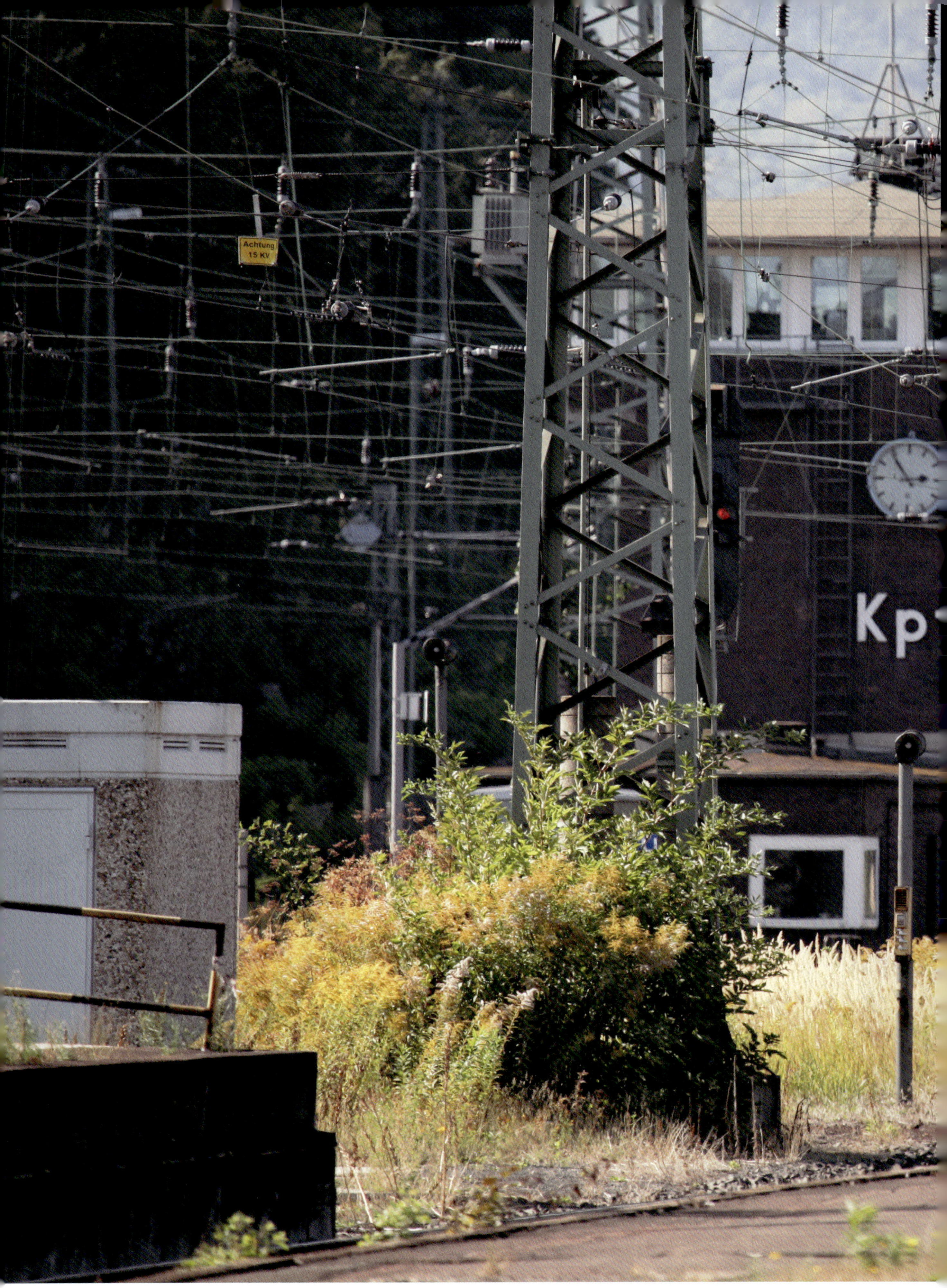
Achtung
15 KV

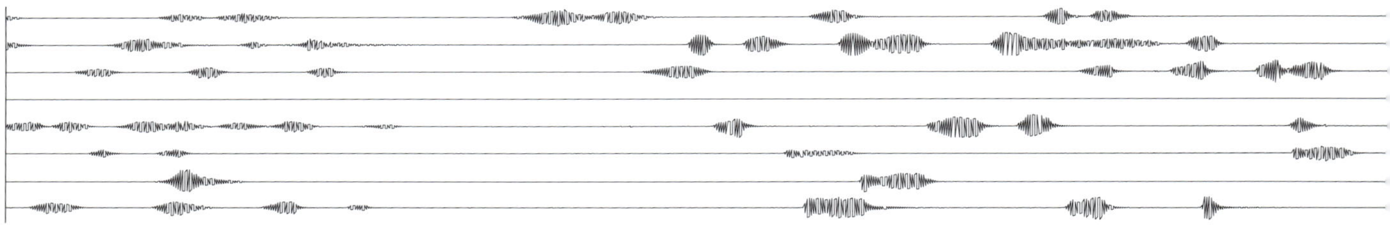

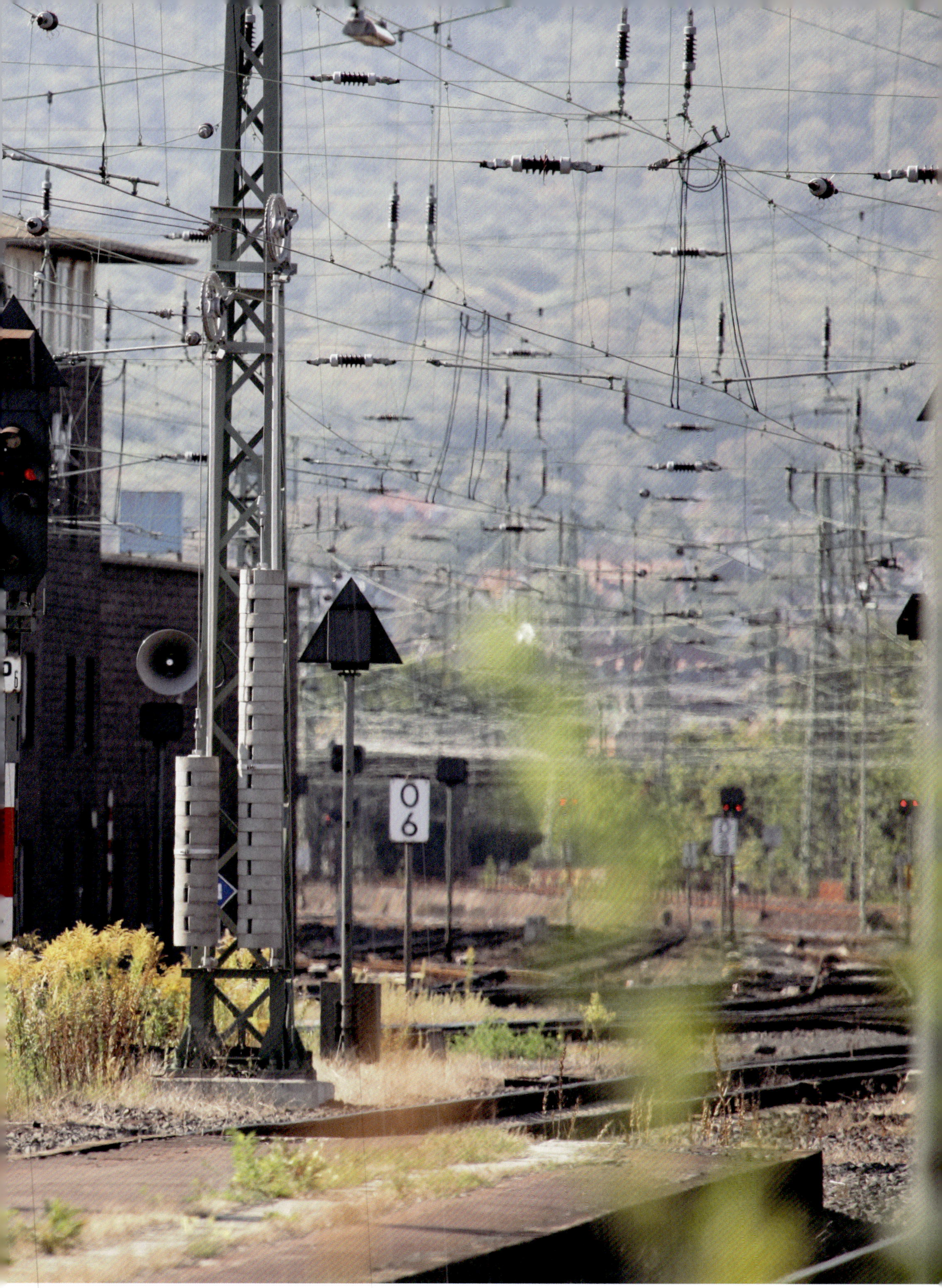
06

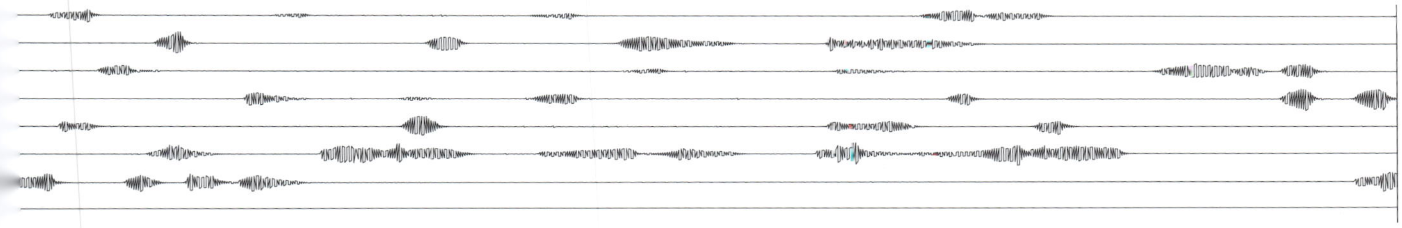

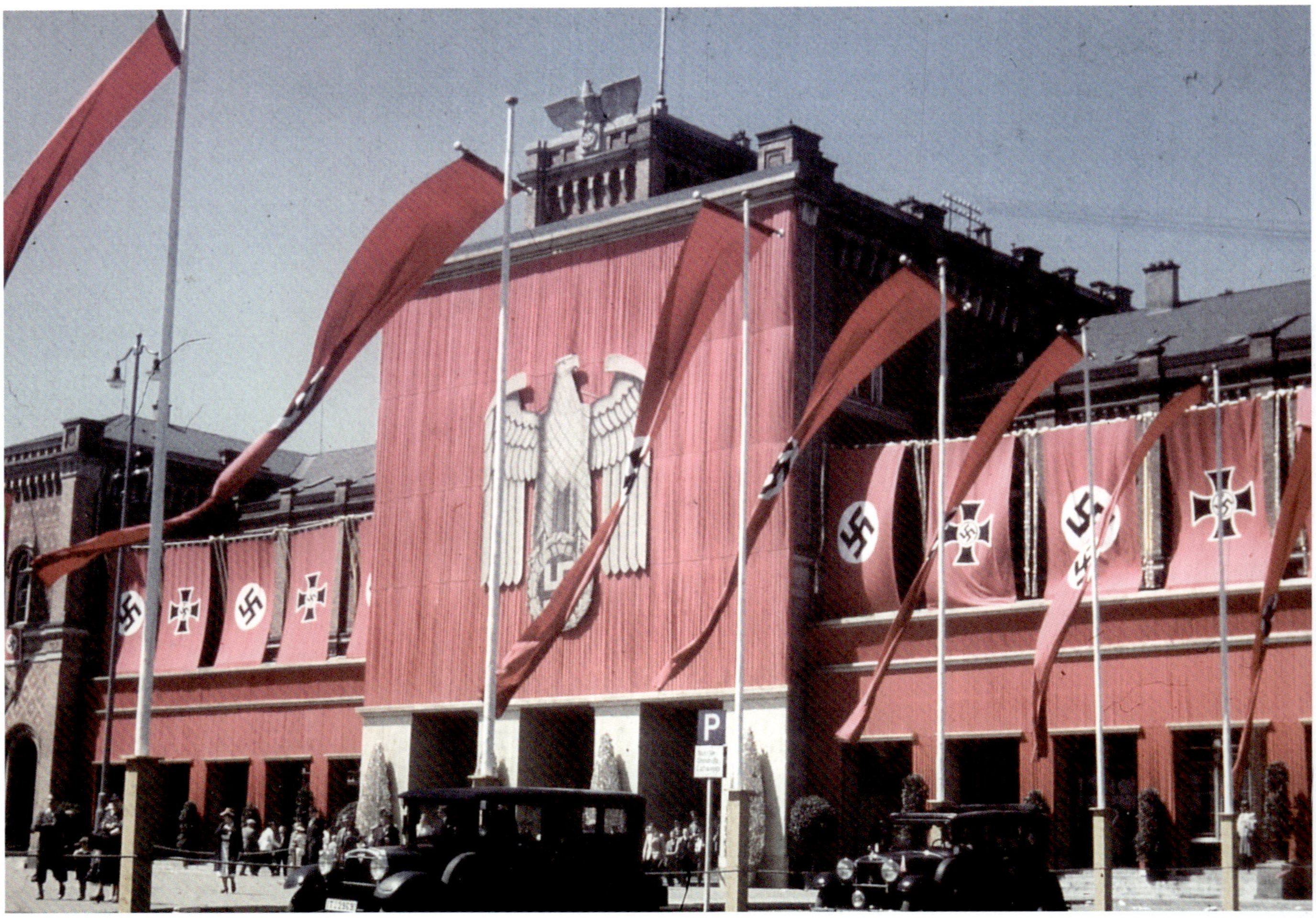

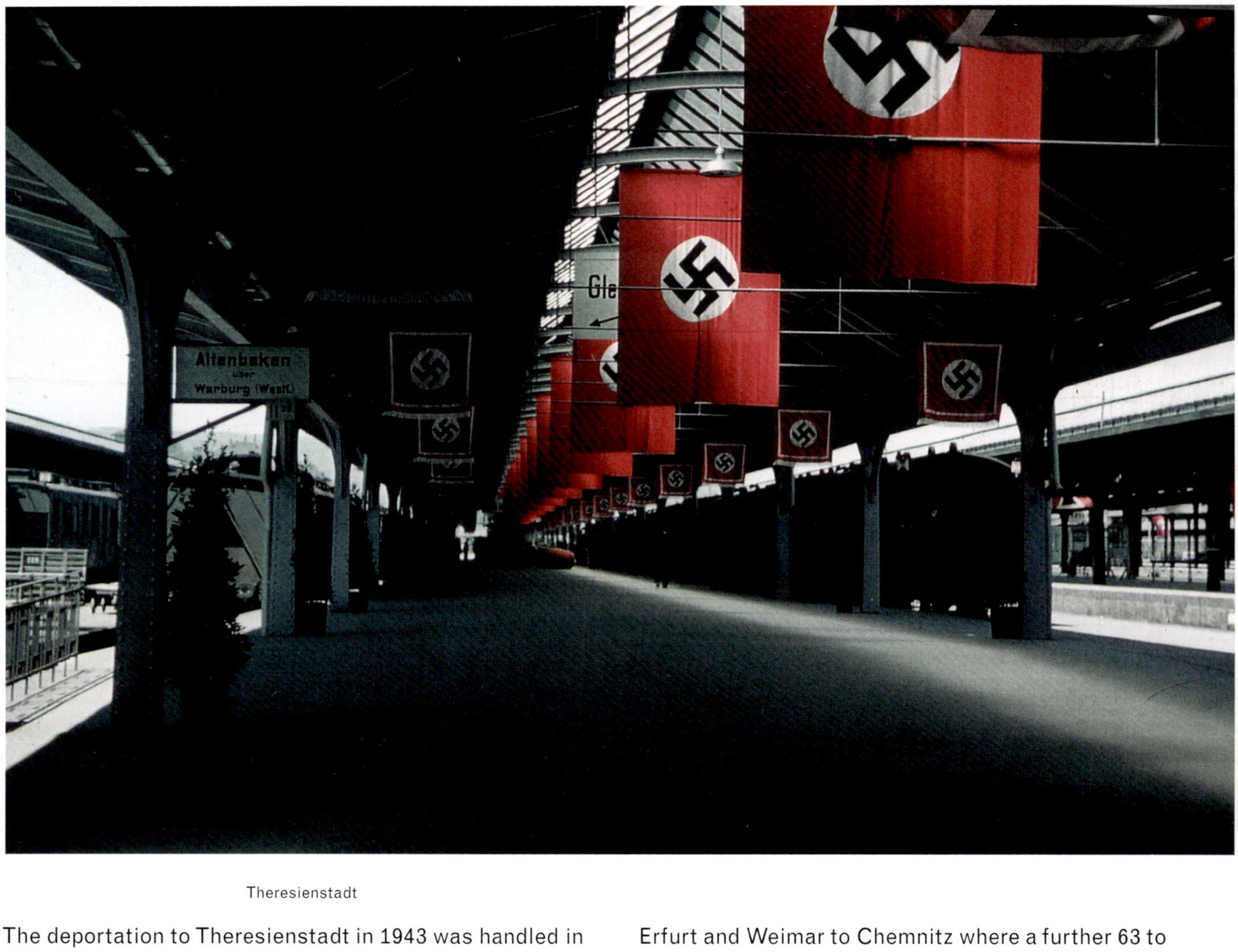

Theresienstadt

The deportation to Theresienstadt in 1943 was handled in the exact same way as the two previous deportations. Some 755 Jewish men and women were taken from their homes to Kassel by train one or two days beforehand. After being registered and searched in the Walter-Hecker school complex on Schillerstraße, they were deported from Kassel Hauptbahnhof. The train *DA 511* traveled over Bebra, Erfurt and Weimar to Chemnitz where a further 63 to 90 Jewish inhabitants of the region were made to board. The next day the train was met in Theresienstadt and registered as *Transport XV–I*. It was the single largest transport from Kassel to Theresienstadt. Only 70 people survived the liberation of Theresienstadt.

Interior and exterior of Kassel Hauptbahnhof decorated with NS symbols on the occasion of the Reichskriegertag in 1939. Courtesy: Stadtarchiv Kassel.

Large scale production of the *Panzer III* tank at the factory site of Henschel & Sohn, Kassel. Photograph: Hebenstreit. Courtesy: Bundesarchiv.

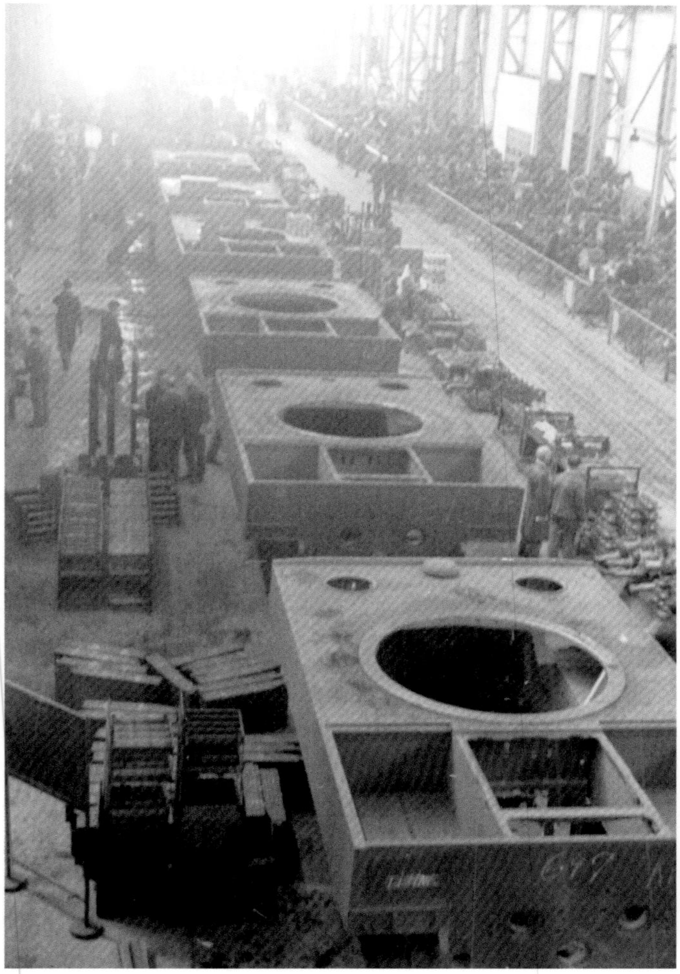

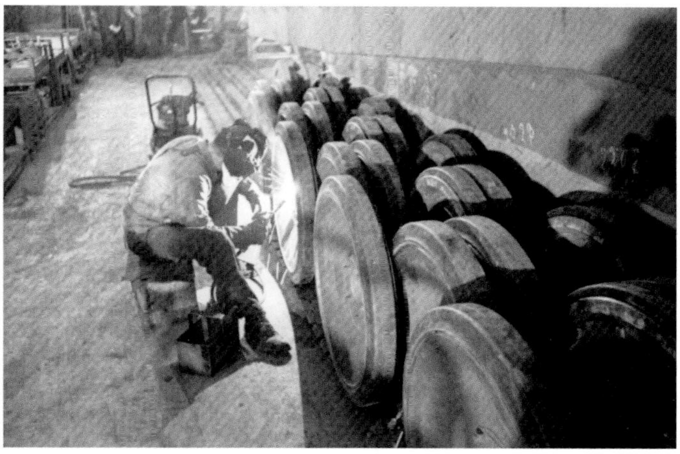

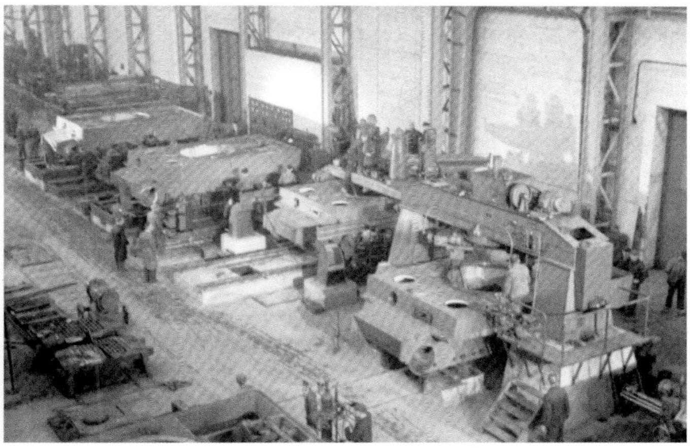

Henschel & Sohn

Henschel & Sohn was established in the early 1800s as a builder of locomotives and during the First World War undertook armament manufacturing as well. By 1942, the company was producing locomotives, tanks, diesel engines, trucks, airplanes and artillery pieces. The tanks it manufactured included the Panzer I, II and III as well as the Panther, Tiger I and Tiger II. The Henschel works at Mittelfeld were primarily devoted to tank assembly and component manufacture. The Mittelfeld Werkes were situated just north of the city centre with strong rail connections to both Kassel-Hauptbahnhof and Kassel-Wilhelmshöhe. In 1942, there were over 6000 forced labourers working on armaments production at Henschel & Sohn.

Cover of the complete score of Pavel Haas' *Study for String Orchestra*, 1943. Courtesy: Boosey & Hawkes Bote & Bock GmbH, Berlin.

Pavel Haas attending the performance of his *Study for String Orchestra* and Egon Ledeč filmed as concert master in Karel Ančerl's Terezín String Orchestra. Filmstills; *Theresienstadt: Ein Dokumentarfilm aus dem jüdischen Siedlungsgebiet*, Kurt Gerron 1944–45. Source: Das Bundesarchiv Filmarchiv. Courtesy: Transit Filmgesellschaft GmbH.

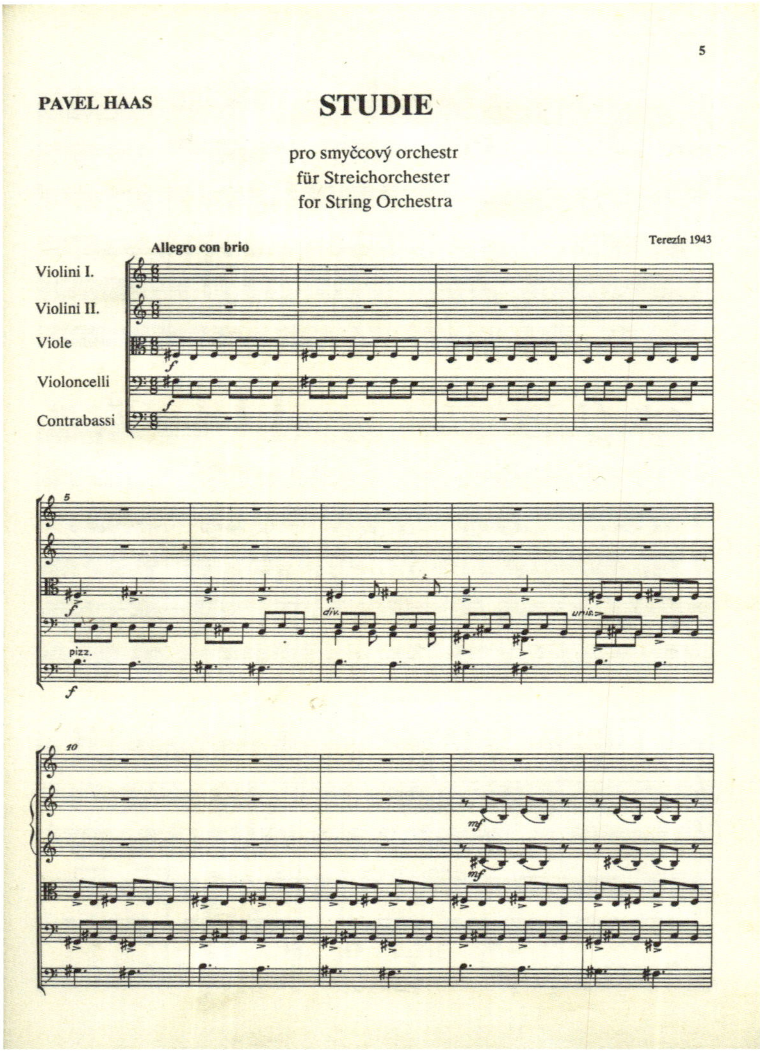

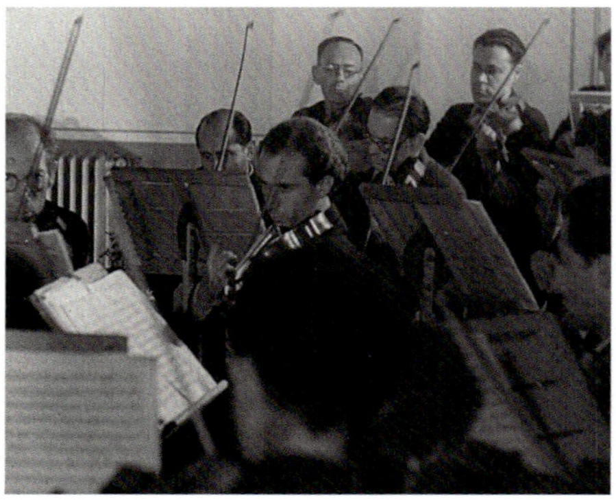

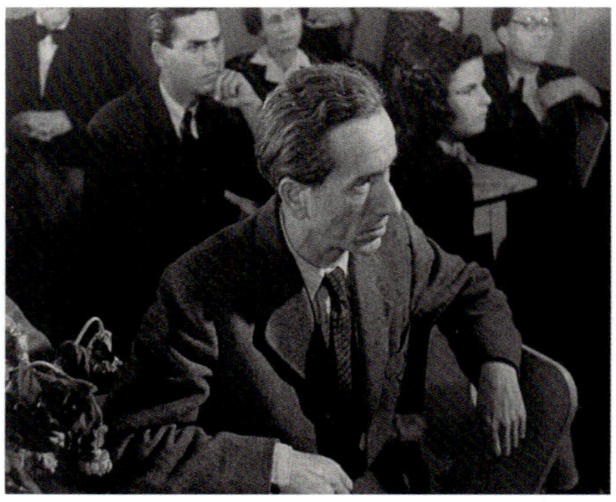

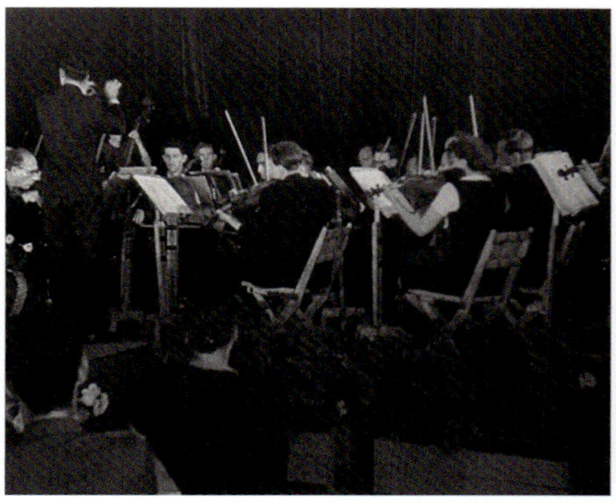

Study for String Orchestra

Towards the end of the propaganda film *Theresienstadt. Ein Dokumentarfilm aus dem Jüdischen Siedlungsgebiet* there is a performance by the Terezín String Orchestra of Pavel Haas' composition *Study for String Orchestra*. Haas is seen in the audience watching the performance and is also shown walking to the stage at the end to congratulate the conductor Karl Ančerl. Shortly after shooting the film, both Haas and the other cast members were sent to Auschwitz where they were murdered upon arrival. Although the scores for the composition were lost in the camp, the conductor and survivor Karl Ančerl managed to find and reassemble the orchestral parts after the war.

Aerial reconnaissance photography showing the centre of Kassel, October 1943. Courtesy: Imperial War Museum.

Restoring tram cables with the ruined Hauptbahnhof in the background, 1945. Courtesy: Stadtmuseum Kassel.

Ruined Hauptbahnhof, 1943. Courtesy: Imperial War Museum.

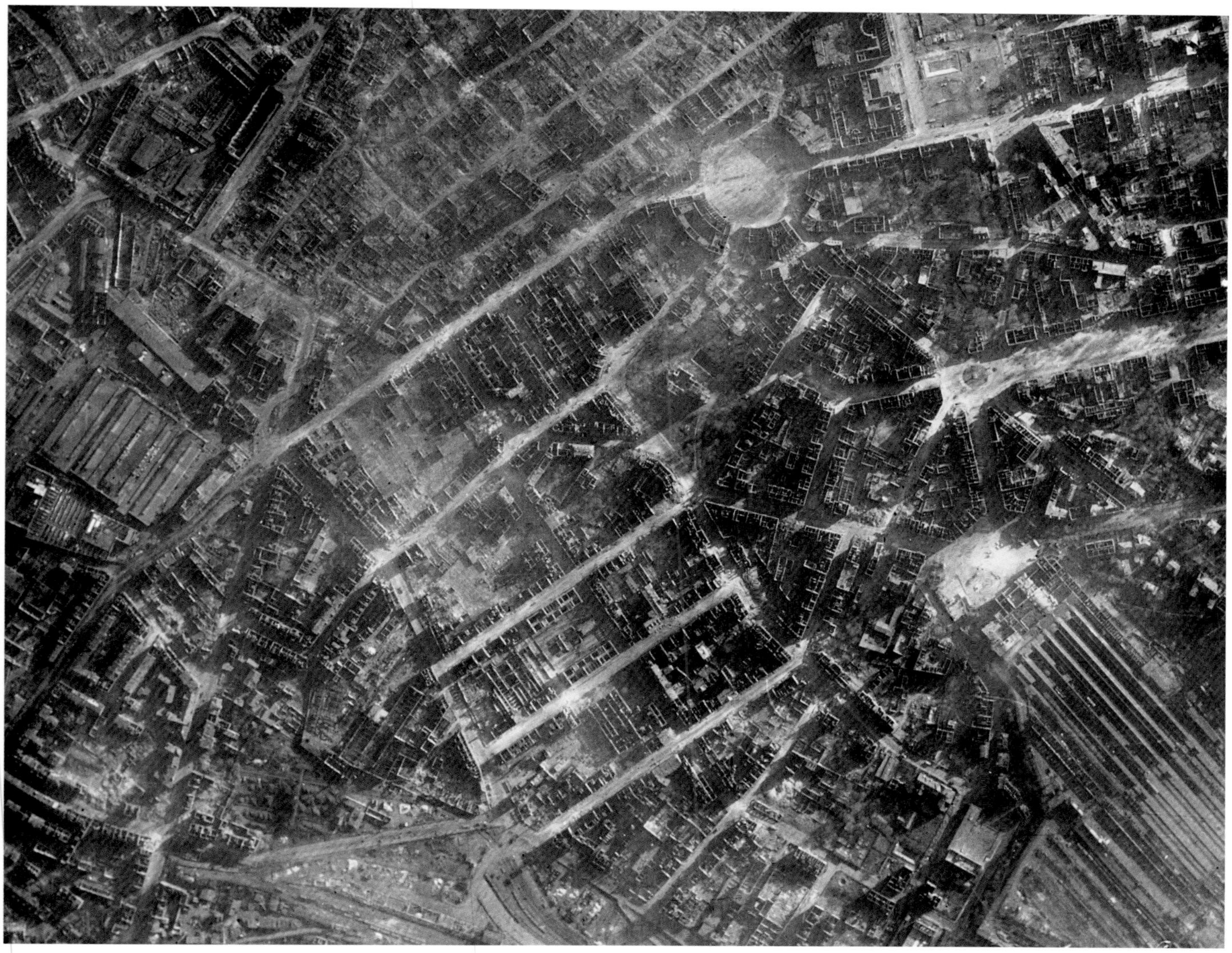

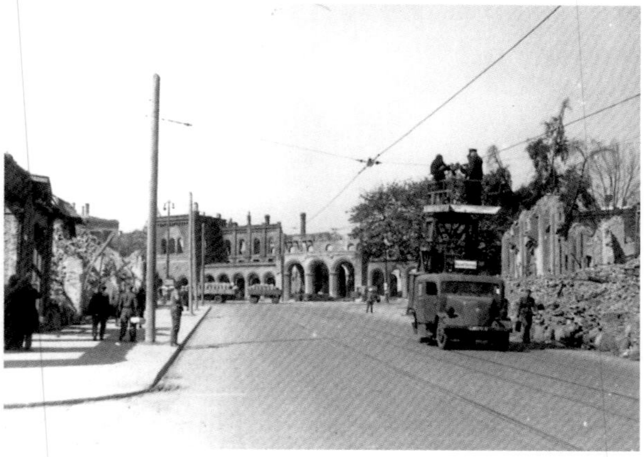

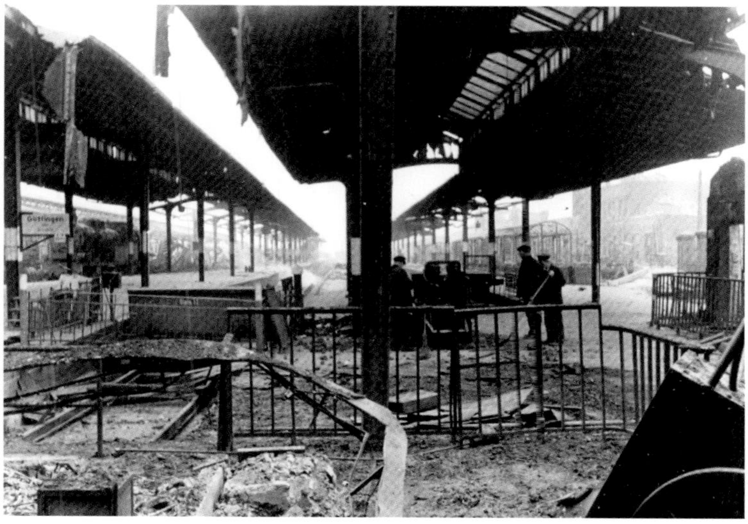

Bombing of Kassel

On the night of 22 October 1943 the Royal Air Force Bomber Command conducted a heavy raid on the centre of Kassel. 569 bombers dropped more than 1,800 tons of bombs, including 460,000 magnesium fire sticks, in a concentrated pattern. The blaze caused a minor firestorm similar in nature to that in Hamburg in July 1943. At least 10,000 people died, 150,000 inhabitants were bombed-out, and the vast majority of the city center was destroyed. This view shows devastated buildings in the vicinity of Königs-platz and the Hauptbahnhof, many of which were still burning seven days after the attack.

Study for Strings

Barbara London

One morning in the late spring of 2012 I caught up with Susan Philipsz at her Berlin studio. She had carefully arranged eight speakers on metal stands around the periphery of her airy workspace. I took my place on a folding chair in the centre of the space, from where I had my first experience of the completed soundtrack for *Study for Strings*. The purposeful notes of a cellist and a violist moved around me. It felt as if the musicians were engaged in a serious conversation, full of dissonant pauses. Each musician seemed to wait politely for the other to complete a thought, and then responded. Playing together but emotionally distanced from each other, they narrated an affecting story. From the pauses, the silences between the notes, I sensed a void where there might otherwise have been some other orchestration.

Talking with Philipsz, I learned that during the preparations for a new installation commissioned by Documenta (13), her researches had led her to *Study for String Orchestra*, a symphony written in 1943 by Pavel Haas. This orchestral piece for twenty-four strings became the genesis of her new sound work. A student of Czech composer Leoš Janáček, Haas wrote *Study for String Orchestra* while interned at the Theresienstadt concentration camp. When the site was beautified in preparation for a visit by the Red Cross in 1944, the authorities decided to produce a propaganda film *Theresienstadt. Ein Dokumentarfilm aus dem jüdischen Siedlungsgebiet*. (Theresienstadt. A Documentary Film from the Jewish Settlement Area). In the film Haas's composition *Study for String Orchestra* is performed by the Terezín String Orchestra conducted by Karl Ančerl. Haas can be seen in the audience watching the performance, and later walking to the stage to congratulate the conductor and receive the applause. Haas and most of the players were subsequently deported to Auschwitz and killed. The score for the composition was presumed lost, but the conductor, Karel Ančerl, survived and managed to find and reassemble the orchestral parts after the war.

By isolating the viola and cello parts, Philipsz effectively pared the Haas symphony down to a duet. An already spare composition became eerily austere. She recorded two musicians playing the respective viola and cello parts one at a time in her studio. Then during the post-production process, she meticulously brought the parts together. With the Kassel installation's multi-channel configuration in mind, she left each recorded note unchanged. Seated in her studio and completely absorbed by the composition—with an occasional glance at the majestic trees outside the windows—I succumbed to the spatial and psychological timbre of the bare, deliberate sounds and silences, and became intensely aware of my physical body perched on the metal chair in the middle of the room. Compared to the concert experience of sitting and listening with others and focusing completely on the performers on stage, this experience was both cerebral and physically more active, as I stood up to mosey around to find a pattern between speakers and sounds. I became keenly aware of the in and out of my breath, and the thoughts coursing through the outer reaches of my brain. Suddenly an inexplicably strong emotion welled up in me and I found myself sobbing. Perhaps the recent passing of my ninety-eight-year-old aunt, the last offspring of a grand-mother who left Germany at the age of fifteen, had triggered this spontaneous sense of being overwhelmed.

I had a different experience in the late summer when I visited Documenta (13) and encountered *Study for Strings* in a new setting. I met Philipsz at a café in Kassel's Hauptbahnhof. We proceeded out into the midday sun and walked away from the station to the farthest end of a platform. She guided me beyond a metal barrier, and we sat down on a simple concrete set of stairs near a workers' shed where we listened to her composition undisturbed. The work emanated from a sound system of eight speakers installed high above on electrical masts around the train tracks. Gazing along the railway line leading

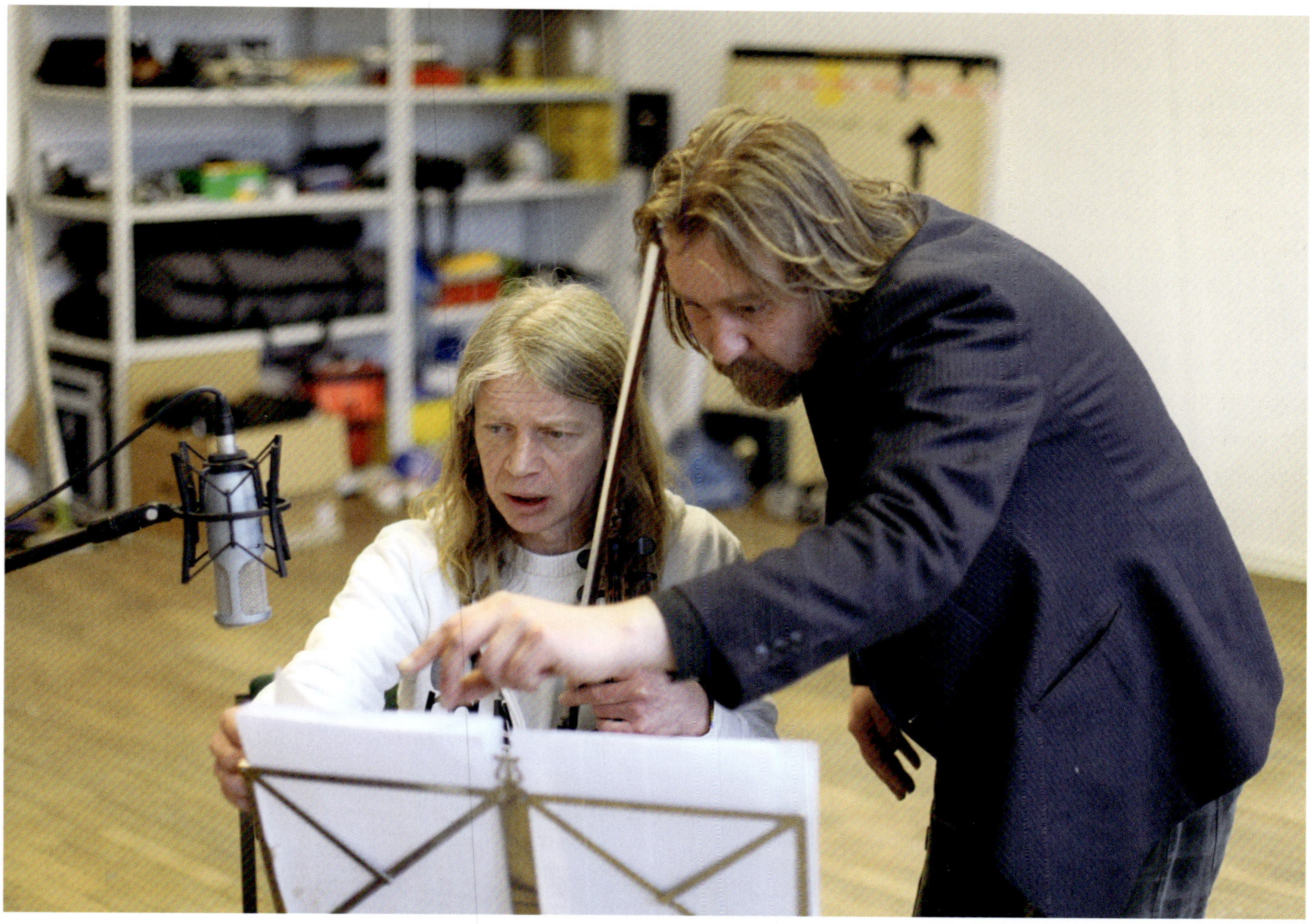

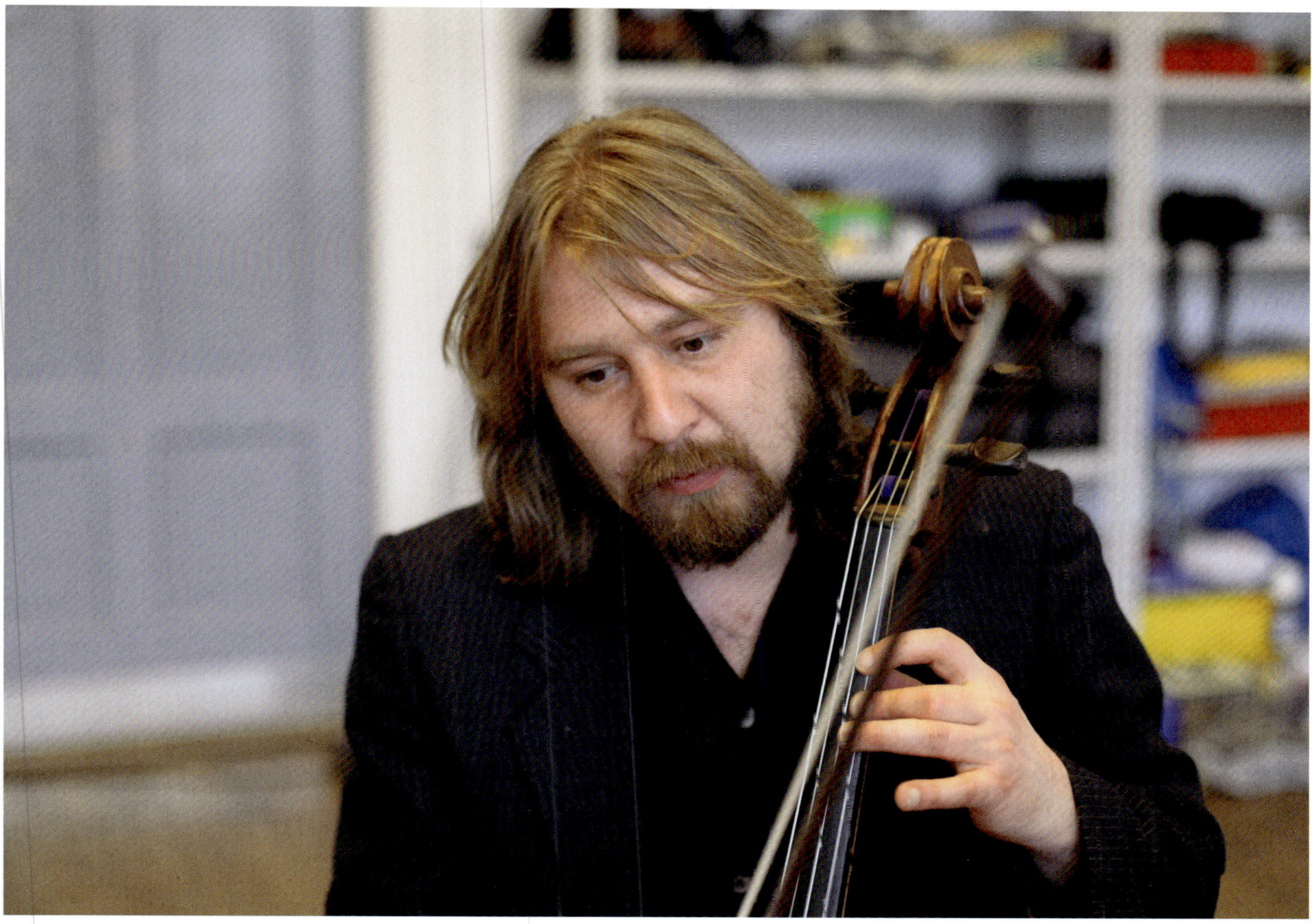

Separated Strings

I asked a viola and cello player to play their parts of the composition separately. The viola and cello parts are more associated with the accompaniment and not with the main melody, so a lot of the original composition is absent and the viola and cello accompaniment is foregrounded. I asked the musicians to record each note of the chromatic scale separately. For example the cello player will identify the first note that appears on his part of the score and then only play that note as it appears across the entire composition, keeping pace but leaving recorded silence between the notes. He then moves to the next note and repeats the process until he has laid down all the notes on twelve separate channels. The exact same process is repeated with the viola player.

away from the station, I again let the dialogue of strings wash over me, with its discrete phrases and weighty pauses. The composition was clearly audible but at the same time felt as though it were occurring somewhere very far away.

Phillipsz pointed out that just to the north of the Hauptbahnhof sit the manufacturing halls and rail networks of the engineering company Henschel & Sohn. By 1942 this German locomotive manufacturer was producing the Tiger I and Tiger II tanks, and had become a significant supplier of armaments to the German army. Around this time there were 6,000 forced labourers working in the Henschel factory. From the very same platforms in 1941 and 1942, three major transports were organized to deport the remaining Jewish families in the Kassel area to ghettos and concentration camps in Majdanek, Sobibor, Treblinka, Izbica, Theresienstadt and Auschwitz.

Time is a crucial element in Philipsz's work. *Study for Strings* was thirteen minutes long, and repeated twice every hour. This rhythm echoed the timetable of trains leaving the station. At regular intervals, the otherworldly notes from the strings intermingled with the blunt 'live' voices that periodically interjected to announce trains ready for departure. As the trains moved past the end of the platform, they disrupted the relative calm of the listener. Gradually, as the train disappeared from view, the sound of the strings re-emerged, rendered even more poignant by the feeling of departure. As summer moved into early autumn during the hundred days of Documenta, the seasonal shift added a further temporal dimension to the pronounced melancholy of *Study for Strings*.

I became acutely aware of how Philipsz had made use of the particular way in which cello and viola strings resonate, their notes reminiscent of the intonation and pain one can hear in the spoken voice. Encouraged to slow down, listeners could sense the fissures, the silences between sounds and the relationship between their physical body and their interior being. Distance and separation became palpable in Philipsz's work, as if the work was fundamentally concerned with what was not there, what could not be experienced; the distance between notes, the distance between times, the separation between the present and the past. The regularity of sounds and movements made you acutely aware of what cannot be retrieved, or controlled, and how memories move in and out of consciousness.

Philipsz shortened the title of Haas's original symphony to reflect the pared down nature of her work. The word 'study' suggests a practice composition in the manner of a piano étude, an exercise for musicians. In Philipsz's case, the word also evokes contemplation, a need to look back at history; a reflective tool to reach into the past, a means of piquing memories lingering deep within us. The word 'strings' has other implications. Beyond its reference to string instruments, the word alludes to an undulating ribbon of time, a train of thought, and to matters of the heart and personal attachments.

As an installation artist, Philipsz builds with sound, one of the most ephemeral of mediums. Pondering the mysterious ways in which sound works to free the human spirit and allows it to soar, I recently listened to Olivier Messiaen's unusual *Quatuor pour la Fin du Temps*, written for four uncommonly combined instruments while he was interned during World War II (at almost exactly the same time that Haas wrote *Study for String Orchestra*). The existential predicament of Haas and Messiaen, their need to compose a response to the utter precariousness of life, generated their respective testimonies to ineffability and to the power of experience beyond words. With *Study for Strings*, Philipsz has created a contemporary equivalent of great pathos and grace, gently reminding its audience of human insignificance before the slow, inevitable march of time.

The Lost Reflection

Voice

Joyous night, O night of love
Your mystic shadows bless us
Starry heavens high above
O joyous night of love

Time is fleet and bears away
The passions that posses us
Far from this enchanted shore
Returning never more

Enjoy while we may
Your beloved caresses
Before the dawn of day
Speeds the moment away

Far away
Far away

Joyous night, O night of love
Your mystic shadows bless us
Starry heavens high above
O joyous night of love

Starry heavens above
Night of ardent caresses
Shine on us, oh night
Oh night of love!

Lowlands

Voice

Lowlands, lowlands, away my John,
Lowlands away I heard them say,
My lowlands away.

I dreamt a dream the other night,
Lowlands, lowlands, away my John,
I dreamt a dream the other night,
My lowlands away.

I dreamt I saw my own true love,
Lowlands, lowlands, away my John,
His hair was wet, his eyes above,
My lowlands away.

I knew my love was drowned and dead,
Lowlands, lowlands, away my John,
He stood so still, no word he said,
My lowlands away.

All dank his hair, all dim his eye,
Lowlands, lowlands, away my John,
I knew that he had said goodbye,
My lowlands away.

All green and wet with weeds so cold,
Lowlands, lowlands, away my John,
Around his form green weeds had hold,
My lowlands away.

'I'm drowned in the lowland seas,' he said,
Lowlands, lowlands, away my John,
'Oh, you an' I will ne'er be wed,'
My lowlands away.

'I shall never kiss you more,' he said,
Lowlands, lowlands, away my John,
'Never kiss you more — for I am dead,'
My lowlands away.

'I will cut my breasts until they bleed.'
Lowlands, lowlands, away my John,
His form had gone — in the green weed,
My lowlands away.

'I will cut away my bonnie hair,
Lowlands, lowlands, away my John,
No other man will think me fair,'
My lowlands away.

I bound the weeper round my head,
Lowlands, lowlands, away my John,
For now I knew my love was dead,
My lowlands away.

My love is drowned in the windy lowlands,
Lowlands, lowlands, away my John,
My love is drowned in the windy lowlands,
My lowlands away.

Voice

Lowlands, lowlands, away my John,
Lowlands away I heard them say,
My lowlands away.

I dreamed a dream the other night,
Lowlands, lowlands, away my John,
My love she came all dressed in white,
My lowlands away.

I dreamed my love came in my sleep,
Lowlands, lowlands, away my John,
Her cheeks were wet her eyes did weep,
My lowlands away.

She came to me as my best bride,
Lowlands, lowlands, away my John,
All dressed in white like some fair bride,
My lowlands away.

And bravely in her bosom fair,
Lowlands, lowlands, away my John,
A red, red rose did my love wear,
My lowlands away.

She made no sound no word she said,
Lowlands, lowlands, away my John,
And then I knew my love was dead,
My lowlands away.

I bound the weeper round my head,
Lowlands, lowlands, away my John,
For now I knew my love was dead,
My lowlands away.

She waved her hand and said goodbye,
Lowlands, lowlands, away my John,
I wiped the tear from out my eye,
My lowlands away.

And then awoke to hear the cry,
Lowlands, lowlands, away my John,
'Oh watch on deck, oh, watch ahoy!'
My lowlands away.

Voice

Lowlands, lowlands, away my John,
Lowlands away I heard them say,
My lowlands away.

I dreamed a dream the other night,
Lowlands, lowlands, away my John,
I dreamt a dream the other night,
My lowlands away.

I dreamed I saw my own true love,
Lowlands, lowlands, away my John,
She flew to me like some young dove,
My lowlands away.

This maid she stood close by my side,
Lowlands, lowlands, away my John,
All dressed in white like some fair bride,
My lowlands away.

She spoke in accents sweet an' low,
Lowlands, lowlands, away my John,
'I love you dear, this well you know',
My lowlands away.

And then she sang in sweetest voice,
Lowlands, lowlands, away my John,
That song which made my heart rejoice,
My lowlands away.

Oh, lowland maids are fair an' true
Lowlands, lowlands, away my John,
This lowland maid she loves you too,
My lowlands away.

And lowland men are strong an' brave,
Lowlands, lowlands, away my John,
The one I love sails o'er the wave,
My lowlands away.

I held her in my fond embrace,
Lowlands, lowlands, away my John,
And kissed her sweet and shinin' face,
My lowlands away.

And then awoke to hear the cry,
Lowlands, lowlands, away my John,
'Rouse out the watch, ho! Watch ahoy!'
My lowlands away.

I See a Darkness

Voice and Piano

Well, you're my friend,
that's what you told me
And can you see
what's inside of me
Many times we've been out drinking
And many times we've shared our thoughts
But did you ever, ever notice,
the kind of thoughts I got
Well you know I have a love,
a love for everyone I know
And you know I have a drive
to live I won't let go
But can you see it's opposition,
comes arising up sometimes
That it's dreadful antiposition,
comes blacking in my mind

And then I see a darkness
And then I see a darkness
And then I see a darkness
And then I see a darkness
And did you know how much I love you
Is a hope that somehow you, you
Can save me from this darkness

Well I hope that someday buddy
We have peace in our lives
Together or apart
Alone or with our wives
And we can stop our whoring
And pull the smiles inside
And light it up forever
And never go to sleep
My best unbeaten brother
This isn't all I see

Oh no, I see a darkness
Oh no, I see a darkness
Oh no, I see a darkness
Oh no, I see a darkness
And did you know how much I love you
Is a hope that somehow you
Can save me from this darkness

Brightly the silver stars
Shine on the water
Softly the gentle breeze
Carries our laughter

My home is far away
For you I'm yearning
Longing to greet the day
Of my returning

I hear you calling me
Your voice enthralling me
Santa Lucia
Santa Lucia

You Are Not Alone

Vibraphone

1 Radio Berlin International, Germany, 1990
2 GTRK Chuvashia, Cheboksary, Russia, ongoing
3 Radio South Africa, South Africa, 1965
4 Radio Peking, China, 1980
5 Serb Republic Radio, External Service, Serbia, 1993
6 GTRK Saratov, Russia, ongoing
7 Radio Argentina al Exterior, Argentina, 1995
8 Radio Mayak, Russia, 1972
9 Swedish Radio P1, Sweden, 1975
10 ELWA, Liberia, 1975
11 Radio Habana, Cuba, 1982
12 Radio Ullan Bator, Mongolia, 1979
13 FEBC, Overseas Service, Philippines, 1964
14 Azerbaijan Radio, Azerbaijan, 1983
15 Voice of the People of Ho Chi Minh City, Vietnam, ongoing
16 Deutschlandfunk, Germany, 1974
17 Radio Normandie, France, 1939
18 Utvarp Föroya, Faroe Islands, 2000
19 Radio Pridnestrovye, Moldova, ongoing
21 Rikisutvarpid, Iceland, 1965
20 Radio Ceylon, Sri Lanka, 1965
22 Murmansk Radio, Russia, 1975
23 Korean Central Broadcasting Station, North Korea, 1980
24 Mother Vietnam (clandestine), Vietnam, 1971
25 Hessischer Rundfunk, Germany, 1975
26 Radio Greenland, Greenland, 1961
27 Bizim Radio (clandestine), Turkey, 1989
28 Kasakh Radio, Kazakhstan, 1978
29 Radio Malaysia Sabah, Malaysia, ongoing
30 Kaliningrad Radio, Russia, 1982
31 Sender Freies Berlin, Germany, 1975

When Day Closes

Voice

Grove of Tuoni, grove of night!
There thy bed of sand is light.
Thither my baby I lead.

Mirth and joy each long hour yields
In the Prince of Tuoni's fields
Tending the Tuonela cattle.

Mirth and joy my babe will know,
Lulled to sleep at evening glow
By the pale Tuonela maiden.

Surely joy hours will hold,
Lying in thy cot of gold,
Hearing the nightjar singing.

Grove of Tuoni, grove of peace!
There all strife and passion cease.
Distant the treacherous world.

Surround Me

Voice and Violin

New Oysters! New Oysters! New Walefleet Oysters!
At a groat a peck, at a groat a peck
Each oyster worth two pence
Fetch us bread and wine that we may eat,
Let us lose no time with such good meat,
A banquet for a prince!

Lachrimae Antiquae (Old Tears)
Lachrimae Antiquae Novae (Old Tears Renewed)
Lachrimae Gementes (Sighing Tears)
Lachrimae Tristes (Sad Tears)
Lachrimae Coactae (Forced Tears)
Lachrimae Amantis (A Lover's Tears)
Lachrimae Verae (True Tears)

The silver swan, who living had no note,
When death approached, unlocked her silent throat.
Leaning her breast upon the reedy shore,
Thus sang her first and last, and sang no more:
'Farewell, all joys! O Death, come close mine eyes!
More geese than swans now live, more fools than wise.'

Weep, O mine eyes, and cease not
Alas, these your spring tides me thinks increase not
O when begin you
To swell so high that I may drown me in you?
That I may drown me in you?

Oh My Love, lov'st thou me?
Then quickly come and save him that dies for thee

Flow, my tears, fall from your springs!
Exiled for ever, let me mourn;
Where night's black bird her sad infamy sings,
There let me live forlorn.

Down vain lights, shine you no more!
No nights are dark enough for those
That in despair their lost fortunes deplore.
Light doth but shame disclose.

Never may my woes be relieved,
Since pity is fled;
And tears and sighs and groans my weary days
Of all joys have deprived.

From the highest spire of contentment
My fortune is thrown;
And fear and grief and pain for my deserts
Are my hopes, since hope is gone.

Hark! you shadows that in darkness dwell,
Learn to contemn light
Happy, happy they that in hell
Feel not the world's despite.

Seven Tears

Voice and Violin

Lachrimae Antiquae (Old Tears)
Lachrimae Antiquae Novae (Old Tears Renewed)
Lachrimae Gementes (Sighing Tears)
Lachrimae Tristes (Sad Tears)
Lachrimae Coactae (Forced Tears)
Lachrimae Amantis (A Lover's Tears)
Lachrimae Verae (True Tears)

New Oysters! New Oysters! New Walefleet Oysters!
At a groat a peck, at a groat a peck
Each oyster worth two pence
Fetch us bread and wine that we may eat,
Let us lose no time with such good meat,
A banquet for a prince!

Oh My Love, lov'st thou me?
Then quickly come and save him that dies for thee

Weep, O mine eyes, and cease not
Alas, these your spring tides me thinks increase not
O when begin you
To swell so high that I may drown me in you?
That I may drown me in you?

The silver swan, who living had no note,
When death approached, unlocked her silent throat.
Leaning her breast upon the reedy shore,
Thus sang her first and last, and sang no more:
'Farewell, all joys! O Death, come close mine eyes!
More geese than swans now live, more fools than wise.'

Flow, my tears, fall from your springs!
Exiled for ever, let me mourn;
Where night's black bird her sad infamy sings,
There let me live forlorn.

Down vain lights, shine you no more!
No nights are dark enough for those
That in despair their lost fortunes deplore.
Light doth but shame disclose.

Never may my woes be relieved,
Since pity is fled.
And tears and sighs and groans my weary days
Of all joys have deprived.

From the highest spire of contentment
My fortune is thrown.
And fear and grief and pain for my deserts
Are my hopes, since hope is gone.

Hark! you shadows that in darkness dwell,
Learn to contemn light
Happy, happy they that in hell
Feel not the world's despite.

Hey ho, to the greenwood now let us go,
Sing hey and ho,
And there shall we find both buck and doe,
Sing hey and ho,
The hart and hind and the little pretty roe,
Sing hey and ho.

We Shall Be All

Voice and Instrumental

Maxwelton's braes are bonnie
Where early fa's the dew
And 'twas there that Annie Laurie
Gave me her promise true.
Gave me her promise true
Which ne'er forgot will be
And for bonnie Annie Laurie
I'd lay me down and die.

Her brow is like the snowdrift
Her throat is like the swan
Her face it is the fairest
That e'er the sun shone on.
That e'er the sun shone on
And dark blue is her e'e
And for bonnie Annie Laurie
I'd lay me down and die.

Like dew on th'gowan lying
Is th' fa' o' her fairy feet
And like the winds in summer sighing
Her voice is low and sweet.
Her voice is low and sweet.
And she's a' the world to me
And for bonnie Annie Laurie
I'd lay me down and die.

I am not dead — I am not dead,
I live a life intense, divine.
Yours be the days forever fled,
But all the morrows shall be mine.

And who by fire, who by water,
Who in the sunshine, who in the night time,
Who by high ordeal, who by common trial,
Who in your merry merry month of May,
Who by very slow decay,
And who shall I say is calling?

And who in her lonely slip, who by barbiturate,
Who in these realms of love, who by something blunt,
And who by avalanche, who by powder,
Who for his greed, who for his hunger,
And who shall I say is calling?

And who by brave assent, who by accident,
Who in solitude, who in this mirror,
Who by his lady's command, who by his own hand,
Who in mortal chains, who in power,
And who shall I say is calling?

Timeline

Voice

H
G#
E

Study for Strings

Viola and Cello

Texts
Sara Arrhenius
Carolyn Christov-Bakargiev
Katrina M. Brown
Maeve Connolly
Steven Connor
Brigitte Franzen
Barbara London
Dieter Roelstraete
Anna Sophia Schultz
Ross Sinclair

Editors
James Lingwood
Brigitte Franzen

Coordinating editor
Eoghan McTigue

Image research
Antonia Bechmann
Eoghan McTigue

Design
Florian Ludwig

Design Assistants
Per Törnberg
Hanne Lippard

Website
Florian Ludwig
Owen Hoskins

Photography
Julian Abrams
Taavetti Alin
Stuart Armitt
Nick Ash
Carl Brunn
Ruth Clark
Mathias Johansson
Andy Keate
Nathan Keay
Eoghan McTigue
Jean Vong
Kai Widell

Image Retouching
Jamie Lemoine

Translations
Paul Bowman

Copy editing
Esther Boehle
Eleanor Nairne

Published by
Verlag der Buchhandlung
Walther König, Köln
Ehrenstraße 4, 50672 Köln

Bibliographic information
published by the Deutsche
Nationalbibliothek

The Deutsche Nationalbibliothek
lists this publication in the
Deutsche Nationalbibliografie;
detailed bibliographic
data are available in the internet
at http://dnb.d-nb.de.

Printed in Germany

Printed by
DZA Druckerei zu
Altenburg GmbH
Gutenbergstr. 1
04600 Altenburg

Distribution

Germany & Europe
Buchhandlung
Walther König, Köln
Ehrenstr. 4, 50672 Köln
Tel. +49 (0) 221 / 20 59 6-53
Fax +49 (0) 221 / 20 59 6-60
verlag@buchhandlung-
walther-koenig.de

Switzerland
AVA Verlagsauslieferungen AG
Centralweg 16
CH-8910 Affoltern a.A.
Tel +41 (44) 762 42 60
Fax +41 (44) 762 42 10
verlagsservice@ava.ch

UK & Ireland
Cornerhouse Publications
70 Oxford Street
GB-Manchester M1 5NH
Fon +44 (0) 161 200 15 03
Fax +44 (0) 161 200 15 04
publications@cornerhouse.org

Outside Europe
D.A.P. / Distributed
Art Publishers, Inc.
155 6th Avenue, 2nd Floor
USA-New York, NY 10013
Fon +1 (0) 212 627 1999
Fax +1 (0) 212 627 9484
eleshowitz@dapinc.com

ISBN 978-3-86335-405-3

Co-published by

Artangel
31 Eyre Street Hill
London EC1R 5EW

Tanya Bonakdar Gallery
521 West 21st Street
New York, NY 10011

Bonniers Konsthall
Torsgatan 19
113 90 Stockholm

Isabella Bortolozzi Galerie
Schöneberger Ufer 61
10785 Berlin

Edinburgh Art Festival
City Art Centre
2 Market Street
Edinburgh EH1 1DE

Ludwig Forum für
Internationale Kunst
Jülicher Straße 97–109
52070 Aachen

Modern Art Oxford
30 Pembroke Street
Oxford OX1 1BP

Museum of
Contemporary Art
Chicago
220 E Chicago Ave
Chicago IL 60611

Pro Arte Foundation
Kalevankatu 4
2nd floor
00100 Helsinki
Finland

Special thanks to

Isabella Bortolozzi
Marta Lusena
Tanya Bonakdar
Ethan Sklar
Claire Pauley
Rob Bowman
Madeleine Grynsztejn
Dominic Molon
Paula Toppila
Tuula Arkio
Sorcha Carey
Stuart Barnes
David Thorp
Verity Slater
Kasper König
Carina Plath
Christoph Platz
Gerard de Geer
Franz König
Christian Posthöfen
Frank Bode
Sebastian Scheithauer
Nikola Jeremic
Immanuel Heidrich
Phil Collins
Maria Cruz
Alasdair Roberts
Will Oldham
Padraig Timoney

Accademia Carrara
Andy Matthews
Melissa Murphy
Baker Library of the Harvard Business School
Basilica Santa Lucia al Sepolcro
Sabine Schumann
bpk Bildagentur für Kunst, Kultur und Geschichte
Dave McCall
British Film Institute
The British Library
Chicago History Museum Research Center
Colin Lindsay
Jessica Collins
The Clothworker's Company
Michael Schmitz
ADDX
Susanne Hartmann
Crous Collection
Maya Buchholz
Deutsches Bundesarchiv / Filmarchiv
Regina Zölßmann
Deutsches Rundfunk Archiv
Melanie Leung
Folger Shakespeare Library
Markus Kien
Funkschau
Nerys Tunnicliffe
Glasgow City Archives and Special Collections
Helen Mavin
Imperial War Museum
Lisa Yun Lee
Jane Adams Hull-House Museum

Library of Congress
Elisabeth Schneider
Boosey & Hawkes Bote & Bock Gmbh
Pinacoteca Nazionale
Princeton Architectural Press
Dagmar Reim, Mark Stuntz
Radio Berlin Brandenburg
Jonas Topooco, Daniel Olsson
Research & Development
Roman Mensing
Ian Brearey
Royal Academy of Music
Michael Mullen
Royal College of Music
Helen Hargest
Shakespeare Birthplace Trust Stratford-upon-Avon
Julie Gardham
Special Collections Department Glasgow University Library
Julia Herdes
Stadtarchiv Kassel
Dr. Alexander Link and
Dr. Barbara Hammes
Stadtmuseum Kassel
Stuart Gilbert Collection at the University of Texas at Austin
Anna Suominen
Tammi Publications
Thorsten Ahrendt and
Daniele Guerlain
Transit Filmgesellschaft mbH
Trustees of the British Museum
Michael Basinski and
Jim Maynard
University of Buffalo